Daniel C. Tofan

General Chemistry Workbook

"Beryllium" Edition

A complete workbook suitable for students enrolled in Advanced Placement, Introductory, or General Chemistry courses

INTELOT Publishing

ISBN 978-0-557-53748-8

Front cover: sample of Cobalt(II) chloride hexahydrate, $CoCl_2 \cdot 6H_2O$
Back cover: crystals of Copper(II) sulfate pentahydrate, $CuSO_4 \cdot 5H_2O$

Cover photo credit: Benjamin Mills (http://www.benjamin-mills.com/) and Ra'ike
(http://commons.wikimedia.org/wiki/Category:Files_by_User:Ra'ike_from_de.wikipedia)

Preface

What is the workbook?

This workbook was designed as a complement to a typical chemistry textbook for beginning students. Its purpose is to present detailed solutions to most types of problems that can be found in a typical Advanced Placement, Introductory Chemistry, or General Chemistry course, and thus it is suitable for high school as well as college level students. There is no "theory" presented, and therefore a textbook, or another comprehensive source of text material, is still necessary.

How is the workbook organized?

The workbook contains a total of 197 learning objectives, grouped in 28 lessons. A lesson represents a major topic, and a learning objective is typically a particular type of problem, that concentrates primarily on one problem solving skill. Before lessons start, there is a math worksheet available, which allows students to practice the algebra employed throughout this book. After an introductory lesson on numbers, units, and measurement, the sequence of the lessons follow an "atoms first" approach, where the structure of matter is introduced and then chemical reactions are expanded upon. Stoichiometry is broken down into several types of problems, and so is the section on solutions and concentration. Thermochemistry and thermodynamics are two separate lessons, so that they can be covered in separate semesters. A new lesson usually builds on some of the previous material, and most learning objectives follow the same trend.

Each lesson starts with a list of the learning objectives covered, and provides several self-study questions whose answers should be understood before proceeding with the solved examples. Then, each learning objective is discussed by showing worked examples. The lesson ends with a worksheet, which allows the student to practice additional problems on the same learning objectives.

This workbook does not necessarily provide exhaustive coverage of all material taught in a full year course. Instead, the workbook tries to focus on the most important topics and learning objectives, while still providing comprehensive coverage of the material. Some topic details have been left out because they are typically further discussed in upper level courses – there is no organic chemistry or biochemistry. At the completion of the two-semester sequence, the typical student should be able to perform above the national average on standardized exams, provided that the entire workbook has been covered in detail.

After the last lesson there is a practice final exam. It is a 50-question test that students can use to prepare for an exam that covers the entire years' worth of material. The practice exam lists questions in multiple choice format and leaves empty space after each question, so that the students can work on the test themselves. An answer sheet is provided for students to write down the answers as they progress through the test. Then, the entire exam is solved in detail, with the full solutions being presented, as well as the list of correct answers.

The workbook contains several appendices, which list useful information, such as equilibrium constants, solubility curves, vapor pressures of water, standard reduction potentials, a complete solution to the algebra worksheet, explanations on how to determine the atomic radius in the three types of cubic unit cells, as well as a detailed periodic table.

How should the workbook be used?

This workbook is probably used best when students work on problems in small groups. They should first reach agreement on the answers to the self-study questions, so that definitions and concepts utilized in the lessons are understood. Then the group should study the worked problems and discuss the solutions among themselves, in order to understand why each solution is the way it is, then work on several examples of the same type. Rather than memorize algorithms and steps, students should be encouraged to generalize each type of problem and retain the chemistry concepts behind it, thus becoming able to apply those concepts to other problems. Not all solved problems have the exact same equivalent in the following worksheet. Sometimes a student will need to combine two or more problem types previously seen in order to arrive to a solution for a new problem. Developing this problem solving skill is essential in introductory chemistry.

The workbook is also ideal for individual study. Most problems include detailed explanations, not just mathematics, in an attempt to offer what most textbooks don't have the space for – a comprehensive treatment of numerous types of problems for each topic.

At the end of each section there is a Self-assessment table, where students should fill in the objective number for each of the objectives covered in the lesson, then rate their understanding of it on a 0-3 numerical scale. Questions that still arise at the completion of the workbook should be written down and then discussed with the teacher.

Best practices

I have found, through several years of class experience using this book, that the best way of teaching with this workbook is to show several worked examples in class, using a tablet computer and a projection system. I created blank copies of the worksheets, in order to solve problems in front of the students and allow them to ask questions. I used Microsoft OneNote 2007 on a tablet PC and wrote my work by hand with the stylus directly on the computer screen. This allowed me to save all notes made during class and post later when necessary. Then, in subsequent class periods, I asked the students to form small groups (3-4 students per group is the ideal number) and work on the worksheets as a group. This proved to be an efficient method and led to increased performance on the part of the students. I noticed drops of 25 to 50% in the failure rate, as well as improved performance on exams, including standardized tests, by up to 20% as class average.

For a more comprehensive description of this method of teaching that uses my workbook, please see my article in the January 2010 issue of the Journal of Chemical Education, on page 47.

I want to hear from you!

While I tried my best to provide an error-free book, there is always the possibility that a few errors may have slipped through unnoticed, since I did not have an editorial team to help proofread this book. If you find such errors, please do not hesitate to email me at *intelot@gmail.com*. Also, suggestions for how to improve this workbook in future editions are more than welcome.

Thank you!

Student opinions

The following student comments are taken from student surveys given over a few semesters through the BlackBoard course management system. Some comments were collected before the solved practice final was included in the present edition. The only editing performed on the comments below was fixing spelling errors, as well as removing student names or course numbers.

A solved practice final (with references to the workbook section that would cover the problem more in depth) would be a welcome addition. A glossary would be helpful.

I can't think of anything more the book needed except maybe some extra tables in the back for constants used in electrochemistry n thermochemistry. I agree that a solved practice final would be an excellent addition to the workbook. The additional length should also prove helpful to future students.

I think that the workbook was good with examples to help do the worksheets, and if you include worked out tests and exams then it will be a lot easier to study. The only time it was hard was when there was a problem on the worksheet that wasn't in the book.

In my opinion, the book is very complete and very well written. Explanations and shown work are great. I have no suggestions. The workbook was extremely helpful.

Overall, the book is an excellent source of information. You could definitely charge more for the book because it was way better than any other chemistry text. People from other Chemistry classes wanted to use my book to study with because it was so detailed and helped you work out every problem. It probably would be a good idea to include some blank pages at the end of each section so students can make notes. Just a few ideas!

I believe a solved practice exam for each section would be helpful. That way you would not have to worry about posting practice exams before the three scheduled exams during the next semester.

I believe the workbook was very helpful, definitely worth the cost. I wish the workbook had been available while taking the first semester.

It is a really great book that helps guide you through the thinking of each kind of problem. There is no way I could have done as well in the class as I have without purchasing this book. The examples were always helpful. I wish there was a workbook like that for all classes.

It was extremely useful and I'm glad I bought one. There were some people who never bought one and in the beginning of the semester they were fine without it, but about halfway through and at the end they were always asking to borrow the book from others.

It really was essential. I did not have the college-recommended text for the class, and found that by using the workbook I had all the information at hand.

Useful book, I wish i had it when I was in the first semester.

The workbook was the bomb.

Worth the money, extremely useful, very helpful.

I liked the workbook a lot, especially with the worked examples.

The workbook was very well structured and made it easy to go back and find the areas that I struggled in. It was also helpful because for every step that was worked out it explained why it was done the way it was. Overall this workbook was a crucial tool in the class.

The workbook was an easy guide to learn how to work out the problems in the course. It makes it easier to see the problem worked out than do a problem yourself.

I honestly believe that this book is responsible for my relative success this semester. The worked examples and the group environment which forced everyone to participate seem to be a much better system than a traditional lecture and listen session. Thanks again for all your help this semester.

I would not have done near as well if I had not bought the workbook. It was worth every penny.

The workbook was a great help. I used it every time I needed to complete a worksheet.

This workbook is exactly what I have always wanted for a course involving mathematics.

Whether for Chemistry, Physics or various incarnations of Math itself, a concise text of this sort with fully explained examples to refer back to would have been invaluable over the course of my college career. The format was perfect. I am very good with formulas, and if I know what elements go into a formula and why, it is much easier for me to memorize and apply them for various problems.

Extremely useful book. Made the course a breeze.

Excellent book, Excellent course, Excellent teacher!

About the author

I earned my Ph.D. in Inorganic Chemistry at Georgetown University between 1997 and 2001, while teaching General Chemistry recitation and laboratory. As a postdoctoral fellow at SUNY Stony Brook between 2001 and 2004, I contributed to the development of software for computer-based assessment in general chemistry, and became familiar with the POGIL teaching techniques. This inspired me to start using collaborative learning methods in the classes that I taught as chemistry faculty at Eastern Kentucky University between 2004 and 2010.

In creating this workbook, I tried to help students learn by doing hands-on work, instead of listening passively to the teacher. In my experience, collaborative learning proved to be far superior to traditional lecture. It is my hope that other instructors will adopt student-centered collaborative learning techniques in their classrooms.

Daniel C. Tofan
Ph.D., Inorganic Chemistry

Acknowledgments

A large amount of gratitude is due to Jennifer Imel, a graduate student in Chemistry at University of Kentucky and newly hired chemistry teacher at East Jessamine High School in Nicholasville, KY. Jennifer helped with various aspects of this book: proof reading, language and formatting corrections, some structure drawing, and class testing using a collaborative learning approach while completing educational research under my guidance. The collection of worksheets that I developed for the past several years, and that Jennifer helped test in the classroom, served as basis for this book.

Table of Contents

Worksheet 0. Mathematics in General Chemistry

Before being able to solve chemistry problems, you need some math skills. Nothing fancy, just college algebra. This worksheet will allow you to practice the math necessary to understand the problems solved in this workbook and to perform your own calculations. After you complete this worksheet on your own, you can check your answers in Appendix J.

1. Compute each of the following:

$$\frac{4}{15} \times \frac{3}{4} =$$

$$(1.25)^{-3} =$$

$$65\% \; of \; 525 =$$

$$55.845 + 2(14.007 + 4 \times 1.008) + 2(32.065 + 4 \times 16.00) =$$

$$\frac{12.01}{6.022 \times 10^{23}} =$$

$$2.18 \times 10^3 - 1.1 \times 10^2 =$$

$$\ln 2^2 =$$

$$\log_3(27) =$$

$$2.18 \times 10^{-18} \times \left(\frac{1}{3^2} - \frac{1}{2^2}\right) =$$

$$\frac{80.912 \times \frac{555}{760}}{0.0821 \times 319} =$$

$$\frac{3 \times 8.315 \times 298}{3.200 \times 10^{-3}} =$$

$$25.4 \times \frac{2.5}{100} \times \frac{1}{295.557} \times \frac{3}{5} \times 79.904 =$$

$$\sqrt[3]{\frac{4 \times 85.4678}{6.022 \times 10^{23} \times 1.63}} =$$

2. Expand the following:

$(x - 2)(x + 2) =$

$\dfrac{a}{b} + \dfrac{c}{d} =$

$\dfrac{2}{a + 1} - \dfrac{1}{a - 1} =$

$\sqrt{64x^4} =$

$\sqrt{3} + \sqrt{27} =$

$\dfrac{a - b}{\dfrac{1}{b} - \dfrac{1}{a}} =$

$x^a \times x^b =$

$\dfrac{x^a}{x^b} =$

$(x^a)^b =$

$\ln(a \times b) =$

$\ln\left(\dfrac{a}{b}\right) =$

$\dfrac{x^{3a+2}}{x^{2a-1}} =$

$\textit{Solve for } E_a : \quad \dfrac{k_1}{k_2} = \dfrac{e^{-\frac{E_a}{RT_1}}}{e^{-\frac{E_a}{RT_2}}}$

3. Solve for x in each equation below:

$$2.56\,x - 3.14 = 9.45$$

$$\frac{3x}{4} = 2$$

$$2(+3) + 3x + 12(-2) = 0$$

$$4x - 9 = 2x + 5$$

$$\frac{x}{2.5} = \frac{14.5}{50}$$

$$42 \text{ is } x\% \text{ of } 256$$

$$15.2 \text{ is } 3.5\% \text{ of } x$$

$$\frac{1}{x} = \frac{1}{10} - 3 \times 0.25$$

$$\frac{0.3611x}{x + 200} = \frac{25}{100}$$

$$\frac{1000x}{256 - 110.98\,x} = 0.500$$

$$\frac{(x-3)^2}{(x+3)^2} = 0.16$$

$$(x - 2)(3x - 4) = 0$$

$$x^2 = 6.5 \times 10^{-5}\,(0.2 - x)$$

$$\begin{cases} 3x + 2y = 8 \\ y = x - 1 \end{cases}$$

$$2^x = 4$$

$$3^x = 1$$

$$\left(\frac{1}{x}\right)^3 = \frac{1}{8}$$

$$\log_{10} x = 1.5$$

$$\ln(2x) = 2.4$$

$$\log(x^2) - \log(10) - 3 = 0$$

$$7 = \ln(5x) + \ln(7x - 2x)$$

$$2^{-x} = \frac{1}{16}$$

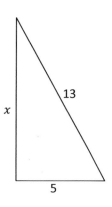

Lesson 1 – Numbers, Units, Measurement

Learning Objectives

In this lesson you will learn:

- To write a number in **scientific notation** and to convert from scientific to normal notation
- To determine the number of **significant figures** (digits) in a **measurement**
- To round off a numeric result to a specific number of **significant digits**
- To report the result of a calculation to the correct number of significant digits
- To convert from a basic **unit** (such as meter) to a smaller or larger unit (such as nanometer) using **SI prefixes**, and vice versa
- To convert between various magnitudes of the same basic unit using SI prefixes (for example from kilometers to millimeters or vice versa)
- To convert between units that involve **powers** (square, cube)
- To convert between any two units using known **conversion factors**
- To determine **accuracy** and **precision** in measurements by calculating **error**, **relative error**, **deviation**, **relative deviation**, and **standard deviation**.

Self-study questions

Before you start studying the worked examples, you should be able to formulate answers to the questions below. Use a textbook of your choice, or an online source of information, to find the answers.

1. Briefly describe the scientific method.
2. What are the components of a measurement?
3. Define unit.
4. What are the base units of the international system (SI)?
5. Define and give examples of derived units.
6. List the metric prefixes and their numerical meaning. Include: k, M, G, T, m, μ, n, p, f, a.
7. What is the difference between mass and weight?
8. What is density?
9. List the three common temperature scales and the relationships between them.
10. What is precision?
11. What is accuracy?
12. What is uncertainty in a measurement?
13. What is a conversion factor?
14. What are significant digits?
15. What is scientific notation?
16. What is the general principle to follow for converting units?

Worked examples

This section contains solved problems that cover the learning objectives listed above. Study each example carefully and make notes in the workbook to check every example that you understood. Repeat several times what you don't understand at first. It should become clearer as you keep working on the examples.

Objective 1.   Determine the number of significant digits in a measurement.

1.   Determine the number of significant digits in each of the values reported below.
- a.   250. kg
- b.   15 book chapters
- c.   1000 miles
- d.   100.1 s
- e.   120 kg
- f.   10.1010 g
- g.   0.002550 kg

Discussion

The following list briefly summarizes the rules for counting significant digits in a measurement:
1.   Significant digits apply only to the results of measurements. Exact numbers, such as those resulting from counting, are said to contain an infinite number of significant digits (sig figs).
2.   All nonzero digits in a measurement are significant.
3.   Zeros between significant digits are always significant. Therefore, "101.203 g" has 6 significant digits.
4.   Leading zeros (those before any other numbers) are never significant. Therefore, "0.000112 km" has 3 significant digits.
5.   Trailing zeros (ones at the end of a number) in numbers containing a decimal point are significant. Therefore "101.00 g" has 5 significant figures.
6.   Trailing zeros in numbers containing no decimal are not to be considered significant. If such zeros need to become significant, scientific notation should be used.

Solutions

- a.   3
- b.   Infinite, as book chapters can be counted, it is not a measurement
- c.   1
- d.   4
- e.   2
- f.   6
- g.   4

Objective 2.   Convert numbers to and from scientific notation.

1.   Convert each number below to scientific notation
- a.   -25,000
- b.   0.0101
- c.   1000
- d.   390
- e.   -50.30
- f. 201×10^3

Discussion

When converting a number to scientific notation, we must keep the same number of significant digits. This makes it easier to understand significant digits, as scientific notation does not use any leading zeros. In scientific notation, all digits shown are significant.

Solutions

a. -2.5×10^4
b. 1.01×10^{-2}
c. 1×10^3
d. 3.9×10^2
e. -5.030×10^1
f. 2.01×10^5

---

2. Convert each number below from scientific notation to normal number notation.
    a. 2.030×10^{-2}
    b. 1.000×10^3
    c. 1.000×10^2
    d. 1.000×10^4
    e. -5.44×10^3
    f. 6.9×10^{-3}

Solutions

a. 0.02030
b. 1000. (note the dot at the end of the number; if the dot isn't there, the number would only have 1 significant digit, while the scientific notation requires 4)
c. 100.0
d. It is not possible to write this number as a decimal AND keep the 4 significant figures; if you write 10000., this has 5 significant digits, which is not allowed either; thus, the number must be kept in scientific notation in order to preserve the precision)
e. -5440
f. 0.0069

Incorrect example: 10.0×10^{-1} is not a correct scientific notation, because it has more than one digit before the decimal point.

Objective 3.   Round the result of a measurement to a given number of significant digits.

1. Round off the following numbers to the specified number of significant digits
    a. 999.6 mL to 3 significant digits
    b. 0.0456610 g to 3 significant digits
    c. 24566 m to 2 significant digits
    d. 6.2 L to 4 significant digits
    e. 3231 miles to 2 significant digits

Discussion

Experimental results sometimes contain more digits than necessary, especially if they are determined through computation, as is the case with density, for example. Such results need to be rounded off to fewer significant digits. When rounding off a number, if the leftmost digit being rounded off is 5 or larger, then the rightmost digit retained in the rounded number is increased by one.

Solutions

a.   999.6 rounds off to 1000, which has only 1 significant digit; in order to report the answer to 3 sig figs, we need scientific notation; thus the answer is $1.00 \times 10^3 \ mL$

b.   0.0457 g or $4.57 \times 10^{-2} \ g$

c.   25000 m or $2.5 \times 10^4 \ m$

d.   It is not possible to increase the precision of a measurement artificially; do not be tempted to write 6.200 L, as we don't know whether the digits after the "2" are really zeros; most likely they are not

e.   3200 miles

---

2.   Determine the results of the calculations below and report them to the appropriate number of digits.

    a.   1.455 g + 26.3 g

    b.   750 K – 273.15 K

    c. $0.02542 \ L \times 0.100 \frac{mol}{L}$

    d. $12.566 \ g \div 3.28 \ cm^3$

    e.   Calculate the average of 3.54 cm, 3.66 cm, 3.51 cm, 3.63 cm, 3.71 cm, 3.42 cm, 3.76 cm, 3.44 cm, 3.55 cm, and 3.36 cm.

Discussion

When adding or subtracting the results of measurements:
1.   Arrange the numbers in a vertical column with the decimal points (or implied decimal points) aligned and compute the answer.
2.   Locate the column farthest to the right that *has a significant digit in it for all the measurements* and round the answer, keeping that place as the last significant digit in the answer.

In other words, for addition or multiplication we retain the **least number of decimals**.

When multiplying or dividing the results of measurements, the answer is rounded keeping the same number of significant digits as the measurement in your problem that has the **smallest** number of significant digits.

Solutions

a.   1.455 g +

    26.3   g

=   27.755 g

We must report the result to the least number of *decimals* (it's an addition) of the two numbers, thus **27.8 g**.

b. 750   K −
     273.15 K
=   476.85 K

The least number of decimals is 0, thus the answer should be rounded up and reported as **477 K**.

c. The unit "L" cancels out:

$$0.02542 \, \cancel{L} \times 0.100 \, \frac{mol}{\cancel{L}} = 0.002542 \, mol$$

The answer needs to be reported to the least number of sig figs (it's a multiplication), which is 3 (in 0.100 mol/L), and thus the answer is $2.54 \times 10^{-3} \, mol$

d.

$$\frac{12.566 \, g}{3.28 \, cm^3} = 3.831097561 \, g/cm^3$$

Because the answer should have the least number of sig figs (3 in the 3.28 cm^3 measurement), the answer is reported as $3.83 \times g/cm^3$

e. The average is (we leave units out for simplicity):

$$\frac{3.54 + 3.66 + 3.51 + 3.63 + 3.71 + 3.42 + 3.76 + 3.44 + 3.55 + 3.36}{10} = 3.558$$

Because we need to keep 3 sig figs (the number 10 is just how many values we have and does not limit sig figs), the answer is **3.56 cm**.

Objective 4.   Convert between a basic unit and smaller or larger units using SI prefixes.

A.   Convert 2.50 m to:
    1.   cm
    2.   mm
    3.   μm
    4.   nm

Discussion

Many SI units are either too Large or too small to be convenient. For that reason, we define prefixes, which change the magnitude of the basic unit using powers of 10, usually in multiples of 3 (positive or negative). The table below lists all the SI prefixes currently defined:

Prefix	Symbol	Factor	Prefix	Symbol	Factor
Yotta	Y	10^{24}	Deci	d	10^{-1}
Zetta	Z	10^{21}	Centi	c	10^{-2}
Exa	E	10^{18}	Milli	m	10^{-3}
Peta	P	10^{15}	Micro	µ	10^{-6}
Tera	T	10^{12}	Nano	n	10^{-9}
Giga	G	10^{9}	Pico	p	10^{-12}
Mega	M	10^{6}	Femto	f	10^{-15}
Kilo	k	10^{3}	Atto	a	10^{-18}
Hecto	h	10^{2}	Zepto	z	10^{-21}
Deka	da	10^{1}	Yocto	y	10^{-24}

From this table we can write relationships between basic units and prefixed units. For example, 1 cm = 0.01 m. This is the same as 1 m = 100 cm.

The general strategy for all unit conversions is to multiply the original measurement by a conversion factor, which equals 1 from a mathematical point of view, but cancels out the original units and leaves the new units in:

$$old\_value \; \cancel{old\_unit} \times \frac{\textbf{number of new\_unit}}{\textbf{equivalent number of } \cancel{old\_unit}} = new\_value \;\; new\_unit$$

The ratio in bold font represents the conversion factor, which relates the old unit to the new unit by using the appropriate numerical values, as you will see below.

In this problem we will use the following conversion factors: $1\;m = 100\;cm = 1000\;mm = 10^6\;\mu m = 10^9\;nm$

This means that the following fractions are all equal to 1:

$$\frac{1\;m}{100\;cm} = \frac{100\;cm}{1\;m} = \frac{1\;m}{1000\;mm} = \frac{1000\;mm}{1\;m} = \frac{1m}{10^6\;\mu m} = \frac{10^6\;\mu m}{1m} = \frac{1\;m}{10^9\;nm} = \frac{10^9\;nm}{1\;m}$$

We will use the ratio that cancels out the undesired unit in each case, leaving the unit we need. That will be our conversion factor in each case.

Solutions

1. We multiply our measurement in *m* by the ratio 100 cm / 1 m, which does not change the value of the measurement (the ratio equals 1), however it does change the units, because the *meters* cancel out. This strategy is used in all unit conversions in order to get rid of the unwanted units and leave the desired ones in place. In the first case, *cm* must be on top and *m* must be on the bottom of the fraction, otherwise your units will not cancel!

$$2.50\;\cancel{m} \times \frac{100\;cm}{1\;\cancel{m}} = \textbf{250.}\,\textbf{\textit{cm}}\;(3\;sig\;figs)$$

2.

$$2.50\;\cancel{m} \times \frac{1000\;mm}{1\;\cancel{m}} = \textbf{2.50} \times \textbf{10}^{\textbf{3}}\;\textbf{\textit{mm}}$$

3.

$$2.50 \; m \times \frac{10^6 \; \mu m}{1 \; m} = 2.50 \times 10^6 \; \mu m$$

4.

$$2.50 \; m \times \frac{10^9 \; nm}{1 \; m} = 2.50 \times 10^9 \; nm$$

B. Convert 420,000,000 bytes to:
   1. kbyte
   2. Mbyte
   3. Gbyte
   4. Tbyte

Solutions

Let's simplify our measurement first: 420,000,000 bytes $= 4.2 \times 10^8$ bytes.

1.

$$4.2 \times 10^8 \; bytes \; \times \frac{1 \; kbyte}{10^3 \; bytes} = 4.2 \times 10^5 \; kbytes$$

2.

$$4.2 \times 10^8 \; bytes \; \times \frac{1 \; Mbyte}{10^6 \; bytes} = 420 \; Mbytes$$

3.

$$4.2 \times 10^8 \; bytes \; \times \frac{1 \; Gbyte}{10^9 \; bytes} = 0.42 \; Gbytes = 4.2 \times 10^{-1} \; Gbytes$$

4.

$$4.2 \times 10^8 \; bytes \; \times \frac{1 \; Tbyte}{10^{12} \; bytes} = 4.2 \times 10^{-4} \; Tbytes$$

Objective 5.   Convert between various magnitudes of the same basic unit using SI prefixes.

Convert:
   1. 325 nm to pm
   2. 32.50 mm to km

Discussion

In order to convert between various magnitudes of the same unit, the best strategy is to go through the base unit first, which means we need two conversion factors.

Solutions

1.

$$325 \; n\!\!\!/m \times \frac{1 \; \cancel{m}}{10^9 \; n\!\!\!/m} \times \frac{10^{12} \; pm}{1 \; \cancel{m}} = 325000 \; pm = \mathbf{3.25 \times 10^5 \; pm}$$

Notice how the first conversion transforms *nm* into *m*, whereas the second converts *m* to *pm*.

2.

$$32.50 \; m\!\!\!/m \times \frac{1 \; \cancel{m}}{10^3 \; m\!\!\!/m} \times \frac{1 \; km}{10^3 \; \cancel{m}} = \mathbf{3.250 \times 10^{-5} \; km}$$

Objective 6.   Convert to and from square units and cubic units.

Convert:
1. $30 \; cm^2$ to m^2
2. $30 \; cm^2$ to μm^2
3. $250 \; cm^3$ to m^3
4. $16 \; km^3$ to mm^3
5. $7.28 \; \frac{g}{cm^3}$ to $\frac{kg}{m^3}$

Discussion

When we convert units that are at a power different than 1 (such as square or cubic), we need to develop conversion factors for these powers, starting from the basic conversion factors.

Solutions

1. $30 \; cm^2$ to m^2

First we develop a conversion factor between square meters and square centimeters:

$$1 \; m = 100 \; cm \Rightarrow (1 \; m)^2 = (100 \; cm)^2 = (100)^2 cm^2 \Rightarrow \mathbf{1 \; m^2 = 10^4 \; cm^2}$$

With this conversion factor we can perform our requested conversion:

$$30 \; \cancel{cm^2} \times \frac{1 \; m^2}{10^4 \; \cancel{cm^2}} = \mathbf{3 \times 10^{-3} \; m^2}$$

2. $30 \; cm^2$ to μm^2

$$1 \; m = 100 \; cm = 10^6 \; \mu m \Rightarrow 1 \; cm = 10^4 \; \mu m \quad (we \; simplify \; the \; factor)$$

$$(1 \; cm)^2 = (10^4 \; \mu m)^2 \Rightarrow 1 \; cm^2 = 10^8 \; \mu m^2$$

$$30 \; \cancel{cm^2} \times \frac{10^8 \; \mu m^2}{1 \; \cancel{cm^2}} = \mathbf{3 \times 10^9 \; \mu m^2}$$

3. 250 cm^3 to m^3

$$1\ m = 100\ cm \Rightarrow (1\ m)^3 = (100\ cm)^3 \Rightarrow 1\ m^3 = 10^6\ cm^3$$

$$250\ \cancel{cm^3} \times \frac{1\ m^3}{10^6\ \cancel{cm^3}} = \mathbf{2.5 \times 10^{-4}\ m^3}$$

4. 16 km^3 to mm^3

$$1\ km = 10^3\ m = 10^3 \times (10^3\ mm) = 10^6\ mm \Rightarrow (1\ km)^3 = (10^6\ mm)^3 \Rightarrow 1 km^3 = 10^{18}\ mm^3$$

$$16\ \cancel{km^3} \times \frac{10^{18}\ mm^3}{1\ \cancel{km^3}} = \mathbf{1.6 \times 10^{19}\ mm^3}$$

5. $7.28\ \frac{g}{cm^3}$ to $\frac{kg}{m^3}$

We will use the conversion factor from problem 3 ($1\ m^3 = 10^6\ cm^3$), as well as this one: 1 kg = 1000 g.

$$7.28\ \frac{\cancel{g}}{\cancel{cm^3}} \times \frac{1\ kg}{1000\ \cancel{g}} \times \frac{10^6\ \cancel{cm^3}}{1\ m^3} = \mathbf{7.28 \times 10^3\ \frac{kg}{cm^3}}$$

Objective 7.   Convert between temperature scales.

Convert the following temperatures:
1.   82 °F to °C
2.   100. °C to °F
3.   263 °C to K
4.   753.6 K to °C

Solutions

We need the relationships between temperature scales:

$$°C = K - 273.15 \quad and \quad °C = (°F - 32) \times \frac{5}{9}$$

1.   82°F to °C:

$$(82 - 32) \times \frac{5}{9} = \frac{250}{9} = 27.777 = \mathbf{28\ °C}$$

2.   100. °C to °F

$$°F = °C \times \frac{9}{5} + 32 = 100 \times \frac{9}{5} + 32 = \mathbf{212\ °F}$$

3.   263 °C to K

$$263 + 273.15 = 536.15 = \mathbf{536\ K}$$

4.   753.6 K to °C

$$753.6 - 273.15 = 480.45 = \mathbf{480.5\ °C}$$

Objective 8.   Convert between other types of units using known conversion factors.

Convert the following units:
1.   4.0 gallons to liters
2.   250 miles to meters and kilometers
3.   36 hours to seconds
4.   75 in to m
5.   2.40 atm to kPa
6. $3.00 \times 10^8 \frac{m}{s}$ to $\frac{miles}{hour}$

Discussion

There are many conversion factors between various units. In general, these conversion factors represent the way certain units are defined, as a function of more basic units. Because conversion factors provide (by definition), as opposed to by measurement) the exact equivalent of a unit in another unit, numerical values of conversion factors never limit the number of significant digits that are to be reported in the final result. The following list gives some of the more common conversion factors.

$$1 \, gal = 3.785 \, L$$
$$1 \, mL = 1 \, cm^3$$
$$1 \, mile = 1609 \, m$$
$$1 \, hour = 3600 \, seconds$$
$$1 \, in = 2.54 \, cm$$
$$1 \, ft = 0.3048 \, m$$
$$1 \, lb = 0.45359 \, kg$$
$$1 \, yard = 0.914 \, m$$
$$1 \, atm = 101325 \, Pa = 760 \, mmHg = 760 \, torr$$
$$1 \, Å = 1 \times 10^{-10} \, m$$
$$1 \, bar = 1 \times 10^5 \, Pa$$
$$1 \, cal = 4.184 \, J$$

Solutions

1.   4.0 gallons to liters

$$4.0 \, gal \times \frac{3.785 \, L}{1 \, gal} = 15.14 \, L = \mathbf{15 \, L}$$

2.   250 miles to meters and kilometers

$$250 \, mi \times \frac{1609 \, m}{1 \, mi} = 402250 \, m = \mathbf{4.0 \times 10^5 \, m}$$

$$4.0 \times 10^5 \, m \times \frac{1 \, km}{1000 \, m} = \mathbf{4.0 \times 10^2 \, km}$$

3.   36 hours to seconds

$$36 \, h \times \frac{3600 s}{1 h} = 129600 \, s = \mathbf{1.3 \times 10^5 \, s}$$

4. 75 in to m

$$75 \; in \; \times \; \frac{2.54 \; cm}{1 \; in} \times \frac{1 \; m}{100 \; cm} = 1.905 \; m = \mathbf{1.9 \; m}$$

5. 2.40 atm to kPa

$$2.40 \; atm \; \times \; \frac{101{,}325 \; Pa}{1 \; atm} \times \frac{1 \; kPa}{1000 \; Pa} = 243.18 \; kPa = \mathbf{243 \; kPa}$$

6. $3.00 \times 10^8 \frac{m}{s}$ to $\frac{miles}{hour}$

$$3.00 \times 10^8 \frac{m}{s} \; \times \; \frac{3600 \; s}{1 \; h} \times \frac{1 \; mi}{1609 \; m} = 671{,}224{,}363 \; \frac{miles}{hour} = \mathbf{6.71 \times 10^8 \frac{miles}{hour}} \; (mph)$$

In all of the above conversions, we limited the number of significant digits reported in the final answer to the number of significant digits in the measurement to convert, and not to the conversion factors themselves!

Objective 9.   Calculate error, percent error, deviation and standard deviation for measurements.

1. In a titration experiment, the following results were obtained for the concentration of an acid solution: 0.124 M, 0.120 M, 0.129 M, 0.125 M, 0.122 M, where M is a concentration unit. The "real" (accepted) concentration of the solution is 0.127 M. Determine the average (mean) concentration, error, relative error, deviations, and standard deviation.

Solution

Average (mean concentration):

$$\frac{0.124 + 0.120 + 0.129 + 0.125 + 0.121}{5} = 0.1238 \; M = \mathbf{0.124 \; M}$$

The error is:

$$Error = average \; experimental \; value - accepted \; value = 0.124 \; M - 0.127 \; M = \mathbf{-0.003 \; M}$$

Relative error:

$$Relative \; error = \frac{Error}{Accepted \; value} \times 100 = \frac{-0.003}{0.127} \times 100 = -2.36 \; \% = \mathbf{-2 \; \%}$$

We calculate deviations for each individual measurement:

$$Deviation = |\; Measured \; value - Average \; value \;|$$

where the | | symbols represent the *absolute* (positive) value of the quantity between them.

Measured value	Deviation	Square of deviation
0.124 M	|0.124-0.124|=0 M	0
0.120 M	|0.120-0.124|=0.004 M	$(.004)^2 = 1.6 \times 10^{-5}$
0.129 M	|0.129-0.124|=0.005 M	$(.005)^2 = 2.5 \times 10^{-5}$
0.125 M	|0.125-0.124|=0.001 M	$(.001)^2 = 1 \times 10^{-6}$
0.121 M	|0.121-0.124|=0.003 M	$(.003)^2 = 9 \times 10^{-6}$

The standard deviation is:

$$St.\,dev. = \sqrt{\frac{\sum (squares\ of\ all\ deviations)}{(number\ of\ measurements - 1)}} = \sqrt{\frac{1.6 \times 10^{-5} + 2.5 \times 10^{-5} + 1 \times 10^{-6} + 9 \times 10^{-6}}{5 - 1}}$$

$$= \sqrt{\frac{5.1 \times 10^{-5}}{4}}$$

$$= 3.57 \times 10^{-3}\ M = \mathbf{4 \times 10^{-3}\ M} \quad (we\ retain\ only\ one\ sig\ fig)$$

Thus, the concentration determined in this experiment should be reported in the following notation:

$$\mathbf{0.124 \pm 0.004\ M}$$

(average value ± standard deviation)

Worksheet 1.   Measurement and units

The problems in this section may be identical or similar to the worked examples above. They may or may not be organized in the same order of learning objectives. The goal is not for you to plug numbers into the same equations, but to work these problems on paper based on your understanding of the topic after seeing a number of solved problems. Work on this section either individually, or in a small group. At the end of the section, rate your understanding of each learning objective using the scale indicated. Discuss your answers with some of your colleagues and try to reach an agreement on what the answers should be.

1. Convert each number below to scientific notation
    a.   2300

    b.   -502.3

    c.   0.005560

    d.   -0.11

    e.   10

2. Convert each number below from scientific notation to normal number notation.
    a. 2.33×10^{-6}

    b. 1.66×10^{4}

    c. -2.56×10^{-4}

    d. -5.00×10^{3}

    e. 2.3333×10^{2}

3. Determine the number of significant digits in each of the values reported in the table below.
    a.   102.4450 g

    b.   10.000 mm

    c.   2300 miles

    d.   3 eggs

    e.   − 23.45 kJ

    f.   0.000224 m

    g. 6.022×10^{23} atoms

4. Round off each of the following numbers to 4 significant digits
    a. 34.579

    b. 193.405

    c. 23.995

    d. 0.003882

    e. 0.023

    f. 2846.5

    g. 7.8354×10^{2}

5. Determine the results of the calculations below and report them to the appropriate number of digits (all are measurements).
    a. 23.225 − 2.69

    b. 27 + 273.15

    c. 59.446 x 30.0

    d. 100. ÷ 2.9988

    e. Calculate the average of 290.4 g, 285.36 g, 291.223 g, and 288.8 g.

6. Convert:
    a. 670.0 mL to L

b.   670.0 mL to μL

c.   59.46 m to mm

d.   59.46 m to dm

e.   2.90 nm to km

f.   2.90 nm to fm

7.   Convert:
   a.   25.96 cm^2 to m^2

   b.   61.2x10^3 cm^2 to μm^2

c. 3.50×10^2 dm^3 to km^3

d. 0.0025 m^3 to nm^3

e. $3.028 \times 10^{-2} \frac{kg}{m^3}$ to $\frac{g}{cm^3}$

8. Convert the following temperatures:
    a. 2266.6 °C to K

    b. 590 °F to °C

    c. 10. K to °C

    d. 220 °C to °F

9. Convert the following units after you look up the appropriate conversion factors:
    a. 2.50 L to gal

    b.   2.0 years to minutes

    c.   655 mL to m^3

    d.   155 lb to kg

    e.   5 ft 7 in to cm

    f.   1160 mmHg to atm

    g. $2.2 \times 10^4 \, \frac{miles}{hour}$ to $\frac{m}{s}$

10. In a lab experiment, the following results were obtained for the mass of an object: 102.25 g, 103.08 g, 101.99 g, 101.80 g, 102.56 g, and 102.66 g. The real mass of the object is 102.45 g. Determine the average (mean) mass, average error, relative error, deviations, and standard deviations.

Self-assessment

Using the scale indicated, rate your understanding of each learning objective at the completion of this lesson. Identify the areas where your understanding is weak or medium and discuss with your class mates and/or instructor. Write down specific questions you still have at the completion of this topic.

Learning objective	Self-assessment 3 = strong, 2 = medium, 1 = weak, 0 = not done
	3 2 1 0
	3 2 1 0
	3 2 1 0
	3 2 1 0
	3 2 1 0
	3 2 1 0
	3 2 1 0
	3 2 1 0
	3 2 1 0

Lesson 2 – Matter and its Forms

Learning Objectives

In this lesson you will learn:

- To distinguish between **elements**, **substances**, and **mixtures**
- To distinguish between and identify features of the three **states of matter**
- To classify chemical elements by type based on their position in the periodic table
- To distinguish between **intensive** and **extensive** properties
- To distinguish between **physical changes** and **chemical changes** (or **physical properties** and **chemical properties**)

Self-study questions

Before you start studying the worked examples, you should be able to formulate answers to the questions below. Use a textbook of your choice, or an online source of information, to find the answers.

1. What is a pure substance?
2. What is a mixture and what types of mixtures are there?
3. What are the three states of matter and what distinguishes them?
4. What is the difference between an element and a compound?
5. List the categories of elements in the periodic table and identify their location.
6. What is a period in the periodic table? What does a period correspond to in terms of electron distribution?
7. What is a group in the periodic table? What can be said about the elements in the same group?
8. How is the group number related to the number of valence electrons for main group elements?
9. What is an intensive property?
10. What is an extensive property?
11. What is a physical change?
12. What is a chemical change?

Worked examples

This section contains several solved examples that cover the learning objectives listed above. Study each example carefully and make notes in the workbook to check every example that you understood. Repeat several times what you don't understand at first. It should become clearer as you keep working on the examples.

Objective 10. Distinguish between pure substances and mixtures. Classify mixtures.

1. Indicate whether each of the following is a pure substance, or a homogeneous / heterogeneous mixture.

Water	Pure substance
Air	Homogeneous mixture
Dirt	Heterogeneous mixture
Copper wire	Pure substance
Stainless steel	Homogeneous mixture
Salad dressing	Heterogeneous mixture
Oxygen gas	Pure substance
Carbon dioxide	Pure substance
Milk	Homogeneous mixture
Brine	Homogeneous mixture
Sparkling water	Heterogeneous mixture

Discussion

Pure substances have the same chemical composition throughout the entire sample. Mixtures are physical combinations of two or more substances, which can be separated through physical means (without altering the chemical composition). Homogeneous mixtures have the same appearance no matter which sample is taken. Milk, for example, is an opaque white liquid, but it looks the same throughout its volume, so it is a homogeneous mixture, at least at macroscopic level (at microscopic level, one could see that milk is actually an emulsion). Sparkling water, at least when it sits in a glass, has gas bubbles coming out of it. If you can identify at least two different states of matter, or two immiscible (*cannot mix*) layers of the same state of matter (such as oil and water), then you have a heterogeneous mixture.

Objective 11. Distinguish between elements and compounds.

1. Indicate whether each of the following is an element or a compound.

Water	Compound
Copper wire	Element
Oxygen gas	Element
Carbon dioxide	Compound
Mercury	Element

Discussion

Whenever a substance contains more than one element in its composition, it is a compound. Elements are the most basic form of matter, containing only one type of atoms.

Objective 12. Distinguish between states of matter.

1.   Indicate true or false for each of the following characteristics of states of matter:

State of matter	Has a fixed volume	Has as fixed shape	Can be compressed or expanded	Has mass
Solid	True	True	False	True
Liquid	True	False	False	True
Gas	False	False	True	True

2.   Indicate whether each of the following is a solid, liquid, or gas in its natural state.

Water	Liquid
Gold	Solid
Copper wire	Solid
Helium	Gas
Carbon dioxide	Gas
Mercury	Liquid

Discussion

You will need to recognize a number of substances and remember their natural state of matter. Lt is part of the learning process in this course.

Objective 13. Classify elements by type.

1.   Classify each element below as a main group metal (M), transition metal (TM), semimetal (S), nonmetal (N), actinide/lanthanide (AL), or noble gas (NG).

Sulfur	N
Silicon	S
Zinc	TM
Oxygen	N
Sodium	M
Mercury	TM
Uranium	AL
Xenon	NG

Discussion

The periodic table in this book has different shadings for metals, nonmetals, and semi-metals (or metalloids). Transition metals, lanthanides, and actinides are also metals, but they generally display slightly different properties than main group metals. Noble gases are nonmetals, but they also have characteristic chemical properties.

Objective 14. Distinguish between intensive properties and extensive properties.

1. Classify each property below as intensive or extensive.

Mass	Extensive
Temperature	Intensive
Color	Intensive
Length	Extensive
Chemical composition	Intensive
Solubility	Extensive

Discussion

An extensive property depends on the quantity of substance subject to measurement. An intensive property is independent of the quantity measured.

Objective 15. Distinguish between chemical changes and physical changes.

1. Classify each property or change below as chemical or physical.

Temperature	Physical
Acidity	Chemical
Caloric content	Chemical
Melting of ice	Physical
Explosion of a bomb	Chemical
Dilution of brine	Physical

Discussion

A physical property (or change) does not imply a change in the internal (chemical) composition of the substance, whereas a chemical property (change) means that the substance is converted into a different substance. Sometimes, the distinction between physical and chemical properties becomes fuzzy, but the definition above will generally be used to make this distinction.

Worksheet 2.   Measurement and matter assessment

Because this lesson was very easy, this worksheet will contain a number of questions in multiple choice format. These are questions that may appear on any test that covers the topics in lessons 1 and 2. Thus, it will be good practice in preparation for an exam. Answer each question by writing the correct answer letter in the space provided to the right of the question text.

1. What is the chemical symbol of the element tin?
    A. Sn
    B. Ti
    C. Tl
    D. Ta

2. What is the name of the group that contains the element bromine?
    A. Alkali metals
    B. Noble gases
    C. Halogens
    D. Alkaline earth metals

3. Which of the following statements does not describe a physical property of chlorine?
    A. The density of chlorine gas at standard temperature and pressure is 3.17 g/L.
    B. Chlorine combines with sodium to form table salt.
    C. The color of chlorine gas is green.
    D. The freezing point of chlorine is -101°C.

4. Which of the following is not an intensive property?
    A. Density
    B. Melting point
    C. Mass
    D. Color

5. Which of the following is not an extensive property?
    A. Diameter
    B. Mass
    C. Color
    D. Volume

6. When measuring various properties of a solid metal block at constant temperature, which measurement will change in numerical value depending on the location where it is taken?
    A. Weight
    B. Volume
    C. Length
    D. Mass

7. Silver is an example of:
    A. A homogeneous mixture
    B. A heterogeneous mixture
    C. A compound
    D. An element

8. Filtered apple juice is an example of:
    A. A homogeneous mixture
    B. A heterogeneous mixture
    C. A compound
    D. An element

9. Salad dressing is an example of:
    A. A homogeneous mixture
    B. A heterogeneous mixture
    C. A compound
    D. An element

10. All of the following elements are nonmetals except
    A. Helium
    B. Nitrogen
    C. Antimony
    D. Sulfur

11. Which of the following is a fundamental SI Unit?
    A. Gram
    B. Centimeter
    C. Second
    D. Kilometer

12. The prefix "deci" corresponds to the number:
    A. 0.1
    B. 0.01
    C. 0.001
    D. 10

13. What symbol corresponds to the factor 10^{-9}?
    A. M
    B. m
    C. µ
    D. n

14. A solid object weighs 8.25 g. When placed into a graduated cylinder containing water, the liquid level rises from 21.25 mL to 26.47 mL. Calculate the density of the object.
    A. 0.633 g/mL
    B. 1.58 g/mL
    C. 0.312 g/mL
    D. 3.21 g/mL

15. Convert 0.004004 to standard scientific notation.
    A. 4004×10^{-6}
    B. 4.004×10^{3}
    C. 4.004×10^{-3}
    D. 4004×10^{6}

16. Convert 1672°C to K.
    A.   897 K
    B.   3042 K
    C.   1945 K
    D.   1399 K

17. Convert 3000. µg to g.
    A. $3 \times 10^{-6}\ g$
    B. $3 \times 10^{6}\ g$
    C. $3.000 \times 10^{-6}\ g$
    D. $3.000 \times 10^{6}\ g$

18. Convert 100 cm^3 to m^3.
    A. $1\ m^3$
    B. $0.01\ m^3$
    C. $10^4\ m^3$
    D. $10^{-4}\ m^3$

19. Which of the following numbers has the greatest number of significant figures?
    A. 6.02×10^{23}
    B.   2,500,000
    C.   0.5040
    D.   0.000201

20. Round off 209.68 to three significant figures.
    A.   209
    B.   209.7
    C.   210
    D.   210.

21. Which measurement is largest?
    A.   100 cm
    B.   10 mm
    C.   0.1 m
    D.   100 dm

Consider the periodic table below for the next 3 questions.

Periodic Table of the Elements

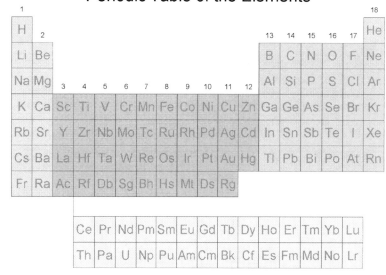

22. How many valence electrons are common for elements in group 17?
    A. 1
    B. 17
    C. 7
    D. They are not all the same

23. Which pair of elements should have the same number of valence electrons?
    A. Na and Cs
    B. Ga and Ge
    C. He and Ne
    D. Rb and Br

24. What is the maximum number of electrons that can be found in the second shell of the element K?
    A. 1
    B. 2
    C. 8
    D. 20

25. What group of elements is indicated by the shaded area in the figure below?
    A. Alkali metals
    B. Nonmetals
    C. Transition metals
    D. Metals

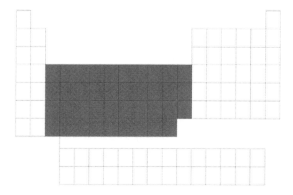

Self-assessment

Using the scale indicated, rate your understanding of each learning objective at the completion of this lesson. Identify the areas where your understanding is weak or medium and discuss with your class mates and/or instructor. Write down specific questions you still have at the completion of this topic.

Learning objective	Self-assessment 3 = strong, 2 = medium, 1 = weak, 0 = not done
	3 2 1 0
	3 2 1 0
	3 2 1 0
	3 2 1 0
	3 2 1 0
	3 2 1 0

Lesson 3 – Basic Atomic Structure

Learning Objectives

In this lesson you will learn:
- To write the chemical symbol of an **isotope**
- To determine the number of **protons** and **neutrons** in the nucleus of an isotope
- To **name** an isotope
- To identify an isotope from certain information given
- To calculate the **average atomic mass** of an element from its natural **isotopic composition**
- To determine the number of **electron shells** found in the **electron cloud** of a given atom
- To determine the number of **valence electrons** for an element
- To write a **Lewis dot symbol** for an element
- To sketch the formation of a simple **ionic compound** when a metal reacts with a nonmetal

Pre-requisite: Matter and its forms.

Self-study questions

Before you start studying the worked examples, you should be able to formulate answers to the questions below. Use a textbook of your choice, or an online source of information, to find the answers.

1. What is an atom made of?
2. What particles are in the nucleus of an atom?
3. What is the atomic number of an element?
4. What is the mass number of an element?
5. What is an isotope?
6. What is meant by isotope abundance?
7. What is the most abundant element on earth?
8. What is the significance of the atomic mass displayed for an element in the periodic table?
9. What is an electron shell?
10. What is meant by valence electrons?
11. What is a Lewis dot symbol?
12. What is an ion?
13. What is ionic bonding?
14. How does an ionic compound form?

Worked examples

This section contains several solved examples that cover the learning objectives listed above. Study each example carefully and make notes in the workbook to check every example that you understood. Repeat several times what you don't understand at first. It should become clearer as you keep working on the examples.

Objective 16. Write isotopic symbols and names for elemental isotopes.

Write the isotopic symbols and names of the three isotopes of hydrogen.

Solutions

Hydrogen has three known isotopes, which differ by the number of neutrons in their nucleus: 0, 1, and 2. Remember:

$$Mass\ number = number\ of\ protons + number\ of\ neutrons$$

$$Atomic\ number = number\ of\ protons$$

$$Isotopic\ symbol: \ _{Atomic\ number}^{Mass\ number}\ Element\ symbol\ (_Z^A E)$$

$$Isotope\ name = element\ name, dash, mass\ number$$

Thus, we can write the symbols and names of these isotopes:

Isotopic symbol	Name
$_1^1 H$	Hydrogen-1 (*protium*)
$_1^2 H$	Hydrogen-2 (*deuterium*)
$_1^3 H$	Hydrogen-3 (*tritium*)

The names given in parentheses are the common names of these isotopes of hydrogen.

Objective 17. Determine the numbers of electrons, protons, and neutrons in the atom of an isotope or isotopic ion.

Determine the number of protons, neutrons, and electrons in each of the following species:
1. $_{12}^{26}Mg$
2. $_{13}^{27}Al^{3+}$
3. $_{35}^{80}Br^-$

Solutions

1. This isotope will have 12 protons, 26-12 = 14 neutrons, and 12 electrons.
2. This is a positive ion and will have 13 protons, 27-13 = 14 neutrons, and 13-3 = 10 electrons.
3. This is a negative ion and will have 35 protons, 80-35=55 neutrons, and 35+1=36 electrons.

Objective 18. Identify an isotope given information about the numbers of particles it contains, or a combination of data.

The table below will be used for objectives 17-19. Complete the table by filling out all the boxes from the information given.

No.	Isotope name	Isotope symbol	Protons	Neutrons	Mass number
1	Carbon-14				
2		$^{18}_{8}O$			
3				10	19
6			25	31	
7			17		37
8			20	20	

Solutions

The answers should be self-explanatory, as in each case the information given is sufficient to let us figure out the rest. Here is the completed table.

No.	Isotope name	Isotope symbol	Protons	Neutrons	Mass number
1	**Carbon-14**	$^{14}_{6}C$	6	8	14
2	Oxygen-18	$^{18}_{8}O$	8	10	18
3	Fluorine-19	$^{19}_{9}F$	9	**10**	**19**
6	Manganese-56	$^{56}_{25}Mn$	**25**	**31**	56
7	Chlorine-37	$^{37}_{17}Cl$	**17**	20	**37**
8	Calcium-40	$^{40}_{20}Ca$	**20**	**20**	40

Objective 19. Calculate the average atomic mass of an element given its isotopic composition.

Calculate the average atomic mass of each element in the table below, given the element's isotopic composition.

No	Element	Isotope 1 mass and abundance	Isotope 2 mass and abundance	Isotope 3 mass and abundance	Isotope 4 mass and abundance	Average atomic mass
1	Cu	Copper-63 62.9296011 amu 69.17%	Copper-65 64.9277937 amu 30.83%	N/A	N/A	
2	Mg	Magnesium-24 23.98504190 amu 78.99%	Magnesium-25 24.98583712 amu 10.00%	Magnesium-26 25.98259304 amu 11.01%	N/A	
3	Fe	Iron-54 53.9396148 amu 5.845%	Iron-56 55.9349421 amu 91.754%	Iron-57 56.9353987 amu 2.119%	Iron-58 57.9332805 amu 0.282%	

Discussion

In each problem, we are given the natural isotopic composition of an element. Copper, for example, has two stable isotopes, Copper-63 and Copper-65. The natural distribution (abundance) of each of the two isotopes is 69.17% and 30.83% respectively. The element copper will always be a mixture of these two isotopes, so the atomic mass of copper that is given in the periodic table must be an average of the masses of its component isotopes.

The exact atomic mass of each isotope has been determined very precisely, as you notice. The mass of each isotope is given in amu (atomic mass units). In order to calculate the average atomic mass of copper, we must take into account the abundance (in percent) of each isotope as well as its mass.

The following formula will calculate the average atomic mass of any element, given its isotopic composition (mass and abundance of each isotope):

$$Average\ atomic\ mass = \sum (Isotope\ mass\ \times isotope\ abundance)$$

We multiply the exact mass of each isotope by its abundance (written as a decimal number), and the sum of all these products will be the average atomic mass of the element.

Solutions

1. $Cu : 62.9296011\ amu \times 0.6917 + 64.9277937\ amu \times 0.3083 = \mathbf{63.55\ amu}$

2. $Mg : 23.98504190\ amu \times 0.7899 + 24.98583712 \times 0.1000 + 25.98259304 \times 0.1101 = \mathbf{24.31\ amu}$

3. $Fe : 53.9396148\ amu \times 0.05845 + 55.9349421\ amu \times 0.91754 + 56.9353987\ amu \times 0.02119 + 57.9332805\ amu \times 0.002820 = \mathbf{55.85\ amu}$

Copy these values in the table above if you wish.

Objective 20. Determine the distribution of electrons in the shells of the atom of an element and the number of valence electrons. Draw the Lewis dot symbol for an element.

For each element below, fill in the boxes with the number of electrons in each shell, its valence electrons, and draw its Lewis dot symbol.
> Hydrogen, Beryllium, Fluorine, Aluminum, Phosphorus, Potassium.

Discussion

The number of electron shells that an atom of an element has corresponds to its period in the periodic table. The main group elements have a number of valence electrons equal to the group number (for groups 1 and 2) or group number minus 10 (for groups 13 through 18). The main groups are those shaded in the schematic periodic table below. All elements in a group have the same number of valence electrons. Thus, the elements chlorine, bromine, and iodine have 7 valence electrons, like fluorine, because they are all in group 17 (and 17-10=7). When we look at electron configurations, you will learn why valence electrons are determined in this way.

The Lewis dot symbol of an element represents the valence electrons, drawn as dots, around the symbol of the atom. For now, it does not really matter how you draw electrons around the symbol, but you will learn more about this too in a future lesson.

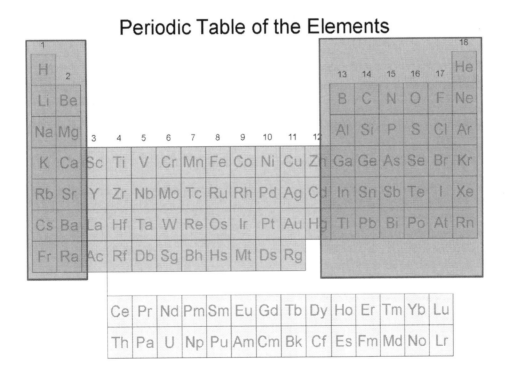

Periodic Table of the Elements

Solution

The table below will help summarize the information presented above.

Element	Shell 1 electrons	Shell 2 electrons	Shell 3 electrons	Shell 4 electrons	Valence electrons	Lewis dot symbol
H	1				1	H•
Be	2	2			2	Be
F	2	7			7	:F:
Al	2	8	3		3	Al•
P	2	8	5		5	:P•
K	2	8	8	1	1	K•

Objective 21. Sketch the formation of simple ionic compounds.

Using Lewis dot symbols (also known as electron dot symbols), show how each pair below, consisting of a metal and a nonmetal, can react and form an ionic compound.
1.   K + Cl
2.   Mg + O
3.   Mg + F
4.   Na + N
5.   Al + S

Discussion

Elements react with each other to form compounds. This is generally because in compounds they achieve a more favorable electron configuration than in their natural state. Metals have a tendency to lose electrons (this is also what makes them good electricity conductors), and nonmetals have a tendency to accept electrons. Thus, a metal and a nonmetal can combine to form a simple ionic compound, which consists of a positive ion (cation) and a negative ion (anion). In doing this, both the metal and the nonmetal achieve a stable configuration of 8 valence electrons, called an octet. This is a noble gas configuration. The cation and the anion are attracted to each other electrostatically, and this attraction is called ionic bond.

The number of electrons lost by the metal must be the same as the number of electrons gained by the nonmetal (conservation of charge). If these numbers don't match, then we need to take more than one metal atom, or one nonmetal atom, or both, in order to reach a common multiplier. This is illustrated in examples 3-5 below.

The names of all these binary ionic compounds are obtained by listing the name of the metal (always first), followed by a modified name of the nonmetal, so that it ends in the suffix –**ide**.

Solutions

1.

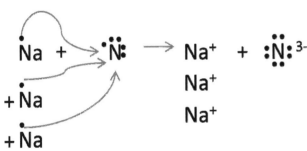

$$K + \; :\overset{\bullet}{\underset{\bullet\bullet}{Cl}}: \longrightarrow K^+ + :\overset{\bullet\bullet}{\underset{\bullet\bullet}{Cl}}:^-$$

Potassium chloride

2.

$$\overset{\bullet\bullet}{Mg} + :\overset{}{\underset{\bullet\bullet}{O}}: \longrightarrow Mg^{2+} + :\overset{\bullet\bullet}{\underset{\bullet\bullet}{O}}:^{2-}$$

Magnesium oxide

3.

$$Mg: + \; \overset{:F:}{\underset{:F:}{}} \longrightarrow Mg^{2+} + :\overset{}{\underset{\bullet\bullet}{F}}:^- + :\overset{}{\underset{\bullet\bullet}{F}}:^-$$

Magnesium fluoride

4.

$$Na + \; \overset{\bullet\bullet}{N}: \longrightarrow Na^+ + :\overset{\bullet\bullet}{\underset{\bullet\bullet}{N}}:^{3-}$$
$$+Na \qquad\qquad Na^+$$
$$+Na \qquad\qquad Na^+$$

Sodium nitride

5.

$$Al\bullet \quad \overset{\bullet\bullet}{\underset{\bullet\bullet}{S}}:$$
$$\quad + \; \overset{}{\underset{\bullet\bullet}{S}}: \longrightarrow 2\,Al^{3+} + 3\,:\overset{}{\underset{\bullet\bullet}{S}}:^{2-}$$
$$Al\bullet \quad \overset{}{\underset{\bullet\bullet}{S}}:$$

Aluminum sulfide

Worksheet 3.   Atomic structure

The exercises and problems in this section will allow you to practice the topic until you understand it well.

1.   Isotopes and isotopic symbols. Complete the table below:

Isotope name	Isotope symbol	Protons	Neutrons	Mass number
	$^{57}_{26}Fe$			
Lithium-5				
		17		37
	$^{60}_{27}Co$			
			55	90
			46	81
		92		235
Copper-63				

2.   Average atomic mass. Complete the table below:

Element	Isotope 1 mass and abundance	Isotope 2 mass and abundance	Isotope 3 mass and abundance	Isotope 4 mass and abundance	Isotope 5 mass and abundance	Average atomic mass
Cl	Chlorine-35 34.969 amu 75.77%	Chlorine-37 36.966 amu 24.23%	N/A	N/A	N/A	
Ti	Titanium-46 45.952633 amu 8.00%	Titanium-47 46.951765 amu 7.30%	Titanium-48 47.947947 amu 73.80%	Titanium-49 48.947871 amu 5.50%	Titanium-50 49.944786 amu 5.40%	

3. Basic electron structure and Lewis dot symbols. Complete the table below:

Element	Shell 1 electrons	Shell 2 electrons	Shell 3 electrons	Shell 4 electrons	Valence electrons	Lewis dot symbol
H						
He						
Li						
Be						
B						
C						
N						
O						
F						
Ne						
Na						
Mg						
Al						
Si						
P						
S						

Cl						
Ar						
K						
Ca						

4. Ionic bond formation. Show how ionic bonds form when the following pairs of elements react and name the compounds formed:

a. Li + S

b. Ca + Cl

c. Al + N

d.   Na + P

e.   Br + Rb

Self-assessment

Using the scale indicated, rate your understanding of each learning objective at the completion of this lesson. Identify the areas where your understanding is weak or medium and discuss with your class mates and/or instructor. Write down specific questions you still have at the completion of this topic.

Learning objective	Self-assessment 3 = strong, 2 = medium, 1 = weak, 0 = not done
	3 2 1 0
	3 2 1 0
	3 2 1 0
	3 2 1 0
	3 2 1 0
	3 2 1 0

Lesson 4 – Classes of Compounds and Nomenclature

Learning Objectives

In this lesson you will learn:
- To distinguish between **ionic** and **covalent compounds**
- To write chemical formulas and names for **oxides**
- To write chemical formulas and names for **hydroxides**
- To write chemical formulas and names for **acids** and their **anions**
- To write chemical formulas and names for **salts** from **cations** and anions
- To write chemical formulas and names for **double salts**
- To write chemical formulas and names for **hydrates**
- To understand the ionic composition of a salt given its chemical formula
- To name a salt given its chemical formula, or to write the chemical formula from its name
- To name **binary covalent compounds**
- To determine why a formula or a name is invalid

Pre-requisite: Matter and its forms; Atomic structure.

Self-study questions

Before you start studying the worked examples, you should be able to formulate answers to the questions below. Use a textbook of your choice, or an online source of information, to find the answers.

1. What is the difference between an ionic compound and a covalent compound?
2. What is a cation?
3. What is an anion?
4. What is the charge of a compound?
5. What happens when a positive charge is removed from a compound?
6. What is an oxide?
7. What is a hydroxide?
8. What is an acid?
9. What types of acids are there (based on their chemical composition)?
10. What is a salt?
11. What is a double salt?
12. What is a hydrate?
13. What is a binary covalent compound?

Worked examples

This section contains several solved examples that cover the learning objectives listed above. Study each example carefully and make notes in the workbook to check every example that you understood. Repeat several times what you don't understand at first. It should become clearer as you keep working on the examples.

Objective 22. Distinguish between ionic compounds and covalent compounds.

For each compound below, indicate whether it is likely to be an ionic or a covalent compound

H_2O	Covalent
NaCl	Ionic
CuO	Ionic
$AlBr_3$	Ionic
CO_2	Covalent
H_2SO_4	Covalent
SiO_2	Covalent

Discussion

In general, metals and nonmetals combine to form ionic compounds. Nonmetals combine with each other to form covalent compounds. Metals do not combine with each other chemically, but they form alloys. Those are mixtures (usually homogeneous), and not compounds. Semimetals (metalloids) also tend to form covalent compounds, regardless of what they combine with.

It is important to learn at this stage how to draw an ionic compound versus a covalent compound. Ionic bonds represent electrostatic attractions between ions of opposite charges. Covalent bonds represent sharing of electrons and are drawn using lines. The sketch below shows the correct way and the incorrect way of drawing potassium chloride, an ionic compound:

There is no bond between potassium and chlorine, so it a serious mistake to draw bonds in ionic compounds. On the other hand, hydrochloric acid is a covalent compound, and it should be drawn using a covalent bond:

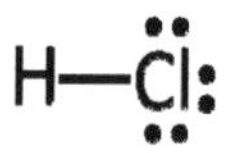

Objective 23. Write formulas and names for metal oxides.

Complete the table below following the examples given in bold.

Metal	Cation formula	Oxide formula	Oxide name
Li	Li^+	Li_2O	Lithium oxide
Mg	Mg^{2+}	MgO	Magnesium oxide
Al	Al^{3+}	Al_2O_3	Aluminum oxide
Zn	Zn^{2+}	ZnO	Zinc Oxide
Cu	Cu^+	Cu_2O	Copper(I) oxide Cuprous oxide
Cu	Cu^{2+}	CuO	Copper(II) oxide Cupric oxide
Fe	Fe^{2+}	FeO	Iron(II) oxide Ferrous oxide
Fe	Fe^{3+}	Fe_2O_3	Iron(III) oxide Ferric oxide

Discussion

An oxide is a binary compound between a metal (or a nonmetal) and oxygen. The oxide ion (O^{2-}) is divalent (its charge is 2 negative), and so the charge of the positive ion (cation) must balance that of the oxide. Thus, a monovalent cation such as Li^+ will need two such cations for each oxide ion in order to form a neutral compound. Notice how in writing the formulas, all we do is balance out the charges, positive and negative, because all compounds are neutral. When we write the formula of a compound, the charges of the individual ions in it are NEVER shown. Thus, $Mg^{2+}O^{2-}$ is incorrect as a formula and you get penalized if write this. It only makes sense to write the two ions separately, but never in a compact chemical formula.

In the case of copper and iron (as well as other metals, primarily transition metals), there is more than one cation possible. You are generally told what these are, as they are not always intuitive. In order to differentiate between the two possible oxides of Cu, we need to indicate the valence of the metal in parenthesis. Thus, Cu_2O is copper(I) oxide, and CuO is copper(II) oxide. Note that the parenthesis starts right after the metal name (there is no space), and the charge of the metal ion is represented by a Roman numeral. This is the correct nomenclature for these cations. In the case of iron, the two cations it makes are charged +2 and +3, and thus the names iron(II) and iron(III).

The second way of naming these compounds is by using the suffixes –*ous* and –*ic*. There is no direct correspondence between these suffixes and the actual charges of the ions. Instead, –*ous* is used for the inferior (lower valence) cation, and –*ic* is used for the superior (higher valence) cation. This, of course, implies only two cations, which is the most common situation anyway. Thus, copper(I) is also called cupr*ous*, and copper(II) is called cupr*ic*. In the case of iron, Fe(II) is ferr*ous*, and Fe(III) is ferr*ic*. In both cases, the Latin name of the element (*cuprum* for Cu, and *ferrum* for Fe) are used to derive the names.

If the metal can only form one cation, then the numeral is not used. It is incorrect (and thus a mistake) to say magnesium(II) oxide, as there is no other cation of magnesium.

These rules apply to hydroxides and salts of metals as well, as you will see in the following examples. The basic rule of thumb is that transition metals form more than one cation, and thus will require numerals for their charge, with the following exceptions:

- Zinc and cadmium are always +2
- Silver is always +1
- Scandium and yttrium are always +3

One exception is important: mercury can have a +1 oxidation state, but it exists as a diatomic ion: Hg_2^{2+}. In its compounds, we name it mercury (I), although we always use the diatomic farm of the ion. For example, mercury (I) chloride is Hg_2Cl_2 and not $HgCl$.

Some metals from the main groups, such as those in periods 5 and higher, can also form more than one cation (examples are Sn, Pb, In, Tl , Bi), and they too require the use of roman numerals in naming their compounds.

Objective 24. Write formulas and names for metal hydroxides.

Complete the table below following the examples given in bold.

Metal	Cation formula	Hydroxide formula	Hydroxide name
Li	Li+	LiOH	**Lithium hydroxide**
Mg	Mg2+	$Mg(OH)_2$	**Magnesium hydroxide**
Al	Al^{3+}	$Al(OH)_3$	Aluminum hydroxide
Zn	Zn2+	$Zn(OH)_2$	Zinc hydroxide
Cu	Cu+	$CuOH$	Copper(I) hydroxide Cuprous hydroxide
	Cu2+	$Cu(OH)_2$	Copper(II) hydroxide Cupric hydroxide

Discussion

Hydroxides are compounds between metal cations and the hydroxide ion (OH^-). They are also known as bases (not all bases are hydroxides, though). The rules described for oxides apply here as well. Since the hydroxide ion is monovalent, most hydroxides will have more than one hydroxide ion in their formulas. When a compound ion, such as hydroxide, is to be taken more than once, it must be written in parenthesis. Thus, the formula $MgOH_2$ is wrong, because it implies that there is one oxygen and two hydrogen atoms in it. It actually has to show that the OH^- ion appears twice. On the other hand, it is incorrect to use parentheses when a compound (polyatomic) ion only appears once. Thus, $Na(OH)$ is wrong and you get penalized if you write it this way.

Objective 25. Write formulas and names for acids.

Name each acid below.

Acid formula	Acid name
HF	Hydrofluoric acid
HCl	Hydrochloric acid
H_2S	Hydrosulfuric acid
HCN	Hydrocyanic acid
HNO_3	Nitric acid
HNO_2	Nitrous acid
H_3PO_4	Phosphoric acid

H_3PO_3	Phosphorous acid
HClO	Hypochlorous acid
$HClO_2$	Chlorous acid
$HClO_3$	Chloric acid
$HClO_4$	Perchloric acid
H_2CO_3	Carbonic acid
H_2SiO_3	Silicic acid
$H_2C_2O_4$	Oxalic acid

Discussion

Acids are compounds of, generally, nonmetals and hydrogen, and they may or may not contain oxygen as well. In the case of acids, it makes most sense to learn their names. There are rules for these names too. If the acid does not contain oxygen in its formula, its name starts with "hydro", followed by the root of the Latin name of the element (typically a nonmetal), and ending in the –*ic* suffix (as in *hydro**chloric***). If the acid contains oxygen (called an oxoacid), then the suffixes –***ous*** and –*ic* are used again, representing the lower and higher number of oxygens in the acid formula. For example, the two common oxoacids of nitrogen are HNO_3 and HNO_2, and their names are nit**r*ic*** (high oxygen, 3) and nitr***ous*** (low oxygen, 2). In the case of phosphorus, the two common acids are H_3PO_4 (phosphor**ic**, high O) and H_3PO_3 (phosphor***ous***, low O). It is not intuitive why this is, and that is the reason why I recommend learning the acids and their names. The word "acid" is added to all acid names.

Certain elements, such as the halogens (except fluorine), make more than 2 acids, four to be exact. Thus, the two suffixes are no longer enough, and for that reason we use prefixes AND suffixes. *Hypo-* means lower, and *Per-* means higher, and thus the four oxoacids known for chlorine have the names **hypo**chlor***ous***, chlor***ous***, chlor**ic**, and **per**chlor**ic**. On the other hand, if only one acid exists for a nonmetal, the suffix –*ic* is used (as in carbon**ic** acid).

Other acids have names that are not derived from the central nonmetal (hydrocyanic, oxalic, etc.), which is one more reason to learn them as such. For more details see Appendix A.

Objective 26. Write formulas and names for anions derived from acids.

For each acid below, write the formulas of the anions resulting from the stepwise removal of hydrogen ions (protons) from the acid. Give the names of the resulting anions.

Acid formula	Acid name	Anion formula	Anion name
HF	Hydrofluoric acid	F^-	Fluoride
HCl	Hydrochloric acid	Cl^-	Chloride
HNO_3	Nitric acid	NO_3^-	Nitrate
HNO_2	Nitrous acid	NO_2^-	Nitrite
HClO	Hypochlorous acid	ClO^-	Hypochlorite
$HClO_2$	Chlorous acid	ClO_2^-	Chlorite
$HClO_3$	Chloric acid	ClO_3^-	Chlorate
$HClO_4$	Perchloric acid	ClO_4^-	Perchlorate
H_2SO_4	Sulfuric acid	HSO_4^-	Hydrogen sulfate
		SO_4^{2-}	Sulfate
HCN	Hydrocyanic acid	CN^-	Cyanide
H_3PO_4	Phosphoric acid	$H_2PO_4^-$	Dihydrogen phosphate
		HPO_4^{2-}	Hydrogen phosphate
		PO_4^{3-}	Phosphate
$HMnO_4$	Permanganic acid	MnO_4^-	Permanganate
CH_3COOH	Acetic acid	CH_3COO^-	Acetate

Discussion

Acids, by definition, are compounds that can donate hydrogen ions (H^+, which are actually just protons) in solution. So what remains from the acid when it donates a charged hydrogen ion? A negative ion, of course (called an anion). Acids that have more than one hydrogen atom in their molecule can form more than one anion, and we learn how to write them all, indicating the correct charges (see the sulfuric and phosphoric acids, for example).

Anions get their own names, because as we will see later, they make salts with other cations, and the names of the anions will determine the names of the salts. The name of an anion is always derived from the acid that the anion itself is derived from. If the acid name ends in –ic, the anion name ends in –ate. If the acid's name ends in –ous, the anion's name ends in –ite. This is the rule. Prefixes (such as **hypo**- and **per**-) are kept as such (see the anions of the four oxoacids of chlorine). If the acid is binary, the salt simply receives the –ide ending.

Of course, acids lose hydrogen ions stepwise (one by one), and so those acids that have more than one hydrogen to begin with (such as phosphoric) will generate anions that still have some hydrogen atoms in them. To differentiate between an anion without hydrogen and one that has some hydrogen in it, we simply add the word "hydrogen" in front of the anion name, as in "*hydrogen* sulfate" or "*hydrogen* phosphate". If there is more than one hydrogen, we use prefixes to indicate how many (as in **dihydrogen** phosphate, $H_2PO_4^-$).

The permanganate ion is similar to the perchlorate ion, even though there are no manganese analogues for all chlorine anions. In the case of acetic acid (and the acetate ion), note the way we are writing the formula. Do not combine it in $C_2H_3O_2H$, for reasons you will understand later (your organic chemistry professor will really appreciate that you followed this advice – in this course, though, it is a requirement, not just advice...)

Objective 27. Write formulas and names for salts.

In the table below, a cation/anion pair is given on each line. Combine the ions together to form a neutral salt, then write the salt's formula and name.

Cation	Anion	Salt formula	Salt name
Li^+	Cl^-	$LiCl$	Lithium chloride
Na^+	HSO_4^-	$NaHSO_4$	Sodium hydrogen sulfate
Li^+	SO_4^{2-}	Li_2SO_4	Lithium sulfate
NH_4^+	I^-	NH_4I	Ammonium iodide
K^+	CrO_4^{2-}	K_2CrO_4	Potassium chromate
K^+	$Cr_2O_7^{2-}$	$K_2Cr_2O_7$	Potassium dichromate
K^+	MnO_4^-	$KMnO_4$	Potassium permanganate
Fe^{2+}	PO_4^{3-}	$Fe_3(PO_4)_2$	Iron(II) phosphate or Ferrous phosphate
Fe^{3+}	PO_4^{3-}	$FePO_4$	Iron(III) phosphate or Ferric phosphate
Zn^{2+}	ClO_4^-	$Zn(ClO_4)_2$	Zinc perchlorate
Na^+	$S_2O_3^{2-}$	$Na_2S_2O_3$	Sodium thiosulfate
Na^+	$S_4O_6^{2-}$	$Na_2S_4O_6$	Sodium tetrathionate

Discussion

A salt is generally made from a metal cation, which comes from a base (hydroxide), and an anion, which comes from an acid. Thus, the name of a salt has two parts: the name of the metal cation (as in hydroxides), followed by the name of the anion. You simply apply what you learned in the previous two objectives in order to name salts. A special case is the ammonium ion, NH_4^+, which obviously is not a metal, but it is a very common polyatomic cation that forms as many salts as a metal cation might.

In the formula of a salt, the basic principle is that the salt is a neutral compound formed by the combination of a cation and an anion. Thus, the salt formula follows the balance of charge principle that we saw in oxides and hydroxides, and charges are not shown in the salt formula, of course, but the ionic composition is implied. Parentheses are used to indicate polyatomic ions that appear more than once in the formula (as in ferrous phosphate), and never used when that number is 1 (as in ferric phosphate).

As you can see, some salts derived from acids you have not seen before (chromate, dichromate, thiosulfate, tetrathionate, etc.) That is ok, the corresponding acids are in many cases not possible to isolate in solution, but we still use their salts. Learn the names of these anions as given.

Objective 28. Write formulas and names for hydrates.

The table below lists some formulas of hydrates (compounds containing water molecules bound to the ions in the solid structure). Give their names.

Formula	Name
$Na_2CO_3 \cdot H_2O$	Sodium carbonate monohydrate
$CuSO_4 \cdot 5\,H_2O$	Copper(II) sulfate pentahydrate
$Na_2CO_3 \cdot 10\,H_2O$	Sodium carbonate decahydrate
$MgSO_4 \cdot 7\,H_2O$	Magnesium sulfate heptahydrate
$Al_2(SO_4)_3 \cdot 12\,H_2O$	Aluminum sulfate dodecahydrate

Discussion

Many salts trap water molecules in their solid form when they crystallize. The water is actually bound relatively strongly to the metal ion(s), and must be taken into account when writing formulas for these crystalline solids (you will see why later). To name such hydrated salts (simply called hydrates), we use the normal name of the salt, followed by the word "hydrate" with a prefix that indicates how many waters the hydrate contains. Remember: mono = 1, di = 2, tri = 3, tetra = 4, penta = 5, hexa = 6, hepta = 7, octa = 8, nona = 9, deca = 10, undeca = 11, dodeca = 12. This should cover all your hydrate naming.

Objective 29. Write formulas and names for double salts.

The table below lists some formulas of double salts (salts containing more than one cation, or more than one anion). Give their names.

Formula	Name
$KAl(SO_4)_2$	Potassium aluminum sulfate
$Fe(NH_4)_2(SO_4)_2$	Iron(II) ammonium sulfate
$ZnCdCl_4$	Zinc cadmium chloride

Discussion

Some salts may contain two different cations (or, rarely, two different anions) in their formula. They just form this way. Not a problem, as we name them as regular salts, by simply indicating the names of both cations (or anions). Thus, $Fe(NH_4)_2(SO_4)_2$ is iron(II) ammonium sulfate, or ferrous ammonium sulfate. How do we know it is iron(II) and not iron(III) just from the formula? We don't. We need to look at the component ions. There are two sulfates, each charged -2, for a total of -4. There are two ammonium ions, each at +1, for a total of +2. The difference is -4 +2 = -2, which must be compensated by something else. There is one iron left, which must be +2. Thus, it is the ferrous and not the ferric ion in this double salt!

Objective 30. Break down an ionic compound into its component ions and name the compound.

For each compound indicated in the table below, write the formulas of the ions that form it, and give its full name.

Compound formula	Component ions	Compound name
Na_2O	Na^+ and O^{2-}	Sodium oxide
$CsOH$	Cs^+ and OH^-	Cesium hydroxide
$AlBr_3$	Al^{3+} and Br^-	Aluminum bromide
$AgNO_3$	Ag^+ and NO_3^-	Silver nitrate
Cu_2SO_4	Cu^+ and SO_4^{2-}	Cuprous sulfate
$Fe_2(HPO_4)_3$	Fe^{3+} and HPO_4^{2-}	Iron(III) hydrogen phosphate

$Zn(CH_3COO)_2$	Zn^{2+} and CH_3COO^-	Zinc acetate

Discussion

Whenever you need to name a compound from a formula, first see what type of compound it is. If it is an acid, there is a finite list of them, so look it up or name it by analogy (bromic acid is the analogous of chloric acid). If it contains a metal (or nonmetal) and oxygen, it is an oxide. If it contains a metal and OH^- groups, it must be a hydroxide. Most inorganic compounds are salts, so you should be able to recognize them. First you recognize the metal, and then you should recognize the anion, which is derived from one of the known acids.

Charges are many times implied. In $AgNO_3$, even if you have not seen the silver ion before, you saw the nitrate ion, charged -1, and thus Ag must be charged +1 in this salt. In $AlBr_3$, the bromide ion is derived from the hydrobromic acid, HBr, and so it is charged -1. Thus, aluminum must be +3. In the zinc acetate, you have seen both ions before.

In $Fe_2(HPO_4)_3$, you should recognize the hydrogen phosphate ion from before. But even if you don't, you can see that iron appears twice and the HPO_4 group three times. This must be because the charges are reversed, iron must be +3 and the anion must be -2. That's because 2(+3) + 3(-2) = 0. Thus, you will deduct that the two ions are Fe^{+3} and HPO_4^{2-}. Apply this general strategy for all formulas. Whenever you are looking at the formula of a salt, oxide, or hydroxide, break it down into ions, recognize any part that you may have seen before, or that you remember an acid containing it (for an anion), write down the correct ions on paper. The name should come naturally after you have it broken down. Practice!

Objective 31. Given a name, write the formula of the compound and the ions that form it.

For each compound name indicated in the table below, write its formula and then the formulas of the ions that the compound consists of.

Compound name	Component ions	Formula
Iron(II) chlorite	Fe^{2+} and ClO_2^-	$Fe(ClO_2)_2$
Iron(III) nitrate	Fe^{3+} and NO_3^-	$Fe(NO_3)_3$
Barium sulfite	Ba^{2+} and SO_3^{2-}	$BaSO_3$
Calcium hydrogen carbonate	Ca^{2+} and HCO_3^-	$Ca(HCO_3)_2$
Ammonium sulfide	NH_4^+ and S^{2-}	$(NH_4)_2S$
Sodium peroxide	Na^+ and O_2^{2-}	Na_2O_2
Sodium superoxide	Na^+ and O_2^-	NaO_2

Discussion

Writing formulas from names is easier. The name already tells you the ions in the compound, so you just write them down, and then combine them to make your neutral salt (or other compound). The peroxide (O_2^{2-}) and superoxide (O_2^-) ions are two special anions, which are forms of oxygen that bind two such oxygen atoms together. We balance the charges as usual in order to write the correct formulas.

Objective 32.   Write names for binary covalent compounds.

Give the name of each binary covalent compound in the table below.

Formula	Name
H_2	Dihydrogen
HCl	Hydrogen chloride
CO	Carbon monoxide
CO_2	Carbon dioxide
PF_3	Phosphorus trifluoride
CCl_4	Carbon tetrachloride
PBr_5	Phosphorus pentabromide
N_2O_4	Dinitrogen tetroxide
P_4O_{10}	Tetraphosphorus decoxide

Discussion

Compounds between nonmetals are covalent, not ionic, and they follow slightly different rules. The following rules applied in naming these:
- Prefixes are used to indicate how many of each element is in the formula
- "mono" is not used in front of the first element, nor in front of the second when the first element is hydrogen (hydrogen ~~mono~~chloride is incorrect, and so is ~~mono~~carbon dioxide)
- When two vowels are adjacent after applying the prefix, such as a and o (or o and o), the first one is dropped (thus, tetr~~a~~oxide and mon~~o~~oxide are incorrect)

Objective 33.   Determine why a given formula is invalid.

Each of the following formulas is invalid. Explain why.
1. $NaCl_2$
2. HSO_4
3. $FeNO_3$
4. $Ag(NO_3)$
5. Cu_3SO_4

Solutions

1. Na is charged +1 (review Lewis dot symbols and ionic compound formation from the previous lesson), and Cl is charged -1, so there is no way you can have $NaCl_2$. The correct formula is $NaCl$.
2. Either this is H_2SO_4 (sulfuric acid) or the hydrogen sulfate ion, HSO_4^-. If the charge is missing, the formula is wrong and has no meaning.
3. The nitrate ion, NO_3^-, is charged -1 obviously, and Fe does not have a +1 cation.
4. The formula will become correct once parentheses are removed (Objective 28).
5. The sulfate ion is charged -2, and thus there is no way you can have 3 of any metal cation.

Objective 34.   Determine why a given name is invalid.

Each of the following names is invalid. Explain why.
1. Iron chloride
2. Sodium perchlorite
3. Calcium carbonatate
4. Nitrogenic acid
5. Sodium(I) bromide
6. Copper dioxide

Solutions

1. Iron has two different cations (+2 and +3), and thus the name of any iron salt must specify which charge it is.
2. There is no such thing as perchlorite. The prefix **per** can only be combined with a suffix that implies high oxygen, which is **ate**, not **ite**.
3. The correct name is carbonate.
4. The correct name is nitric.
5. Sodium can only have a +1 cation, and thus sodium(I) is redundant and incorrect.
6. Copper dioxide implies a formula like CuO_2, even though these rules apply to nonmetal compounds (sometimes they are accepted for metal compounds too, but not in this course). Also, such a formula would mean that there is a Cu^{4+} ion in there, and there is no such ion for copper.

Worksheet 4.   Formulas and Nomenclature

The exercises and problems in this section will allow you to practice the topic until you understand it well.

1.   Complete the table below:

Metal	Cation	Oxide formula	Oxide name
Na			
K			
Cs			
Rb			
Be			
Ca			
Sr			
Ba			
Co	Co^{2+}		
Cr	Cr^{3+}		
Ti	Ti^{3+}		
Mn	Mn^{2+}		
	Mn^{4+}		

2.   Complete the table below:

Metal	Cation	Hydroxide formula	Hydroxide name
Na			
K			
Cs			
N/A	NH_4^{+}		
Be			

Ca			
Sr			
Ba			
Co	Co^{2+}		
Cr	Cr^{3+}		
Ti	Ti^{3+}		
Fe	Fe^{2+}		
	Fe^{3+}		
Pb	Pb^{2+}		
	Pb^{4+}		

3. Complete the table below:

Acid formula	Acid name	Anion formula	Anion name
HBr			
HI			
HBrO			
$HBrO_2$			
$HBrO_3$			
$HBrO_4$			
H_2SO_3			
H_3PO_3			
			does not form a 3- anion

H_2CO_3			
$H_2C_2O_4$	Oxalic acid		

4. Complete the table below:

Cation	Anion	Salt formula	Salt name
NH_4^+	HSO^{3-}		
NH_4^+	SO_3^{2-}		
Mg^{2+}	F^-		
Mg^{2+}	HCO_3^-		
Mg^{2+}	CO_3^{2-}		
Al^{3+}	Br^-		
Al^{3+}	HSO_4^-		
Al^{3+}	SO_4^{2-}		
Cu^+	SO_4^{2-}		
Cu^{2+}	SO_4^{2-}		
Ag^+	NO_3^-		
Ti^{3+}	SiO_3^{2-}		
Ca^{2+}	N^{3-}		
Ca^{2+}	$C_2O_4^{2-}$		
Ca^{2+}	CH_3COO^-		
Na^+	P^{3-}		
Na^+	CN^-		

Ni^{2+}	ClO_3^-		
Na^+	HPO_4^{2-}		
K^+	ClO_4^-		

5. Write the correct name for each of the following:
    a. $CaMg(CO_3)_2$

    b. $(NH_4)_2Ni(SO_4)_2$

    c. $Na_2CO_3 \cdot H_2O$

    d. $Fe(NO_3)_3 \cdot 9H_2O$

    e. $SnCl_2 \cdot 2H_2O$

6. For each compound indicated by name below, write the constituent ions, then write the correct chemical formula:

    a. iron (II) chlorite

    b. iron (III) nitrate

    c. sodium sulfite

    d. calcium carbonate

    e. ammonium cyanide

    f. cupric oxide

    g. manganese(II) dihydrogen phosphate

    h. titanium(III) bromide

    i. sodium peroxide

    j. sodium dihydrogen phosphate

    k. calcium silicate

    l. nickel (II) phosphate

    m. copper(II) acetate

    n. lithium perchlorate

o. zinc hydroxide

p. silver iodide

q. silver dichromate

r. calcium dichromate

s. titanium(IV) oxide

t. ammonium nitrite

7. Write the name of each compound below:

Formula	Name
N_2O_5	
SF_4	
NBr_3	
Cl_2O	
Br_2	
P_4O_6	
H_2O	
Cl_2O_5	
Cl_2O_7	
Cl_2O_3	

8. In each case below, determine whether the formula or name given is valid (can correspond to an actual compound) or not. Explain each answer. Provide a corrected formula and/or name for each invalid case.

a. $FeCl$

b. BaO_2

c. H_2PO_4

d. $Ca(SO_4)$

e. $Fe_2(PO_4)_3$

f. $NaAl(OH)_4$

g. $FeClBr$

h. H_2Cl

i. $NH_4H_2PO_4$

j. FSO_4

k. $GoCl_3$

l.   Carbon bisoxide

m.   Sulfic acid

n.   Monohydrogen monobromide

o.   Sodium tellurate

p.   Manganese hydroxide

q.   Sodium potassium phthalate

r.   Sodium hydrogen sulfurate

s.   Plumbic oxide

Self-assessment

Using the scale indicated, rate your understanding of each learning objective at the completion of this lesson. Identify the areas where your understanding is weak or medium and discuss with your class mates and/or instructor. Write down specific questions you still have at the completion of this topic.

Learning objective	Self-assessment 3 = strong, 2 = medium, 1 = weak, 0 = not done
	3 2 1 0
	3 2 1 0
	3 2 1 0
	3 2 1 0
	3 2 1 0
	3 2 1 0
	3 2 1 0
	3 2 1 0
	3 2 1 0
	3 2 1 0
	3 2 1 0
	3 2 1 0
	3 2 1 0

Lesson 5 – Oxidation Numbers and Balancing Simple Redox Reactions

Learning Objectives

In this lesson you will learn:

- To assign an **oxidation number** to any element in a compound
- To **balance a simple chemical reaction** by inspection
- To identify the **oxidizing agent** and the **reducing agent** in a **redox reaction**
- To use the **activity series** of metals to predict which metals will react with compounds of another metal

Pre-requisites: Atomic structure; Classes of compounds.

Self-study questions

Before you start studying the worked examples, you should be able to formulate answers to the questions below. Use a textbook of your choice, or an online source of information, to find the answers.

1. What is an oxidation number (or oxidation state)?
2. In general, metals have positive or negative oxidation numbers?
3. In general, nonmetals have positive or negative oxidation numbers?
4. What is true about the sum of all oxidation numbers in a neutral compound?
5. What is true about the sum of all oxidation numbers in an ion?
6. What is a chemical reaction?
7. What do we call the species shown on the left side of the arrow in a chemical reaction?
8. What do we call the species shown on the right side of the arrow in a chemical reaction?
9. What must be the same on each side of a balanced chemical reaction?
10. What is an oxidation?
11. What is a reduction?
12. What is a redox reaction?
13. Where do electrons go in a redox reaction?
14. What is an oxidizing agent?
15. What is a reducing agent?
16. What is the activity series and how is it useful?

Worked examples

This section contains several solved examples that cover the learning objectives listed above. Study each example carefully and make notes in the workbook to check every example that you understood. Repeat several times what you don't understand at first. It should become clearer as you keep working on the examples.

Objective 35. Assign oxidation numbers to elements in a compound.

In the table below are given formulas of various compounds. Indicate the oxidation number of <u>each element in each compound</u>.

No.	Compound	Oxidation numbers
1	H_2	$H = 0$
2	H_2O	$H = +1, \quad O = -2$
3	LiH	$Li = +1, \quad H = -1$
4	Na_2O_2	$Na = +1, \quad O = -1$
5	NaO_2	$Na = +1, \quad O = -0.5$
6	F_2O	$F = -1, \quad O = +2$
7	Fe_2O_3	$Fe = +3, \quad O = -2$
8	H_2SO_4	$H = +1, \quad S = +6, \quad O = -2$
9	$CaSiO_3$	$Ca = +2, \quad Si = +4, \quad O = -2$
10	$Cr_2O_7^{2-}$	$Cr = +6, \quad O = -2$
11	$S_4O_6^{2-}$	$S = +2.5, \quad O = -2$
12	$(NH_4)_2SO_4$	$N = -3, \quad H = +1, \quad S = +6, \quad O = -2$

Discussion

First, remember the rules for assigning oxidation numbers to elements, which apply in the order written:
1. Element in its natural state = 0 (Cu, H_2, etc.)
2. Hydrogen = +1, except in hydrides (-1)
3. Fluorine = -1
4. Oxygen = -2, except in peroxides and superoxides, and in combinations with F (+2)
5. Metals as cations = +n, depending on the charge of the metal ion (Na^+ = +1, Ca^{2+} = +2, etc.)
6. The sum of all oxidation numbers of elements in a compound is zero
7. The sum of all oxidation numbers of elements in a polyatomic ion is equal to the total charge of the ion

Solutions

Let's discuss each example:

1. Rule 1 applies
2. Rules 2 and 4 apply
3. Rules 2 and 5 apply; LiH is a hydride, and thus the metals gets the positive charge
4. Sodium peroxide: Na = +1, and O = x ; 2(+1) + 2x = 0 (rule 6). Thus, x = O = -1, which is what oxygen gets in peroxides.
5. Sodium superoxide: Na = +1, and O = x ; (+1) + 2x = 0 (rule 6). Thus, x = O = -0.5, which is what oxygen gets in superoxides.
6. Rules 3 and 4 apply; F is more electronegative than O (you will learn why later) and it always gets a negative oxidation number
7. Straightforward: O = -2 (rule 4), and Fe = x ; 2(x) + 3(-2) = 0 (rule 6). Thus, x = Fe = +3.
8. H = +1, and O = -2 (rules 2 and 4). Let sulfur be x. Rule 6: 2(+1) + x + 4(-2) = 0. Thus, x = S = +6.
9. Ca = +2, O = -2. Thus: +2 + x + 3(-2) = 0 ; x = Si = +4.
10. O = -2. Let Cr be x. Rule 7 applies, as this is a charged ion: 2(x) + 7(-2) = -2 ; 2x = 12 ; x = Cr = +6.
11. O = -2, S = x ; 4x + 6(-2) = -2 ; 4x = 10 ; x = S = +2.5
12. Here, we are dealing with two polyatomic ions, so let's break the salt down into ions: there are two NH_4^+ ions and one SO_4^{2-} ion in the formula of the sale. We will treat them separately to assign oxidation numbers:
    a. In SO_4^{2-}, S = +6 and O = -2 as we saw before
    b. In NH_4^+ we do the math, as H is +1 and N is the unknown: x + 4(+1) = +1 ; x = N = -3 ; voila!

Notice how oxidation numbers are written with the sign in front of the number (+2), whereas charges on ions are written with the sign after the number (2+).

You can now assign an oxidation number to any element in any compound… or almost ☺

Objective 36. Balance a simple chemical reaction.

Each equation below represents a chemical reaction. Balance each equation by visual inspection.

1. $Na + O_2 \rightarrow Na_2O$
2. $Al + MgO \rightarrow Al_2O_3 + Mg$
3. $(NH_4)_2Cr_2O_7 \rightarrow Cr_2O_3 + N_2 + H_2O$
4. $C_2H_6 + O_2 \rightarrow CO_2 + H_2O$

Solutions

When we balance chemical equations, we must have the same number of each type of atom on each side. Here is the step-by-step strategy.

1. $Na + O_2 \rightarrow Na_2O$

    Always start with the most complicated formula and leave the simplest entities at the end. In this case Na will be balanced last, as it won't interfere with anything. We have 2 oxygens on the left and one on the right, so we double that:

    $$Na + O_2 \rightarrow 2Na_2O$$

Now, we have 4 Na on the right, so we need 4 on the left:
$$4Na + O_2 \rightarrow 2Na_2O$$
Balanced!

2. $Al + MgO \rightarrow Al_2O_3 + Mg$

    Let's balance O first:
    $$Al + 3MgO \rightarrow Al_2O_3 + Mg$$

    Next, Mg:
    $$Al + 3MgO \rightarrow Al_2O_3 + 3Mg$$

    Finally, Al:
    $$2Al + 3MgO \rightarrow Al_2O_3 + 3Mg$$

    Balanced!

3. $(NH_4)_2Cr_2O_7 \rightarrow Cr_2O_3 + N_2 + H_2O$

    Starting with the most complicated, $(NH_4)_2Cr_2O_7$, we count 2 N's, 8 H's, 2 Cr's, and 7 O's. We have 2 Cr's on the right, so we'll leave that alone. We fix hydrogens:

    $$(NH_4)_2Cr_2O_7 \rightarrow Cr_2O_3 + N_2 + 4H_2O$$

    And, in one step, we seem to have fixed the oxygens too. Balanced!

4. $C_2H_6 + O_2 \rightarrow CO_2 + H_2O$

    Starting with the most complicated, C_2H_6, we see 2 C's and 6 H's. We fix C and H in one step:

    $$C_2H_6 + O_2 \rightarrow 2CO_2 + 3H_2O$$

    Now, we count all oxygens on the right and we get 7. Hmm, oxygens come in twos on the left (as O_2), so it looks like we need a fraction:

    $$C_2H_6 + \frac{7}{2}O_2 \rightarrow 2CO_2 + 3H_2O$$

    This would give us a balanced equation. But, at this stage, we want all coefficients to be integers, and for that reason we multiply everything by 2:

    $$2C_2H_6 + 7O_2 \rightarrow 4CO_2 + 6H_2O$$

    A bit more complicated, but still very doable.

Apply this strategy and you will be able to balance most chemical reactions now.

Objective 37. Identify oxidizing agents and reducing agents in a simple redox reaction.

Each equation below represents a redox reaction. Identify the oxidizing and reducing agent in each reaction.

1. $K + S \rightarrow K_2S$

2. $CH_4 + O_2 \rightarrow CO_2 + H_2O$

3. $(NH_4)_2Cr_2O_7 \rightarrow Cr_2O_3 + N_2 + H_2O$

Discussion

In a redox reaction, certain elements change their oxidation numbers. Redox means reduction-oxidation. Reduction means gaining electrons, and oxidation means losing electrons. Because electrons are negatively charged particles, reduction leads to a decrease in the oxidation state (number), and oxidation means an increase on the oxidation number. An oxidizing agent is the entity that <u>oxidizes something else</u>, and in the process it <u>gets reduced</u>. In contrast, a reducing agent is an entity that <u>reduces something else</u>, and in the process it <u>gets oxidized</u>. Let's analyze each reaction and see what's happening. What we do is we assign oxidation numbers to all elements before and after the reaction (on each side of the arrow), and we track what changes and how.

Solutions

1. Before (left): K = 0, S = 0 ; after (right): K = +1, S = -2. In this reaction, K gets oxidized and S gets reduced. Thus, K is the reducing agent, and S is the oxidizing agent.

2. Before (left): C = -4 (see rules again), H = +1, O = 0 ; after (right): C = +4, O = -2 (in CO_2), H = +1, O = -2 (in H_2O). C went from -4 to +4 (got oxidized), and O went from 0 to -2 in both compounds, so it got reduced. Oxidizing agent is O_2 (the molecule), and reducing agent is CH_4 (we always take the entire compound as the "agent", not just the element changing oxidation number).

3. Left: N = -3, H = +1, Cr = +6, O = -2 (0). Right: Cr = +3, O = -2, N = 0, H = +1, O = -2. So, it looks like Cr is getting reduced (+6 to +3) and some (not all) oxygen is getting oxidized (-2 to 0). But both elements are in the same compound, ammonium dichromate. So, $(NH_4)_2Cr_2O_7$ is both oxidizing and reducing agent, because it decomposes in a redox reaction. This type of reaction, where the same compound undergoes <u>both oxidation and reduction</u>, is called **disproportionation**.

Objective 38. Use the activity series to predict which metals will react with salts of other metals or binary acids.

Using the activity series of metals, predict the products of each reaction below, or write N/R if no reaction is expected.

1. $Zn + CuSO_4$
2. $Mg + HCl$
3. $Cu + HCl$
4. $Cu + AgNO_3$

Discussion

Consult the activity series of metals in 0The rule of thumb is the following: if metal 1 is above metal 2 (or hydrogen) in the activity series, then metal 1 in its free state will react with a compound of metal 2 (or hydrogen) and switch places, freeing up metal 2 (or hydrogen) in elemental form.

Solutions

1. Zn is above Cu in the series, so the reaction will proceed as such:

$$Zn + CuSO_4 \rightarrow ZnSO_4 + Cu$$

2. Mg is above H in the series, so it will react with the acid:

$$Mg + 2HCl \rightarrow MgCl_2 + H_2$$

3. Cu is below H in the series, so it will not react (note: oxoacids will generally react with metals below H in the activity series, but will not free up hydrogen; instead, their reactions are more complicated).

$$Cu + HCl \rightarrow N/R$$

4. Cu is above Ag in the series, so it will react as well. Of course, we need to balance any chemical equation we write, at any moment:

$$Cu + 2AgNO_3 \rightarrow Cu(NO_3)_2 + 2Ag$$

How do we know that Cu(II) is the product, and not Cu(I) ? Well, it's not that simple, in general the most common or stable cation forms. For Cu, it is the +2 cation.

Worksheet 5.   Oxidation numbers and balancing simple reactions

The exercises and problems in this section will allow you to practice the topic until you understand it well.

1. Assign oxidation numbers to <u>each element</u> in <u>each of the following</u> compounds:

    a. Dioxygen

    b. Sodium chloride

    c. Sodium hydride

    d. Barium peroxide

    e. Potassium superoxide

    f. Sulfurous acid

    g. Phosphoric acid

    h. Phosphorous acid

    i. Iron (II) oxide

    j. Calcium carbonate

    k. Cupric oxide

    l. Lithium perchlorate

    m. Chromate ion

    n. Permanganate ion

    o. Thiosulfate ion

2. Balance each reaction below, then indicate how oxidation and reduction occurs, and which species serve as oxidation and reduction agents. If no oxidation and reduction occur, indicate that.

    a. $Na + Cl_2 \rightarrow NaCl$

b. $K + S \rightarrow K_2S$

c. $Mg + N_2 \rightarrow Mg_3N_2$

d. $H_2O_2 \rightarrow H_2O + O_2$

e. $K_2O_2 + H_2O \rightarrow KOH + H_2O_2$

f. $NH_4NO_3 \rightarrow N_2O + H_2O$

g. $Mg + B_2O_3 \rightarrow B + MgO$

h. $PCl_5 + H_2O \rightarrow H_3PO_4 + HCl$

i. $Na_3P + H_2O \rightarrow NaOH + PH_3$

j. $C_2H_6 + O_2 \rightarrow CO_2 + H_2O$

3.   Complete and balance each of the reactions below or indicate N/R if no reaction should occur.

a. $Mg + HCl$

b. $Cu + HCl$

c. $Zn + CuSO_4$

d. $Zn + Al_2(SO_4)_3$

e. $Cu + NiSO_4$

f. $Cu + AgNO_3$

g. $Cu + Hg(NO_3)_2$

h. $Al + MnCl_2$

i. $Zn + H_2SO_4$

Self-assessment

Using the scale indicated, rate your understanding of each learning objective at the completion of this lesson. Identify the areas where your understanding is weak or medium and discuss with your class mates and/or instructor. Write down specific questions you still have at the completion of this topic.

Learning objective	Self-assessment 3 = strong, 2 = medium, 1 = weak, 0 = not done
	3 2 1 0
	3 2 1 0
	3 2 1 0
	3 2 1 0

Lesson 6 – Chemical Reactions in Solution

Learning Objectives

In this lesson you will learn:

- To write the formula of the **conjugate base** of an acid
- To write the formula of the **conjugate acid** of a base
- To determine whether a compound will **dissolve** in water
- To write a chemical equation for the **dissociation of an acid** in aqueous solution
- To write a chemical equation for the **dissociation of a base** in aqueous solution
- To write a chemical equation for the **dissociation of a salt** in aqueous solution
- To classify chemical reactions
- To write **molecular**, **ionic**, and **net ionic equations** for chemical reactions

Pre-requisites: Classes of compounds.

Self-study questions

Before you start studying the worked examples, you should be able to formulate answers to the questions below. Use a textbook of your choice, or an online source of information, to find the answers.

1. What is a conjugate base?
2. What is a conjugate acid?
3. What is an insoluble compound?
4. What is the meaning of the solubility rules?
5. Give an example of a family of salts that are always soluble.
6. Give an example of a family of salts that are almost always insoluble.
7. What is meant by *dissociation*?
8. When an acid dissociates in water, what type of ions appear?
9. When a base dissociates in water, what type of ions appear?
10. When a salt dissociates in water, what type of ions appear?
11. What is a combination (synthesis) reaction?
12. What is a decomposition reaction?
13. What is a neutralization reaction?
14. What is a redox reaction?
15. What is a disproportionation reaction?
16. What is a single exchange reaction?
17. What is a double exchange reaction?
18. What is a precipitation reaction?
19. What is a molecular equation for a chemical reaction?
20. What is an ionic equation?
21. What is a net ionic equation?
22. What are spectator ions?
23. What is a precipitate?

Worked examples

This section contains several solved examples that cover the learning objectives listed above. Study each example carefully and make notes in the workbook to check every example that you understood. Repeat several times what you don't understand at first. It should become clearer as you keep working on the examples.

Objective 39. Identify acid/conjugate base pairs.

For each acid in the table below, write the formula of its conjugate base.

Acid	Conjugate base
HCl	Cl^-
HCN	CN^-
H_2SO_4	HSO_4^-
$H_2PO_4^-$	HPO_4^{2-}
CH_3COOH	CH_3COO^-

Discussion

The conjugate base of an acid is the entity that remains after the acid donates a proton. We have seen this before. In the case of polyprotic acids, the conjugate base is the one that differs by just one proton. Acid anions can act as acids too (as in the case of the dihydrogen phosphate ion) and get their own conjugate bases.

Objective 40. Identify base/conjugate acid pairs.

For each base in the table below, write the formula of its conjugate acid.

Base	Conjugate acid
NH_3	NH_4^+
OH^-	H_2O
S^{2-}	HS^-
SO_4^{2-}	HSO_4^-
PO_4^{3-}	HPO_4^{2-}

Discussion

The conjugate acid of a base is the entity that forms when the base accepts a proton (H^+). Again, the base/conjugate acid pair must differ by only one proton. So, in the case of phosphoric acid, there are three separate acid/conjugate base pairs, and three base/conjugate acid pairs, depending on how we write them.

Common mistake: Is H_2S/S^{2-} an acid/conjugate base pair? No, because they differ by two protons.

Objective 41. Use solubility rules to determine whether a compound is soluble in water.

For each compound in the table below, indicate whether it is expected to be soluble or insoluble in water, based on solubility rules.

Compound	Solubility in water
NaCl	Soluble (rules 1, 4)
AgCl	Insoluble (rules 4, 5)
$Ba(NO_3)_3$	Soluble (rule 3)
$BaSO_4$	Insoluble (rule 6)
$CuCO_3$	Insoluble (rule 9)
$Fe(OH)_2$	Insoluble (rule 7)
Na_3PO_4	Soluble (rule 1)
$(NH_4)_2CO_3$	Soluble (rule 1)
$Ca(HCO_3)_2$	Soluble (rule 2)
$KMnO_4$	Soluble (rule 1)

Discussion

Let's summarize solubility rules that we applied to the table above:

1. Salts containing Group I elements are soluble (Li^+, Na^+, K^+, Cs^+, and Rb^+). Exceptions to this rule are extremely rare (one is $KClO_4$, which is slightly soluble). Salts containing the ammonium ion (NH_4^+) are also soluble.

2. Acids are soluble. Salts containing hydrogen (acidic salts) are soluble. Example: $Ca(HCO_3)_2$. Exceptions are some hydrogen phosphates of transition metals.

3. Salts containing the nitrate ion (nitrates) are always soluble. Same for chlorates, perchlorates, acetates.

4. Halides (except fluorides) are generally soluble. Important exceptions to this rule are halide salts of Ag^+, Pb^{2+}, and Hg_2^{2+}. Thus, $AgCl$, $PbBr_2$, and Hg_2Cl_2 are all insoluble.

5. Most silver salts are insoluble. $AgNO_3$ and $AgCH_3COO$ are common soluble salts of silver; virtually anything else is insoluble. Ag_2SO_4 and AgF are slightly soluble.

6. Most sulfate salts are soluble. Important exceptions to this rule include $BaSO_4$, $PbSO_4$, and $SrSO_4$.

7. Most hydroxides are only slightly soluble. Hydroxides of Group I elements are soluble. Hydroxides of Group II elements (Mg, Ca, Sr, and Ba) are slightly soluble. Hydroxides of transition metals and Al^{3+} are insoluble. Thus, $Fe(OH)_3, Al(OH)_3, Co(OH)_2$ are not soluble.

8. Most sulfides of transition metals are highly insoluble. Thus, CdS, FeS, ZnS, Ag_2S are all insoluble. Arsenic, antimony, bismuth, and lead sulfides are also insoluble.

9. Carbonates are generally insoluble, including group II carbonates (Ca, Sr, and Ba).

10. Chromates are frequently insoluble. Examples: $PbCrO_4, BaCrO_4$

11. Phosphates are frequently insoluble. Examples: $Ca_3(PO_4)_2$, Ag_3PO_4

12. Fluorides are frequently insoluble. Examples: BaF_2, MgF_2, PbF_2.

Objective 42. Write a reaction for the dissociation of an acid in aqueous solution.

For each acid listed below, write a balanced chemical reaction that illustrates its dissociation in aqueous solution. When an acid has *more than one hydrogen* in its molecule, write all dissociation steps.
1. Hydrochloric acid
2. Perbromic acid
3. Sulfuric acid
4. Phosphoric acid

Discussion

When an acid dissolves in water, it generally dissociates, meaning it breaks down into hydrogen ions and the remaining anions. This dissociation is stepwise, meaning each hydrogen ion is given off one by one (for polyprotic acids). Since the hydrogen ion is nothing but a proton, it cannot exist in solution by itself, and thus it attaches itself to a water molecule to form the hydronium ion, H_3O^+. For that reason, we use water as a reactant to help out with the dissociation of the acid.

Solutions

1. $HCl + H_2O \rightarrow H_3O^+ + Cl^-$

2. $HBrO_4 + H_2O \rightarrow H_3O^+ + BrO_4^-$

3. First dissociation step: $H_2SO_4 + H_2O \rightarrow H_3O^+ + HSO_4^-$

   Second dissociation step: $HSO_4^- + H_2O \rightleftharpoons H_3O^+ + SO_4^{2-}$

4.   First dissociation step: $H_3PO_4 + H_2O \rightleftharpoons H_3O^+ + H_2PO_4^-$

Second dissociation step: $H_2PO_4^- + H_2O \rightleftharpoons H_3O^+ + HPO_4^{2-}$

Third dissociation step: $HPO_4^{2-} + H_2O \rightleftharpoons H_3O^+ + PO_4^{3-}$

You will learn the reason for using the double arrow in some of these reactions later in this course.

Objective 43. Write a reaction for the dissociation of a base in aqueous solution.

For each base listed below, write a balanced chemical reaction that illustrates its dissociation in aqueous solution. If the base is not soluble in water, use an *equilibrium symbol* (double arrow) instead of a simple arrow.
   1.   Sodium hydroxide
   2.   Calcium hydroxide
   3.   Aluminum hydroxide
   4.   Ammonium hydroxide

Solutions

With bases, the situation is simpler, as they release hydroxide ions, which exist by themselves in solution (no water is needed as reactant), and the dissociation usually happens in one step.
   1. $NaOH \rightarrow Na^+ + OH^-$

   2. $Ca(OH)_2 \rightarrow Ca^{2+} + 2OH^-$

   3. $Al(OH)_3 \rightleftharpoons Al^{3+} + 3OH^-$

   4. $NH_4OH \rightarrow NH_4^+ + OH^-$

Note how in the case of aluminum hydroxide we used a double arrow, because aluminum hydroxide is insoluble in water (see solubility), and thus only very little of it actually dissociates.

Objective 44. Write a reaction for the dissociation of a salt in aqueous solution.

For each salt listed below, write a balanced chemical reaction that illustrates its dissociation in aqueous solution. If the salt is not soluble in water, write N.R.
   1.   Sodium chloride
   2.   Magnesium sulfate
   3.   Aluminum chloride
   4.   Potassium phosphate
   5.   Potassium dichromate
   6.   Calcium hydrogen carbonate
   7.   Barium sulfate
   8.   Ammonium nitrate
   9.   Silver iodide
   10. Ferric sulfate

Solutions

1. $NaCl \rightarrow Na^+ + Cl^-$

2. $MgSO_4 \rightarrow Mg^{2+} + SO_4^{2-}$

3. $AlCl_3 \rightarrow Al^{3+} + 3Cl^-$

4. $K_3PO_4 \rightarrow 3K^+ + PO_4^{3-}$

5. $K_2Cr_2O_7 \rightarrow 2K^+ + Cr_2O_7^{2-}$

6. $Ca(HCO_3)_2 \rightarrow Ca^{2+} + 2HCO_3^-$

7. $BaSO_4 \rightarrow N.R.$

8. $NH_4NO_3 \rightarrow NH_4^+ + NO_3^-$

9. $AgI \rightarrow N.R.$

10. $Fe_2(SO_4)_3 \rightarrow 2Fe^{3+} + 3SO_4^{2-}$

The key here is, again, to recognize the ions that the salt is made of, and then write down those dissociated ions, unless the salt is insoluble.

Common mistake: $K_2Cr_2O_7 \rightarrow 2K^+ + 2Cr^{6+} + 7O^{2-}$. See the problem?

Objective 45. Classify chemical reactions by type.

For each chemical reaction numbered below, put a checkmark in the box corresponding to each type of chemical reaction. Most reactions correspond to more than one category. The reactions are balanced for your convenience.

1. $2H_2 + O_2 \rightarrow 2H_2O$

2. $Fe + 2HCl \rightarrow FeCl_2 + H_2$

3. $H_2SO_4 + Ba(OH)_2 \rightarrow BaSO_4 + 2H_2O$

4. $CuCl_2 + Na_2CO_3 \rightarrow CuCO_3 + 2NaCl$

5. $(NH_4)_2Cr_2O_7 \xrightarrow{heat} N_2 + Cr_2O_3 + 4H_2O$

6. $Na_2O + H_2O \rightarrow 2NaOH$

7. $2H_2O_2 \rightarrow 2H_2O + O_2$

8. $P_4O_6 + 2O_2 \rightarrow P_4O_{10}$

9. $CuCO_3 + H_2SO_4 \rightarrow CuSO_4 + CO_2 + H_2O$

Reaction #	Combination (synthesis)	Decomposition	Neutralization	Transfer of proton	Transfer of electrons (redox)	Disproportionation	Single exchange	Double exchange	Precipitation	Liquid formation	Gas formation
1	✓				✓					✓	
2					✓		✓				✓
3			✓	✓					✓	✓	
4								✓	✓		
5		✓			✓	✓					✓
6	✓			✓							
7		✓			✓	✓				✓	✓
8	✓				✓						
9				✓				✓		✓	✓

Discussion

1. Two reactants combine into a single product (synthesis or combination), and the oxidation numbers change (redox). The product is liquid water.
2. Oxidation numbers change (redox), and iron displaces hydrogen gas from the acid (see activity series)
3. An acid neutralizes a base, where protons react with hydroxide ions to form water (see in next lesson); also, barium sulfate is insoluble, so it precipitates.
4. Copper and sodium exchange places, and copper carbonate precipitates.
5. Ammonium dichromate decomposes when heated. We studied this reaction as a redox as well, and we saw how it is a disproportionation reaction. Since the reaction proceeds at high heat (and produces even more heat), the water resulted is in vapor form, not liquid.
6. The reaction is a combination, and protons are transferred from water to the oxide ion in the sodium oxide, to form hydroxide ions.
7. Disproportionation with formation of a gas and liquid water.
8. Combination and redox. P_4O_{10} is a solid but the reaction does not happen in solution, so this reaction is not a precipitation.
9. Copper and hydrogen exchange places, and an intermediate product is carbonic acid, H_2CO_3. But this acid is very unstable and it decomposes at room temperature into CO_2 and H_2O.

Objective 46. Given two reactants in solution, write a molecular equation, an ionic equation, and a net ionic equation for their reaction in solution.

For each pair of reactants below, write a complete balanced chemical reaction, a balanced ionic equation, and a net ionic equation.
1. Sodium hydroxide and sulfuric acid
2. Barium nitrate and sodium sulfate
3. Potassium chloride and iron (II) sulfate
4. Plumbous nitrate and hydrochloric acid
5. Cupric acetate and rubidium hydroxide

Solutions

The chemical reactions we have seen so far are written as molecular equations. That means that we show the formulas of the reactants and products in the equation. In this section, we break down everything into ions, as we know that acids, bases, and salts dissociate in aqueous solutions, and they exist, and react, as ions. For each pair of reactants above we will write a molecular equation, a complete ionic equation, and a net ionic equation to show what really happens at molecular and ionic level. We need to start by predicting the products of each reaction.

1. Sodium hydroxide and sulfuric acid

An acid and a base will react to form a salt and water, because the hydrogen ions and the hydroxide ions combine to form the stable product water. The balanced molecular equation is the following:

$$2NaOH + H_2SO_4 \rightarrow Na_2SO_4 + 2H_2O$$

The second step is to break everything down into ions, except insoluble salts and compounds that are not ionic, such as water. For these reactions, we will start showing the states too. We use **aq** for a species that is dissolved in water, **s** for an insoluble precipitate, **l** for a liquid such as water, and **g** for a gas. States are shown in parentheses as subscripts to the right of the compound formula.

The result will be a complete ionic equation:

$$2Na^+{}_{(aq)} + 2OH^-{}_{(aq)} + 2H^+{}_{(aq)} + SO_4^{2-}{}_{(aq)} \rightarrow 2Na^+{}_{(aq)} + SO_4^{2-}{}_{(aq)} + 2H_2O_{(l)}$$

Notice that:
- We took into account the coefficients of the balanced equation, so two $NaOH$ formula units will result in two of each ion, sodium and hydroxide
- We dissociated sulfuric acid completely, for simplicity (we know by now that it is stepwise and that intermediate ions also form)
- We wrote H^+ instead of the real H_3O^+, also for simplicity
- We do not dissociate water because it is not an ionic compound
- Some ions appear on both sides of the equation, in exactly the same state

The last observation above is what leads us to the final step, writing a net ionic equation. Ions that are in solution before AND after the reaction do not really participate in the reaction. We call them spectator ions. If we treat the ionic equation as a mathematical equation, then the spectator ions will cancel out as follows:

$$2\cancel{Na^+}_{(aq)} + 2OH^-_{(aq)} + 2H^+_{(aq)} + \cancel{SO_4^{2-}}_{(aq)} \rightarrow 2\cancel{Na^+}_{(aq)} + \cancel{SO_4^{2-}}_{(aq)} + 2H_2O_{(l)}$$

Note that spectator ions MUST BE in exactly the same number, and same state, on both sides of the equation in order to cancel out. The result of this cancelation is our net ionic equaiton:

$$2OH^-_{(aq)} + 2H^+_{(aq)} \rightarrow 2H_2O_{(l)}$$

Or to simplify,

$$OH^-_{(aq)} + H^+_{(aq)} \rightarrow H_2O_{(l)}$$

Basically, this is showing us that mixing a base with an acid leads to neutralization of both, but it is the hydrogen ions and the hydroxide ions that really react with each other. The sodium cations and the sulfate anions simply stay in solution before and after the reaction. This means that ANY soluble base can react with ANY acid and the result will be the formation of water (unless the salt formed is insoluble).

2. Barium nitrate and sodium sulfate

This will be a double exchange reaction. Molecular equation:

$$Ba(NO_3)_2 + Na_2SO_4 \rightarrow BaSO_4 + 2NaNO_3$$

Ionic equation:

$$Ba^{2+}_{(aq)} + 2\cancel{NO_3^-}_{(aq)} + 2\cancel{Na^+}_{(aq)} + SO_4^{2-}_{(aq)} \rightarrow BaSO_{4\,(s)} + 2\cancel{Na^+}_{(aq)} + 2\cancel{NO_3^-}_{(aq)}$$

Net ionic equation:

$$Ba^{2+}_{(aq)} + SO_4^{2-}_{(aq)} \rightarrow BaSO_{4\,(s)}$$

Here, because barium sulfate is insoluble, it precipitates from the solution, and thus it is not dissociated, which prevents us from canceling out the barium ions and the sulfate ions. The net ionic equation is the formation of solid barium sulfate from its ions. This means that ANY soluble barium salt can react with ANY soluble sulfate (or sulfuric acid) and will lead to the same net ionic equation.

3. Potassium chloride and iron (II) sulfate

Molecular:

$$2KCl + FeSO_4 \rightarrow K_2SO_4 + FeCl_2$$

Ionic:

$$2\cancel{K^+}_{(aq)} + 2\cancel{Cl^-}_{(aq)} + \cancel{Fe^{2+}}_{(aq)} + \cancel{SO_4^{2-}}_{(aq)} \rightarrow 2\cancel{K^+}_{(aq)} + \cancel{SO_4^{2-}}_{(aq)} + \cancel{Fe^{2+}}_{(aq)} + 2\cancel{Cl^-}_{(aq)}$$

Net ionic: there isn't one, because all salts in the reaction are soluble, and all ions cancel out. What this means is that if you tried this reaction in lab, you probably won't see any visible change after mixing the two reactants. It happens.

4. Plumbous nitrate and hydrochloric acid

Plumbous means a lead cation. Lead forms Pb^{2+} and Pb^{4+}, and plumbous is the lower valence one (also the more common and more stable of the two). The higher valence cation would be called plumbic.

Molecular:
$$Pb(NO_3)_2 + 2HCl \rightarrow PbCl_2 + 2HNO_3$$

Ionic:
$$Pb^{2+}{}_{(aq)} + 2\cancel{NO_3^-}{}_{(aq)} + \cancel{2H^+}{}_{(aq)} + 2Cl^-{}_{(aq)} \rightarrow PbCl_2{}_{(s)} + \cancel{2H^+}{}_{(aq)} + 2\cancel{NO_3^-}{}_{(aq)}$$

Net ionic:
$$Pb^{2+}{}_{(aq)} + 2Cl^-{}_{(aq)} \rightarrow PbCl_2{}_{(s)}$$

5. Cupric acetate and rubidium hydroxide

Molecular:
$$Cu(CH_3COO)_2 + 2RbOH \rightarrow Cu(OH)_2 + 2RbCH_3COO$$

Ionic:
$$Cu^{2+}{}_{(aq)} + 2\cancel{CH_3COO^-}{}_{(aq)} + 2\cancel{Rb^+}{}_{(aq)} + 2OH^-{}_{(aq)} \rightarrow Cu(OH)_2{}_{(s)} + 2\cancel{Rb^+}{}_{(aq)} + 2\cancel{CH_3COO^-}{}_{(aq)}$$

Net ionic:
$$Cu^{2+}{}_{(aq)} + 2OH^-{}_{(aq)} \rightarrow Cu(OH)_2{}_{(s)}$$

Worksheet 6.   Chemical reactions

The exercises and problems in this section will allow you to practice the topic until you understand it well.

1. For each acid below, write the formula of its conjugate base.
    a. HF

    b. H_2CO_3

    c. HNO_2

    d. HPO_4^{2-}

    e. HCOOH

    f. H_2O

2. For each base below, write the formula of its conjugate acid.
    a. O^{2-}

    b. HS^-

    c. HCO_3^-

    d. H_2O

    e. ClO_2^-

    f. N_2H_4

3. Write balanced equations to show how each acid indicated dissociates when dissolved in water.
    a. Hydrobromic acid

    b. Perchloric acid

    c. Sulfurous acid

    d. Phosphoric acid

4. Write balanced equations to show how each base indicated below dissociates when dissolved in water.
    a. Lithium hydroxide

    b. Strontium hydroxide

    c. Ferric hydroxide

    d. Cupric hydroxide

5. Show how each salt below dissociates in aqueous solution. If the salt is insoluble, indicate N/R (no reaction).
   a. Sodium chloride

   b. Magnesium sulfate

   c. Aluminum chloride

   d. Potassium phosphate

   e. Potassium dichromate

   f. Calcium hydrogen carbonate

   g. Barium sulfate

   h. Ammonium nitrate

   i. Silver iodide

   j. Ferrous sulfate

   k. Ferric sulfate

   l. Cupric acetate

   m. Sodium perchlorate

   n. Mercurous nitrate

   o. Sodium hydrogen phosphate

6. Write a complete chemical equation, an ionic equation and a net ionic equation for each of the following reactions:
   a. silver nitrate and sodium chloride

    b.   potassium sulfate and barium chloride

    c.   aluminum chloride and sodium sulfate

    d.   ammonium sulfide and cadmium sulfate

    e.   iron(III) nitrate and sodium carbonate

    f.   cupric sulfate and sodium carbonate

Self-assessment

Using the scale indicated, rate your understanding of each learning objective at the completion of this lesson. Identify the areas where your understanding is weak or medium and discuss with your class mates and/or instructor. Write down specific questions you still have at the completion of this topic.

Learning objective	Self-assessment 3 = strong, 2 = medium, 1 = weak, 0 = not done
	3 2 1 0
	3 2 1 0
	3 2 1 0
	3 2 1 0
	3 2 1 0
	3 2 1 0
	3 2 1 0
	3 2 1 0

Lesson 7 – Balancing Redox Reactions in Solution

Learning Objectives

In this lesson you will learn:

- To balance more complex **redox reactions** using the **half reactions method**

Pre-requisites: Classes of compounds; Oxidation numbers and balancing simple redox reactions.

Self-study questions

Before you start studying the worked examples, you should be able to formulate answers to the questions below. Use a textbook of your choice, or an online source of information, to find the answers.

1. What is a redox reaction?
2. What is a half reaction?
3. What is an oxidation?
4. What is a reduction?
5. What ions are present in relatively large amounts in an acidic solution?
6. What ions are present in relatively large amounts in a basic solution?
7. What is true about all redox reactions as far as electrons are concerned?
8. Why do we balance redox reactions?

Worked examples

This section contains several solved examples that cover the learning objectives listed above. Study each example carefully and make notes in the workbook to check every example that you understood. Repeat several times what you don't understand at first. It should become clearer as you keep working on the examples.

Objective 47. Balance redox reactions in solution using the half reactions method.

We will use the template table below in order to better understand the stepwise balancing process. The numbers in bold represent the order in which the table should be filled. Each reaction takes place in either acidic or basic solution. Balance the following redox reactions using the half-reaction method.

1. $H_2O_2 + Co^{2+} \rightarrow Co^{3+} + H_2O$ (acidic solution)

2. $Fe^{2+} + Cr_2O_7^{2-} \rightarrow Fe^{3+} + Cr^{3+}$ (acidic solution)

3. $Mn^{2+} + H_2O_2 \rightarrow MnO_2 + H_2O$ (basic solution)

4. $ClO_3^- + Cl^- \rightarrow Cl_2 + ClO_2$ (basic solution)

(No.)	(Reaction)							
Multipliers	Half reactions							
3	1							
4	2							
Sum of two half reactions	5							
Balanced reaction	6							
Element oxidized	7	From 8	To 9	Element reduced	10	From 11	To 12	
Oxidizing agent 13		14		Reducing agent 15			16	

Discussion

There are several things to notice about these reactions:
- They are not complete (some products are missing)
- They all involve oxidation and reduction
- They require an acidic or basic medium to proceed.

Since these reactions are more difficult to balance than others you have seen so far, we employ a special method for redox reactions, called the half reactions method. Basically, we split each redox reaction in two half reactions, based on the reactants and the products. These will end up being the oxidation and the reduction, but we won't know for sure which is which until we balance them. The fact that the reactions happen in acidic or basic solution means that they generally require (or sometimes produce) H^+ ions (in an acidic solution) or OH^- ions (in a basic solution), but never both. Let's start balancing step by step, following the order indicated in the table above, which we will fill for each reaction we balance.

1. $H_2O_2 + Co^{2+} \rightarrow Co^{3+} + H_2O$ (acidic solution)

First, we split the reaction in two half reactions, each indicating what each reactant converts into. Clearly, H_2O_2 will convert to H_2O, and Co^{2+} will convert to Co^{3+} (conservation of matter). We then balance each half reaction as follows:
1. We balance atoms **other than H and O** first
2. We balance **oxygens** next, by adding H_2O (if in acidic solution) or OH^- (if in basic solution)
3. We balance **hydrogens** next, by adding H^+ (if in acidic solution) or H_2O (if in basic solution)
4. We balance **charge** as the last step, by adding electrons to the side that has excess positive charges.

First half reaction:

$$H_2O_2 \rightarrow H_2O$$

The right side is lacking oxygens, so we add a water molecule to it:

$$H_2O_2 \rightarrow H_2O + H_2O \quad \text{(which becomes } H_2O_2 \rightarrow 2H_2O)$$

Now we have introduced more hydrogens, so we need to balance hydrogens on the left. In acidic solution, there are H^+ ions available, of course, and so that is what we will use:

$$2H^+ + H_2O_2 \rightarrow 2H_2O$$

Now all atoms are balanced, but not the charge. The left side has two positive charges while the right side has none. We balance the charge by adding two electrons (negative charges) on the left:

$$2e^- + 2H^+ + H_2O_2 \rightarrow 2H_2O \quad (this\ is\ the\ reduction)$$

Now this half reaction is balanced. We move on to the second half reaction:

$$Co^{2+} \rightarrow Co^{3+}$$

Atoms are already balanced, so we only need to balance the charge:

$$Co^{2+} \rightarrow Co^{3+} + e^- \quad (this\ is\ the\ oxidation)$$

We put these balanced half reactions in boxes labeled 1 and 2 in the table. Next we need to balance the overall reaction from the two half reactions. In the first one, 2 electrons are needed (they are a reactant). In the second one, one electron is released (product). The first reaction is a reduction, and the second is an oxidation. But, the number of electrons exchanged must be the same, so the second half reaction must be multiplied by 2 in order to supply the 2 electrons needed by the first. Thus, in boxes 3 and 4 in the table we put "×1" and "×2". These will be the multipliers needed to obtain the full reaction. So far the table looks as follows:

1	$H_2O_2 + Co^{2+} \rightarrow Co^{3+} + H_2O$	Acidic
Multipliers	Half reactions	
× 1	$2e^- + 2H^+ + H_2O_2 \rightarrow 2H_2O$	
× 2	$Co^{2+} \rightarrow Co^{3+} + e^-$	

Next, we add up the two half reactions, multiplied by their respective coefficients. In adding reactions, all reactants go together and all products go together:

$$\cancel{2e^-} + 2H^+ + H_2O_2 + 2Co^{2+} \rightarrow 2H_2O + 2Co^{3+} + \cancel{2e^-} \quad (box\ 5)$$

The purpose here is to cancel out the electrons, which must be present in equal numbers on both sides of the arrow. If they don't, you have made a mistake and must fix it. The resulting equation represents the balanced redox reaction:

$$2H^+ + H_2O_2 + 2Co^{2+} \rightarrow 2H_2O + 2Co^{3+} \quad (box\ 6)$$

Now you see why acidic solution is important – acid is in fact a reactant. Next, we identify the elements being oxidized and reduced. Clearly, Co is oxidized from +2 to +3. As we have seen before, O is the element being reduced, from -1 in H_2O_2 to -2 in H_2O. Finally, the oxidizing agent is H_2O_2, and the reducing agent is Co^{2+}. The complete table should now look like this:

1	$H_2O_2 + Co^{2+} \rightarrow Co^{3+} + H_2O$						Acidic
Multipliers	Half reactions						
× 1	$2e^- + 2H^+ + H_2O_2 \rightarrow 2H_2O$						
× 2	$Co^{2+} \rightarrow Co^{3+} + e^-$						
Sum of two half reactions	$\cancel{2e^-} + 2H^+ + H_2O_2 + 2Co^{2+} \rightarrow 2H_2O + 2Co^{3+} + \cancel{2e^-}$						
Balanced reaction	$2H^+ + H_2O_2 + 2Co^{2+} \rightarrow 2H_2O + 2Co^{3+}$						
Element oxidized	Co	From +2	To +3	Element reduced	O	From -1	To -2
Oxidizing agent	H_2O_2			Reducing agent		Co^{2+}	

2. $Fe^{2+} + Cr_2O_7^{2-} \rightarrow Fe^{3+} + Cr^{3+}$ (acidic solution)

First half reaction:

$$Cr_2O_7^{2-} \rightarrow Cr^{3+}$$

First we balance the chromium atoms:

$$Cr_2O_7^{2-} \rightarrow 2Cr^{3+}$$

Then, the right side is lacking oxygens, so we add a water molecule to it:

$$Cr_2O_7^{2-} \rightarrow 2Cr^{3+} + 7H_2O$$

Now we have introduced 14 hydrogens on the right, so we need to add hydrogen ions to the left:

$$14H^+ + Cr_2O_7^{2-} \rightarrow 2Cr^{3+} + 7H_2O$$

Now all atoms are balanced, but not the charge. The left side has 12 positive charges total, while the right side has 6. We balance the charge by adding 6 electrons (negative charges) on the left:

$$6e^- + 14H^+ + Cr_2O_7^{2-} \rightarrow 2Cr^{3+} + 7H_2O$$

Now everything is balanced. We move on to the second half reaction:

$$Fe^{2+} \rightarrow Fe^{3+}$$

Atoms are already balanced, so we only need to balance the charge:

$$Fe^{2+} \rightarrow Fe^{3+} + e^-$$

Multipliers: reaction 1 needs 6 electrons, and reaction 2 produces 1, so the multipliers will be "×1" and "×6". The rest of the table should be straightforward:

2	$Fe^{2+} + Cr_2O_7^{2-} \rightarrow Fe^{3+} + Cr^{3+}$						Acidic
Multipliers	Half reactions						
× 1	$6e^- + 14H^+ + Cr_2O_7^{2-} \rightarrow 2Cr^{3+} + 7H_2O$						
× 6	$Fe^{2+} \rightarrow Fe^{3+} + e^-$						
Sum of two half reactions	$\cancel{6e^-} + 14H^+ + Cr_2O_7^{2-} + 6Fe^{2+} \rightarrow 2Cr^{3+} + 7H_2O + 6Fe^{3+} + \cancel{6e^-}$						
Balanced reaction	$14H^+ + Cr_2O_7^{2-} + 6Fe^{2+} \rightarrow 2Cr^{3+} + 7H_2O + 6Fe^{3+}$						
Element oxidized	Fe	From +2	To +3	Element reduced	Cr	From +6	To +3
Oxidizing agent		$Cr_2O_7^{2-}$		Reducing agent		Fe^{2+}	

3. $Mn^{2+} + H_2O_2 \rightarrow MnO_2 + H_2O$ (basic solution)

Balancing in basic solution is similar, except that in a basic solution we do not have hydrogen ions. What is available for using to help balance the redox reaction are water molecules and hydroxide ions.

First half reaction:

$$Mn^{2+} \rightarrow MnO_2$$

We need to balance oxygens (since manganese is already balanced). In basic solution, we add OH^- ions to the side lacking oxygens. Then we will add water on the opposite side to balance hydrogens. Here is a strategy that works very well: once you identify how many oxygens are lacking, add double that number of OH^- ion to the lacking side, then add half of that (meaning the original number) of water molecules to the other side. Here, we lack 2 oxygens on the left. Thus, we will add $4OH^-$ to the left, and $2H_2O$ to the right:

$$4OH^- + Mn^{2+} \rightarrow MnO_2 + 2H_2O$$

See, in one step we balance both oxygens and hydrogens. This only leaves charges to be balanced:

$$4OH^- + Mn^{2+} \rightarrow MnO_2 + 2H_2O + 2e^-$$

Second half reaction:

$$H_2O_2 \rightarrow H_2O$$

We apply the same strategy (cannot add H^+ as we did in example 1), so we add $2OH^-$ to the right, and $1H_2O$ to the left:

$$H_2O + H_2O_2 \rightarrow H_2O + 2OH^-$$

We notice that water is on both sides of the equation, so we cancel it out right away, as well as balance the charge:

$$2e^- + H_2O_2 \rightarrow 2OH^-$$

This now gives us the second half reaction, balanced. Notice how the electrons involved are the same, 2 in each, so the multipliers will be 1 and 1. Here is the final table:

3	$Mn^{2+} + H_2O_2 \rightarrow MnO_2 + H_2O$							Basic
Multipliers	Half reactions							
× 1	$4OH^- + Mn^{2+} \rightarrow MnO_2 + 2H_2O + 2e^-$							
× 1	$2e^- + H_2O_2 \rightarrow 2OH^-$							
Sum of two half reactions	$4OH^- + Mn^{2+} + \cancel{2e^-} + H_2O_2 \rightarrow MnO_2 + 2H_2O + \cancel{2e^-} + 2OH^-$							
Balanced reaction	$4OH^- + Mn^{2+} + H_2O_2 \rightarrow MnO_2 + 2H_2O + 2OH^-$							
Element oxidized	Mn	From	+2	To	+4	Element reduced	O	From -1	To -2
Oxidizing agent			H_2O_2			Reducing agent		Mn^{2+}	

4. $ClO_3^- + Cl^- \rightarrow Cl_2 + ClO_2$ (basic solution)

Here, we have 4 species containing Cl, so how do we determine the two half reactions? It is safe to assume that the chlorate ion is converted into chlorine dioxide, and the chloride into free chlorine. Everything else applies the same as in the previous example, and thus you should obtain this table:

4	$ClO_3^- + Cl^- \rightarrow Cl_2 + ClO_2$							Basic
Multipliers	Half reactions							
× 2	$e^- + H_2O + ClO_3^- \rightarrow ClO_2 + 2OH^-$							
× 1	$2Cl^- \rightarrow Cl_2 + 2e^-$							
Sum of two half reactions	$\cancel{2e^-} + 2H_2O + 2ClO_3^- + 2Cl^- \rightarrow 2ClO_2 + 4OH^- + Cl_2 + \cancel{2e^-}$							
Balanced reaction	$2H_2O + 2ClO_3^- + 2Cl^- \rightarrow 2ClO_2 + 4OH^- + Cl_2$							
Element oxidized	Cl in Cl^-	From	-1	To	0	Element reduced	Cl in ClO_3^-	From +5	To +4
Oxidizing agent			ClO_3^-			Reducing agent		Cl^-	

Worksheet 7.   Balancing redox reactions

The exercises and problems in this section will allow you to practice the topic until you understand it well.

Balance each redox reaction below using the half reaction method. Complete all tables as in the examples above.

1	$S_2O_3^{2-} + I_2 \rightarrow S_4O_6^{2-} + I^-$						Acidic	
Multipliers	Half reactions							
Sum of two half reactions								
Balanced reaction								
Element oxidized		From	To	Element reduced		From	To	
Oxidizing agent				Reducing agent				

2	$Bi(OH)_3 + SnO_2^{2-} \rightarrow SnO_3^{2-} + Bi$						Basic	
Multipliers	Half reactions							
Sum of two half reactions								
Balanced reaction								
Element oxidized		From	To	Element reduced		From	To	
Oxidizing agent				Reducing agent				

3	$Cr_2O_7^{2-} + C_2O_4^{2-} \rightarrow Cr^{3+} + CO_2$						Acidic	
Multipliers	Half reactions							
Sum of two half reactions								
Balanced reaction								
Element oxidized		From	To	Element reduced		From	To	
Oxidizing agent				Reducing agent				

4	$CN^- + MnO_4^- \rightarrow CNO^- + MnO_2$					Basic
Multipliers	Half reactions					
Sum of two half reactions						
Balanced reaction						
Element oxidized		From	To	Element reduced		From	To
Oxidizing agent				Reducing agent		

5	$Cu + NO_3^- \rightarrow Cu^{2+} + NO$					Acidic
Multipliers	Half reactions					
Sum of two half reactions						
Balanced reaction						
Element oxidized		From	To	Element reduced		From	To
Oxidizing agent				Reducing agent		

6	$Br_2 \rightarrow BrO_3^- + Br^-$					Basic
Multipliers	Half reactions					
Sum of two half reactions						
Balanced reaction						
Element oxidized		From	To	Element reduced		From	To
Oxidizing agent				Reducing agent		

7	$MnO_4^- + Fe^{2+} \rightarrow Fe^{3+} + Mn^{2+}$					Acidic	
Multipliers	Half reactions						
Sum of two half reactions							
Balanced reaction							
Element oxidized		From	To	Element reduced		From	To
Oxidizing agent				Reducing agent			

Self-assessment

Using the scale indicated, rate your understanding of each learning objective at the completion of this lesson. Identify the areas where your understanding is weak or medium and discuss with your class mates and/or instructor. Write down specific questions you still have at the completion of this topic.

Learning objective	Self-assessment 3 = strong, 2 = medium, 1 = weak, 0 = not done
	3 2 1 0

Lesson 8 – Predicting Products of Chemical Reactions

Learning Objectives

In this lesson you will learn:

- How to write equations to represent **common chemical properties** of metals, nonmetals, metal and nonmetal oxides, hydroxides, acids, and salts
- How to **predict products** of reactions between various **classes of inorganic compounds**

Pre-requisites: Classes of compounds; Chemical reactions in solution; Balancing chemical reactions.

Self-study questions

Before you start studying the worked examples, you should be able to formulate answers to the questions below. Use a textbook of your choice, or an online source of information, to find the answers.

1. What is an oxide?
2. What are acidic oxides?
3. What are basic oxides?
4. Why are some oxides called anhydrides?
5. What is a hydroxide?
6. Are there bases other than hydroxides? Give examples.
7. What is an acid?
8. What is meant by neutralization?
9. What is a salt?
10. What is the activity series?

Worked examples

This section contains several solved examples that cover the learning objectives listed above. Study each example carefully and make notes in the workbook to check every example that you understood. Repeat several times what you don't understand at first. It should become clearer as you keep working on the examples.

Objective 48. Write chemical reactions characteristic to metals.

Predict the products of, and balance the following chemical reactions involving metals:

1. $Na + Cl_2$
2. $Mg + O_2$
3. $Cs + H_2O$
4. $Al + Fe_2O_3$
5. $Mg + HCl$
6. $Zn + CuSO_4$

Solutions

1. $2Na + Cl_2 \rightarrow 2NaCl$
   Metals react with nonmetals to form simple ionic salts.

2. $2Mg + O_2 \rightarrow 2MgO$
   Metals react with oxygen to make oxides.

3. $2Cs + 2H_2O \rightarrow 2CsOH + H_2$
   Metals (from groups 1 and 2, and Al) react with water to form hydroxides and hydrogen.

4. $2Al + Fe_2O_3 \rightarrow 2Fe + Al_2O_3$
   Metals react with compounds of other metals, such as oxides, if they are above in the activity series.

5. $Mg + 2HCl \rightarrow MgCl_2 + H_2$
   Metals above H in the activity series replace it from acids.

6. $Zn + CuSO_4 \rightarrow ZnSO_4 + Cu$
   Zn is above Cu so it replaces it in compounds.

Objective 49. Write chemical reactions characteristic to nonmetals.

Predict the products of, and balance the following chemical reactions involving nonmetals:

1. $H_2 + Na$
2. $C + O_2$
3. $N_2 + H_2$
4. $H_2 + Cl_2$
5. $Cl_2 + NaOH$
6. $Cl_2 + NaBr$

Solutions

1. $H_2 + 2Na \rightarrow 2NaH$

    Hydrogen reacts with metals in groups 1 and 2 to form hydrides.

2. $C + O_2 \rightarrow CO_2$

    Nonmetals react with oxygen to make nonmetal oxides.

3. $N_2 + 3H_2 \rightarrow 2NH_3$
4. $H_2 + Cl_2 \rightarrow 2HCl$

    Hydrogen reacts with many nonmetals to form nonmetal hydrides, some of which are acids, others are bases.

5. $Cl_2 + 2NaOH \rightarrow NaCl + NaClO + H_2O$

    Halogens (except fluorine) react with solutions of alkali (hydroxides of group 1 metals, sometimes group 2 as well) to disproportionate and form salts (and water), in this case chloride (Cl = -1) and hypochlorite (Cl = +1).

6. $Cl_2 + 2NaBr \rightarrow 2NaCl + Br_2$

    Halogens higher in the group react with salts of halogens lower in the group to displace the latter from their salts.

Objective 50. Write chemical reactions characteristic to oxides.

Predict the products of, and balance the following chemical reactions involving oxides:

1. $CaO + H_2O$
2. $SO_2 + H_2O$
3. $Cl_2O_7 + H_2O$
4. $CaO + SO_3$
5. $MgO + HCl$
6. $CO_2 + NaOH$
7. $P_4O_6 + O_2$
8. $FeCl_2 + Cl_2$

Solutions

1. $Na_2O + H_2O \rightarrow 2NaOH$

    Metal oxides react with water to form bases (hydroxides). For this reason, metal oxides are also called basic oxides. Only metals from groups 1 and 2 actually give this reaction.

2. $SO_2 + H_2O \rightarrow H_2SO_3$

Nonmetal oxides react with water to form acids. What acid is formed is a different issue, considering that most nonmetals have more than one oxoacid. The rule is that the acid formed is one in which the oxidation number of the metal is the same as in the oxide.

Here, S is +4 in SO_2, so it must make an acid in which its oxidation number remains +4. Sulfur has two common oxoacids: H_2SO_4 and H_2SO_3. In the former, S is +6, and in the latter, S is +4 (right?). Thus, sulfurous acid is the product when sulfur dioxide reacts with water. What oxide of S will give sulfuric acid when reacted with water?

3. $Cl_2O_7 + H_2O \rightarrow 2HClO_4$

The same discussion as above applies here. There are several oxides and acids of chlorine, so the one that maintains the oxidation number is formed. Here, Cl is +7 in both.

4. $CaO + SO_3 \rightarrow CaSO_4$

Metal oxides and nonmetal oxides react and form salts. Just like above, the salt formed is the one where the oxidation numbers of both metal and nonmetal are conserved.

5. $Fe_2O_3 + 6HCl \rightarrow 2FeCl_3 + 6H_2O$

Metal oxides react with acids to form salts and water. The metal stays in the same oxidation state.

6. $CO_2 + 2NaOH \rightarrow Na_2CO_3 + H_2O$

Nonmetal oxides react with hydroxides just like with metal oxides, but water is also a product now.

7. $P_4O_6 + 2O_2 \rightarrow P_4O_{10}$
    $2FeCl_2 + Cl_2 \rightarrow 2FeCl_3$

Oxides (and other binary salts) of nonmetals (and metals) in a lower oxidation state will react with oxygen, or a nonmetal, to form the same type of compound in a superior oxidation state. Here, P goes from +3 to +5, and Fe goes from +2 to +3. This is because oxygen and halogens are powerful oxidants.

Objective 51. Write chemical reactions characteristic to hydroxides.

Predict the products of and balance the following chemical reactions involving hydroxides:

1. $NaOH + NH_4Cl$

2. $NaOH + CuSO_4$

3. $Cu(OH)_2 \xrightarrow{heat}$

4. $Ca(OH)_2 + H_3PO_4$

Solutions

1. $NaOH + NH_4Cl \rightarrow NaCl + NH_3 + H_2O$

   Strong bases (such as those of groups 1 and 2 metals) react with salts of other metals (or ammonium) to free up weaker bases. In this case, the weak base NH_4OH is formed, which is unstable and decomposes into ammonia (NH_3, also a weak base) and water.

2. $2NaOH + CuSO_4 \rightarrow Cu(OH)_2 + Na_2SO_4$

   Strong bases react with metal salts that form weak or insoluble bases. In this case $Cu(OH)_2$ is an insoluble base and precipitates from solution.

3. $Cu(OH)_2 \xrightarrow{heat} CuO + H_2O$

   Hydroxides of certain metals (primarily transition metals) decompose when heated, forming the metal oxide (same oxidation state) and water (vapor).

4. $3Ca(OH)_2 + 2H_3PO_4 \rightarrow Ca_3(PO_4)_3 + 6H_2O$

   Bases and acids react to neutralize each other and form salts and water. Of course, the cation and anion combine to form the corresponding salt, as we have seen before.

Objective 52. Write chemical reactions characteristic to acids.

Predict the products of, and balance the following chemical reactions involving acids:

1. $HCl + Fe$

2. $H_2SO_4 + CuO$

3. $HCl + AgNO_3$

4. $H_2SO_4 + NaCl$

Solutions

1. $2HCl + Fe \rightarrow FeCl_2 + H_2$

Acids react with metals above H in the activity series to form salts (usually in low oxidation states) and hydrogen.

2. $H_2SO_4 + CuO \rightarrow CuSO_4 + H_2O$

Acids react with metal oxides to form salts and water.

3. $HCl + AgNO_3 \rightarrow AgCl_{(s)} + HNO_3$

Acids react with salts of other acids when a precipitate can form (AgCl is insoluble).

4. $H_2SO_{4\,(l)} + 2NaCl_{(s)} \rightarrow Na_2SO_4 + HCl_{(g)}$

Strong, concentrated acids react with solid salts of more volatile acids (such as HCl) to free up such acids.

Objective 53. Write chemical reactions characteristic to salts.

Predict the products of, and balance the following chemical reactions involving salts:

1. $CaCO_3 \xrightarrow{\text{heat}}$

2. $Na_2SO_4 + BaCl_2$

3. $CaCO_3 + HCl$

4. $FeCl_3 + NaOH$

Solutions

1. $CaCO_3 \xrightarrow{\text{heat}} CaO + CO_2$

Salts of certain unstable acids (such as carbonic) decompose when heated, to form the two oxides.

2. $Na_2SO_4 + BaCl_2 \rightarrow BaSO_4 + 2NaCl$

Salts generally react with each other if an insoluble compound can be formed (in this case barium sulfate).

3. $CaCO_3 + 2HCl \rightarrow CaCl_2 + CO_2 + H_2O$

Salts of weak acids, such as carbonic, react with stronger acids to make new salts and free up the weak acids. In this case, carbonic acid, H_2CO_3, would be the product, but it is unstable and decomposes.

4. $FeCl_3 + 3NaOH \rightarrow Fe(OH)_3 + 3NaCl$

Same pattern as in the properties of hydroxides, example 2.

Worksheet 8.   Predicting products of chemical reactions

The exercises and problems in this section will allow you to practice the topic until you understand it well.

Predict the products and balance each chemical reaction below.

1. $Al + O_2$

2. $Na + S$

3. $K + H_2O$

4. $Fe + HBr$

5. $Al + ZnSO_4$

6. $H_2 + O_2$

7. $Br_2 + NaOH$

8. $H_2 + S$

9. $CO + O_2$

10. $CO_2 + H_2O$

11. $N_2O_5 + H_2O$

12. $SO_3 + CaO$

13. $SO_2 + NaOH$

14. $BaO + HNO_3$

15. $Na_2O + H_2O$

16. $NaOH + FeCl_2$

17. $LiOH + H_3PO_4$

18. $HBr + Zn$

19. $H_2SO_4 + Fe$

20. $CuO + HCl$

21. $Na_2CO_3 + CH_3COOH$

22. $BaCl_2 + H_2SO_4$

23. $Fe_2(SO_4)_3 + Na_3PO_4$

24. $CaCO_3 \xrightarrow{\text{heat}}$

25. $Ca + Se$

26. $Na_2O + SO_2$

27. $Br_2 + NaI$

28. $P_4O_{10} + H_2O$

29. $Hg_2(NO_3)_2 + NaCl$

Self-assessment

Using the scale indicated, rate your understanding of each learning objective at the completion of this lesson. Identify the areas where your understanding is weak or medium and discuss with your class mates and/or instructor. Write down specific questions you still have at the completion of this topic.

Learning objective	Self-assessment 3 = strong, 2 = medium, 1 = weak, 0 = not done
	3 2 1 0
	3 2 1 0
	3 2 1 0
	3 2 1 0
	3 2 1 0
	3 2 1 0

Lesson 9 – Formulas, Moles, Chemical Composition

Learning Objectives

In this lesson you will learn:

- To determine the **number of particles** in a given number of **molecules** or **formula units** of a compound
- To determine the number of particles in a given amount (in **moles**) of a compound
- To calculate the **molar mass** of a compound (including a hydrate)
- To convert **mass to moles** and **moles to mass**
- To convert moles to number of particles and vice versa
- To convert the mass of a **hydrate** into moles of **anhydrous** salt and moles of water
- To convert the mass of a hydrate into numbers of ions and water molecules
- To convert the mass of a hydrate into numbers of atoms of each element
- To determine the **mass percent composition** of a compound
- To write the **empirical formula** of a compound and the relationship between empirical and **molecular formula**
- To determine the empirical formula and molecular formula of a compound from mass percent composition
- To determine the empirical and molecular formula of a compound from **products of combustion** or other type of reaction

Pre-requisites: Atomic structure; Classes of compounds; Oxidation numbers and balancing simple redox reactions.

Self-study questions

Before you start studying the worked examples, you should be able to formulate answers to the questions below. Use a textbook of your choice, or an online source of information, to find the answers.

1. What is the difference between a molecule and a formula unit? What types of compounds are associated with each? (in terms of chemical bonding)
2. What is a mole?
3. What is molar mass?
4. What is a hydrate?
5. What is meant by anhydrous?
6. What is meant by mass percent composition?
7. What is a molecular formula?
8. What is an empirical formula?
9. What is a combustion reaction?

Worked examples

This section contains several solved examples that cover the learning objectives listed above. Study each example carefully and make notes in the workbook to check every example that you understood. Repeat several times what you don't understand at first. It should become clearer as you keep working on the examples.

Objective 54. Understand the mole. Distinguish between molecules and "formula units".

Indicate the meaning of the formulas and coefficients in front of each compound below:

Compound	What particles and how many
1 H_2O	1 molecule of H_2O
1 NaCl	1 formula unit of NaCl = 1 Na^+ ion and 1 Cl^- ion
5 HCl	5 HCl molecules
10 $CaCl_2$	10 formula units of $CaCl_2$ = 10 Ca^{2+} ions and 20 Cl^- ions
3 Na_2SO_4	3 formula units of Na_2SO_4 = 6 Na^+ ions and 3 SO_4^{2-} ions
2 $FePO_4$	2 $FePO_4$ units = 2 Fe^{3+} ions and 2 PO_4^{3-} ions
25 CO_2	25 CO_2 molecules

Discussion

Formula units apply to ionic compounds, and molecules exist only for covalent compounds (review Objective 22). Thus, for ionic compounds we consider their component ions and their ratio in the formula unit, whereas for covalent compounds we take them as a whole, because their molecules are normally not dissociated except in certain conditions that are not the focus of this chapter.

Objective 55. Determine the number of moles of particles in a given amount of a compound.

Given the amounts of each compound below, determine the number of moles of each element, as well as the number of moles of ions if the compound is ionic.

Amount of compound	Moles of each element	Moles of each ion where applicable
1.0 mol H_2O	2.0 mol H atoms and 1.0 mol O atoms	Not ionic
5.0 mol H_2SO_4	10. mol H atoms, 5.0 mol S atoms, and 20. mol O atoms	Not ionic
2.5 mol $Ca(NO_3)_2$	2.5 mol Ca atoms, 5.0 mol N atoms, and 15 mol O atoms	2.5 mol Ca^{2+} and 5.0 mol NO_3^-
12 mol $FeCl_3$	12 mol Fe atoms, 36 mol Cl atoms	12 mol Fe^{3+} ions, 36 mol Cl^- ions
2.0 mol $Al_2(SO_4)_3$	4.0 mol Al atoms, 6.0 mol S atoms, 24 mol O atoms	4.0 mol Al^{3+} ions, 6.0 mol SO_4^{2-} ions

Objective 56. Calculate the molar mass of a compound (including hydrates).

Calculate the molar mass of each compound below to two decimals:

1. CO_2

2. $Fe(NO_3)_3$

3. $Fe(NH_4)_2(SO_4)_2$

4. $CuSO_4 \cdot 5H_2O$

Solutions

1. $CO_2 : 12.01 + 2(16.00) = 44.01$ g/mol

2. $Fe(NO_3)_3 : 55.845 + 3(14.007 + 3 \times 16.00) = 241.86$ g/mol

3. $Fe(NH_4)_2(SO_4)_2 : 55.845 + 2(14.007 + 4 \times 1.008) + 2(32.065 + 4 \times 16.00) = 284.05$ g/mol

4. $CuSO_4 \cdot 5H_2O : 63.546 + 32.065 + 4 \times 15.999 + 5 \times (2 \times 1.008 + 15.999) = 249.69$ g/mol

Objective 57. Convert from mass to moles and vice versa.

Convert each given mass of a compound into an amount in moles.

1. 125.4 g Cl_2

2. 88.02 g CO_2

3. 25.6 g $CuSO_4$

4. 455 g $Al_2(SO_4)_3$

Solutions

1. 125.4 g Cl_2

$$125.4 \text{ g } Cl_2 \times \frac{1 \text{ mol } Cl_2}{70.906 \text{ g}} = 1.769 \text{ mol } Cl_2$$

2. 88.02 g CO_2

$$88.02 \text{ g } CO_2 \times \frac{1 \text{ mol } CO_2}{44.01 \text{ g}} = 2.000 \text{ mol } CO_2$$

3. 0.256 g $CuSO_4$

$$0.256 \text{ g } CuSO_4 \times \frac{1 \text{ mol } CuSO_4}{159.61 \text{ g}} = 1.60 \times 10^{-3} \text{ mol } CuSO_4$$

4. 455 g $Al_2(SO_4)_3$

$$455 \text{ g } Al_2(SO_4)_3 \times \frac{1 \text{ mol } Al_2(SO_4)_3}{342.15 \text{ g}} = 1.33 \text{ mol } Al_2(SO_4)_3$$

Convert each given amount of a compound into mass.

5. 2.0 mol H_2SO_4

6. 3.5 mol H_2O

7. 14.2 mol Na_2CO_3

8. 10.0 mol $(NH_4)_2Cr_2O_7$

Solutions

5. 2.00 mol H_2SO_4

$$2.00 \text{ mol } H_2SO_4 \times \frac{98.078 \text{ g}}{1 \text{ mol } H_2SO_4} = 196 \text{ g } H_2SO_4$$

6. 3.50 mol H_2O

$$3.50 \text{ mol } H_2O \times \frac{18.015 \text{ g}}{1 \text{ mol } H_2O} = 196 \text{ g } H_2O$$

7. 14.2 mol Na_2CO_3

$$14.2 \text{ mol } Na_2CO_3 \times \frac{105.99 \text{ g}}{1 \text{ mol } Na_2CO_3} = 1.51 \times 10^3 \text{ g } Na_2CO_3 = 1.51 \text{ kg } Na_2CO_3$$

8. 10.0 mol $(NH_4)_2Cr_2O_7$

$$3.50 \text{ mol } (NH_4)_2Cr_2O_7 \times \frac{252.065 \text{ g}}{1 \text{ mol } (NH_4)_2Cr_2O_7} = 2.52 \times 10^3 \text{ g } (NH_4)_2Cr_2O_7 = 2.52 \text{ kg } (NH_4)_2Cr_2O_7$$

Objective 58. Convert from moles to number of particles and vice versa.

Convert each given amount of compound (in moles) into numbers of atoms of each element, and into numbers of ions where applicable.

1. 3.0 mol S_8

2. 2.5×10^{-2} mol CO_2

3. 4.5 mol Al_2S_3

4. 8.5 mol $Fe_3(PO_4)_2$

Solutions

1 mole contains 6.022×10^{23} particles (atoms, ions, molecules, whatever the case may be). Although the ionic compounds contain actual ions, many questions you may encounter will ask about numbers of atoms of particular elements, and so we treat these compounds from both points of view.

1. 3.0 mol S_8

    a. $\text{mol } S_8 \times \frac{8 \text{ mol S atoms}}{1 \text{ mol } S_8} \times \frac{6.022 \times 10^{23} \text{ atoms}}{1 \text{ mol S atoms}} = 1.5 \times 10^{25}$ atoms of S

2. 2.5×10^{-2} mol CO_2

$$2.5 \times 10^{-2} \text{ mol } CO_2 \times \frac{1 \text{ mol C}}{1 \text{ mol } CO_2} \times \frac{6.022 \times 10^{23} \text{ atoms}}{1 \text{ mol C}} = 1.5 \times 10^{22} \text{ atoms of C}$$

$$2.5 \times 10^{-2} \text{ mol } CO_2 \times \frac{2 \text{ mol O}}{1 \text{ mol } CO_2} \times \frac{6.022 \times 10^{23} \text{ atoms}}{1 \text{ mol O}} = 3.0 \times 10^{22} \text{ atoms of O}$$

3. 4.5 mol Al_2S_3

$$4.5 \text{ mol } Al_2S_3 \times \frac{3 \text{ mol S}}{1 \text{ mol } Al_2S_3} \times \frac{6.022 \times 10^{23} \text{ atoms}}{1 \text{ mol S}} = 8.1 \times 10^{24} \text{ atoms of S } or \text{ } S^{2-} \text{ ions}$$

$$4.5 \text{ mol Al}_2\text{S}_3 \times \frac{2 \text{ mol Al}}{1 \text{ mol Al}_2\text{S}_3} \times \frac{6.022 \times 10^{23} \text{ atoms}}{1 \text{ mol Al}} = 5.4 \times 10^{24} \text{ atoms of Al } or \text{ Al}^{3+} \text{ ions}$$

4. $8.5 \text{ mol Fe}_3(\text{PO}_4)_2$

$$8.5 \text{ mol Fe}_3(\text{PO}_4)_2 \times \frac{3 \text{ mol Fe}}{1 \text{ mol Fe}_3(\text{PO}_4)_2} \times \frac{6.022 \times 10^{23} \text{ atoms}}{1 \text{ mol Fe}} = 1.5 \times 10^{25} \text{ atoms of Fe } or \text{ Fe}^{2+} \text{ ions}$$

$$8.5 \text{ mol Fe}_3(\text{PO}_4)_2 \times \frac{2 \text{ mol P}}{1 \text{ mol Fe}_3(\text{PO}_4)_2} \times \frac{6.022 \times 10^{23} \text{ atoms}}{1 \text{ mol P}} = 1.0 \times 10^{25} \text{ atoms of P}$$

$$8.5 \text{ mol Fe}_3(\text{PO}_4)_2 \times \frac{8 \text{ mol O}}{1 \text{ mol Fe}_3(\text{PO}_4)_2} \times \frac{6.022 \times 10^{23} \text{ atoms}}{1 \text{ mol O}} = 4.1 \times 10^{25} \text{ atoms of O}$$

$$8.5 \text{ mol Fe}_3(\text{PO}_4)_2 \times \frac{2 \text{ mol PO}_4^{3-} \text{ ions}}{1 \text{ mol Fe}_3(\text{PO}_4)_2} \times \frac{6.022 \times 10^{23} \text{ ions}}{1 \text{ mol PO}_4^{3-} \text{ ions}} = 1.0 \times 10^{25} \text{ PO}_4^{3-} \text{ ions}$$

Objective 59. Convert a mass of hydrate into moles of anhydrous salt and water.

Given a mass of each hydrated salt below, convert into moles of hydrate, moles of anhydrous salt, and moles of water.

No.	Hydrate	Given mass	Moles hydrate	Moles anhydrous salt	Moles water
1	$CuSO_4 \cdot 5H_2O$	25.458 g	0.10196	0.10196	0.50980
2	$Al_2(SO_4)_3 \cdot 12 H_2O$	850.94 g	1.5241	1.5241	18.289

Solutions

1. $25.458 \text{ g CuSO}_4 \cdot 5\text{H}_2\text{O}$

$$25.458 \text{ g CuSO}_4 \cdot 5\text{H}_2\text{O} \times \frac{1 \text{ mol CuSO}_4 \cdot 5\text{H}_2\text{O}}{249.685 \text{ g}} = 0.10196 \text{ mol CuSO}_4 \cdot 5\text{H}_2\text{O}$$

$$0.10196 \text{ mol CuSO}_4 \cdot 5\text{H}_2\text{O} \times \frac{1 \text{ mol CuSO}_4}{1 \text{ mol CuSO}_4 \cdot 5\text{H}_2\text{O}} = 0.10196 \text{ mol CuSO}_4$$

$$0.10196 \text{ mol CuSO}_4 \cdot 5\text{H}_2\text{O} \times \frac{5 \text{ mol H}_2\text{O}}{1 \text{ mol CuSO}_4 \cdot 5\text{H}_2\text{O}} = 0.50980 \text{ mol H}_2\text{O}$$

2. $850.94 \text{ g Al}_2(\text{SO}_4)_3 \cdot 12 \text{ H}_2\text{O}$

$$850.94 \text{ g Al}_2(\text{SO}_4)_3 \cdot 12 \text{ H}_2\text{O} \times \frac{1 \text{ mol Al}_2(\text{SO}_4)_3 \cdot 12 \text{ H}_2\text{O}}{558.334 \text{ g}} = 1.5241 \text{ mol Al}_2(\text{SO}_4)_3 \cdot 12 \text{ H}_2\text{O}$$

$$1.5241 \text{ mol Al}_2(\text{SO}_4)_3 \cdot 12 \text{ H}_2\text{O} \times \frac{1 \text{ mol Al}_2(\text{SO}_4)_3}{1 \text{ mol Al}_2(\text{SO}_4)_3 \cdot 12 \text{ H}_2\text{O}} = 1.5241 \text{ mol Al}_2(\text{SO}_4)_3$$

$$1.5241 \text{ mol Al}_2(\text{SO}_4)_3 \cdot 12 \text{ H}_2\text{O} \times \frac{12 \text{ mol H}_2\text{O}}{1 \text{ mol Al}_2(\text{SO}_4)_3 \cdot 12 \text{ H}_2\text{O}} = 18.289 \text{ mol H}_2\text{O}$$

Objective 60. Convert a mass of hydrate into numbers of ions and water molecules.

Given a mass of each hydrated salt below, convert into numbers of ions and water molecules.

No.	Hydrate	Given mass	Numbers of ions	Number of water molecules
1	$CuSO_4 \cdot 5H_2O$	25.458 g	$6.140 \times 10^{22}\ Cu^{2+}\ ions$ $6.140 \times 10^{22}\ SO_4^{2-}\ ions$	$3.070 \times 10^{23}\ H_2O\ molecules$
2	$Al_2(SO_4)_3 \cdot 12\ H_2O$	850.94 g	$1.836 \times 10^{24}\ Al^{3+}\ ions$ $2.753 \times 10^{24}\ SO_4^{2-}\ ions$	$1.101 \times 10^{25}\ H_2O\ molecules$

Solutions

We will use the previously determined numbers of moles in these calculations (because the masses given in the problem are the same).

1. $CuSO_4 \cdot 5H_2O \rightarrow Cu^{2+} + SO_4^{2-} + 5H_2O$

$$0.10196\ mol\ CuSO_4 \cdot 5H_2O \times \frac{1\ mol\ Cu^{2+}}{1\ mol\ CuSO_4 \cdot 5H_2O} \times \frac{6.022 \times 10^{23}\ ions}{1\ mol\ Cu^{2+}} = 6.140 \times 10^{22}\ Cu^{2+}\ ions$$

$$0.10196\ mol\ CuSO_4 \cdot 5H_2O \times \frac{1\ mol\ SO_4^{2-}}{1\ mol\ CuSO_4 \cdot 5H_2O} \times \frac{6.022 \times 10^{23}\ ions}{1\ mol\ SO_4^{2-}} = 6.140 \times 10^{22}\ SO_4^{2-}\ ions$$

$$0.50980\ mol\ H_2O \times \frac{6.022 \times 10^{23}\ molecules}{1\ mol\ H_2O} = 3.070 \times 10^{23}\ H_2O\ molecules$$

2. $Al_2(SO_4)_3 \cdot 12\ H_2O \rightarrow 2Al^{3+} + 3SO_4^{2-} + 12H_2O$

$$1.5241\ mol\ Al_2(SO_4)_3 \cdot 12\ H_2O \times \frac{2\ mol\ Al^{3+}}{1\ mol\ Al_2(SO_4)_3 \cdot 12\ H_2O} \times \frac{6.022 \times 10^{23}\ ions}{1\ mol\ Al^{3+}} = 1.836 \times 10^{24}\ Al^{3+}\ ions$$

$$1.5241\ mol\ Al_2(SO_4)_3 \cdot 12\ H_2O \times \frac{3\ mol\ SO_4^{2-}}{1\ mol\ Al_2(SO_4)_3 \cdot 12\ H_2O} \times \frac{6.022 \times 10^{23}\ ions}{1\ mol\ SO_4^{2-}} = 2.753 \times 10^{24}\ SO_4^{2-}\ ions$$

$$18.289\ mol\ H_2O \times \frac{6.022 \times 10^{23}\ molecules}{1\ mol\ H_2O} = 1.101 \times 10^{25}\ H_2O\ molecules$$

Objective 61. Convert a mass of hydrate into numbers of atoms of each element.

Given a mass of each hydrated salt below, convert into moles and numbers of atoms of each element contained.

No.	Hydrate	Given mass	Numbers of atoms of each element
1	$CuSO_4 \cdot 5H_2O$	25.458 g	6.140×10^{22} Cu atoms, 6.140×10^{22} S atoms, 5.526×10^{23} O atoms, 6.124×10^{23} H atoms
2	$Al_2(SO_4)_3 \cdot 12 H_2O$	850.94 g	1.836×10^{24} Al atoms, 2.753×10^{24} S atoms, 2.203×10^{25} O atoms, 2.203×10^{25} H atoms

Solutions

We will use the previously determined number of moles in these calculations (masses are the same).

1.

$$0.10196 \text{ mol } CuSO_4 \cdot 5H_2O \times \frac{1 \text{ mol Cu}}{1 \text{ mol } CuSO_4 \cdot 5H_2O} \times \frac{6.022 \times 10^{23} \text{ atoms}}{1 \text{ mol Cu}} = 6.140 \times 10^{22} \text{ Cu atoms}$$

$$0.10196 \text{ mol } CuSO_4 \cdot 5H_2O \times \frac{1 \text{ mol S}}{1 \text{ mol } CuSO_4 \cdot 5H_2O} \times \frac{6.022 \times 10^{23} \text{ atoms}}{1 \text{ mol S}} = 6.140 \times 10^{22} \text{ S atoms}$$

$$0.10196 \text{ mol } CuSO_4 \cdot 5H_2O \times \frac{9 \text{ mol O}}{1 \text{ mol } CuSO_4 \cdot 5H_2O} \times \frac{6.022 \times 10^{23} \text{ atoms}}{1 \text{ mol O}} = 5.526 \times 10^{23} \text{ O atoms}$$

$$0.10196 \text{ mol } CuSO_4 \cdot 5H_2O \times \frac{10 \text{ mol H}}{1 \text{ mol } CuSO_4 \cdot 5H_2O} \times \frac{6.022 \times 10^{23} \text{ atoms}}{1 \text{ mol H}} = 6.124 \times 10^{23} \text{ H atoms}$$

2.

$$1.5241 \text{ mol } Al_2(SO_4)_3 \cdot 12 H_2O \times \frac{2 \text{ mol Al}}{1 \text{ mol } Al_2(SO_4)_3 \cdot 12 H_2O} \times \frac{6.022 \times 10^{23} \text{ atoms}}{1 \text{ mol Al}} = 1.836 \times 10^{24} \text{ Al atoms}$$

$$1.5241 \text{ mol } Al_2(SO_4)_3 \cdot 12 H_2O \times \frac{3 \text{ mol S}}{1 \text{ mol } Al_2(SO_4)_3 \cdot 12 H_2O} \times \frac{6.022 \times 10^{23} \text{ atoms}}{1 \text{ mol S}} = 2.753 \times 10^{24} \text{ S atoms}$$

$$1.5241 \text{ mol } Al_2(SO_4)_3 \cdot 12 H_2O \times \frac{24 \text{ mol O}}{1 \text{ mol } Al_2(SO_4)_3 \cdot 12 H_2O} \times \frac{6.022 \times 10^{23} \text{ atoms}}{1 \text{ mol O}} = 2.203 \times 10^{25} \text{ O atoms}$$

$$1.5241 \text{ mol } Al_2(SO_4)_3 \cdot 12 H_2O \times \frac{24 \text{ mol H}}{1 \text{ mol } Al_2(SO_4)_3 \cdot 12 H_2O} \times \frac{6.022 \times 10^{23} \text{ atoms}}{1 \text{ mol H}} = 2.203 \times 10^{25} \text{ H atoms}$$

Objective 62. Determine the elemental mass percent composition of a compound.

Determine the elemental mass percent composition of each compound in the table below:

Compound	Elemental mass percent composition
$KMnO_4$	24.74 % K , 34.76 % Mn , 40.50 % O
$Al_2(SO_4)_3$	15.77 % Al , 28.12 % S , 56.11 % O

Discussion

The elemental mass percent composition is calculated as follows:

$$mass\ \%\ of\ element\ X = \frac{mass\ of\ X\ in\ compound}{mass\ of\ compound} \times 100$$

All compounds have a fixed elemental composition, so it is not necessary to specify a mass. We can use any mass, and we will assume 1 mole of each compound, because we know the molar mass. Thus, as we saw before:

$$1\ mol\ KMnO_4\ contains\ 1\ mol\ K, 1\ mol\ Mn, and\ 4\ mol\ O$$
$$1\ mol\ Al_2(SO_4)_3\ contains\ 2\ mol\ Al, 3\ mol\ S, and\ 12\ mol\ O$$

Solutions

$KMnO_4$:

$$\% K = \frac{39.0983\ g\ K}{158.0339\ g\ KMnO_4} \times 100 = 24.74\ \%$$

$$\% Mn = \frac{54.938\ g\ Mn}{158.0339\ g\ KMnO_4} \times 100 = 34.76\ \%$$

$$\% O = \frac{63.9976\ g\ O}{158.0339\ g\ KMnO_4} \times 100 = 40.50\ \%$$

$Al_2(SO_4)_3$:

$$\% Al = \frac{53.9631\ g\ Al}{342.1509\ g\ Al_2(SO_4)_3} \times 100 = 15.77\ \%$$

$$\% S = \frac{96.195\ g\ S}{342.1509\ g\ Al_2(SO_4)_3} \times 100 = 28.12\ \%$$

$$\% O = \frac{191.9928\ g\ O}{342.1509\ g\ Al_2(SO_4)_3} \times 100 = 56.11\ \%$$

Objective 63. Write an empirical formula for a compound and relate it to the molecular formula.

For each compound formula in the table below, write its empirical formula, and a relationship between the empirical and molecular formula.

Compound	Empirical formula	Relation to molecular formula
H_2O	H_2O	$(H_2O)_1 = H_2O$
$Na_2C_2O_4$	$NaCO_2$	$(NaCO_2)_2 = Na_2C_2O_4$
$C_6H_{12}O_6$	CH_2O	$(CH_2O)_6 = C_6H_{12}O_6$
NH_4NO_2	NH_2O	$(NH_2O)_2 = N_2H_4O_2 = NH_4NO_2$

As you can see, the molecular formula is a multiple of the empirical formula, and in most cases the two are the same.

Objective 64. Determine the empirical formula and molecular formula of a compound from elemental mass percent composition.

From the elemental mass percent composition of each compound below, determine its empirical formula. When the molar mass is given, determine the molecular formula of the compound as well.
1.   76.0% C, 12.8% H, and 11.2% O (molar mass = 284.5 g/mol)
2.   12.7% Al, 19.7% N, and 67.6% O

Solutions

The empirical formula of a compound can be determined if the elemental mass percent composition is known. The molecular formula can also be determined if the molar mass of the compound is known, otherwise it cannot.

In these examples, we will assume exactly 100.000 g of compound, so that from the mass percentages we infer the mass in grams of each element. The principle is the following: to determine the empirical formula we need the ratios between the elements in the compound. That ratio represents atoms for a molecule (or formula unit), and also represents moles for a mole of compound. Thus, if we convert the mass of each element into moles, and then we calculate the ratios of these moles, we will have the empirical formula.

1.   76.0% C, 12.8% H, and 11.2% O (molar mass = 284.5 g/mol)

We assume 100.0 g compound, so we have 76.0 g C, 12.8 g H, and 11.0 g O.
Next we convert these masses to moles:

$$76.0 \text{ g C} \times \frac{1 \text{ mol C}}{12.01 \text{ g}} = 6.33 \text{ mol C}$$

$$12.8 \text{ g H} \times \frac{1 \text{ mol H}}{1.008 \text{ g}} = 12.7 \text{ mol H}$$

$$11.2 \text{ g O} \times \frac{1 \text{ mol O}}{16.00 \text{ g}} = 0.700 \text{ mol O}$$

Now we have the ratios between moles of elements:

$$C : H : O = 6.33 : 12.7 : 0.700$$

But these are not numbers we want to see in a formula, so in order to attempt to make them integers, we divide them all by the lowest of them:

$$C: \frac{6.33}{0.700} = 9.04 \; ; \; H: \frac{12.7}{0.700} = 18.1 \; ; \; O: \frac{0.700}{0.700} = 1$$

Since these numbers are experimentally determined, they will not have exact integer values, but they are close enough. Thus, our empirical formula is:

$$C_9H_{18}O$$

We have the molar mass of the compound, so we can determine the molecular formula. Remember, the molecular formula will be of the form:

$$(C_9H_{18}O)_n$$

Thus:

$$n = \frac{\text{molar mass of compound}}{\text{molar mass of empirical formula}} = \frac{284.5 \text{ g/mol}}{142.24 \text{ g/mol}} = 2.00$$

So, the molecular formula is:

$$C_{18}H_{36}O_2$$

2. 12.7% Al, 19.7% N, and 67.6% O

In 100.0 g compound we have 12.7 g Al, 19.7 g N, and 67.6 g O.

Convert to moles:

$$12.7 \text{ g Al} \times \frac{1 \text{ mol Al}}{26.98 \text{ g}} = 0.471 \text{ mol Al}$$

$$19.7 \text{ g N} \times \frac{1 \text{ mol N}}{14.01 \text{ g}} = 1.41 \text{ mol N}$$

$$67.6 \text{ g O} \times \frac{1 \text{ mol O}}{16.00 \text{ g}} = 4.23 \text{ mol O}$$

Convert to smallest integer ratios:

$$Al : \frac{0.471}{0.471} = 1 \; ; \; N : \frac{1.41}{0.471} = 2.99 \; ; \; O : \frac{4.23}{0.471} = 8.98$$

So it looks like the empirical formula is AlN_3O_9. We don't have the molar mass in this case, so we cannot calculate the molecular formula. But: by looking at the empirical formula, and knowing that Al has a valence of 3, we can infer that the compound is very likely $Al(NO_3)_3$, right? This is aluminum nitrate, which we have seen before. Eureka!

Objective 65. Determine the empirical and molecular formula of a compound from products of combustion or other type of reaction.

1. Combustion analysis of an unknown compound containing only carbon and hydrogen produced 4.554 g of CO_2 and 2.322 g of H_2O. What is the empirical formula of the compound?
2. Combustion analysis of 2.400 g of an unknown compound containing carbon, hydrogen, and oxygen produced 4.171 g of CO_2 and 2.268 g of H_2O. What is the empirical formula of the compound?

Solutions

In a combustion reaction, a compound is burned in oxygen. If the compound contains C and H, the products will be CO_2 and H_2O. If the compound also contains O, products are the same, just that less external O_2 is needed for combustion. The analysis is the same: we measure how much CO_2 and H_2O is formed, and we work back to determine the moles of C and H (and O by difference if that is the case) in order to determine the empirical formula.

1. The products are 4.554 g of CO_2 and 2.322 g H_2O.

First we determine how much C and H (in moles) are in these products:

$$4.554 \text{ g CO}_2 \times \frac{1 \text{ mol CO}_2}{44.01 \text{ g}} \times \frac{1 \text{ mol C}}{1 \text{ mol CO}_2} = 0.1035 \text{ mol C}$$

$$2.322 \text{ g H}_2O \times \frac{1 \text{ mol H}_2O}{18.02 \text{ g}} \times \frac{2 \text{ mol H}}{1 \text{ mol H}_2O} = 0.2578 \text{ mol H}$$

All the carbon and hydrogen comes from the combustion of the compound and they are the only elements in it, so we proceed with the ratios:

$$C: \frac{0.1035}{0.1035} = 1 \quad ; \quad H: \frac{0.2578}{0.1035} = 2.49$$

This gives us $CH_{2.5}$. Since we want integers, a simple multiplication by 2 gives us the empirical formula: C_2H_5

2. We start with 2.400 g compound and we end up with 4.171 g of CO_2 and 2.268 g H_2O.

We start with the same calculation:

$$4.171 \text{ g CO}_2 \times \frac{1 \text{ mol CO}_2}{44.01 \text{ g}} \times \frac{1 \text{ mol C}}{1 \text{ mol CO}_2} = 0.09477 \text{ mol C}$$

$$2.268 \text{ g H}_2O \times \frac{1 \text{ mol H}_2O}{18.02 \text{ g}} \times \frac{2 \text{ mol H}}{1 \text{ mol H}_2O} = 0.2518 \text{ mol H}$$

The compound also contains O, but the oxygen combines with external oxygen used in combustion so we can't use the O in CO_2 and H_2O in the calculation. Instead, we will find the oxygen in the original compound by difference, since we know the starting mass. To do that, we need to know what mass of C and H was in the compound so we need two additional calculations:

$$0.09477 \text{ mol C} \times \frac{12.01 \text{ g}}{1 \text{ mol C}} = 1.138 \text{ g C}$$

$$0.2518 \text{ g H} \times \frac{1.008 \text{ g}}{1 \text{ mol H}} = 0.2538 \text{ g H}$$

The mass of oxygen will be the difference:

$$2.400 \text{ g compound} - 1.138 \text{ g C} - 0.2538 \text{ g H} = 1.008 \text{ g O}$$

Now we can determine the moles of oxygen:

$$1.008 \text{ g O} \times \frac{1 \text{ mol O}}{16.00 \text{ g}} = 0.06300 \text{ mol O}$$

Finally, the ratios of moles:

$$\text{C:} \frac{0.09477}{0.06300} = 1.50 \quad ; \quad \text{H:} \frac{0.2518}{0.06300} = 4.00 \quad ; \quad \text{O:} \frac{0.06300}{0.06300} = 1$$

Empirical formula is $C_{1.5}H_4O$, or rather $C_3H_8O_2$

Worksheet 9.   Formulas, moles, composition

The exercises and problems in this section will allow you to practice the topic until you understand it well.

1. Indicate the meaning of the formulas and coefficients in front of each compound below:

Compound	What particles and how many
1 H_2SO_4	
2 $MgCl_2$	
6 HF	
6 K_3PO_4	
4 $Al_2(SO_4)_3$	

2. Given the amounts of each compound below, determine the number of moles of each element, as well as the number of moles of ions if the compound is ionic.

Amount of compound	Moles of each element	Moles of each ion where applicable
2 mol H_2SO_4		
1 mol $MgCl_2$		
4 mol HF		
6 mol K_3PO_4		
5 mol $Al_2(SO_4)_3$		

3. Calculate the molar mass of each compound below:

a. H_3PO_4

b. CaC_2O_4

c. $Na_2Cr_2O_7 \cdot 2H_2O$

d. $KAl(SO_4)_2$

4. Convert each given mass of a compound into an amount in moles.
    a. 125.4 g Br_2

    b. 0.8802 g Na_2CO_3

    c. 25.6 g $KAl(SO_4)_2$

    d. 455 g HNO_3

5. Convert each given amount of a compound into mass.
    a. 2.0 mol $CaCO_3$

    b. 5.0 mol $Ba(NO_3)_2$

    c. 0.025 mol $Fe_2(SO_4)_3$

6. Convert each given amount of compound (in moles) into numbers of atoms of each element, and into numbers of ions where applicable.

    a. 2.0 mol $CaCO_3$

    b. 5.0 mol $Ba(NO_3)_2$

c. 2.5 mol $Fe_2(SO_4)_3$

d. 10 mol $(NH_4)_3PO_4$

7. Given a mass of each hydrated salt below, convert into moles of hydrate, moles of anhydrous salt, and moles of water.

No.	Hydrate	Given mass	Moles hydrate	Moles anhydrous salt	Moles water
1	$Na_2Cr_2O_7 \cdot 2H_2O$	0.1458 g			
2	$FeSO_4 \cdot 7H_2O$	11.456 g			

8. Given a mass of each hydrated salt below, convert into numbers of ions and water molecules.

No.	Hydrate	Given mass	Numbers of ions	Number of water molecules
1	$Na_2Cr_2O_7 \cdot 2H_2O$	0.1458 g		
2	$FeSO_4 \cdot 7H_2O$	11.456 g		

9. Given a mass of each hydrated salt below, convert into moles and numbers of atoms of each element contained.

No.	Hydrate	Given mass	Numbers of atoms of each element
1	$Na_2Cr_2O_7 \cdot 2H_2O$	0.1458 g	
2	$FeSO_4 \cdot 7H_2O$	11.456 g	

10. Determine the elemental mass percent composition of each compound in the table below:

Compound	Elemental mass percent composition
$CaCl_2$	
Na_2CO_3	
$Al(ClO_3)_3$	
$Fe_3(PO_4)_2$	

11. For each compound formula in the table below, write its empirical formula, and a relationship between the empirical and molecular formula.

Compound	Empirical formula	Relation to molecular formula
H_2SO_4		
P_4O_{10}		
C_3H_6		
Hg_2Cl_2		

12. From the elemental mass percent composition of each compound below, determine its empirical formula. When the molar mass is given, determine the molecular formula of the compound as well.
    a. 85.6% C and 14.4% H

    b. 43.4% Na, 11.3% C, 45.3% O

    c. 87.5% N and 12.5% H (molar mass = 32.0 g/mol)

    d.   40.00% C, 6.71% H, 53.29% O (molar mass = 180.2 g/mol)

13. When a 0.500 g sample of a compound containing carbon, hydrogen, and oxygen is combusted in air, it gives 1.341 g of CO_2 and 0.329 g of H_2O. The compound has a molecular weight of 162 g/mol. Determine its molecular formula.

Self-assessment

Using the scale indicated, rate your understanding of each learning objective at the completion of this lesson. Identify the areas where your understanding is weak or medium and discuss with your class mates and/or instructor. Write down specific questions you still have at the completion of this topic.

Learning objective	Self-assessment 3 = strong, 2 = medium, 1 = weak, 0 = not done
	3 2 1 0
	3 2 1 0
	3 2 1 0
	3 2 1 0
	3 2 1 0
	3 2 1 0
	3 2 1 0
	3 2 1 0
	3 2 1 0
	3 2 1 0
	3 2 1 0
	3 2 1 0

Lesson 10 – Solutions and Concentration

Learning Objectives

In this lesson you will learn:

- To calculate the **mass percent composition** of a **solution**
- To calculate the **volume percent composition** of a solution
- To calculate the **content of a solution** from the mass percent composition
- To calculate the composition of a **saturated solution** of a compound at a given **temperature**
- To calculate the **solubility** of a compound from the mass percent composition of a saturated solution
- To calculate the **molarity** (molar concentration) of a solution
- To calculate the **molarity of each** ion in a solution
- To calculate the quantity of solute needed to make a solution of given (target) molarity
- To calculate the molarity of a solution after **dilution**
- To calculate the volume of **stock solution** needed to make a solution of given (target) molarity
- To calculate the molarity of a solution made by **mixing two solutions** of the same compound
- To calculate the molarity of a solution made by mixing two solutions containing a **common ion**
- To calculate the **molality** of a solution
- To calculate the quantity of a compound and solvent needed to make a solution of given (target) molality

Pre-requisites: Classes of compounds; Formulas, moles, chemical composition.

Self-study questions

Before you start studying the worked examples, you should be able to formulate answers to the questions below. Use a textbook of your choice, or an online source of information, to find the answers.

1. What is a solution? What are the components of a solution?
2. What is meant by mass percent composition?
3. What is meant by volume percent composition?
4. What is a saturated solution?
5. What is solubility?
6. What is molarity?
7. What is meant by dilution? What stays constant during dilution?
8. What is a stock solution?
9. What is molality?

Worked examples

This section contains several solved examples that cover the learning objectives listed above. Study each example carefully and make notes in the workbook to check every example that you understood. Repeat several times what you don't understand at first. It should become clearer as you keep working on the examples.

Objective 66. Calculate the mass percent composition of a solution.

1. Calculate the mass percent composition of each solution below:
   a. 23.56 g NaCl dissolved in 95.44 g H_2O
   b. 134 g $Ca(NO_3)_2$ dissolved in 125 g H_2O

Solutions

Since these compounds dissolve in water, the mass percent composition will be straightforward:

a.

$$\% \, NaCl = \frac{23.56 \; g \; NaCl}{(23.56 \, + \, 95.44)g \; solution} \times 100 = 19.80 \, \% \;\; ; \;\; \% \, H_2O = 80.20 \, \%$$

b.

$$\% \, Ca(NO_3)_2 = \frac{134 \; g \; Ca(NO_3)_2}{(134 + 125)g \; solution} \times 100 = 51.7 \, \% \;\; ; \;\; \% \, H_2O = 48.3 \, \%$$

2. What mass of $CaCl_2$ must be dissolved in water in order to make a solution that is 12.5% Ca^{2+}?

Solution

Here, instead of the percent of a full compound, we are given the mass percent of just one ion. We need 25 g Ca^{2+} in 100. g solution so let's work with these masses. We cannot obtain pure calcium ions, so we must use a compound that contains them, in this case calcium chloride (remember dissociation of salts, Objective 44). We convert the ions into the full compound with the help of moles:

$$12.5 \; g \; Ca^{2+} \times \frac{1 \; mol \; Ca^{2+}}{40.078 \; g} \times \frac{1 \; mol \; CaCl_2}{1 \; mol \; Ca^{2+}} \times \frac{110.984 \; g}{1 \; mol \; CaCl_2} = 34.62 \; g \; CaCl_2$$

Thus if we dissolve 34.62 g $CaCl_2$ in (100 − 34.62) = 65.38 g H_2O, we get a solution that contains 12.5% Ca^{2+} ions.

3. What mass of $CaCl_2$ must be added to 200.0 g H_2O in order to make a solution that is 12.5% Ca^{2+}?

Solution

Now we know that we must use 200. g water and some calcium chloride in order to make a solution that still contains 12.5% Ca^{2+} ions by mass. Again, we cannot add pure calcium ions to water, but must use calcium chloride, so let x be the mass of calcium chloride that we need.

We need to find out how much in this mass of x is just calcium ions, so we work with moles:

$$x \; g \; CaCl_2 \times \frac{1 \; mol \; CaCl_2}{110.984 \; g} \times \frac{1 \; mol \; Ca^{2+}}{1 \; mol \; CaCl_2} \times \frac{40.048 \; g}{1 \; mol \; Ca^{2+}} = 0.3611x \; g \; Ca^{2+}$$

This is the same thing as finding the mass percent composition of $CaCl_2$: it contains 36.11% Ca, so the mass of Ca^{2+} in x g of $CaCl_2$ is 0.3611 x g.

Thus, the ratio between the mass of the calcium ions ($0.3611\, x$) and the mass of the entire solution (x plus the 200. g water) must equal 12.5%:

$$\frac{0.3611x}{x + 200} = \frac{12.5}{100} = 0.125$$

So let's solve for x :

$$0.3611x = 0.125\, (x + 200) = 0.125x + 25 \quad \Rightarrow \quad 0.2361x = 25 \quad \Rightarrow \quad x = 105.9\, g\; CaCl_2$$

Is the result reasonable? Let's check. Since we determined that calcium chloride is 36.11% calcium ions, the mass of Ca^{2+} in the 105.9 g $CaCl_2$ is:

$$105.9\, g\; CaCl_2 \times \frac{36.11}{100} = 38.24\, g\; Ca^{2+}$$

The mass of the solution is:

$$105.9\, g\; CaCl_2 + 200.0\, g\; H_2O = 305.9\, g\; solution$$

Mass percent calcium ions:

$$\frac{38.24\, g\; Ca^{2+}}{305.9\, g\; solution} \times 100 = 12.50\, \%\; Ca^{2+}$$

Objective 67. Calculate the volume percent composition of a solution.

1. Calculate the volume percent composition of a solution made by mixing 25.0 mL water with 125.0 mL ethanol and 50.0 mL acetone

2. What volume of ethanol needs to be added to 165 mL water in order to make a solution that is 40.0% ethanol by volume?

Solutions

Volume percent composition is the same as mass percent composition but for liquids, which are more easily measured by volume.

1.

$$water = \frac{25.0\, mL}{(25.0 + 125.0 + 50.0)\, mL} \times 100 = 12.5\%\; by\; volume$$

$$ethanol = \frac{125.0\, mL}{(25.0 + 125.0 + 50.0)\, mL} \times 100 = 62.5\%\; by\; volume$$

$$acetone = \frac{50.0\, mL}{(25.0 + 125.0 + 50.0)\, mL} \times 100 = 25.0\%\; by\; volume$$

2. Let x be the volume of ethanol. Thus:

$$\frac{x}{165 + x} = \frac{40.0}{100} = 0.400 \quad \Rightarrow \quad x = 0.4(165 + x) = 66 + 0.4x \quad \Rightarrow \quad 0.6x = 66 \quad \Rightarrow \quad x = 110.\, mL\; ethanol$$

Is the result reasonable?

$$\frac{110.\,mL\ ethanol}{275\ mL\ mixture} \times 100 = 40.0\%$$

Objective 68. Calculate the content of a solution from mass percent composition.

Calculate the mass and mass percent of:
1. Sodium ions in 50.0 g solution that is 10.0% Na_2CO_3 by mass
2. Bromide ions in 25.4 g solution that is 2.5% $FeBr_3$ by mass

Solutions

1. We need the mass and the mass percent of sodium in this solution. We convert the mass of sodium carbonate to mass of sodium (as ions):

$$50.0\ g\ solution \times \frac{10.0\ g\ Na_2CO_3}{100\ g\ solution} = 5.00\ g\ Na_2CO_3$$

$$5.00\ g\ Na_2CO_3 \times \frac{1\ mol\ Na_2CO_3}{105.99\ g} = 0.0472\ mol\ Na_2CO_3$$

$$0.0472\ mol\ Na_2CO_3 \times \frac{2\ mol\ Na^+}{1\ mol\ Na_2CO_3} = 0.0944\ mol\ Na^+$$

$$0.0944\ mol\ Na^+ \times \frac{22.99\ g\ Na^+}{1\ mol\ Na^+} = 2.17\ g\ Na^+$$

And now the mass percent:

$$\frac{2.17\ g\ Na^+}{50.0\ g\ solution} \times 100 = 4.34\%\ Na^+$$

Does the result make sense? Yes, if the solution is 10% in sodium carbonate, then 4.34% sodium seems right.

2. Same calculation for the mass of bromine. I will do it in one long equation:

$$25.4\ g\ solution \times \frac{2.5\ g\ FeBr_3}{100\ g\ solution} \times \frac{1\ mol\ FeBr_3}{295.557\ g} \times \frac{3\ mol\ Br^-}{1\ mol\ FeBr_3} \times \frac{79.904\ g}{1\ mol\ Br^-} = 0.515\ g\ Br^-$$

$$\frac{0.515\ g\ Br^-}{25.4\ g\ solution} \times 100 = 2.03\%\ Br^-$$

Does the result make sense? Yes, the solution is 2.5% $FeBr_3$, and bromine represents most of the mass of the solute, so 2.03% seems right.

Objective 69. Calculate the composition of a saturated solution of a salt at a given temperature.

Calculate the mass percent composition of each saturated solution below. Obtain the solubility of the salt from the solubility chart provided in Appendix D.
1. KCl at 60°C
2. $NaNO_3$ at 5°C

Solutions

The chart we are referred to is called a solubility chart. It contains solubility curves, which tell us how much of a compound dissolves in exactly 100 g of water at a given temperature between 0 and 100 °C. The solubility of a salt generally increases with temperature, but a few have the opposite effect. When given a certain temperature, we determine the solubility of a given salt from the chart, by intersecting the temperature line with the solubility curve. Of course, for temperatures other than every 10°C, we would need to construct our own line.

1. KCl at 60°C.

From the chart, we estimate the solubility of KCl at 60°C to be 43 g per 100 g water (since the y scale has divisions every 10 g, we can only estimate to the nearest gram). Thus:

$$\frac{43\ g\ KCl}{(43+100)g\ solution} \times 100 = 30.1\%\ KCl, \quad and\ thus\ 69.9\%\ H_2O$$

2. $NaNO_3$ at 5°C.

5°C does not have a line drawn on the chart, so we make one (try on paper) and we estimate the solubility as 76g $NaNO_3$ per 100 g H_2O (you may disagree if you'd like). Thus:

$$\frac{76g\ NaNO_3}{(76+100)g\ solution} \times 100 = 43.2\%\ NaNO_3, \quad and\ 56.8\%\ H_2O$$

Objective 70. Calculate the solubility of a compound from the mass percent composition of a saturated solution.

Calculate the solubility of each compound below in water from the mass percent composition of the solution (temperature not specified).
1. A saturated solution containing 47.6% $MgSO_4$ by mass
2. A saturated solution containing 35.2% NaCl by mass.

Solutions

Here, we calculate the solubility of a salt, in grams of salt per 100 g of water, from the mass percent composition. We work backwards:

1. A saturated solution containing 47.6% $MgSO_4$ by mass

47.6% $MgSO_4$ by mass means that a saturated solution will contain 47.6 g $MgSO_4$ and 52.4 g H_2O in each 100.0 g solution. We need to set up a proportion in order to find the solubility as defined above:

$$\frac{47.6 \ g \ MgSO_4}{52.4 \ g \ H_2O} = \frac{x \ g \ MgSO_4}{100.0 \ g \ H_2O}$$

This is true because solubility is directly proportional, so we need to find the mass of solute that will dissolve in 100 g water. Solving for x we get:

$$x = \frac{47.6 \ x \ 100.0}{52.4} = 90.8 \ g \ MgSO_4 \ per \ 100.0 \ g \ water$$

2.   A saturated solution containing 35.2% NaCl by mass.

$$\frac{35.2 \ g \ NaCl}{64.8 \ g \ H_2O} = \frac{x \ g \ NaCl}{100.0 \ g \ H_2O} \quad \Rightarrow \quad x = \frac{35.2 \times 100.0}{64.8} = 54.3 \ g \ NaCl \ per \ 100.0 \ g \ water$$

Objective 71. Calculate the molarity of a solution when a compound is dissolved in water.

Calculate the molarity of each solution below.
1.   3.0 mol H_2SO_4 in 500. mL of solution.
2.   25.64 g NaOH in 2000.0 mL of solution.
3.   3.456 g $CuSO_4 \cdot 5H_2O$ in 250.00 mL solution.

Solutions

Molarity, or molar concentration, represents the number of moles of solute per liter of solution:

$$Molarity = \frac{moles \ of \ solute}{volume \ of \ solution \ (in \ L)} \quad ; \quad M = \frac{n}{V}$$

Units for molarity are mol/L, or simply M (a 1.0 M solution contains 1.0 mol of solute per liter).

1.   3.0 mol H_2SO_4 in 500. mL of solution. All volumes in mL must be converted to L.

$$M = \frac{3.0 \ mol}{0.500 \ L \ solution} = 6.0 \frac{mol}{L} \ (M)$$

2.   25.64 g NaOH in 2000.0 mL of solution.

$$25.64 \ g \ NaOH \ \times \ \frac{1 \ mol \ NaOH}{40.00 \ g} = 0.6410 \ mol \ NaOH$$

$$M = \frac{0.6401 \ mol}{2.0000 \ L} = 0.3205 \ M$$

3.   3.456 g $CuSO_4 \cdot 5H_2O$ in 250.00 mL solution.

$$3.456 \ g \ CuSO_4 \cdot 5H_2O \ \times \frac{1 \ mol \ CuSO_4 \cdot 5H_2O}{249.685 \ g} = 0.01384 \ mol \ CuSO_4 \cdot 5H_2O$$

$$M = \frac{0.01384 \ mol}{0.250 \ L} = 0.05537 \ M$$

Do not worry about the water from the hydrate here; the volume of solution is 250 mL, which incorporates the little amount of water that comes from the hydrate.

Objective 72. Calculate the molarity of each ion in a solution.

Calculate the molar concentration of each ion in each of the following solutions:

1.   0.125 M $NaCl$
2.   0.340 M $FeBr_3$
3.   0.250 M $Al_2(SO_4)_3$

Solutions

When we are given the molar concentration of a salt, it refers to the moles of the entire salt per liter of solution. But as we know, soluble salts dissociate into ions. An important quantity is the molarity of each ion in solution, because, as we have seen in net ionic equations, it is the ions that do the work in a reaction (and we need solutions to do some work for us, not to just sit there). So, the actual concentration of ions in solution depends on how many ions are in each formula unit of a salt.

1.   0.125 M $NaCl$

$$NaCl \xrightarrow{in \ water} Na^+_{(aq)} + Cl^-_{(aq)}$$

Since there are 1 of each ion per formula unit of NaCl, the concentrations of each ion is the same as that of the entire salt. So this solution is 0.125 M in Na$^+$ and also 0.125 M in Cl$^-$.

2.   0.340 M $FeBr_3$

$$FeBr_3 \xrightarrow{in \ water} Fe^{3+}_{(aq)} + 3Br^-_{(aq)}$$

We're not going to do dimensional analysis for such simple things. The solution is 0.340 M in Fe^{3+} and 1.02 M in Br^-.

3.   0.250 M $Al_2(SO_4)_3$

Clearly, 0.500 M in Al^{3+} and 0.750 M in SO_4^{2-}.

Objective 73. Calculate the quantity of solute in a given volume of solution of known concentration.

Calculate the following:
1. How many moles and mmoles of $MgCl_2$ are found in 60.0 mL of 0.100 M solution?
2. How many grams of KOH are found in 35.0 mL of 2.50 M solution?
3. How many grams of Fe^{2+} are found in 75.0 mL of 0.250 M solution of $FeSO_4$?

Solutions

1. How many moles of $MgCl_2$ is found in 60.0 mL of 0.100 M solution?

$$M = \frac{n}{V} \Rightarrow n = MV = 0.100\frac{mol}{L} \times 60.0 \; mL \times \frac{1 \; L}{1000 \; mL} = 6.00 \times 10^{-3} \; mol = 6.00 \; mmol \; MgCl_2$$

Yes, get used to working in mmol, as they will be the more convenient unit for most calculations. If we use mmol, then we don't need to convert mL to L anymore, as you'll see.

2. How many grams of KOH are found in 35.0 mL of 2.50 M solution?
$$n = MV = 2.50\frac{mol}{L} \times 35.0 \; mL = 87.5 \; mmol \; KOH$$

$$87.5 \; mmol \; KOH \times \frac{1 \; mol}{1000 \; mmol} \times \frac{56.106 \; g}{1 \; mol \; KOH} = 4.91 \; g \; KOH$$

3. How many grams of Fe^{2+} are found in 75.0 mL of 0.250 M solution of $FeSO_4$?
$$n = 0.250\frac{mol}{L} \times 75.0 \; mL = 18.75 \; mmol \; FeSO_4$$

$$18.75 \; mmol \; FeSO_4 \times \frac{1 \; mol}{1000 \; mmol} \times \frac{1 \; mol \; Fe^{2+}}{1 \; mol \; FeSO_4} \times \frac{55.845 \; g \; Fe^{2+}}{1 \; mol \; Fe^{2+}} = 1.05 \; g \; Fe^{2+}$$

Objective 74. Calculate the quantity of a compound needed to make a solution of given (target) molarity.

Calculate the mass of compound needed to make each solution below and describe how the solution should be made.
1. 250.0 mL of 0.757M $NaNO_3$
2. The mass of $CuSO_4 \cdot 5H_2O$ needed to make 125 mL solution of 0.200 M Cu^{2+} ?

Solutions

To make a solution of anything from a solid, we need to weigh the compound and dissolve in pure water, adjusting the volume to the required quantity. This is done typically in volumetric flasks. In order to find the mass of compound needed, we calculate the moles and convert to mass.

1. 250.0 mL of 0.757M $NaNO_3$

$$n = MV = 0.757 \frac{mol}{L} \times 250.0 \; mL = 189.25 \; mmol \; NaNO_3$$

$$189.25 \; mmol \; NaNO_3 \times \frac{1 \; mol}{1000 \; mmol} \times \frac{84.995 \; g}{1 \; mol \; NaNO_3} = 16.085 \; g \; NaNO_3$$

So, we dissolve 16.1 g $NaNO_3$ in water, adjust the total solution volume to 250.0 mL in a volumetric flask, and we have the solution requested.

2. The mass of $CuSO_4 \cdot 5H_2O$ needed to make 125 mL solution of 0.200 M Cu^{2+} ?

$$n = MV = 0.200 \frac{mol}{L} \times 125 \; mL = 25.0 \; mmol \; Cu^{2+}$$

$$25.0 \; mmol \; Cu^{2+} \times \frac{1 \; mol}{1000 \; mmol} \times \frac{1 \; mol \; CuSO_4 \cdot 5H_2O}{1 \; mol \; Cu^{2+}} \times \frac{249.685 \; g}{1 \; mol \; CuSO_4 \cdot 5H_2O} = 6.24 \; g \; CuSO_4 \cdot 5H_2O$$

We weigh $6.24 \; g \; CuSO_4 \cdot 5H_2O$ on a balance, dissolve in water, adjust to 125 mL in a volumetric flask, and we have a solution that is 0.200 M in Cu^{2+}.

Objective 75. Calculate the molarity of a solution after dilution.

Each solution below is diluted. Calculate the new molarity in each case.
   1. 10.00 mL of 2.00 M $NaOH$ is diluted to 500.0 mL total.
   2. 12.55 mL water is added to 2.45 mL of 6.00 M H_2SO_4.

Solutions

When a solution is diluted, we add water to it to increase its volume, and thus make it less concentrated (more diluted). What does not change in this process is the number of moles of solute, as we only add solvent. So if we denote (1) as the quantities before dilution, and (2) the quantities after dilution, we can write:
$$n = M_1 V_1 = M_2 V_2$$

This is called the dilution formula and it is very convenient to use in problems. Given three quantities, we solve for the fourth, whatever that maybe.

1. 10.00 mL of 2.00 M $NaOH$ is diluted to 500.0 mL total.

We know the volume and the molarity before dilution, as well as the volume after dilution. We solve for M_2, right?

$$M_1 V_1 = M_2 V_2 \quad \Rightarrow \quad M_2 = \frac{M_1 V_1}{V_2} = \frac{2.00 \; M \times 10.00 \; mL}{500.0 \; mL} = 0.0400 \; M$$

Since volumes cancel out we do not need any conversion in liters, and we get molar units as the final answer.

2. 12.55 mL water is added to 2.45 mL of 0.7500 M H_2SO_4.

We know the initial volume and molarity, and we know how much solvent (water) is added.

$$M_1V_1 = M_2V_2 \Rightarrow M_2 = \frac{M_1V_1}{V_2} = \frac{0.750\ M \times 2.45\ mL}{(2.45 + 12.55)\ mL} = \frac{0.750\ M \times 2.45\ mL}{15.00\ mL} = 0.123\ M$$

Objective 76.   Calculate the volume or molarity of stock solution needed to make a solution of given (target) molarity.

In each case below, a solution of a certain concentration needs to be prepared from a more concentrated (stock) solution available. Calculate the volume of stock solution or the molarity of the stock solution as needed.
1. 250.00 mL of 0.122 M HCl made from 11.5 M stock HCl
2. 500.00 mL of 0.400 M NaOH made by diluting 20.9 mL stock NaOH

Solutions

1. 250.00 mL of 0.122 M HCl made from 11.5 M HCl

$$M_1V_1 = M_2V_2 \Rightarrow V_1 = \frac{M_2V_2}{M_1} = \frac{0.122\ M \times 250.00\ mL}{11.5\ M} = 2.65\ mL\ stock\ solution$$

2. 500.00 mL of 0.400 M NaOH made from 9.54 M NaOH

$$M_1V_1 = M_2V_2 \Rightarrow M_1 = \frac{M_2V_2}{V_1} = \frac{0.400\ M \times 500.00\ mL}{20.9\ mL} = 9.57\ M$$

Objective 77.   Calculate the molarity of a solution made by mixing two solutions of the same compound.

In each case below, two solutions of the same compound, but of different concentrations, are mixed. Calculate the concentration of the resulting solution.
1. 25.0 mL of 0.125 M HCl and 75.0 mL of 0.334 M HCl
2. 200. mL of 0.200 M $CuSO_4$ and 200. mL of 0.400 M $CuSO_4$

Solutions

When two solutions of the same compound are mixed, the volumes add up, and the moles of solute from the two solutions also add up. So the final concentration would be:

$$Final\ molarity = \frac{total\ moles\ of\ solute}{total\ volume\ of\ solution}$$

1. 25.0 mL of 0.125 M HCl and 75.0 mL of 0.334 M HCl

$$M = \frac{n_1 + n_2}{V_1 + V_2} = \frac{M_1V_1 + M_2V_2}{V_1 + V_2} = \frac{0.125\ M \times 25.0\ mL + 0.334\ M \times 75.0\ mL}{25.0\ mL + 75.0\ mL} = 0.28175 = 0.282\ M$$

Does the answer make sense? Yes, the resulting molarity should be between those of the solutions mixed, and it should be closer to that of the solution taken in a larger amount.

2. 200. mL of 0.200 M $CuSO_4$ and 200. mL of 0.400 M $CuSO_4$

Do we need to calculate this one? I am going to say that the final concentration will be 0.300 M. Figure out why!

Objective 78. Calculate the molarity of a solution made by mixing two solutions containing a common ion.

In the case below, two solutions of different compounds containing a common ion are mixed. Calculate the concentration of each ion in the resulting solution.
     75.4 mL of 0.228 M HNO_3 and 46.8 mL of 0.148 M $Ca(NO_3)_2$

Solution

Here, we mix solution of different compounds, which have a common ion. First we need to make sure that the solutes do not react with each other once mixed, as that would be a different story. Then, we calculate the concentration of each ion separately, and after that we look at the dilution. When the solutions are mixed, everything inside occupies the entire new volume.

First solution: 0.228 M HNO_3 will be 0.228 M in H^+ and 0.228 M in NO_3^- (Objective 72).

Similarly, second solution: 0.148 M in $Ca(NO_3)_2$ will be 0.148 M in Ca^{2+} and 0.296 M in NO_3^-.

The common ion is nitrate. This means that when the solutions are mixed, the moles of nitrate from both sources need to be added up and divided by the new volume (Objective 77). The other ions, hydrogen and calcium, come only from one source, and so they are only subject to a dilution (Objective 75). Here are the calculations:

$$M_{NO_3^-} = \frac{M_1V_1 + M_2V_2}{V_1 + V_2} = \frac{0.228\ M \times 75.4\ mL + 0.296\ M \times 46.8\ mL}{75.4\ mL + 46.8\ mL} = 0.254\ M\ NO_3^-$$

H^+ comes only from solution 1:

$$M_{H^+} = \frac{M_1V_1}{V_1 + V_2} = \frac{0.228\ M \times 75.4\ mL}{75.4\ mL + 46.8\ mL} = 0.141\ M\ H^+$$

Ca^{2+} comes only from solution 2:

$$M_{Ca^{2+}} = \frac{M_2V_2}{V_1 + V_2} = \frac{0.148\ M \times 46.8\ mL}{75.4\ mL + 46.8\ mL} = 0.0566\ M\ Ca^{2+}$$

Do these answers make sense?

Objective 79.   Calculate the molality of a solution.

Calculate the molality of each solution prepared as described below.
1.   23.56 g NaCl dissolved in 124.81 g H_2O.
2.   26.458 g $CuSO_4 \cdot 5H_2O$ dissolved in 200.00 g H_2O

Solutions

Molality is another way of expressing concentration:

$$molality\ (m) = \frac{number\ of\ moles\ of\ solute}{mass\ of\ solvent\ (in\ kg)}$$

Units for molality are mol/kg (implying solvent), or simply m. There are two crucial differences between molarity and molality: the denominator of the fraction for molality has <u>mass</u>, not volume, and it refers to <u>solvent</u>, not solution. Also, the units must be **kg**! Molarity can be converted into molality if the density of the solution is known. This will be learned later in this course.

1.   23.56 g NaCl dissolved in 124.81 g H_2O.

$$\frac{23.56\ g\ NaCl}{58.44\ g/mol} = 0.4031\ mol\ NaCl$$

$$m = \frac{0.4031\ mol}{0.12481\ kg\ water} = 3.230\ m$$

2.   26.458 g $CuSO_4 \cdot 5H_2O$ dissolved in 200.00 g H_2O

Here, a hydrate is dissolved in water, and the water from the hydrate will mix with the water solvent, and needs to be added as such. Thus, we need to figure out the mass of water in the given mass of hydrate (Objective 59).

$$\frac{26.458\ g\ CuSO_4 \cdot 5H_2O}{249.685\ g/mol} = 0.10196\ mol\ CuSO_4 \cdot 5H_2O = 0.10196\ mol\ CuSO_4\ and\ 0.50980\ mol\ H_2O$$

$$0.50980\ mol\ H_2O \times 18.015\ \frac{g}{mol} = 9.1840\ g\ H_2O$$

Total mass of water: $200.00\ g + 9.1840\ g = 209.18\ g = 0.20918\ kg\ water\ (solvent)$

$$m = \frac{0.10196\ mol\ CuSO_4}{0.20918\ kg\ water} = 0.48743\ m \quad (5\ sig\ figs\ neded)$$

Objective 80. Calculate the quantity of a compound and solvent needed to make a solution of given (target) molality.

1. Calculate the mass of compound and that of solvent needed to make 256.00 g of 0.500 m $CaCl_2$

Solution

Here we know the total mass of the target solution (256 g) and its molality, 0.500 m.

$$m = \frac{moles\ of\ CaCl_2}{mass\ of\ water\ (kg)}$$

Let x be the moles of the $CaCl_2$ we need. The mass of $CaCl_2$ will be:

$$x\ moles\ CaCl_2 \times 110.98\frac{g}{mol} = 110.98x \quad (in\ g)$$

The mass of the water will be the mass of the solution minus the mass of the calcium chloride:

$$mass\ of\ water\ \ (kg) = \frac{256g\ solution - 110.98x\ g\ CaCl_2}{1000\ g/kg}$$

We plug these values into the molality equation and solve for x:

$$m = \frac{x}{\dfrac{256 - 110.98\ x}{1000}} = \frac{1000x}{256 - 110.98\ x} = 0.500$$

$$1000x = 0.5(256 - 110.98\ x) = 128 - 55.49x$$

$$1055.49\ x = 128 \quad \Rightarrow \quad x = 0.1213\ moles\ CaCl_2$$

$$0.1213\ moles\ CaCl_2 \times 110.98\frac{g}{mol} = 13.46\ g\ CaCl_2$$

$$m_{H_2O} = 256.00 - 13.46 = 242.54\ g\ H_2O$$

Result check:

$$m = \frac{0.1213\ mol}{0.24254\ kg\ H_2O} = 0.500$$

Worksheet 10.   Solutions and Concentration

The exercises and problems in this section will allow you to practice the topic until you understand it well.

1.   Calculate the mass percent composition of a solution made by dissolving 13.26 g ferrous sulfate dissolved in 156.34 g water.

2.   What mass of silver nitrate must be dissolved in 80.0 g water in order to make a solution that is 9.5% Ag^+ by mass?

3.   What mass of aluminum sulfate must be added to 135g water in order to make a solution that is 16.5% sulfate ions by mass?

4.   A solution is 5.0% water and 95.0% ethanol by volume. What volume of water must be added in order to reduce the percent of ethanol to 25.0%?

5.   Calculate the mass percent of aluminum in 455.5 g of solution that contains 11.5% aluminum sulfate by mass.

6. Calculate the mass of nitrate ions in 150.0 g solution that contains 5.00% calcium nitrate by mass.

7. Calculate the mass percent composition of each saturated solution below. Obtain the solubility of the salt from the chart provided.

    a. KNO_3 at 50 °C

    b. $MgBr_2$ at 20°C

    c. NH_4Cl at 85°C

8. Calculate the solubility of aluminum sulfate in a saturated solution that is 11.5% aluminum sulfate by mass.

9. Calculate the molarity of a solution of 22.6 g of sucrose ($C_{12}H_{22}O_{11}$) in 100.0 mL solution.

10. Calculate the molarity of a solution of 1.225 g $FeSO_4 \cdot 6H_2O$ in 50.0 mL solution.

11. Calculate the molar concentration of each ion in each of the following solutions:
    a. 0.205 M HNO_3

    b. 0.110 M sodium carbonate

    c. 0.450 M magnesium phosphate

12. Calculate the moles and mass of sodium ions in 250.00 mL of 0.336 M sodium sulfate.

13. What mass of $NaNO_3$ would be required to prepare 250.0 mL of a 0.547 M solution?

14. What mass of ferrous sulfate heptahydrate is needed to make 2.00 L of 0.0750 M solution?

15. Water is added to 25.0 mL of a 0.476 M solution of potassium nitrate until the volume is exactly 500.0 mL. What is the concentration of the final solution?

16. You have 55.0 mL of a 0.825 M hydrochloric acid solution and you want to dilute it to exactly 0.100 M. What is the volume of the resulting solution? How much water should you add?

17. 55.2 mL of 0.412 M solution of potassium permanganate is mixed with 63.5 mL of 0.182 M potassium permanganate. Calculate the concentration of the final solution.

18. 66.2 mL of 0.238 M solution of calcium nitrate is mixed with 50.5 mL of 0.405 M calcium nitrate. Calculate the concentrations of calcium ions and nitrate ions in the final solution.

19. 16.5 g of solid magnesium chloride is dissolved in 450. mL of 0.456 M hydrochloric acid. Calculate the concentration of chloride ions in the final solution, assuming no change in volume.

20. Calculate the molality of a solution made by dissolving 114.5 g calcium nitrate in 325.0 g water.

21. Calculate the molality of a solution made by dissolving 12.45 g magnesium sulfate heptahydrate in 85.00 g water.

22. Calculate the masses of sucrose ($C_{12}H_{22}O_{11}$) and water necessary to make 750.0 g of 1.45 m solution.

Self-assessment

Using the scale indicated, rate your understanding of each learning objective at the completion of this lesson. Identify the areas where your understanding is weak or medium and discuss with your class mates and/or instructor. Write down specific questions you still have at the completion of this topic.

Learning objective	Self-assessment 3 = strong, 2 = medium, 1 = weak, 0 = not done
	3 2 1 0
	3 2 1 0
	3 2 1 0
	3 2 1 0
	3 2 1 0
	3 2 1 0
	3 2 1 0
	3 2 1 0
	3 2 1 0
	3 2 1 0
	3 2 1 0
	3 2 1 0
	3 2 1 0
	3 2 1 0
	3 2 1 0

Lesson 11 – Basic Stoichiometry

Learning Objectives

In this lesson you will learn:

- To calculate the **moles of products** made when starting with a **given amount of reactant**
- To calculate the **moles of reactants** needed to produce a **given amount of product**
- To calculate the **mass of products** made when starting with a given **mass of reactant**
- To calculate the **mass of reactants** needed to produce a given **mass of product**
- To calculate the **yield** of a reaction
- To calculate the amount of reactant needed given a specific reaction yield
- To determine the **limiting** and **excess reactant** in a reaction
- To calculate the mass of product made in a reaction involving a **limiting reactant**

Pre-requisites: Balancing chemical reactions; Predicting products of chemical reactions; Formulas, moles, chemical composition.

Self-study questions

Before you start studying the worked examples, you should be able to formulate answers to the questions below. Use a textbook of your choice, or an online source of information, to find the answers.

1. What is a reactant?
2. What is a product?
3. Can you perform calculations using an unbalanced chemical equation? Explain.
4. What is meant by stoichiometry?
5. What is the yield of reaction?
6. What is a limiting reactant?
7. What is an excess reactant?
8. How do you know that a problem needs to be solved using the concept of limiting reactant?

Worked examples

This section contains several solved examples that cover the learning objectives listed above. Study each example carefully and make notes in the workbook to check every example that you understood. Repeat several times what you don't understand at first. It should become clearer as you keep working on the examples.

Objective 81. Calculate the moles of products made when starting with a given amount of reactant.

> Calculate the moles of each product made in the reaction below, starting with 2.4 mol NaOH.
> $$NaOH + CuSO_4 \rightarrow Cu(OH)_2 + Na_2SO_4$$

Solution

Chemical reactions need to be balanced before we can do any calculations on them. Once balanced, if we know the starting amount of a reactant, we can calculate everything else: how much of the other reactant(s) is needed, and what quantity of product(s) is made. This type of calculation based on the coefficients of the balanced chemical; equation is called stoichiometry.

Balanced reaction: $2NaOH + CuSO_4 \rightarrow Cu(OH)_2 + Na_2SO_4$

$$2.4 \; mol \; NaOH \times \frac{1 \; mol \; Cu(OH)_2}{2 \; mol \; NaOH} = 1.2 \; mol \; Cu(OH)_2$$

The same calculation applies to the other product, which will form in the same amount, as it has the same stoichiometric coefficient as $Cu(OH)_2$.

Objective 82. Calculate the moles of reactants needed to produce a given amount of product.

> Calculate the moles of each reactant needed in the reaction below, in order to make 24 mol H_3PO_4.
> $$P_4O_{10} + H_2O \rightarrow H_3PO_4$$

Solution

Balanced reaction: $P_4O_{10} + 6H_2O \rightarrow 4H_3PO_4$

The calculation applies backwards as well:
$$24 \; mol \; H_3PO_4 \times \frac{1 \; mol \; P_4O_{10}}{4 \; mol \; H_3PO_4} = 6 \; mol \; P_4O_{10} \; needed$$

$$24 \; mol \; H_3PO_4 \times \frac{6 \; mol \; H_2O}{4 \; mol \; H_3PO_4} = 36 \; mol \; H_2O \; needed$$

Objective 83. Calculate the mass of product made when starting with a given mass of reactant.

> Calculate the mass of each product made in the reaction below, starting with 13.45 g Fe_2O_3.
> $$Al + Fe_2O_3 \rightarrow Fe + Al_2O_3$$

Solution

Balanced reaction: $2Al + Fe_2O_3 \rightarrow 2Fe + Al_2O_3$

Any quantities other than moles given in a stoichiometry problem must be converted to moles.

$$13.45 \; g \; Fe_2O_3 \times \frac{1 \; mol \; Fe_2O_3}{159.69 \; g} = 0.08423 \; mol \; Fe_2O_3$$

$$0.08423 \; mol \; Fe_2O_3 \times \frac{2 \; mol \; Fe}{1 \; mol \; Fe_2O_3} \times \frac{55.845 \; g}{1 \; mol \; Fe} = 9.407 \; g \; Fe \; produced$$

$$0.08423 \; mol \; Fe_2O_3 \times \frac{1 \; mol \; Al_2O_3}{1 \; mol \; Fe_2O_3} \times \frac{101.96 \; g}{1 \; mol \; Al_2O_3} = 8.588 \; g \; Al_2O_3 \; produced$$

Objective 84. Calculate the mass of reactant needed to produce a given mass of product.

Calculate the mass of each reactant needed in the reaction below, in order to make 50.44 g $CaCO_3$.
$$CaO + CO_2 \rightarrow CaCO_3$$

Solution

$$50.44 \; g \; CaCO_3 \times \frac{1 \; mol \; CaCO_3}{100.09 \; g} = 0.5040 \; mol \; CaCO_3$$

From the stoichiometry, we notice that all reactants and products have coefficients of 1, thus we need 0.5040 mol of each reactant.

$$0.5040 \; mol \; CaO \times 56.077 \; \frac{g}{mol} = 28.26 \; g \; CaO \; needed$$

$$0.5040 \; mol \; CO_2 \times 44.01 \; \frac{g}{mol} = 22.18 \; g \; CO_2 \; needed$$

Objective 85. Calculate the yield of a reaction.

The reaction below is started with 25.4 kg H_2 and 98.4 kg NH_3 are obtained. Calculate the reaction yield.
$$N_2 + H_2 \rightarrow NH_3$$

Solution

Not all reactions proceed to completion, and so sometimes we obtain a smaller quantity of product than is stoichiometrically possible. The percent yield is:

$$reaction \; yield = \frac{quantity \; produced}{theoretical \; quantity} \times 100$$

Let's determine how much product should be made in this reaction, given the starting quantity of one reactant. The fact that the quantity is given in kg is not an issue, as we can work in kmol just as well as in mol. First we balance the reaction:

$$N_2 + 3H_2 \rightarrow 2NH_3$$

$$25.4 \ kg \ H_2 \times \frac{1 \ kmol \ H_2}{2.016 \ kg} \times \frac{2 \ kmol \ NH_3}{3 \ kmol \ H_2} \times \frac{17.031 \ kg \ NH_3}{1 \ kmol \ NH_3} = 143 \ kg \ NH_3$$

The fact that only 98.4 kg NH_3 are obtained means that the reaction is not 100% efficient (does not go to completion). The yield is:

$$\% \ yield = \frac{98.4 \ kg \ NH_3}{143 \ kg \ NH_3} \times 100 = 68.8 \ \%$$

Objective 86. Calculate the amount of reactant needed given a specific reaction yield.

In the reaction below, the target mass of one product is given, as well as the percent yield. If the percent yield for this reaction is 65.0%, how many grams of $KClO_3$ are needed to produce 42.0 g of O_2?
$$KClO_3 \rightarrow KCl + O_2 \ .$$

Solution

Now we need to work backwards. We know the yield and the mass of product, and we need to calculate the mass of reactant needed.

Balanced reaction: $2KClO_3 \rightarrow 2KCl + 3O_2$. Since the mass of product obtained is less than the theoretical (because the yield is not 100%), let's find the theoretical mass (by rearranging the formula for yield):

$$theoretical \ quantity = \frac{quantity \ produced}{reaction \ yield} \times 100 = \frac{42.0 \ g \ O_2}{65.0} \times 100 = 64.6 \ g \ O_2$$

The stoichiometry calculations apply to the theoretical mass of product needed, which needs to be in mol:

$$\frac{64.6 \ g \ O_2}{32.00 \ g/mol} = 2.02 \ mol \ O_2$$

Stoichiometry:

$$2.02 \ mol \ O_2 \times \frac{2 \ mol \ KClO_3}{3 \ mol \ O_2} \times \frac{122.55 \ g \ KClO_3}{1 \ mol \ KClO_3} = 165 \ g \ KClO_3 \ needed$$

This is the mass of reactant that will produce the given mass of O_2 in the conditions given.

Objective 87. Determine the limiting reactant and excess reactant in a reaction.

In each reaction below, the quantities of reactants being mixed are given. Determine the limiting and excess reactant in each case, and the mass of reactant in excess.
1. $Na_2O + H_2O \rightarrow NaOH$; start with 24.5 g Na_2O and 36.2 g H_2O
2. $Mg + Fe_2O_3 \rightarrow Fe + MgO$; start with 20.0 kg Mg and 50.0 kg Fe_2O_3

Solutions

As you have seen so far, only the quantity of one reactant is needed in order to calculate everything else in a reaction based on stoichiometry. When a problem gives you the quantities of both reactants, you are dealing with a limiting reactant problem. Let's see what this means.

1. Balance: $Na_2O + H_2O \rightarrow 2\,NaOH$; start with 24.5 g Na_2O and 36.2 g H_2O

We always start by converting masses to moles:

$$\frac{24.5\ g\ Na_2O}{61.979\ g/mol} = 0.395\ mol\ Na_2O$$

$$\frac{36.2\ g\ H_2O}{18.015\ g/mol} = 2.01\ mol\ H_2O$$

The reaction is now balanced, and you can see that each mole of Na_2O reacts with one mole of H_2O. Considering the amounts given in the problem, it is clear that not all of them will react:

$$0.395\ mol\ Na_2O\ \times \frac{1\ mol\ H_2O}{1\ mol\ Na_2O} = 0.395\ mol\ H_2O$$

This is saying that for 0.395 mol Na_2O we need 0.395 mol H_2O. We have 2.01 mol H_2O at our disposal. Not all of it will react. Only the 0.395 mol will react, because the smaller amount of Na_2O limits the amount of H_2O that can react. We say that Na_2O is the limiting reactant in this problem. On the other hand, H_2O is in excess, so we call it the excess reactant. How much excess of H_2O is left over?

$$2.01\ mol - 0.395\ mol = 1.62\ mol\ H_2O\ in\ excess$$

As mass:

$$1.62\ mol\ H_2O\ \times 18.015\frac{g}{mol} = 29.1\ g\ H_2O\ in\ excess$$

2. $Mg + Fe_2O_3 \rightarrow Fe + MgO$; start with 20.0 kg Mg and 50.0 kg Fe_2O_3

Balance reaction:

$$3Mg + Fe_2O_3 \rightarrow 2Fe + 3MgO$$

Convert to kmoles:

$$\frac{20.0\ kg\ Mg}{24.305\ g/mol} = 0.822\ kmol\ Mg$$

$$\frac{50.0 \; kg \; Fe_2O_3}{159.69 \; g/mol} = 0.313 \; kmol \; Fe_2O_3$$

This time, since the stoichiometry is no longer 1 to 1, it is not obvious from these amounts of reactants which one is limiting, so we will need to calculate that using one of them:

$$0.822 \; kmol \; Mg \times \frac{1 \; kmol \; Fe_2O_3}{3 \; kmol \; Mg} = 0.274 \; kmol \; Fe_2O_3 \; needed$$

We need 0.274 kmol Fe_2O_3 and we have 0.313 kmol, so Fe_2O_3 must be in excess, and Mg is limiting. You could have determined the limiting reactant starting with Fe_2O_3 as well:

$$0.313 \; kmol \; Fe_2O_3 \times \frac{3 \; kmol \; Mg}{1 \; kmol \; Fe_2O_3} = 0.939 \; kmol \; Mg \; needed$$

If you did this instead, you'd notice that we need 0.939 kmol of Mg, but we only have 0.822 kmol, so the conclusion is the same.

Amount of excess:
$$0.313 - 0.274 \; = \; 0.039 \; kmol \; Fe_2O_3 = 6.23 \; kg \; Fe_2O_3$$

Objective 88.   Calculate the mass of product made in a reaction involving a limiting reactant.

Determine the mass of each product made in the previous problem.

Solution

Once we determine the limiting reactant in a problem, it is that amount that is used to calculate the amounts of products formed. In the problem above, Mg was limiting, in the amount of 0.822 kmol.

$$0.822 \; kmol \; Mg \; \times \frac{3 \; kmol \; MgO}{3 \; kmol \; Mg} \times 40.304 \frac{kg}{kmol} = 33.1 \; kg \; MgO$$

$$0.822 \; kmol \; Mg \; \times \frac{2 \; kmol \; Fe}{3 \; kmol \; Mg} \times 55.845 \frac{kg}{kmol} = 30.6 \; kg \; Fe$$

Do the answers make sense? If they are correct, the mass of all reactants (minus any excess) should equal the mass of all products. Verify!

Worksheet 11.   Basic stoichiometry

The exercises and problems in this section will allow you to practice the topic until you understand it well.

1.   Several chemical reactions are given below. Balance each one. Then, an amount in moles, or a mass in grams, of either a reactant or a product is given. Fill out the empty boxes in each table with the correct amounts (in moles) and masses of the other reactants and/or products, according to the stoichiometry of each reaction.

    a. $NaOH + H_2SO_4 \rightarrow Na_2SO_4 + H_2O$

$NaOH$	H_2SO_4	Na_2SO_4	H_2O
	0.556 moles		

    b. $N_2 + H_2 \rightarrow NH_3$

N_2	H_2	NH_3
		35.45 g

c. $PCl_5 + H_2O \rightarrow H_3PO_4 + HCl$

PCl_5	H_2O	H_3PO_4	HCl
12.98 g			

d. $CaCO_3 + HCl \rightarrow CaCl_2 + H_2O + CO_2$

$CaCO_3$	HCl	$CaCl_2$	H_2O	CO_2
				0.500 moles

e. $Cu + NO_3^- + H^+ \rightarrow Cu^{2+} + NO + H_2O$

Cu	NO_3^-	Cu^{2+}	NO	H_2O
1.332 g				

2. Several chemical reactions are given below. Balance each one. Then, an amount in moles or a mass in grams of a reactant is given, as well as the mass or amount of a product made. From this information, determine the percent yield of the reaction. Alternatively, the percent yield may be given, and the mass of reactant needs to be calculated.

a. $(NH_4)_2Cr_2O_7 \rightarrow N_2 + Cr_2O_3 + H_2O$

$(NH_4)_2Cr_2O_7$	H_2O	% yield
2.558 g	0.699 g	

b. $H_2 + Br_2 \rightarrow HBr$

Br_2	HBr	% yield
23.55 g	18.95 g	

c. $Ca + H_2O \rightarrow Ca(OH)_2 + H_2$

H_2O	$Ca(OH)_2$	% yield
	5.668 g	76.5%

3. Several chemical reactions are given below. Balance each one. Then, the masses of two reactants are given. Determine which reactant is limiting and which reactant is in excess and by how much, then calculate the mass of the product indicated..

   a. $Ca + H_2O \rightarrow Ca(OH)_2 + H_2$

Ca	H_2O	Limiting reactant	Excess reactant and mass	Mass H_2
4.56 g	10.00 g			

   b. $H_2 + N_2 \rightarrow NH_3$

H_2	N_2	Limiting reactant	Excess reactant and mass	Mass NH_3
5.00 g	5.00 g			

Self-assessment

Using the scale indicated, rate your understanding of each learning objective at the completion of this lesson. Identify the areas where your understanding is weak or medium and discuss with your class mates and/or instructor. Write down specific questions you still have at the completion of this topic.

Learning objective	Self-assessment 3 = strong, 2 = medium, 1 = weak, 0 = not done
	3 2 1 0
	3 2 1 0
	3 2 1 0
	3 2 1 0
	3 2 1 0
	3 2 1 0
	3 2 1 0
	3 2 1 0

Lesson 12 – Solution Stoichiometry

Learning Objectives

In this lesson you will learn:
- To calculate the **volume of solution** of given concentration consumed in an **acid-base titration**
- To calculate the **concentration** of a starting solution or the **purity of a sample** in an acid-base titration
- To calculate the volume of solution of given concentration consumed in a **redox titration**
- To calculate the **purity** or **percent composition** of a sample in a redox titration
- To determine the **limiting** and **excess** reactant in a reaction in solution
- To calculate the quantity of product made in a **precipitation reaction** in solution

Pre-requisites: Solutions and concentration; Basic stoichiometry.

Self-study questions

Before you start studying the worked examples, you should be able to formulate answers to the questions below. Use a textbook of your choice, or an online source of information, to find the answers.

1. What is a titration? Give examples.
2. What is a redox titration?
3. What is the difference between stoichiometry as you learned it in the previous section and stoichiometry in solution?
4. What is the meaning of concentration?
5. What is a limiting reactant?
6. What is an excess reactant?
7. What is a precipitation reactant?

Worked examples

This section contains several solved examples that cover the learning objectives listed above. Study each example carefully and make notes in the workbook to check every example that you understood. Repeat several times what you don't understand at first. It should become clearer as you keep working on the examples.

Objective 89. Calculate the volume of solution of given concentration consumed in an acid-base titration.

> 1. Calculate the volume of 0.250 M solution of NaOH needed to titrate 5.00 mL solution of 0.336 M H_2SO_4.

Solution

Titrations are stoichiometric reactions in solution. What we learned in the previous lesson applies here as well, but now we are dealing with reactants in solution rather than pure, so the concept of concentration comes into play again. The balanced reaction always comes first:

$$2NaOH + H_2SO_4 \rightarrow Na_2SO_4 + 2H_2O$$

The amount of H_2SO_4 that needs to be titrated:

$$n = MV = 0.336\ M \times 5.00\ mL = 1.68\ mmol\ H_2SO_4$$

Stoichiometry:

$$1.68\ mmol\ H_2SO_4 \times \frac{2\ mol\ NaOH}{1\ mol\ H_2SO_4} = 3.36\ mmol\ NaOH\ needed$$

Volume of solution needed:

$$V = \frac{n}{M} = \frac{3.36\ mmol}{0.250\ mol/L} = 13.44\ mL\ NaOH\ solution$$

> 2. Calculate the volume of 0.100 M solution of NaOH needed to titrate 0.345 g potassium hydrogen phthalate ("KHP").

Solution

"KHP" is an abbreviation (P is not phosphorus here), its actual formula is $KHC_8H_4O_4$. It is a monoprotic acid used as a standard, because it is very stable and can be weighed precisely. If we write the reaction using the abbreviation KHP, it should look like this:

$$KH"P" + NaOH \rightarrow KNa"P" + H_2O$$

Where $KNa"P"$ would be the double salt potassium sodium phthalate ($KNaC_8H_4O_4$). The molar mass of KHP is thus 204.22 g/mol (verify).

The amount of KHP that needs to be titrated:

$$\frac{0.345\ g\ KHP}{204.22\ g/mol} = 0.001689\ mol = 1.69\ mmol\ KHP$$

Stoichiometry:

$$1.69\ mmol\ KHP \times \frac{1\ mol\ NaOH}{1\ mol\ KHP} = 1.69\ mmol\ NaOH\ needed$$

Volume of solution needed:

$$V = \frac{n}{M} = \frac{1.69 \; mmol}{0.100 \; mol/L} = 16.9 \; mL \; NaOH \; solution$$

---

3. Calculate the volume of 2.000 M solution of HBr needed to titrate 1.556 g LiOH · H_2O.

Solution

Now we are titrating a hydrated base. Reaction:

$$LiOH + HBr \rightarrow LiBr + H_2O$$

The amount of base that needs to be titrated:

$$\frac{1.556 \; g \; LiOH \cdot H_2O}{41.964 \; g/mol} = 0.03708 \; mol = 37.08 \; mmol \; LiOH \cdot H_2O = 37.08 \; mmol \; LiOH$$

We have 1 to 1 stoichiometry, so we need 0.03708 mol HBr. As solution:

$$V = \frac{n}{M} = \frac{37.08 \; mmol}{2.000 \; mol/L} = 18.54 \; mL \; HBr \; solution$$

Objective 90. **Calculate the concentration of a starting solution or the purity of a sample in an acid-base titration.**

1. A volume of 10.00 mL solution of H_3PO_4 requires 22.45 mL of 0.1050 M $NaOH$ in a complete titration. Calculate the concentration of the H_3PO_4 solution.

Solution

In a titration, a polyprotic acid is completely neutralized:

$$H_3PO_4 + 3NaOH \rightarrow Na_3PO_4 + 3H_2O$$

Moles of base consumed:

$$n = mV = 0.1050 \; M \; \times 22.45 \; mL = 2.357 \; mmol \; NaOH$$

Stoichiometry:

$$2.357 \; mmol \; NaOH \times \frac{1 \; mol \; H_3PO_4}{3 \; mol \; NaOH} = 0.7858 \; mmol \; H_3PO_4 \; needed$$

Concentration:

$$M = \frac{n}{V} = \frac{0.7858 \; mmol}{10.00 \; mL} = 0.0786 \; M$$

2. A 0.988 g sample of impure KHP requires 18.50 mL of 0.2510 M $NaOH$ in a complete titration. Calculate the purity of the KHP sample.

Solution

Moles of base consumed:

$$n = mV = 0.2510 \, M \, \times 18.50 \, mL = 4.644 \, mmol \, NaOH$$

Amount of KHP titrated will be 4.644 mmol (as in the previous problem that used KHP).

Mass of KHP in sample:

$$4.644 \, mmol \, KHP \, \times 204.22 \frac{g}{mol} = 948.29 \, mg = 0.9483 \, g \, pure \, KHP$$

Purity of sample:

$$\frac{0.9483 \, g \, KHP}{0.988 \, g \, sample} \times 100 = 96.0 \, \%$$

Objective 91. Calculate the volume of solution of given concentration consumed in a redox titration.

1. Calculate the volume of 0.02500 M solution of $K_2Cr_2O_7$ needed to titrate 20.00 mL solution of 0.1225 M Fe^{2+} in acidic medium.

Solution

A redox titration is just like an acid-base titration, except that the reaction taking place is a redox reaction and not a neutralization one.

In solution, $K_2Cr_2O_7$ is dissociated:

$$K_2Cr_2O_7 \xrightarrow{in \ water} 2K^+{}_{(aq)} + Cr_2O_7^{2-}{}_{(aq)}$$

It is the dichromate ion that reacts with Fe^{2+} in acidic medium. We balanced the redox reaction previously (Objective 47):

$$14H^+ + Cr_2O_7^{2-} + 6Fe^{2+} \rightarrow 2Cr^{3+} + 7H_2O + 6Fe^{3+}$$

All we have to do is apply stoichiometry, once we have a balanced reaction.

$$20.00 \, mL \, \times 0.1225 \, M = 2.450 \, mmol \, Fe^{2+}$$

$$2.450 \, mmol \, Fe^{2+} \times \frac{1 \, mol \, Cr_2O_7^{2-}}{6 \, mol \, Fe^{2+}} = 0.4083 \, mmol \, Cr_2O_7^{2-} = 0.4083 \, mmol \, K_2Cr_2O_7$$

$$\frac{0.4083 \, mmol \, K_2Cr_2O_7}{0.02500 \, mol/L} = 16.33 \, mL \, K_2Cr_2O_7 \, solution$$

Objective 92. Calculate the purity or percent composition of a sample in a redox titration.

1. A 0.325 g sample containing Fe^{2+} requires 11.55 mL of 0.01813 M $K_2Cr_2O_7$ in a redox titration conducted in acidic solution. Calculate the percent iron in the sample.

Solution

$$11.55 \; mL \; \times 0.01813 \frac{mol}{L} = 0.2094 \; mmol \; K_2Cr_2O_7 \; (or \; Cr_2O_7^{2-} \; ions)$$

$$0.2094 \; mmol \; K_2Cr_2O_7 \; \times \frac{6 \; mol \; Fe^{2+}}{1 \; mol \; Cr_2O_7^{2-}} \times 55.845 \frac{g}{mol} = 70.164 \; mg \; Fe^{2+}$$

$$\frac{70.164 \; mg \; Fe^{2+}}{325 \; mg \; sample} \times 100 = 21.6 \; \% \; Fe^{2+} \; in \; a \; sample$$

Objective 93. Determine the limiting reactant and excess reactant in a reaction in solution.

Determine the limiting reactant and the amount of excess reactant when the following solutions are mixed:
1. 44 mL of 1.0 M H_2SO_4 and 56 mL of 1.5 M KOH.

Solution

$$44 \; mL \; \times 1.0 \; M = 44 \; mmol \; H_2SO_4$$
$$56 \; mL \; \times 1.5 \; M = 84 \; mmol \; KOH$$

$$H_2SO_4 + 2KOH \; \rightarrow K_2SO_4 + 2H_2O$$

$$44 \; mmol \; H_2SO_4 \times \frac{2 \; mol \; KOH}{1 \; mol \; H_2SO_4} = 88 \; mmol \; KOH \; needed$$

We have only 84 mmol KOH, so KOH is the limiting reactant, thus sulfuric acid is in excess. Let's see by how much:

$$84 \; mmol \; KOH \times \frac{1 \; mol \; H_2SO_4}{2 \; mol \; KOH} = 42 \; mmol \; H_2SO_4 \; needed$$

Excess amount is: 44 – 42 = 2 mmol H_2SO_4. As a volume, this excess will be:

$$\frac{2 \; mmol \; H_2SO_4}{1.0 \; mol/L} = 2.0 \; mL \; solution \; of \; H_2SO_4$$

Objective 94. Calculate the quantity of product made in a precipitation reaction in solution.

Calculate the mass of precipitate made when the following solutions are mixed:
   1.   9.56 mL of 0.112 M $AgNO_3$ and 6.33 mL of 0.215 M $CaCl_2$.

Solution

$$CaCl_2 + 2AgNO_3 \rightarrow 2AgCl_{(s)} + Ca(NO_3)_2$$

The precipitate is AgCl (review solubility rules, Objective 41).

$$9.56 \; mL \; \times 0.112 \; M = 1.07 \; mmol \; AgNO_3$$
$$6.33 \; mL \; \times 0.215 \; M = 1.36 \; mmol \; CaCl_2$$

$$1.07 \; mmol \; AgNO_3 \times \frac{1 \; mol \; CaCl_2}{2 \; mol \; AgNO_3} = 0.535 \; mmol \; CaCl_2 \; needed$$

We have more $CaCl_2$ than is needed, so $AgNO_3$ is the limiting reactant. We will use it to find the mass of precipitate formed:

$$1.07 \; mmol \; AgNO_3 \times \frac{2 \; mol \; AgCl}{2 \; mol \; AgNO_3} \times 143.32 \frac{g}{mol} = 153 \; mg \; AgCl \; precipitate \; formed$$

Worksheet 12. Solution stoichiometry

The exercises and problems in this section will allow you to practice the topic until you understand it well.

1. What volume of 0.260 M Na_2S is needed to react with 25.00 mL of 0.315 M $AgNO_3$?

$$Na_2S + 2Ag_2NO_3 \rightarrow 2NaNO_3 + Ag_2S$$

$$2(0.260 M \ Na_2S \cdot v) = (0.315 M \cdot 25.00 mL)$$

$$\boxed{v = 15.1 \ mL \ of \ Na_2S}$$

2. When excess of 0.500 M $AgNO_3$ is added to 125 mL of 0.300 M NH_4Cl, what mass of precipitate is formed?

3. What volume of 0.550 M hydrochloric acid is needed to react with 25.00 mL of 0.217 M potassium hydroxide?

4. In an acid-base titration, 23.74 mL of 0.500 M potassium hydroxide reacts with 50.00 mL of sulfuric acid solution. What is the concentration of the acid solution?

$$2 KOH + H_2SO_4 \rightarrow K_2SO_4 + 2H_2O$$

$$\frac{23.74 mL \cdot 0.500 M}{2} = 50mL \cdot X$$

$$X = .1187 M\ H_2SO_4$$

$$[H_2SO_4] = 0.1187 M$$

5. Determine the volume of 0.0300 M phosphoric acid required to neutralize 25.00 mL of 0.0150 M calcium hydroxide.

6. A 1.651 g sample of KHP requires 11.33 mL of 0.301 M $NaOH$ in a complete titration. Calculate the purity of the KHP sample.

$$1.651 g\ KHP \cdot \frac{1 mol\ KHP}{(40 + 1.008 + 30.9)\ g} = 0.02296\ mol\ KHP$$

$$\frac{X moles}{11.33 mL} \cdot \frac{10^3 mL}{1L} = 0.301 M$$

$$X = 0.00341\ moles\ NaOH \cdot \frac{1 mol\ KHP}{1 mol\ NaOH} = 0.00341\ mol\ KHP$$

$$\frac{0.00341}{0.02296} \cdot 100 = 14.85\%$$

$$KHP + NaOH \rightarrow KOH + NaHP$$

7. Calculate the volume of 0.100 M NaOH solution necessary to completely titrate a 0.358 g sample of pure oxalic acid ($H_2C_2O_4$).

$NaOH + H_2C_2O_4 \rightarrow H_2O + NaHC_2O_4$

$$0.358g \; H_2C_2O_4 \cdot \frac{mol \; Oxalic \; acid}{(2 \cdot 1.008 + 2 \cdot 12 + 4 \cdot 16) \, g} = 0.00398 \; mol \; H_2C_2O_4$$

8. Calculate the volume of 0.0412 M solution of $KMnO_4$ needed to titrate 0.289 g $FeSO_4 \cdot 7H_2O$ in acidic medium (the reducing agent is the ferrous ion, and the products are Mn^{2+} and Fe^{3+}).

9. 20.00 mL of 0.250 M $BaCl_2$ are added to 15.00 mL of 0.160 M H_2SO_4. Calculate the mass of precipitate formed (and give its identity).

$BaCl_{2(aq)} + H_2SO_{4(aq)} \rightarrow BaSO_{4(s)} + 2HCl_{(aq)}$

$0.250 M = \frac{x}{20.00 mL} \cdot \frac{10^3 mL}{1L}$

$x = 0.005 \; mol \; BaCl_2 \cdot \frac{1 mol \; BaSO_4}{1 mol \; BaCl_2} = 0.005 \; mol \; BaSO_4$

$0.160 M = \frac{x}{15 mL} \cdot \frac{10^3 mL}{1L}$

$x = 0.0024 \; mol \; H_2SO_4 \cdot \frac{1 mol \; BaSO_4}{1 mol \; H_2SO_4} = 0.0024 \; mol \; BaSO_4 \cdot \frac{(137 + 32 + 4 \cdot 16) \, g}{1 mol \; BaSO_4}$

$\boxed{= 0.5598 g \; BaSO_4}$

10. When 100.00 mL of 0.200 M NaOH and 100.00 mL of 0.200 M $CuSO_4$ are mixed, 0.805 g of a precipitate are formed. Show the complete chemical reaction and calculate the yield of the reaction.

$$2NaOH_{(aq)} + CuSO_{4(aq)} \rightarrow Na_2SO_{4(aq)} + Cu(OH)_{2(s)}$$

$0.200 M \; NaOH = \dfrac{x \; mole}{100mL} \cdot \dfrac{10^3 mL}{1L}$ $0.2 M \; CuSO_4 \cdot \dfrac{x \; mol}{100mL} \cdot \dfrac{10^3 mL}{1L}$

$X = 0.02 \; mol \; NaOH$ $\Big\}$ limiting $0.04 \; mol \; NaOH$
$\quad \; 0.01 \; mol \; CuSO_4$ $\underline{\quad\quad\quad}$ $X = 0.02 \; mol \; CuSO_4$

$0.02 \; mol \; NaOH \cdot \dfrac{1 \; mol \; Cu(OH)_2}{2 \; mol \; NaOH} \cdot \dfrac{(63 + 2(16 + 1.008))}{1 \; mol \; Cu(OH)_2} \; Cu(OH)_2 = 0.970 \; g$

$\dfrac{0.805g}{0.970g} \cdot 100 = 82.99 \; \% \quad yield.$

Self-assessment

Using the scale indicated, rate your understanding of each learning objective at the completion of this lesson. Identify the areas where your understanding is weak or medium and discuss with your class mates and/or instructor. Write down specific questions you still have at the completion of this topic.

Learning objective	Self-assessment 3 = strong, 2 = medium, 1 = weak, 0 = not done
	3 2 1 0
	3 2 1 0
	3 2 1 0
	3 2 1 0
	3 2 1 0
	3 2 1 0

Lesson 13 – Electron Structure and Periodic Properties

Learning Objectives

In this lesson you will learn:

- To distinguish between the concepts of **shell, subshell, orbital**
- To determine the **electronic configuration** of an element
- To determine the electronic configuration of a **monoatomic ion**
- To determine the possible values for the four **quantum numbers**
- To determine whether a set of quantum numbers is valid
- To calculate the **frequency, wavelength**, and **energy** of **light**
- To calculate the energy involved in **electron jumps** between **energy levels** and the **wavelength** of light emitted or absorbed
- To determine the order of increasing or decreasing **atomic radii** in a series
- To determine the order of **ionic radii** in a series
- To determine the order of increasing or decreasing **electronegativity** in a series
- To determine the order of increasing or decreasing **ionization energy** in a series
- To determine the biggest jump between **consecutive ionization energies** of a given element
- To identify elements that display similar properties in a series
- To identify elements likely to form ionic or covalent bonds in a series

Pre-requisite: Atomic structure.

Self-study questions

Before you start studying the worked examples, you should be able to formulate answers to the questions below. Use a textbook of your choice, or an online source of information, to find the answers.

1. What is an electron shell?
2. What is a subshell?
3. What is an orbital?
4. Which of the above is the most precise "location" for an electron?
5. What is meant by electron configuration?
6. What are quantum numbers?
7. What are electron energy levels?
8. What is frequency?
9. What is wavelength?
10. Why does light have energy?
11. What is meant by atomic radius?
12. What is meant by ionic radius?
13. What is electronegativity?
14. What is meant by electron affinity?
15. What is ionization energy?
16. How many ionization energies can an atom of an element have?
17. What is the difference between ionic and covalent bonds?

Worked examples

This section contains solved problems that cover the learning objectives listed above. Study each example carefully and make notes in the workbook to check every example that you understood. Repeat several times what you don't understand at first. It should become clearer as you keep working on the examples.

Objective 95. Distinguish between shells, subshells, orbitals, electrons. Assign quantum numbers to shells and subshells.

> For each electron shell, indicate how many subshells it has, how many orbitals are in each subshell, and how many total electrons exist in each subshell and each shell. Give the quantum numbers associated with shells, subshells, and orbitals.

Energy level (shell)	Subshell #	Number of Orbitals in subshell	Number of electrons per subshell	Number of electrons per shell
1 $n = 1$	1 $l = 0$	1 $m_l = 0$	2	2
2 $n = 2$	1 $l = 0$	1 $m_l = 0$	2	8
	2 $l = 1$	3 $m_l = -1,0,1$	6	
3 $n = 3$	1 $l = 0$	1 $m_l = 0$	2	18
	2 $l = 1$	3 $m_l = -1,0,1$	6	
	3 $l = 2$	5 $m_l = -2,-1,0,1,2$	10	
4 $n = 4$	1 $l = 0$	1 $m_l = 0$	2	32
	2 $l = 1$	3 $m_l = -1,0,1$	6	
	3 $l = 2$	5 $m_l = -2,-1,0,1,2$	10	
	4 $l = 3$	7 $m_l = -3,-2,-1,0,1,2,3$	14	

Explanations

An energy level (shell) contains subshells. Shells correspond to the **principal** quantum number, n, and have integer values (1,2,3...). A shell contains subshells. Subshells correspond to the **angular momentum** quantum number, l. Each value of l designates a subshell. The number of subshells in a shell is equal to the shell number (see in table), because quantum number l has values from 0 to n-1, which is n values total.

A subshell contains orbitals. Orbitals correspond to the **magnetic** quantum number, m_l. The values of m_l depend on the value of l and range from $-l$ to $+l$. The number of orbitals in a subshell equals the number of values that m_l can take. Each value of m_l (for a given l, or subshell) represents an orbital of a different shape. For example, in shell 3, subshell labeled 2 (in the series 0, 1, 2), m_l can be -2, -1, 0, +1, +2, thus a total of 5 values. Subshell corresponds to the d orbitals, and there are 5 d orbitals, each with a different shape (or orientation in space).

An orbital can contain a maximum of 2 electrons, which means that each subshell, and then each shell, can contain a certain number of electrons in total (in table). The **spin** quantum number, m_s, corresponds to the two possible spins of an electron (clockwise and counter clockwise), having the values $+\frac{1}{2}$ and $-\frac{1}{2}$.

Shells correspond to periods in the periodic table. Subshells correspond to "blocks" (**s** block, **p** block, **d** block, **f** block), because they group orbitals of the same type. The number of groups in a block in the periodic table corresponds to the number of electrons that can be contained in each subshell: 2 in the **s** block, 6 in the **p** block, 10 in the **d** block, and 14 in the **f** block. Each element differs from the previous one by one electron. There is a very close relationship between electronic structure of the elements and the periodic table, which allows us to easily determine the electron configuration of an element.

Objective 96. Write the electron configuration of an atom of a given element.

Write the electron configuration for each element below:

1. He
2. Li
3. O
4. Mg
5. P
6. K
7. Cr
8. Co
9. Cu

Discussion

The easiest way to write the electronic configuration of an element is to go across the periodic table left to right, starting with hydrogen, and put electrons in shells and subshells. Remember:

- The shell number is the period number (and it is the number that goes in front of the lower case letter)
- The subshell is the block, written as the lower case letter (s, p, d, f)
- The number of electrons in each subshell is the number of element boxes you count in each block of the periodic table until you reach your element
- d subshells fill after the previous s subshell fills (3d fills after 4s, 4d after 5s, etc.)
- f subshells fill after the previous two s subshells fill (4f fills after 6s and 5f after 7s)
- Orbitals of the same type get one electron each, and only after all have 1 electron a second electron can fill the first orbital in the group
- Configurations such as $s^2 d^4$ and $s^2 d^9$ are unstable and they become $s^1 d^5$ and $s^1 d^{10}$ respectively.

In the image below, the four blocks are shaded in different colors. Helium is misplaced in this representation due to its chemical similarity to the other elements in group 18 (noble gases). It really belongs to the **s** block.

Periodic Table of the Elements

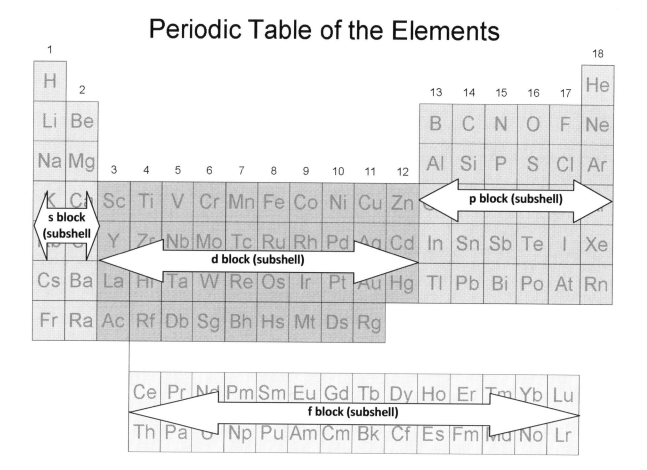

Solutions

1. He : $1s^2$
2. Li : $1s^2 2s^1$
3. O : $1s^2 2s^2 2p^4$
4. Mg : $1s^2 2s^2 2p^6 3s^2$
5. P : $1s^2 2s^2 2p^6 3s^2 3p^3$
6. K : $1s^2 2s^2 2p^6 3s^2 3p^6 4s^1$
7. Cr : $1s^2 2s^2 2p^6 3s^2 3p^6 4s^1 3d^5$
8. Co : $1s^2 2s^2 2p^6 3s^2 3p^6 4s^2 3d^7$
9. Cu : $1s^2 2s^2 2p^6 3s^2 3p^6 4s^1 3d^{10}$

Objective 97. Draw an orbital diagram for an atom of a given element.

Draw an orbital diagram for each element below, showing how orbitals fill with electrons:

1. N
2. Cl
3. K
4. Cr

Solutions

We draw boxes representing orbitals, in order of increasing energy. Then we put electrons in orbitals according to the electron configuration of each element, following the rules mentioned in the previous objective.

1. N

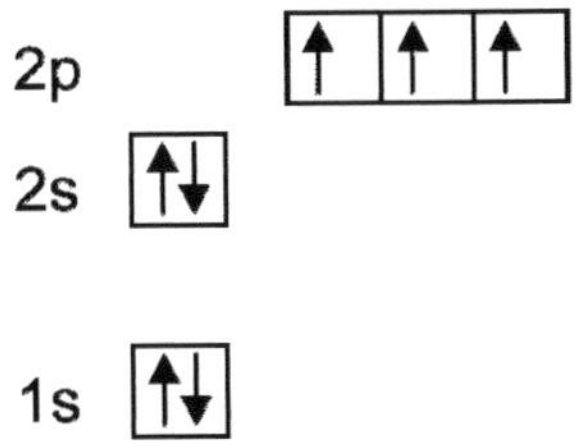

2p   ↑ | ↑ | ↑
2s   ↑↓

1s   ↑↓

2. Cl

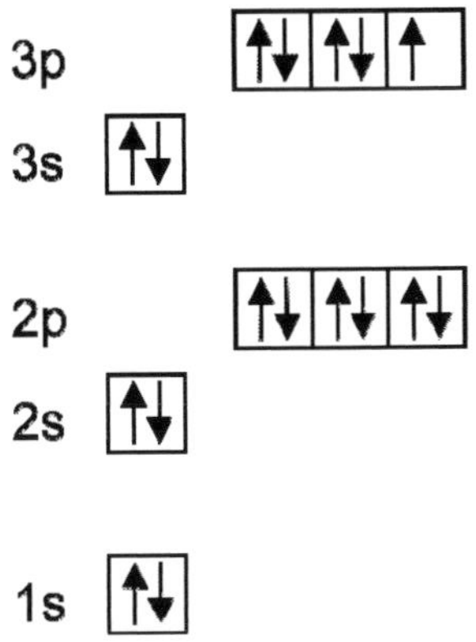

3p   ↑↓ | ↑↓ | ↑
3s   ↑↓

2p   ↑↓ | ↑↓ | ↑↓
2s   ↑↓

1s   ↑↓

3. K

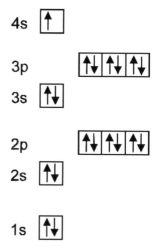

4. Cr

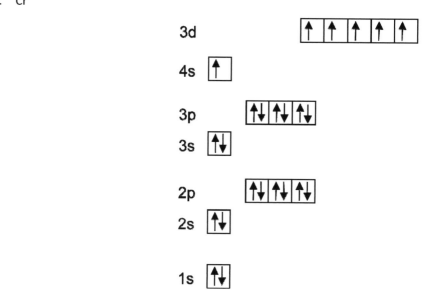

Objective 98. Write the electron configuration of a monoatomic ion.

Write the electron configuration for each ion below:

1. Na^+
2. Cl^-
3. Cu^{2+}
4. Ce^{3+}

Solutions

As a general rule, when we write an electron configuration for an ion, we remove the appropriate number of electrons from the highest occupied shell. For transition metals, s electrons are removed first, and then d electrons if necessary. The same applies to lanthanides and actinides (f electrons are removed last).

1. $Na^+ : 1s^2 2s^2 2p^6$
2. $Cl^- : 1s^2 2s^2 2p^6 3s^2 3p^6$
3. $Cu^{2+} : 1s^2 2s^2 2p^6 3s^2 3p^6 4s^0 3d^9$
4. $Ce^{3+} : 1s^2 2s^2 2p^6 3s^2 3p^6 4s^2 3d^{10} 5s^2 4d^{10} 5p^6 6s^0 5d^0 4f^1$

Objective 99. Show ionic bond formation using orbital diagrams and electron movement.

Show how ionic bonding forms between aluminum and nitrogen by drawing the electron orbital diagrams and showing how electrons move from the metal to the nonmetal.

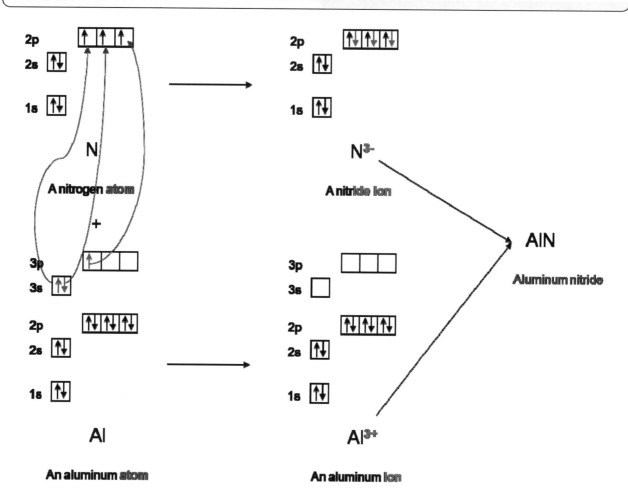

Objective 100.   Write possible values for quantum numbers.

Write all possible values for the following quantum numbers:
1.   When $n = 5$, what are the possible values for l ?
2.   When $l = 3$, what are the possible values for m_l ?
3.   When $m_l = -2$, what are the possible values for m_s ?

Solutions

1. $n = 5 : l\ can\ be\ 0, 1, 2, 3, 4$

2. $l = 3 : m_l\ can\ be -3, -2, -1, 0, +1, +2, +3$

3. $m_l = -2 : m_s\ can\ be +\frac{1}{2} or -\frac{1}{2}$

Objective 101.   For a given electron, write its complete set of 4 quantum numbers.

In each example below, a full or partial orbital diagram is shown. Give the set of 4 quantum numbers that defines the electron circled.

1.   The electron in red, circled (second from left):

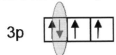

2.   The electron in red, circled (second from right):

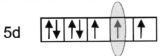

Solutions

1.   This is a 3p electron, so $n = 3$ and $l = 1$. Since the electron shown is in the first p orbital, we will assign it the quantum number $m_l = -1$. Since the spin is pointing down, we will assign the quantum number it $m_s = -\frac{1}{2}$.

2. $n = 5$, $l = 2$ (d orbital), $m_l = +1$ (fourth value), $m_s = \frac{1}{2}$ (spin up)

Objective 102.   Determine whether a given set of quantum numbers is valid.

Determine whether each of the following set of 4 quantum numbers is valid. If not, explain why.

1. $n = 2$, $l = 2$, $m_l = 0$, $m_s = -\frac{1}{2}$

2. $n = 3$, $l = 0$, $m_l = -1$, $m_s = +\frac{1}{2}$

3. $n = 4$, $l = 3$, $m_l = 2$, $m_s = 1$

4. $n = 4$, $l = 1$, $m_l = 1$, $m_s = -\frac{1}{2}$

Solutions

1. $n = 2$, $l = 2$, $m_l = 0$, $m_s = -\frac{1}{2}$

The value of l is invalid. When $n = 2$, l can be 0 or 1 (in shell 2, there can be only s and p orbitals).

2. $n = 3$, $l = 0$, $m_l = -1$, $m_s = +\frac{1}{2}$

The value of m_l is invalid. When $l = 0$, m_l can only be 0 (there can be only one s orbital).

3. $n = 4$, $l = 3$, $m_l = 2$, $m_s = 1$

The value of m_s is invalid. m_s can only be $\pm\frac{1}{2}$.

4. $n = 4$, $l = 1$, $m_l = 1$, $m_s = -\frac{1}{2}$

This is a valid set of quantum numbers. They identify the electron circled below (in the 4p subshell):

4p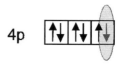

Objective 103.   Calculate the frequency, wavelength, and energy of light.

1. What is the wavelength (in nm) and energy of ultraviolet light with $v = 2.4 \times 10^{15}$ s^{-1}?

Solution

$$\lambda = \frac{c}{v} = \frac{3.00 \times 10^8 \ m/s}{2.4 \times 10^{15} \ /s} \times \frac{10^9 \ nm}{1 \ m} = 125 \ nm$$

$$E = hv = 6.636 \times 10^{-34} \ J \ s \ \times 2.4 \times 10^{15} \ s^{-1} = 1.6 \times 10^{-18} \ J$$

2. What is the frequency and energy of light that has a wavelength of 2200 Angstroms?

Solution

$$v = \frac{c}{\lambda} = \frac{3.00 \times 10^8 \ m/s}{2200 \ \mathring{A}} \times \frac{10^{10} \mathring{A}}{1 \ m} = 1.4 \times 10^{15} \ s^{-1}$$

$$E = hv = 6.636 \times 10^{-34} \ J \ s \ \times 1.4 \times 10^{15} \ s^{-1} = 9.3 \times 10^{-19} \ J$$

Objective 104.   Calculate the energy involved in electron jumps between energy levels and the wavelength of light emitted.

Calculate the energy and the wavelength of light emitted or absorbed when an electron jumps from:
1. $n = 6 \ to \ n = 4$
2. $n = 1 \ to \ n = 3$

Solutions

We will use Rydberg's equation:

$$\Delta E = R_H \left(\frac{1}{n_i^2} - \frac{1}{n_f^2} \right)$$

where ΔE is the change in energy when an electron jumps between energy levels, R_H is Rydberg's constant for hydrogen ($2.18 \times 10^{-18} \ J$), n_i is the initial level number, and n_f is the final level number.

1. $n = 6 \text{ to } n = 4$

$$\Delta E = R_H \left(\frac{1}{n_i^2} - \frac{1}{n_f^2}\right) = 2.18 \times 10^{-18} J \times \left(\frac{1}{6^2} - \frac{1}{4^2}\right) = 2.18 \times 10^{-18} J \times \left(\frac{1}{36} - \frac{1}{16}\right) = -7.57 \times 10^{-20} J$$

The negative sign implies (by convention) that the energy is being released. In this case, it comes in the form of light. When we calculate the wavelength, we drop the negative sign, as we know that light will be emitted:

$$E = \frac{hc}{\lambda} \Rightarrow \lambda = \frac{hc}{\Delta E} = \frac{6.636 \times 10^{-34} J \, s \times 3.00 \times 10^8 \, m/s}{7.57 \times 10^{-20} J} = 2.63 \times 10^{-6} \, m = 2630 \, nm$$

When an electron jumps from a higher level to a lower level, light will be emitted.

2. $n = 1 \text{ to } n = 3$

$$\Delta E = R_H \left(\frac{1}{n_i^2} - \frac{1}{n_f^2}\right) = 2.18 \times 10^{-18} J \times \left(\frac{1}{1^2} - \frac{1}{3^2}\right) = 2.18 \times 10^{-18} J \times \left(1 - \frac{1}{9}\right) = 1.94 \times 10^{-18} J$$

$$E = \frac{hc}{\lambda} \Rightarrow \lambda = \frac{hc}{\Delta E} = \frac{6.636 \times 10^{-34} J \, s \times 3.00 \times 10^8 \, m/s}{1.94 \times 10^{-18} J} = 1.03 \times 10^{-7} \, m = 103 \, nm$$

When an electron jumps from a lower level to a higher level, it needs (absorbs) light (energy) in order to do so (the value of the energy was positive, which means absorbed).

Objective 105. Determine the order of increasing or decreasing atomic radii in a series.

Determine the order of increasing atomic radius for the following elements:

1. S, O, Se
2. Be, B, N
3. Mg, Sr, Ca

Solutions

Atomic radius (size of atoms really) generally decreases left to right across the periodic table, and increases when going down in a group.

1. $O < S < Se$
2. $N < B < Be$
3. $Mg < Ca < Sr$

Objective 106. Determine the order of ionic radii in a series.

Determine the order of increasing ionic radius for the following ions:

1. Na^+, Mg^{2+}, Al^{3+}
2. P^{3-}, S^{2-}, Cl^-
3. *series 1 and 2 above, compared to each other*

Solutions

Ionic radius (size of ions) generally decreases from left to right across the periodic table, but increases sharply when going from metals to nonmetals (semimetals are not likely to form ions), to decrease again as we go from left to right. Ionic radius increases when going down in a group just like atomic radius does.

1. $Al^{3+} < Mg^{2+} < Na^+$
2. $Cl^- < S^{2-} < P^{3-}$
3. *series 1 and series 2*

Ions in series 2 will all be larger than those in series 1, because for elements in the same period, anions are usually much larger than cations, due to their extra electron shell.

Objective 107. Determine the order of increasing or decreasing electronegativity in a series.

Arrange the following elements in the order of decreasing electronegativity:
1. Cl, Na, Si
2. Br, F, Cl
3. C, O, Ge

Solutions

Electronegativity increases left to right and from down up in the periodic table. Thus, fluorine is the most electronegative element.

1. $Cl > Si > Na$
2. $F > Cl > Br$
3. $O > C > Ge$

Objective 108. Determine the order of increasing or decreasing ionization energy in a series.

Arrange the following elements in the order of increasing ionization energy:
1. O, Ne
2. Mg, Sr
3. Cr, K
4. Br, Sb

Solutions

Ionization energy generally increases left to right (nonmetals have a harder time losing electrons than metals do), but decreases slightly down a group (larger metals lose electrons easier than smaller metals).

1. $O < Ne$
2. $Sr < Mg$
3. $K < Cr$
4. $Sb < Br$

Objective 109. Determine the biggest jump between consecutive ionization energies of a given element.

For each of the elements below, show schematically how the first six ionization energies are expected to vary.
1. Na
2. Al

Solution

The first 6 ionization energies represent the amount of energy it takes to remove each of 6 electrons from the atom of an element. Sodium has one valence electron, and it will give it up relatively easily to form a Na^+ ion, but it will not give up easily any further electrons, so there will be a big gap between the first and the second ionization energy for sodium:

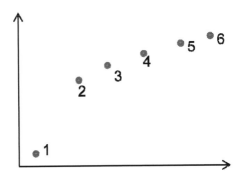

Aluminum will give up three electrons easily, but not another three, so for aluminum the gap will be between the third and the fourth ionization energies. The same reasoning can be applied to any other element.

Objective 110.   Identify elements that display similar properties in a series.

Which of the following series of elements display similar chemical properties?
1.   Al, Be
2.   F, O, N, C
3.   Ca, Ba, Sr
4.   I, Cl, Br

Solution

Series 1 displays similar properties because of the diagonal relationships. Series 3 and 4 displays similar properties because the elements are in the same group. Series 2 will not have similar properties.

Objective 111.   Identify elements likely to form ionic bonds or covalent bonds in a series.

For each pair of elements given below, indicate whether they are likely to form a covalent or an ionic bond:
1.   Na and H
2.   O and S
3.   P and Cl
4.   Cu and O

Solution

Review Objective 22.

1.   Na and H : metal and nonmetal, likely to form an ionic compound
2.   O and S : two nonmetals, likely to form a covalent compound
3.   Mg and Zn : two metals, not likely to form a compound
4.   Cu and O : metal and nonmetal, likely to form an ionic compound

Worksheet 13.   Electron structure and periodic properties

The exercises and problems in this section will allow you to practice the topic until you understand it well.

1.   For each of the first 36 elements, complete the following table.

Element	Orbital Diagram	Electron Configuration	# of valence electrons

Daniel C. Tofan

2. Write the electron configuration for each ion below:
   a. Ca^{2+}

   b. P^{3-}

   c. Cu^+

   d. Fe^{3+}

   e. O^{2-}

3. Write all possible values for the following quantum numbers:
   a. When $n = 6$, what are the possible values for l ?

   b. When $l = 2$, what are the possible values for m_l ?

   c. When $m_l = 1$, what are the possible values for m_s ?

4. Refer to the orbital diagrams in problem 1. Give the set of 4 quantum numbers that characterize each electron described.

    a. The **last** (rightmost) electron drawn for an atom of Ne

    b. The middle **d** electron drawn for an atom of Cr

    c. The second spin down **p** electron drawn for an atom of Cl

5. Determine whether each of the following set of 4 quantum numbers is valid. If not, explain why.

    a. $n = 1$, $l = 0$, $m_l = 0$, $m_s = 0$

    b. $n = 6$, $l = 2$, $m_l = 0$, $m_s = -\frac{1}{2}$

    c. $n = 4$, $l = -3$, $m_l = -3$, $m_s = +\frac{1}{2}$

    d. $n = 4$, $l = 4$, $m_l = 0$, $m_s = -\frac{1}{2}$

6. What is the wavelength (in nm) and energy of gamma rays with $v = 3.5 \times 10^{20}$ s^{-1}?

7. What are the frequency and the energy of light that has a wavelength of 445 nm?

8. What are the frequency and the energy of light that has a wavelength of 1100 Angstroms?

9. Calculate the energy and the wavelength of light emitted or absorbed when an electron jumps from:

    a. $n = 1\ to\ n = 5$

    b. $n = 2\ to\ n = 3$

    c. $n = 6\ to\ n = 2$

10. Determine the order of increasing atomic radius for the following elements:

    a.   Na, Rb, Cs, Li

    b.   Ca, Ar, S, Cl

    c.   P, Bi, Al, Sb

11. Determine the order of increasing ionic radius for the following ions:

    a. $Ba^{2+},\ Sr^{2+}, Ca^{2+}, Mg^{2+}$

    b. $O^{2-},\ N^{3-},\ F^{-}$

    c. $Ca^{2+},\ K^{+},\ Ga^{3+}$

    d. $As^{3-},\ Br^{-},\ Se^{2-}$

    e.   *series* **d** *and* **c** *above, compared to each other*

12. Arrange the following elements in the order of increasing electronegativity:
    a. He, Li, O, C

    b. Se, O, S

    c. Cs, Na, K, Rb, Li

    d. Mg, Si, Al, Ne, Cl

    e. Ba, H, Kr, F

13. Which of the following series of elements display similar chemical properties?
    a. H, Li, Cs

    b. Ne, Ar, Xe

    c. Se, Te

    d. Na, Mg, Al, Si

14. For each pair of elements given below, indicate whether they are likely to form a covalent or an ionic bond:
    a. C and H

    b. Si and O

    c. F and Na

    d. O and F

    e. Ca and Se

15. For each of the elements below, show schematically how the first seven ionization energies are expected to vary.
    a. Ca

b. Si

c. K

d. S

e. P

Self-assessment

Using the scale indicated, rate your understanding of each learning objective at the completion of this lesson. Identify the areas where your understanding is weak or medium and discuss with your class mates and/or instructor. Write down specific questions you still have at the completion of this topic.

Learning objective	Self-assessment 3 = strong, 2 = medium, 1 = weak, 0 = not done			
	3	2	1	0
	3	2	1	0
	3	2	1	0
	3	2	1	0
	3	2	1	0
	3	2	1	0
	3	2	1	0
	3	2	1	0
	3	2	1	0
	3	2	1	0
	3	2	1	0
	3	2	1	0
	3	2	1	0
	3	2	1	0
	3	2	1	0
	3	2	1	0
	3	2	1	0

Lesson 14 – Covalent Bonding and Lewis Structures

Learning Objectives

In this lesson you will learn:

- To write the formula of a **covalent compound** from its name
- To draw the **Lewis structure** for a compound
- To draw reasonable Lewis structures and assign **formal charges** to atoms in a Lewis structure

Pre-requisites: Atomic structure; Electron Structure and Periodic Properties.

Self-study questions

Before you start studying the worked examples, you should be able to formulate answers to the questions below. Use a textbook of your choice, or an online source of information, to find the answers.

1. What is covalent bonding?
2. What is the difference between an ionic compound and a covalent compound?
3. What is a Lewis structure?
4. What is the octet rule? Why do elements tend to obey this rule when making compounds?
5. Can certain elements have more than an octet? Which ones?
6. What are formal charges?

Worked examples

This section contains solved problems that cover the learning objectives listed above. Study each example carefully and make notes in the workbook to check every example that you understood. Repeat several times what you don't understand at first. It should become clearer as you keep working on the examples.

Objective 112. Write the formula of a covalent compound from its name.

Write the formula of each compound indicated:
1. carbon tetrachloride
2. tetraphosphorus hexoxide
3. dinitrogen pentoxide
4. selenium trioxide

Solutions:

1. CCl_4

2. P_4O_6

3. N_2O_5

4. SeO_3

Objective 113. Draw a Lewis structure for a covalent compound.

Draw a reasonable Lewis structure for each of the following compounds:
1. F_2
2. HCl
3. CO_2
4. SO_2
5. SO_3
6. NO_2

Discussion

When drawing a Lewis structure for a compound, I find it easier to start with the Lewis dot symbols for all elements. Then, I build single bonds between atoms, using unpaired electrons on each one whenever possible. Double bonds are also needed at times in order to make an octet for each atom. Finally, electrons can be moved around in order to accomplish a reasonable structure.

Solutions

1. F_2

Here, each fluorine atom has one unpaired electron. By sharing that electron with the equivalent one from the other fluorine atom, a single bond is formed, and each fluorine has an octet.

2. HCl

$$H \overset{\cdot\cdot}{\underset{\cdot\cdot}{:}} \overset{\cdot\cdot}{\underset{\cdot\cdot}{Cl}} : \qquad H - \overset{\cdot\cdot}{\underset{\cdot\cdot}{Cl}} :$$

Again, by pairing up the single electron from hydrogen with the unpaired electron from chlorine, a single bond can be formed.

3. CO_2

$$\overset{\cdot\cdot}{\underset{\cdot\cdot}{O}} :: C :: \overset{\cdot\cdot}{\underset{\cdot\cdot}{O}} \qquad \overset{\cdot\cdot}{\underset{\cdot\cdot}{O}} = C = \overset{\cdot\cdot}{\underset{\cdot\cdot}{O}}$$

Carbon has 4 electrons, and oxygen has 6. Each needs an octet to become stable. Single bonds would not be sufficient in this case. If each oxygen shares two electrons with two from carbon, then all three atoms make an octet through the use of two double bonds.

4. SO_2

Both oxygen and sulfur come with 6 valence electrons. Sulfur can have more than an octet, but oxygen cannot. A structure with two double bonds is possible, which would leave one pair of electrons on the sulfur (10 electrons total). A better structure is the one above. The oxygen left of the sulfur can share two electrons and make a double bond with the sulfur. The oxygen below the sulfur can keep its 6 electrons, and a lone pair from sulfur can be moved around to serve as a single bond instead. This keeps sulfur with an octet. In the next objective you will see that several equivalent structures are possible for the same molecule.

5. SO_3

From the SO_2 molecule, we add an oxygen, which keeps its 6 electrons, and we move the lone pair on sulfur to make a single bond to the third oxygen. This gives all atoms an octet.

6. NO_2

In this structure, the best we can do is a double bond and a single bond. We are unable to give nitrogen an octet because the total number of electrons is odd (6+6+5=17). Thus, the nitrogen dioxide molecule will have an unpaired electron on the nitrogen.

Objective 114.   Write resonance structures for a covalent compound. Determine formal charges on atoms in a Lewis structure.

For each of the following covalent compounds or polyatomic ions, draw possible resonance Lewis structures and assign formal charges to each atom.

1. SO_3

2. N_2O

3. PO_4^{3-}

Solutions

In some of the structures above, we used a combination of a double bond and a single bond. By moving the double bond around, we can obtain resonance structures.

1. SO_3

There is no particular reason to place the double bond on the particular oxygen atom we chose in the previous objective. We can move that bond on any of the other two (we need to move a lone pair at the same time). This gives us three individual Lewis structures, which are all equivalent. These are resonance structures.

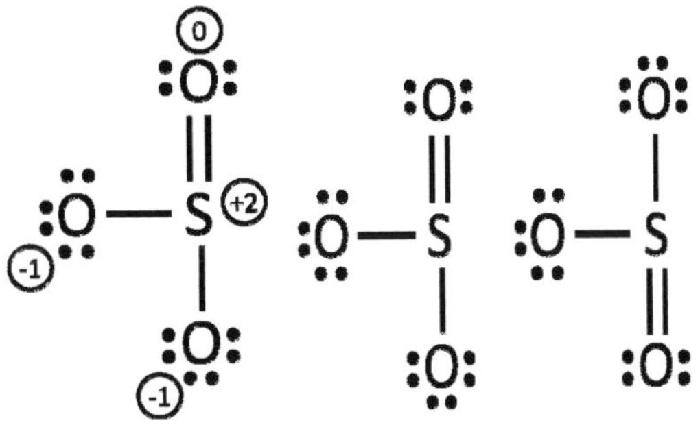

When we assign formal charges to atoms in a Lewis structure, we count one electron per bond around each atom (as if we split bonds into individual atoms). Formal charge is:

$$formal\ charge = valence\ electrons\ of\ the\ nonbonded\ atom - electrons\ currently\ around\ the\ atom$$

Thus, an oxygen with 3 lone pairs and one single bond is said to have 7 electrons around it. The formal charge is: 6 valence electrons – 7 electrons currently around the atom = -1. For sulfur, we count 1 electron per single bond and 2 electrons per double bond. Formal charge = 6 valence electrons – 4 electrons currently around S = +2. And so on. I only show formal charges for one structure in each series where they are equivalent, you can fill in the rest.

Formal charges are indicated in small circles by each atom. The sum of all formal charges in a Lewis structure representing a molecule or a polyatomic ion must equal 0 for a neutral molecule, or the charge of the ion.

2. NO_2

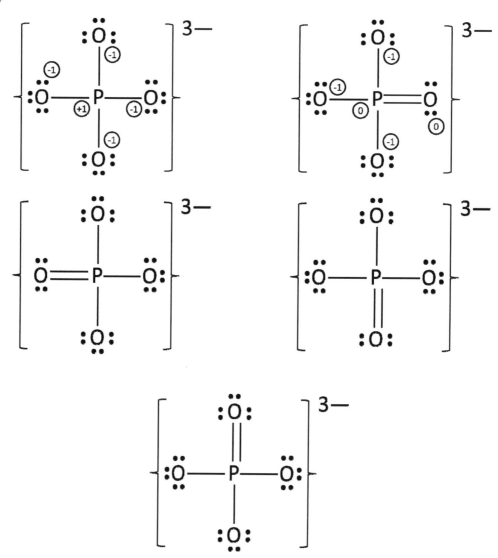

3. PO_4^{3-}

Because phosphorus can have more than an octet (since it has empty **d** orbitals), five resonance structures are possible, by using one double bond that can be moved around on each of the 4 oxygens, as well as a structure that contains 4 single bonds. An octet for each atom can be ensured by using four equivalent single bonds. Which of these structures is better? We can't really say. In general, it is preferable to minimize the number of formal charges, so structures 2-5, which have 3 non-zero formal charges, would be preferred. On the other hand, measurements indicate that all P – O bonds are equivalent in size, indicating that structure 1 is more plausible. In reality, there is always a mix between various possible Lewis structures for any molecule or ion. What we learn here is how to draw reasonable structures from the information we have at hand.

Worksheet 14.   Covalent bonding and Lewis structures

The exercises and problems in this section will allow you to practice the topic until you understand it well.

1.   Write the formula of each compound indicated:
   a.   Dihydrogen monoxide

   b.   Dichlorine heptoxide

   c.   Sulfur trioxide

   d.   Tricarbon octahydride

   e.   Tetraphosphorus decoxide

2.   Complete the table below:

Compound	Name	Lewis structure showing all non-zero formal charges on each atom
H_2		
H_2O		
NO		
N_2O		
CO		

SiO_2		
SCl_4		
SCl_6		
BrF_3		
BrF_5		
ClO_2		
NF_3		
ICl_3		

3. Show resonance structures and formal charges for each of the following species:

    a. N_2O

    b. CO_3^{2-}

    c. NO_3^-

    d. ClO_3^-

Self-assessment

Using the scale indicated, rate your understanding of each learning objective at the completion of this lesson. Identify the areas where your understanding is weak or medium and discuss with your class mates and/or instructor. Write down specific questions you still have at the completion of this topic.

Learning objective	Self-assessment 3 = strong, 2 = medium, 1 = weak, 0 = not done
	3 2 1 0
	3 2 1 0
	3 2 1 0

Lesson 15 –   Molecular Structure

Learning Objectives

In this lesson you will learn:

- To determine the **polarity** of a **covalent bond**
- To determine the **electron geometry** and **molecular geometry** of a molecule, including names and **bond angles**
- To determine the type of **hybridization** for an atom in a molecule
- To draw a **molecular orbital diagram** for a binary covalent molecule. Write the **molecular electron configuration** and calculate the **bond order**

Pre-requisites: Covalent Bonding and Lewis Structures.

Self-study questions

Before you start studying the worked examples, you should be able to formulate answers to the questions below. Use a textbook of your choice, or an online source of information, to find the answers.

1. What is a covalent bond?
2. What is the difference between a polar and a nonpolar covalent bond?
3. What are bond angles?
4. What are lone pairs?
5. What is hybridization?
6. What is a dipole moment?
7. What is a molecular orbital?
8. What is bond order?
9. What is the difference between *diamagnetic* and *paramagnetic*?
10. What is a *sigma* bond?
11. What is a *pi* bond?

Worked examples

This section contains solved problems that cover the learning objectives listed above. Study each example carefully and make notes in the workbook to check every example that you understood. Repeat several times what you don't understand at first. It should become clearer as you keep working on the examples.

Objective 115. Determine the polarity of a covalent bond.

Indicate whether a covalent bond between each of the atoms indicated is expected to be polar and justify your answer.

1. H—H
2. H—Cl
3. H—P
4. Cl—Br
5. F—S

Solutions

1. H—H : nonpolar, because the two atoms are identical
2. H—Cl : polar
3. H—P : nonpolar, because the two elements have the same electronegativity value
4. Cl—Br : polar
5. F—S : polar

Objective 116. Determine the electron geometry and molecular geometry of a molecule, including names and bond angles.

For each of the compounds below, sketch the 3D geometry of the molecule, indicate the name of the electron and molecular geometry, and give the bond angles around the central atom. Indicate whether the molecule has an overall dipole moment, and if so give its direction.

1. CO_2
2. H_2O
3. SO_2
4. SCl_4
5. $XeCl_2$
6. ICl_4^-

Solutions

1. CO_2

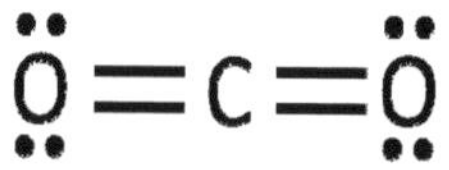

Carbon has no lone pairs left. The electron and molecular geometries are both linear, and the O—C—O bond angle is 180°. Because the two carbon-oxygen bonds, although polar, are opposite each other, there is no overall dipole moment, so we say that the carbon dioxide molecule is **nonpolar**.

2. H_2O

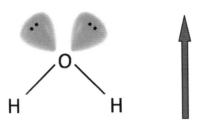

Oxygen has two lone pairs. They will each occupy an orbital. The electron geometry of the molecule is tetrahedral (4 electron pairs total around oxygen, including the lone pairs and the bonds). The molecular geometry is bent (only the bonds are taken into account). The H—O—H bond angle is 105° (slightly distorted from a tetrahedral angle of 109°). Because oxygen is a lot more electronegative than hydrogen, there is an overall dipole moment pointing towards the oxygen. We say that the water molecule is **polar**.

3. SO_2

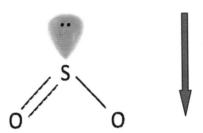

Sulfur has a lone pair of electrons in an orbital. The electron geometry of the molecule is trigonal planar (3 electron pairs total, including the lone pair and the bonds – a double bond is counted as if it were a single bond).The molecular geometry is bent (only the bonds are taken into account). O—S—O bond angle is 120° (in reality, a little less, due to the repulsion from the lone electron pair). There is a dipole moment pointing towards the oxygens and the molecule is polar.

4. SCl_4

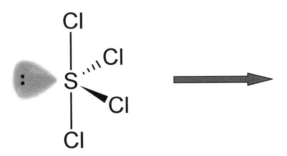

The electron geometry is trigonal bypiramidal (5 electron pairs). The molecular geometry is see-saw. Cl—S—Cl bond angles are 180° (top and bottom, or axial, chlorines), 120° (equatorial chlorines, within the horizontal plane), and 90° (one axial and one equatorial chlorine). Because the two equatorial S-Cl bonds do not cancel each other out, there is an overall dipole moment. These values are actually a little distorted again, due to electron pair repulsion.

5. $XeCl_2$

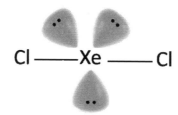

The electron geometry is trigonal bypiramidal (5 electron pairs around Xe). The molecular geometry is linear (the lone pairs occupy the equatorial positions, as this geometry ensures the maximum distance between them). The Cl—S—Cl bond angle is 180°. The Xe-Cl bonds are polar, but the geometry cancels out the polarities and the molecule has no overall dipole moment.

6. ICl_4^-

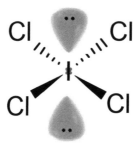

This is an ion, so we account for the additional electron, which puts 8 electrons on iodine. Four electrons are engaged in single bonds, and the other four form 2 lone pairs. There are a total of 6 pairs around iodine, so the electron geometry is octahedral. The molecular geometry is square planar (the lone pairs are positioned opposite each other). Bond angles are 90° and 180°, depending on which chlorines you include in the bond angle. In this case too, the molecule has no dipole moment.

Objective 117.   Determine the type of hybridization for an atom in a molecule.

Determine the hybridization of the atom(s) in bold in each of the molecules below. Indicate the number of σ and π bonds in each molecule.

1. **CH$_4$**

2. **H$_2$C=C=CH$_2$**

3. **H$_3$C—C≡CH**

4. **SO$_2$**

5. **PCl$_5$**

6. **SF$_6$**

Solutions

The common hybridization states are: sp, sp^2, sp^3, sp^3d, sp^3d^2 (in the order of increasing numbers of orbitals available for bonding, from 2 to 6). Atoms involved in double bonds generally are hybridized sp^2, and those involved in triple (or two double) bonds are hybridized sp. Single bonds are σ bonds. A double bond consists of one σ and one π bond. A triple bond consists of one σ and two π bonds.

1. CH_4 : carbon is sp^3. 4 σ bonds.
2. $H_2C=C=CH_2$: carbons 1 and 3 are sp^2, carbon 2 (middle) is sp. 6 σ bonds and 2 π bonds.
3. $H_3C—C\equiv CH$: carbon 1 is sp^3, carbons 2 and 3 are sp. 6 σ bonds and 2 π bonds.
4. SO_2 : S is sp^2 (needs 3 hybrid orbitals for the σ bonds and one p orbital for the π bond). 3 σ bonds and 1 π bond.
5. PCl_5 : P is sp^3d. 5 σ bonds.
6. SF_6 : S is sp^3d^2. 6 σ bonds.

Objective 118. Draw a molecular orbital diagram for a binary covalent molecule. Write the molecular electron configuration and calculate the bond order.

For each of the binary molecules below, draw a complete molecular orbital (MO) diagram, write the MO electron configuration, and calculate the bond order in the molecule. Indicate whether the molecule is expected to be paramagnetic or diamagnetic.
   1. H_2
   2. O_2
   3. C_2
   4. O_2^{2-}

Solutions

Atomic orbitals combine and split into **bonding** and **antibonding** molecular orbitals. The arrangement of these molecular orbitals depends on the original atomic orbitals. They then occupy with electrons following the same rules as atomic orbitals do.

1. H_2

Each H atom has one 1s orbital carrying one electron. The two 1s orbitals combine to form *sigma* molecular orbitals:

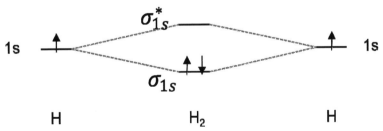

The molecular orbital electron configuration will be: $(\sigma_{1s})^2$. We put the symbol for each molecular orbital in parentheses, then we indicate the number of electrons occupying the set of orbitals. Empty orbitals need not be listed. The bond order is:

$$bond\ order = \frac{number\ of\ bonding\ electrons - number\ of\ antibonding\ electrons}{2} = \frac{2-0}{2} = 1$$

Bonding electrons are those occupying bonding orbitals, and antibonding electrons are those occupying antibonding orbitals. This signifies that the hydrogen molecule (H_2) should have one single bond, which corresponds to what we already knew.

2. O_2

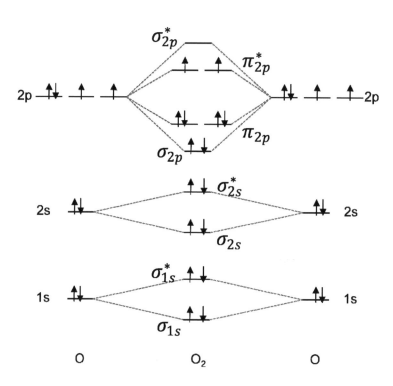

MO electron configuration: $(\sigma_{1s})^2(\sigma_{1s}^*)^2(\sigma_{2s})^2(\sigma_{2s}^*)^2(\sigma_{2p})^2(\pi_{2p})^4(\pi_{2p}^*)^2$. Bond order:

$$bond\ order = \frac{10-6}{2} = 2$$

Note that you can exclude subshells that are completely filled with bonding and antibonding electrons (in this case, the MO's resulting from the 1s and 2s subshells, because they have equal numbers of bonding and antibonding electrons) and only count the electrons in partially filled subshells, in this case 2p:

$$bond\ order = \frac{6-2}{2} = 2$$

A bond order of 2 implies a double bond between the two atoms in the molecule, which is what we expect when we draw the Lewis structure for O_2.

3. C_2

The diagram for C_2 is similar to that for O_2 except the order of the *sigma* and *pi* bonding (not the antibonding ones) orbitals resulting from the combination of 2p atomic orbitals is reversed (this happens for B, C, and N):

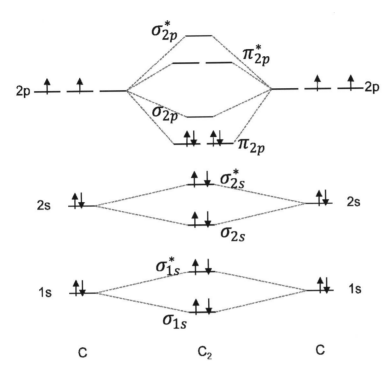

The MO electron configuration is: $(\sigma_{1s})^2(\sigma_{1s}^*)^2(\sigma_{2s})^2(\sigma_{2s}^*)^2(\pi_{2p})^4$. Bond order:

$$bond\ order = \frac{4-0}{2} = 2$$

4. O_2^{2-}

This is the peroxide ion. The diagram is similar to that of the oxygen molecules. Two extra electrons are added to account for the 2- charge (they do not belong to the oxygen atoms, but will exist in the ion).

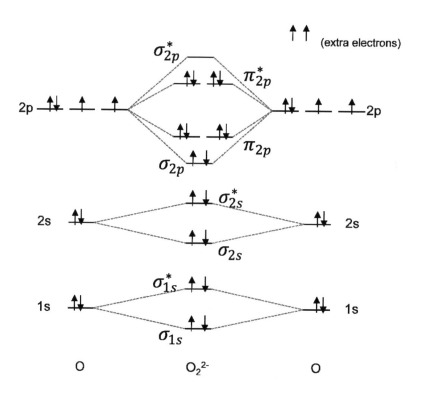

MO electron configuration: $(\sigma_{1s})^2(\sigma_{1s}^*)^2(\sigma_{2s})^2(\sigma_{2s}^*)^2(\sigma_{2p})^2(\pi_{2p})^4(\pi_{2p}^*)^4$. Bond order:

$$bond\ order = \frac{6-4}{2} = 1$$

Worksheet 15.　Molecular structure

1.　Complete the tables below for each compound indicated

　　　a.　　BF_3

Lewis structure	3D geometry	Electron geometry name
		Molecular geometry name
		Bond angles
Hybridization of central atom	Dipole moment	

　　　b.　　SiH_4

Lewis structure	3D geometry	Electron geometry name
		Molecular geometry name
		Bond angles
Hybridization of central atom	Dipole moment	

　　　c.　　HCN

Lewis structure	3D geometry	Electron geometry name
		Molecular geometry name
		Bond angles
Hybridization of central atom	Dipole moment	

d. SCl_6

Lewis structure	3D geometry	Electron geometry name
		Molecular geometry name
		Bond angles
Hybridization of central atom	Dipole moment	

e. $XeCl_4$

Lewis structure	3D geometry	Electron geometry name
		Molecular geometry name
		Bond angles
Hybridization of central atom	Dipole moment	

f. PF_5

Lewis structure	3D geometry	Electron geometry name
		Molecular geometry name
		Bond angles
Hybridization of central atom	Dipole moment	

g. SO_3

Lewis structure	3D geometry	Electron geometry name
		Molecular geometry name
		Bond angles
Hybridization of central atom	Dipole moment	

h. F_2O

Lewis structure	3D geometry	Electron geometry name
		Molecular geometry name
		Bond angles
Hybridization of central atom	Dipole moment	

i. ClO_3^-

Lewis structure	3D geometry	Electron geometry name
		Molecular geometry name
		Bond angles
Hybridization of central atom	Dipole moment	

j. NH_3

Lewis structure	3D geometry	Electron geometry name
		Molecular geometry name
		Bond angles
Hybridization of central atom	Dipole moment	

k. ICl_5

Lewis structure	3D geometry	Electron geometry name
		Molecular geometry name
		Bond angles
Hybridization of central atom	Dipole moment	

l. PO_4^{3-}

Lewis structure	3D geometry	Electron geometry name
		Molecular geometry name
		Bond angles
Hybridization of central atom	Dipole moment	

2. For each of the binary molecules below, draw a complete molecular orbital (MO) diagram, write the MO electron configuration, and calculate the bond order in the molecule. Indicate whether the molecule is expected to be paramagnetic or diamagnetic.

   a. N_2

   b. F_2

c.　　CO

d.　　O_2^-

e. O_2^+

f. Ne_2

3. Which of the following molecules does not contain an sp^2 hybridized carbon atom?
    a. H_3C-CH_3

    b. H_3C-CH=CH_2

    c. CH_3-CH=CH-CH_2OH

    d. CH_3CH=O

    e. CH_4

4. In which of the following species is C not sp hybridized?
    a. CO_2

    b.   HCOOH

    c.   CO

    d. C_2H_2

Self-assessment

Using the scale indicated, rate your understanding of each learning objective at the completion of this lesson. Identify the areas where your understanding is weak or medium and discuss with your class mates and/or instructor. Write down specific questions you still have at the completion of this topic.

Learning objective	Self-assessment 3 = strong, 2 = medium, 1 = weak, 0 = not done
	3 2 1 0
	3 2 1 0
	3 2 1 0
	3 2 1 0

Lesson 16 – Thermochemistry

Learning Objectives

In this lesson you will learn:

- To write **thermochemical equations** representing the **formation** of a compound from its elements
- To calculate the **enthalpy change** of a reaction from **standard enthalpies of formation**
- To calculate the **heat absorbed** or **released** in a chemical reaction
- To calculate the **enthalpy of combustion** of a compound from the heat released
- To determine the enthalpy change in a chemical reaction using **Hess's Law**
- To calculate the **temperature change** of a substance or solution when it absorbs or releases heat
- To calculate the final temperature when two substances or solutions of different initial temperatures are mixed
- To calculate the **heat capacity** of a calorimeter or use the given heat capacity to determine the final temperature
- To calculate the heat released in a **neutralization** reaction
- To calculate the heat released or absorbed when a substance is **dissolved** in water
- To calculate the **heat of combustion** of a compound from **calorimetric data**

Pre-requisites: Balancing chemical reactions; Solutions and concentration.

Self-study questions

Before you start studying the worked examples, you should be able to formulate answers to the questions below. Use a textbook of your choice, or an online source of information, to find the answers.

1. What is heat?
2. What is enthalpy?
3. What is the standard enthalpy of formation?
4. What is the convention for expressing heat absorbed versus released?
5. What is an exothermic process?
6. What is an endothermic process?
7. What is a combustion reaction?
8. What is heat capacity?
9. What is specific heat?
10. What is a neutralization reaction?
11. What is meant by calorimetry?

Worked examples

This section contains solved problems that cover the learning objectives listed above. Study each example carefully and make notes in the workbook to check every example that you understood. Repeat several times what you don't understand at first. It should become clearer as you keep working on the examples.

Objective 119. Write a chemical equation that represents the formation of a compound from its elements and look up its enthalpy of formation.

Write a chemical equation that represents the formation of each compound below from its constituent elements, then look up its enthalpy of formation and give the source.

1. H_2O
2. C_2H_5OH
3. H_2SO_4

Solutions

1. H_2O

$$H_{2\,(g)} + \frac{1}{2}O_{2\,(g)} \rightarrow H_2O_{(l)} \quad ; \quad \Delta H_f^o = -285.8\ kJ/mol$$

2. C_2H_5OH

$$2C_{(s)} + 3H_{2\,(g)} + \frac{1}{2}O_{2\,(g)} \rightarrow C_2H_5OH_{(l)} \quad ; \quad \Delta H_f^o = -277.7\ kJ/mol$$

3. H_2SO_4

$$H_{2\,(g)} + \frac{1}{8}S_{8\,(s)} + 2O_{2\,(g)} \rightarrow H_2SO_{4\,(l)} \quad ; \quad \Delta H_f^o = -814\ kJ/mol$$

Source: McMurry/Fay, "Chemistry", 5th Edition, Prentice Hall.

The formation of a compound from its elements, and its enthalpy, refers to exactly 1 mol of product, hence the fractional coefficients.

Objective 120. Calculate the enthalpy change of a reaction from standard enthalpies of formation.

Calculate the enthalpy change in each of the reactions below from the standard enthalpies of formation of reactants and products (look up these values).

1. $H_{2\,(g)} + C_2H_{4\,(g)} \rightarrow C_2H_{6\,(g)}$

2. $C_2H_{2\,(g)} + \frac{5}{2}O_{2\,(g)} \rightarrow 2CO_{2\,(g)} + H_2O_{(l)}$

Solutions

The enthalpy change in a chemical reaction can be calculated from the standard enthalpies of formation of all reactants and all products, each multiplied by their stoichiometric coefficients:

$$\Delta H° = \sum \Delta H_f^o(products) - \sum \Delta H_f^o\ (reactants)$$

1. $H_{2\,(g)} + C_2H_{4\,(g)} \rightarrow C_2H_{6\,(g)}$

$$\Delta H^\circ = \left(1 \text{ mol } C_2H_6 {}_{(g)}\right)$$
$$\times \Delta H_f^\circ \left(C_2H_6 {}_{(g)}\right) - \left(\left(1 \text{ mol } H_2 {}_{(g)}\right) \times \Delta H_f^\circ \left(H_2 {}_{(g)}\right) + \left(1 \text{ mol } C_2H_4 {}_{(g)}\right) \times \Delta H_f^\circ \left(C_2H_4 {}_{(g)}\right)\right)$$

$$\Delta H^\circ = \left(1 \text{ mol } C_2H_6 {}_{(g)}\right) \times \left(-84.7 \frac{kJ}{mol}\right) - \left(1 \text{ mol } H_2 {}_{(g)}\right) \times \left(0 \frac{kJ}{mol}\right) - \left(1 \text{ mol } C_2H_4 {}_{(g)}\right) \times \left(52.3 \frac{kJ}{mol}\right)$$

$$\Delta H^\circ = -32.4 \text{ kJ}$$

This is the standard enthalpy change for the reaction above, when the amounts of compounds reacted are equal to the stoichiometric coefficients. The enthalpy change for a reaction is measured in kJ and not kJ/mol as some books mistakenly indicate, as it refers to the entire reaction, not a particular compound.

2. $C_2H_2 {}_{(g)} + \frac{5}{2} O_2 {}_{(g)} \rightarrow 2CO_2 {}_{(g)} + H_2O {}_{(l)}$

$$\Delta H^\circ = \left(2 \text{ mol } CO_2 {}_{(g)}\right) \times \Delta H_f^\circ \left(CO_2 {}_{(g)}\right) + \left(1 \text{ mol } H_2O {}_{(l)}\right)$$

$$\times \Delta H_f^\circ \left(H_2O {}_{(l)}\right) - \left(\left(1 \text{ mol } C_2H_2 {}_{(g)}\right) \times \Delta H_f^\circ \left(C_2H_2 {}_{(g)}\right) + \left(\frac{5}{2} \text{ mol } O_2 {}_{(g)}\right) \times \Delta H_f^\circ \left(O_2 {}_{(g)}\right)\right)$$

$$\Delta H^\circ = \left(2 \text{ mol } CO_2 {}_{(g)}\right) \times \left(-393.5 \frac{kJ}{mol}\right) + \left(1 \text{ mol } H_2O {}_{(l)}\right) \times \left(-285.8 \frac{kJ}{mol}\right) - \left(1 \text{ mol } C_2H_2 {}_{(g)}\right) \times \left(226.7 \frac{kJ}{mol}\right)$$

$$- \left(\frac{5}{2} \text{ mol } O_2 {}_{(g)}\right) \times \left(0 \frac{kJ}{mol}\right)$$

$$\Delta H^\circ = -1299.5 \text{ kJ}$$

Objective 121. Calculate the heat absorbed or released in a chemical reaction given a specific quantity of reactant or product.

1. Calculate the amount of heat absorbed or released in each the reaction below, given the standard enthalpy change and starting with 24.02 g carbon.

$$5C_{(s)} + 2SO_2 {}_{(g)} \rightarrow CS_2 {}_{(l)} + 4CO_2 {}_{(g)} \; ; \; \Delta H^\circ = 239.9 \, kJ$$

Solution

The enthalpy of the reaction above corresponds to the amounts of reactants (and products) in the balanced chemical equation, as written. This means that when 5 moles of C react, the reaction absorbs (then enthalpy is positive) 239.9 kJ. For our given amount, we need to do a stoichiometric calculation:

$$24.02 \, g \, C \times \frac{1 \, mol \, C}{12.01 \, g} \times \frac{239.9 \, kJ}{5 \, mol \, C} = 95.96 \, kJ \, absorbed$$

Objective 122. Calculate the enthalpy of combustion of a compound from the heat released.

1. When 100.0 g of ethanol (C_2H_5OH) is burned in air, 2260 kJ of heat is liberated. Calculate the heat of combustion of ethanol in kJ/mol.

Solution

The combustion of ethanol represents its reaction with oxygen:

$$C_2H_5OH_{(l)} + 3O_{2\,(g)} \rightarrow 2CO_{2\,(g)} + 3H_2O_{(s)}$$

The enthalpy of combustion of ethanol will be the enthalpy change of this reaction, as written, when 1 mole of ethanol reacts. Our given quantity is different:

$$\frac{100.\,g\ C_2H_5OH_{(l)}}{46.068\ g/mol} = 2.17\ mol\ C_2H_5OH$$

Since the heat released (or absorbed) in a reaction is proportional to the quantity of reactant, it is easiest to just do a proportion:

$$\frac{2260\ kJ}{2.17\ mol} = \frac{x}{1\ mol} \quad \Rightarrow \quad x = \frac{2260\ kJ \times 1\ mol}{2.17\ mol} = 1040\ kJ/mol$$

Objective 123. Determine the enthalpy change in a chemical reaction using Hess's Law.

1. From the following enthalpies of reaction:

$$CH_3OH_{(l)} + \frac{3}{2}O_{2\,(g)} \rightarrow CO_{2\,(g)} + 2H_2O_{(l)} \qquad \Delta H°_1 = -726.4\ kJ \quad (1)$$

$$C_{(s)} + O_{2\,(g)} \rightarrow CO_{2\,(g)} \qquad\qquad\qquad\qquad \Delta H°_2 = -393.5\ kJ \quad (2)$$

$$H_{2\,(g)} + \frac{1}{2}O_{2\,(g)} \rightarrow H_2O_{(l)} \qquad\qquad\qquad \Delta H°_3 = -285.8\ kJ \quad (3)$$

Calculate the enthalpy of formation of methanol from its elements:

$$C_{(s)} + 2H_{2\,(g)} + \frac{1}{2}O_{2\,(g)} \rightarrow CH_3OH_{(l)} \qquad\qquad (4)$$

Solution

Another method of determining the enthalpy change of a reaction is if a series of steps are known, which when added together (like redox half reactions) result in our desired reaction. In these problems, we are given a series of reactions and their enthalpies, and we need to calculate the enthalpy of a final reaction, which has common reactants and products with the ones given. This method is called Hess' Law.

We need to combine reactions (1), (2) and (3) to give us (4). We look at reactants and products that appear in (4) and we locate them in the other set. It seems that if we inverse (1), $CH_3OH_{(l)}$ will become a product. If we take (2) as is, we get the $C(graphite)$ as reactant. Finally, since we need $2H_{2\,(g)}$, we can multiply (3) by 2. The enthalpies of (1), (2) and (3) change in the same way that we change the reactions: $\Delta H°_1$ gets inversed (becomes positive), $\Delta H°_2$ stays the same, and $\Delta H°_3$ is multiplied by two. The new set looks like this:

$$CO_{2\,(g)} + 2H_2O_{(l)} \rightarrow CH_3OH_{(l)} + \frac{3}{2}O_{2\,(g)} \quad \Delta H = -\Delta H°_1$$

$$C_{(s)} + O_{2\,(g)} \rightarrow CO_{2\,(g)} \quad \Delta H = \Delta H°_2$$

$$2H_{2\,(g)} + O_{2\,(g)} \rightarrow 2H_2O_{(l)} \quad \Delta H = 2\Delta H°_3$$

Now we add the three reactions together:

$$CO_{2\,(g)} + 2H_2O_{(l)} + C_{(s)} + O_{2\,(g)} + 2H_{2\,(g)} + O_{2\,(g)} \rightarrow CH_3OH_{(l)} + \frac{3}{2}O_{2\,(g)} + CO_{2\,(g)} + 2H_2O_{(l)}$$

After canceling out everything that is redundant, we get:

$$C_{(s)} + 2H_{2\,(g)} + \frac{1}{2}O_{2\,(g)} \rightarrow CH_3OH_{(l)} \qquad\qquad (4)$$

Thus, the enthalpy change of (4) will be the sum of the changed enthalpies of reactions 1-3:

$$\Delta H_4^o = -\Delta H°_1 + \Delta H°_2 + 2\Delta H°_3 = 726.4 + (-393.5) + 2(-285.8) = -238.7 \ kJ$$

Objective 124.   Calculate the temperature change of a substance or solution when it absorbs or releases heat.

1. A quantity of water weighing 254 g, initially at 22.0 °C, absorbs 2.45 kJ of heat. What is the temperature reached by the water?

Solution

The calorimetry formula allows us to relate heat to mass of substance, temperature change, and a constant for each substance called specific heat:

$$Q = m \times s \times \Delta T$$

The specific heat of water is $4.18 \frac{J}{g\,K}$ (look it up). The magnitude of the Kelvin is the same of the degree Celsius, and so we can use °C instead of K for any temperature difference.

$$\Delta T = \frac{Q}{ms} = \frac{2450 \ J}{254 \ g \ \times 4.18 \frac{J}{g\,K}} = 2.31 \ °C$$

This is the change in temperature, so the final temperature is: $22.0 + 2.31 = 24.3\,°C$

> 2. How much heat is needed to raise the temperature of 45.2 g Cu by 50.0 °C?

Solution

$$Q = m \times s \times \Delta T = 45.2\ g\ \times 0.385\ \frac{J}{g\ K} \times 50.0\ K = 870. J$$

Here, we used the specific heat of Cu, of course (look it up).

Objective 125. Calculate the final temperature when two substances or solutions of different initial temperatures are mixed.

> 1. 25.0 g of water at 25.0 ° is mixed with 75.0 g water at 75.0 °C. What is the final temperature reached after mixing?

Solution

When two quantities of (same or different) substance(s) at different temperatures are put together, heat is transferred from the hot substance to the cold substance until equilibrium is reached:

$$Q_{hot} = Q_{cold} \quad (heat\ released\ by\ hot\ substance = heat\ absorbed\ by\ cold\ substance)$$

$$m_{hot} \times s \times \left(T_{hot} - T_{eq}\right) = m_{cold} \times s \times \left(T_{eq} - T_{cold}\right)$$

We set up the equations this way so that both heats are positive in value. We need to solve for T_{eq} :

$$m_{hot}T_{hot} - m_{hot}T_{eq} = m_{cold}T_{eq} - m_{cold}T_{cold}$$

$$m_{hot}T_{hot} + m_{cold}T_{cold} = (m_{cold} + m_{hot})T_{eq}$$

$$T_{eq} = \frac{m_{hot}T_{hot} + m_{cold}T_{cold}}{m_{cold} + m_{hot}} = \frac{25.0\ g\ \times 298.1\ K + 75.0\ g\ \times 348.1\ K}{25.0\ g + 75.0\ g} = 335.5\ K = 62.4\,°C$$

Here, because we are dealing with actual temperatures and not differences, we must use K and not °C (to prevent values such as 0°C to invalidate the calculation).

Does the answer make sense? Yes, we are mixing a little cold water with 3 times that mass of hot water, so the final temperature should lie closer to that of the hot water.

> 2. 28.0 g water is at 4.0 °C. How much hot water (at 90.0°C) is needed for the final temperature to reach 32°C?

Solution

Here, the unknown is the mass of hot water.

$$m_{hot} \times s \times (T_{hot} - T_{eq}) = m_{cold} \times s \times (T_{eq} - T_{cold})$$

$$m_{hot} \times (90.0 - 32.0)°C = 28.0 \ g \ \times (32.0 - 4.0)°C$$

$$m_{hot} = \frac{28.0 \ g \ \times 28.0 \ °C}{58.0 \ °C} = 13.5 \ g \ hot \ water \ (90°C)$$

Does the answer make sense? Yes, the target temperature is considerably closer to that of the cold water than to that of the hot water, so a smaller mass of hot water should be needed.

Objective 126. Calculate the heat capacity of a calorimeter or use the given heat capacity to determine the final temperature.

1. A calorimeter contains 125 g water at 25.0°C. 125 g water at 85.0°C is added, and soon thereafter the final temperature is 44.0°C. Calculate the heat capacity of the calorimeter.

Solution

The calorimeter is the device that holds the water, and being made out of matter, it should absorb heat as well. In the previous problem we neglected that heat. Now, we are going to determine the heat capacity of the calorimeter.

Heat released by hot water: $Q_{hot} = m_{hot} \times s \times (T_{hot} - T_{eq})$
Heat absorbed by cold water: $Q_{cold} = m_{cold} \times s \times (T_{eq} - T_{cold})$

Heat absorbed by the calorimeter: $Q_{cal} = C_{cal} \times (T_{eq} - T_{cold})$

where C_{cal} is the heat capacity of the calorimeter (characteristic to the object, not per unit of mass as specific heat is). Thus:

$$m_{hot} \times s \times (T_{hot} - T_{eq}) = m_{cold} \times s \times (T_{eq} - T_{cold}) + C_{cal} \times (T_{eq} - T_{cold})$$

$$m_{hot} \times s \times (T_{hot} - T_{eq}) - m_{cold} \times s \times (T_{eq} - T_{cold}) = C_{cal} \times (T_{eq} - T_{cold})$$

$$C_{cal} = \frac{m_{hot} \times s \times (T_{hot} - T_{eq}) - m_{cold} \times s \times (T_{eq} - T_{cold})}{T_{eq} - T_{cold}}$$

We can still use temperature in °C as if they were K (they are all differences), but the specific heat of water no longer cancels out.

$$C_{cal} = \frac{125g \times 4.18 \ \frac{J}{g \ K} \times (85.0 - 44.0)K - 125g \times 4.18 \ \frac{J}{g \ K} \times (44.0 - 25.0)K}{(44.0 - 25.0)K} = 605 \ \frac{J}{K}$$

2.   In a calorimeter with a heat capacity of 250. J/K, a block of Cu weighing 258 g and at a temperature of 227°C is placed into 245 g water at 27°C. What is the final temperature reached?

Solution

Heat released by copper block: $Q_{Cu} = m_{Cu} \times s_{Cu} \times (T_{Cu} - T_{eq})$

Heat absorbed by water: $Q_w = m_w \times s_w \times (T_{eq} - T_w)$

Heat absorbed by the calorimeter: $Q_C = C_C \times (T_{eq} - T_w)$ (same temperature as the water inside)

$$Q_{Cu} = Q_w + Q_C$$

$$m_{Cu} \times s_{Cu} \times (T_{Cu} - T_{eq}) = m_w \times s_w \times (T_{eq} - T_w) + C_C \times (T_{eq} - T_w)$$

$$m_{Cu} \times s_{Cu} \times T_{Cu} \ + \ m_w \times s_w \times T_w \ + \ C_C \times T_w = m_w \times s_w \times T_{eq} \ + \ m_{Cu} \times s_{Cu} \times T_{eq} \ + \ C_C \times T_{eq}$$

$$T_{eq} = \frac{m_{Cu} \times s_{Cu} \times T_{Cu} \ + \ m_w \times s_w \times T_w \ + \ C_C \times T_w}{m_w \times s_w \ + \ m_{Cu} \times s_{Cu} \ + \ C_C}$$

We will leave out the units for simplicity, after converting temperatures in K: 127°C = 400.K and 27°C = 300. K

$$T_{eq} = \frac{258 \times 0.385 \times 500. \ + 245 \times 4.18 \times 300. \ + \ 250. \times 300.}{245 \times 4.18 \ + \ 258 \times 0.385 \ + \ 250.} = 314 \ K = 41°C$$

As you can see, water has a very high specific heat, meaning that it can absorb a lot of heat without changing its temperature too much. A very hot (227 °C) block of copper of comparable mass only caused a 14°C change (the calorimeter absorbed heat too, of course, but much less).

Objective 127.   Calculate the heat released in a neutralization reaction.

1.   The enthalpy change when a strong acid is neutralized by strong base is –56.1 kJ/mol. If 12.0 mL of 6.00 M HBr at 25.0°C is mixed with 30.0 mL of 2.50 M NaOH, also at 25.0°C, what will the maximum temperature reached by the resulting solution? Assume that there is no heat loss to the container, that the specific heat of the final solution is 4.18 J/g K, and that the density of the final solution is 1.00 g/mL.

Solution

In this case the source of heat is the reaction of neutralization:

$$HBr + NaOH \ \rightarrow NaBr + H_2O$$

The amounts of reactants are:

$$12.0 \ mL \ \times 6.00 \ M = 72.0 \ mmol \ HBr$$

$$30.0 \; mL \times 2.50 \; M = 75.0 \; mmol \; NaOH$$

From this information we can see that HBr is the limiting reactant. Thus, the amount of heat produced will be:

$$56.1 \; \frac{kJ}{mol} \times 72.0 \; mmol \times \frac{1 \; mol}{1000 \; mmol} \times \frac{1000 \; J}{1 \; kJ} = 4040 \; J \; of \; heat$$

This heat is used to raise the temperature of the entire solution:

$$mass \; solution = volume \; solution \times density \; of \; solution = 42.0 \; mL \times 1.00 \frac{g}{mL} = 42.0 \; g$$

$$\Delta T = \frac{Q}{m \; s} = \frac{4040 \; J}{42.0 \; g \times 4.18 \; \frac{J}{g \; K}} = 23.0 \; K = 23.0 \; ^{\circ}C$$

The final temperature of the solution will be 25.0 + 23.0 = 48.0 °C.

Objective 128. Calculate the heat released or absorbed when a substance is dissolved in water.

1. The heat of solvation of ammonium nitrate is 26.2 kJ/mol. If a 5.368 g sample of NH_4NO_3 is added to 40.00 g of water in a calorimeter at 23.5°C, what is the minimum temperature reached by the solution? specific heat of water = 4.18 J/g·°C; heat capacity of the calorimeter = 250. J/°C

Solution

The positive value for the heat of solvation of ammonium nitrate means that when it dissolves, this salt absorbs heat, and so the solution cools. The calculations are similar:

$$5.368 \; g \; NH_3NO_3 \times \frac{1 \; mol}{80.043 \; g} \times \frac{26200 \; J}{mol} = 1757 \; J \; absorbed$$

$$Q = ms\Delta T + C\Delta T = (ms + C)\Delta T$$

$$\Delta T = \frac{Q}{m \; s + C} = \frac{1757 \; J}{(5.368 + 40.00)g \times 4.18 \; \frac{J}{g \; K} + 250 \frac{J}{K}} = 4.00 \; K = 4.00 \; ^{\circ}C$$

This heat is absorbed, so the temperature will go down:

$$23.5 \; ^{\circ}C - 4.00 \; ^{\circ}C = 19.5 \; ^{\circ}C$$

Objective 129.   Calculate the heat of combustion of a compound from calorimetric data.

1. A 0.1946 g piece of magnesium metal is burned in a constant-volume calorimeter that has a heat capacity of 1349 J/°C. The calorimeter contains 500. g of water and the temperature rise is 1.40°C. Calculate the heat of combustion of magnesium metal in kJ/g, given that the specific heat of water = 4.184 J/g·°C.

Solution

The source of the heat is the magnesium being burned, and the heat is transferred to the water and the calorimeter.

$$Q = ms\Delta T + C\Delta T = (ms + C)\Delta T$$

$$Q = \left(500.\,g \times 4.18\frac{J}{g\,K} + 1349\frac{J}{K}\right) \times 1.40\,K = 4815\,J$$

$$\frac{0.1946\,g\,Mg}{24.305\,g/mol} = 8.007 \times 10^{-3}\,mol\,Mg$$

Heat of combustion:

$$\frac{4815\,J}{8.007 \times 10^{-3}\,mol} = 601330\frac{J}{mol} = 601.3\frac{kJ}{mol}$$

This is a very large heat, but it is normal for a combustion reaction.

Worksheet 16. Thermochemistry

The exercises and problems in this section will allow you to practice the topic until you understand it well.

1. Write a chemical equation that represents the formation of each compound below from its constituent elements, then look up its enthalpy of formation and give the source.
    a. $NaNO_3$

    b. H_3PO_4

2. Balance and calculate the enthalpy change in each of the reactions below from the standard enthalpies of formation of reactants and products (look up these values).
    a. $C_2H_4 \text{ (g)} + O_2 \text{ (g)} \rightarrow CO_2 \text{ (g)} + H_2O \text{ (l)}$

    b. $H_2S \text{ (g)} + O_2 \text{ (g)} \rightarrow SO_2 \text{ (g)} + H_2O \text{ (l)}$

3. From the data in the previous problem, calculate the amount of heat released when 69.78 g C_2H_4 is combusted in air.

4. From the data in the previous problem, calculate the mass of C_2H_4 that will produce 666 kJ of heat.

5. When 10.0 g of n-propanol (C_3H_7OH) is burned in air, 334 kJ of heat is liberated. Calculate the heat of combustion of n-propanol in kJ/mol.

6. From the following enthalpies of reaction:

$$2Al_{(s)} + \frac{3}{2}O_{2\,(g)} \rightarrow Al_2O_{3\,(s)} \quad \Delta H°_1 = -1601 \; kJ \quad (1)$$

$$2Fe_{(s)} + \frac{3}{2}O_{2\,(g)} \rightarrow Fe_2O_{3\,(s)} \quad \Delta H°_2 = -821 \; kJ \quad (2)$$

Calculate the enthalpy of the following reaction:

$$2Al_{(s)} + Fe_2O_{3\,(s)} \rightarrow Al_2O_{3\,(s)} + 2Fe_{(s)} \quad (3)$$

7. From the following enthalpies of reaction:

$$2C_2H_{6\,(g)} + 7O_{2\,(g)} \rightarrow 4CO_{2\,(g)} + 6H_2O_{(l)} \quad \Delta H°_1 = -3119.6 \; kJ \quad (1)$$

$$C_{(s)} + O_{2\,(g)} \rightarrow CO_{2\,(g)} \qquad\qquad\qquad \Delta H°_2 = -393.5 \; kJ \quad (2)$$

$$H_{2\,(g)} + \frac{1}{2}O_{2\,(g)} \rightarrow H_2O_{(l)} \qquad\qquad \Delta H°_3 = -285.8 \; kJ \quad (3)$$

Calculate the enthalpy of the following reaction:

$$2C_{(s)} + 3H_{2\,(g)} \rightarrow C_2H_{6\,(g)} \qquad\qquad (4)$$

8. A mass of water of 98.5 g, initially at 82.0 °C, is allowed to cool to 25.5°C. What is the quantity of heat released?

9. A 50.0 g block of iron, initially at 15.0°C, absorbs 880 J of heat. What is its final temperature?

10. 50.0 g of water at 15.0 ° is mixed with 80.0 g water at 85.0 °C. What is the final temperature reached after mixing?

11. 125 g of water is at 90.0 °C. How much water at 5.0°C must be added in order to reach a final temperature of 30.0°C?

12. A calorimeter contains 50.0 g water at 22.0°C. 50.0 g water at 82.0°C is added, and soon thereafter the final temperature is 48.0°C. Calculate the heat capacity of the calorimeter.

13. In a calorimeter with a heat capacity of 350 J/K, a block of silver weighing 158 g and at a temperature of 195°C is placed into 340. g water at 22.5°C. What is the final temperature reached?

14. The enthalpy change when a strong monoprotic acid is neutralized by a strong monoacidic base is −56.1 kJ/mol. If 135 mL of 0.450 M HI at 23.15°C is mixed with 145 mL of 0.500 M NaOH, also at 23.15°C, what will the maximum temperature reached by the resulting solution? Assume that there is no heat loss to the container, that the specific heat of the final solution is 4.18 J/g·°C, and that the density of the final solution is 1.05 g/mL.

15. The heat of solvation of ammonium chloride is 15.2 kJ/mol. If an 8.224 g sample of NH_4Cl is added to 85.0 mL of water in a calorimeter at 24.5°C, what is the minimum temperature reached by the solution? Constants: specific heat of water = 4.18 J/g·°C; heat capacity of the calorimeter = 450. J/°C

Self-assessment

Using the scale indicated, rate your understanding of each learning objective at the completion of this lesson. Identify the areas where your understanding is weak or medium and discuss with your class mates and/or instructor. Write down specific questions you still have at the completion of this topic.

Learning objective	Self-assessment 3 = strong, 2 = medium, 1 = weak, 0 = not done
	3 2 1 0
	3 2 1 0
	3 2 1 0
	3 2 1 0
	3 2 1 0
	3 2 1 0
	3 2 1 0
	3 2 1 0
	3 2 1 0
	3 2 1 0
	3 2 1 0

Lesson 17 – Gas Laws

Learning Objectives

In this lesson you will learn:

- To convert between various **units of pressure**
- To calculate the **pressure** or **volume** of a gas using **Boyle's Law**
- To calculate the **volume** or **temperature** of a gas using **Charles' Law**.
- To calculate the **pressure** or **temperature** of a gas using **Gay-Lussac's Law**
- To calculate the **volume** or **amount** of a gas using **Avogadro's Law**
- To calculate a parameter of a gas using the **combined gas law** when 5 parameters are known
- To calculate a parameter of a gas using the **ideal gas law** when 3 parameters are known
- To calculate the **molar mass** or **density** of an ideal gas using the ideal gas law
- To calculate the **partial pressure** and **molar fraction** of a gas in a mixture
- To calculate the **root mean square speed** of the molecules of an ideal gas
- To calculate quantities of reactants or products using **gas stoichiometry**

Pre-requisites: Units and measurement; Stoichiometry.

Self-study questions

Before you start studying the worked examples, you should be able to formulate answers to the questions below. Use a textbook of your choice, or an online source of information, to find the answers.

1. How is a gas different than the other states of matter?
2. What is pressure?
3. What are the various units for pressure?
4. What are the units for temperature that we must use in gas laws?
5. What does Boyle's law say?
6. What does Charles' law say?
7. What does Gay-Lussac's law say?
8. What does Avogadro's law say?
9. What does Dalton's law say?
10. What is mole fraction?
11. What is partial pressure?
12. What are the units for the density of a gas?
13. What is the root mean square speed?

Worked examples

This section contains solved problems that cover the learning objectives listed above. Study each example carefully and make notes in the workbook to check every example that you understood. Repeat several times what you don't understand at first. It should become clearer as you keep working on the examples.

Objective 130.   Convert between various units of pressure.

Convert the following pressure values into the given units:

1.   730 mmHg to atm
2.   2.45 atm to Pa
3.   3.2 kbar to mmHg

Solutions

1.   730 mmHg to atm

$$730 \; mmHg \; \times \; \frac{1 \; atm}{760 \; mm \; Hg} = 0.96 \; atm$$

2.   2.45 atm to Pa

$$2.45 \; atm \; \times \; \frac{101325 \; Pa}{1 \; atm} = 2.48 \times 10^5 \; Pa$$

3.   3.2 bar to mmHg

$$3.2 \; bar \; \times \; \frac{100000 \; Pa}{1 \; bar} \times \frac{1 \; atm}{101325 \; Pa} \times \frac{760 \; mmHg}{1 \; atm} = 2400 \; mm \; Hg$$

Objective 131.   Calculate the pressure or volume of a gas using Boyle's Law.

1.   A gas occupying a volume of 725 mL at a pressure of 0.970 atm is allowed to expand at constant temperature until its pressure reaches 0.541 atm. What is its final volume?

Solution

There are quite a few gas laws, as you surely noticed. Which one should you use in a numerical problem involving gases depends of course on what is given in the problem and what the question is. Read the text of the problem carefully, write down the variables and the unknown, and choose the appropriate equation.

We are given a volume and a pressure, and the gas expands at constant temperature; therefore, we use Boyle's law:

$$P_1 V_1 = P_2 V_2$$

$$V_2 = \frac{P_1 V_1}{P_2} = \frac{0.970 \; atm \; \times 725 \; mL}{0.541 \; atm} = 1300 \; mL = 1.30 \; L$$

2.   A sample of air occupies 3.8 L when the pressure is 1.2 atm. What pressure is required in order to compress it to 0.075 L?

Solution

$$P_1 V_1 = P_2 V_2$$

$$P_2 = \frac{P_1 V_1}{V_2} = \frac{1.2 \; atm \; \times 3.8 \; L}{0.075 \; L} = 61 \; atm$$

Objective 132. Calculate the volume or temperature of a gas using Charles' Law.

1. A sample of gas has a volume of 1.68 liters at 1 atmosphere pressure and 158 K. What is its volume at STP?

Solution

In these problems, the pressure is constant, and the volume and temperature vary. We use Charles' law. All temperatures must be in K. STP represents 0°C (273.15 K) and 1.00 atm. All temperatures must be in Kelvin for gas law problems.

$$\frac{V_1}{T_1} = \frac{V_2}{T_2} \quad \Rightarrow \quad V_2 = \frac{V_1 T_2}{T_1} = \frac{1.68\ L \times 273\ K}{158\ K} = 2.90\ L$$

Does the answer make sense? Yes, a gas expands when the temperature rises.

2. A 9.4 L volume of methane gas is heated from 25 °C at constant pressure. At what temperature will the gas occupy 32.5 L?

Solution

$$\frac{V_1}{T_1} = \frac{V_2}{T_2} \quad \Rightarrow \quad T_2 = \frac{T_1 V_2}{V_1} = \frac{298\ K \ \times 32.5\ L}{9.4\ L} = 1030\ K = 757\ ^\circ C$$

Objective 133. Calculate the pressure or temperature of a gas using Gay-Lussac's Law.

1. If a gas has a pressure of 0.873 atm at 196°C, what is its pressure at 37.2°C?

Solution

In these problems, the volume is constant, and the pressure and temperature vary. We use Gay-Lussac' law. All temperatures must be in K.

$$\frac{P_1}{T_1} = \frac{P_2}{T_2} \quad \Rightarrow \quad P_2 = \frac{P_1 T_2}{T_1} = \frac{0.873\ atm \times 310\ K}{469\ K} = 0.577\ atm$$

Does the answer make sense? Yes, when the temperature is lowered, the pressure decreases.

2. A certain amount of gas at 25°C and at a pressure of 0.600 atm is contained in a glass vessel. Suppose that the vessel can withstand a pressure of 4.00 atm. How high can you raise the temperature of the gas without bursting the vessel?

Solution

$$\frac{P_1}{T_1} = \frac{P_2}{T_2} \quad \Rightarrow \quad T_2 = \frac{T_1 P_2}{P_1} = \frac{298\ K \ \times 4.00\ atm}{0.600\ atm} = 1986\ K = 1713\ ^\circ C$$

Objective 134.   Calculate the volume or amount of a gas using Avogadro's Law.

1.   A flexible container has 0.025 mol of gas in it and its volume is 2.4 L. If 0.045 mol of gas is added to the container at constant pressure and temperature, what is the new volume of the gas?

Solution

Avogadro's law says that the volume of a gas is proportional to the number of moles at constant pressure, or that the pressure is proportional to the number of moles at constant volume.

$$\frac{V_1}{n_1} = \frac{V_2}{n_2} \quad \Rightarrow \quad V_2 = \frac{V_1 n_2}{n_1} = \frac{2.4\ L\ \times (0.025 + 0.045)\ mol}{0.025\ mol} = 6.7\ L$$

Objective 135.   Calculate a parameter of a gas using the combined gas law when 5 parameters are known.

1.   A gas-filled balloon having a volume of 4.50 L at 1.05 atm and 25°C is allowed to rise to the stratosphere, where the temperature and pressure are -23°C and 4.00×10^{-3} atm, respectively. Calculate the final volume of the balloon.

Solution

The combined gas law allows calculating one parameter (volume, pressure, or temperature) when all three change. You will recognize this type of problem from the data, because 5 values must be known in order to determine the 6th.

The unknown is the final volume, and the "combined gas law" can be used:

$$\frac{P_1 V_1}{T_1} = \frac{P_2 V_2}{T_2} \quad \Rightarrow \quad V_2 = \frac{P_1 V_1 T_2}{T_1 P_2} = \frac{1.05\ atm\ \times 4.50\ L\ \times 250\ K}{298\ K\ \times 4.00 \times 10^{-3}\ atm} = 991\ L$$

This is a huge volume, because the pressure is very low.

2.   A small container of gas was allowed to expand into a much larger one. If the small container had a volume of 325 ml at 3.6 atmospheres pressure and 25°C and the large container had a volume of 6830 ml and a final pressure of 0.180 atmospheres, what was the final temperature of the gas?

Solution

The unknown is the final temperature:

$$\frac{P_1 V_1}{T_1} = \frac{P_2 V_2}{T_2} \quad \Rightarrow \quad T_2 = \frac{P_2 V_2 T_1}{P_1 V_1} = \frac{0.180\ atm\ \times 6830\ mL\ \times 298\ K}{3.6\ atm\ \times 325\ mL} = 313\ K = 40.\,°C$$

3. A sample of gas with a volume of 436 ml at 1.43 atmospheres pressure and a temperature of 25°C is allowed to expand to a volume of 1.68 liters at a temperature of 15°C. What is the final pressure of the gas?

Solution

$$\frac{P_1V_1}{T_1} = \frac{P_2V_2}{T_2} \quad \Rightarrow \quad P_2 = \frac{P_1V_1T_2}{T_1V_2} = \frac{1.43\ atm\ \times 436\ mL\ \times 288\ K}{298\ K\ \times 1680\ mL} = 0.359\ atm$$

Objective 136. Calculate a parameter of a gas using the ideal gas law when 3 parameters are known.

1. A sample of nitrogen gas kept in a container of volume 2.3 L and at a temperature of 32°C exerts a pressure of 4.7 atm. Calculate the number of moles of gas present.

Solution

The ideal gas law refers to a stationary state of a gas (nothing changes). It allows to calculate one of the gas parameters (pressure, temperature, volume, or number of moles) when the other 3 are known. R is the ideal gas constant.

$$PV = nRT \quad \Rightarrow \quad n = \frac{PV}{RT} = \frac{4.7\ atm\ \times 2.3\ L}{0.0821\ \frac{L\ atm}{mol\ K}\ \times 305\ K} = 0.43\ mol$$

2. Given that 6.90 moles of carbon monoxide gas are present in a container of volume 30.4 L, what is the pressure of the gas (in atm) if the temperature is 62°C?

Solution

$$P = \frac{nRT}{V} = \frac{6.9\ mol\ \times 0.0821\ \frac{L\ atm}{mol\ K} \times 335\ K}{30.4\ L} = 6.25\ atm$$

3. What volume will 5.60 moles of sulfur hexafluoride gas occupy if the temperature and pressure of the gas are 128°C and 9.40 atm?

Solution

$$V = \frac{nRT}{P} = \frac{5.60\ mol\ \times 0.0821\ \frac{L\ atm}{mol\ K} \times 401\ K}{9.40\ atm} = 19.6\ L$$

Objective 137. Calculate the molar mass or density of an ideal gas using the ideal gas law.

1. At 741 torr and 27°C, 4.18 g of a gas occupy a volume of 2.40 L. What is the molar mass of the gas?

Solution

The molar mass (M below) of a gas is related to the density (d), pressure, and temperature of a gas through a derivation of the ideal gas law:

$$P = \frac{nRT}{V} = \frac{mRT}{MV} = \frac{m}{V} \times \frac{RT}{M} = \frac{dRT}{M}$$

$$M = \frac{dRT}{P} = \frac{mRT}{VP} = \frac{4.18\ g \times 0.0821\ \frac{L\ atm}{mol\ K} \times 300.\ K}{2.40L \times 741\ torr \times \frac{1\ atm}{760\ torr}} = 44.0\ \frac{g}{mol}\ (perhaps\ CO_2)$$

2. Calculate the density of hydrogen bromide gas in g/L at 733 mmHg and 46°C.

Solution

$$d = \frac{MP}{RT} = \frac{80.912\ \frac{g}{mol} \times 733\ mmHg \times \frac{1\ atm}{760\ mmHg}}{0.0821\ \frac{L\ atm}{mol\ K} \times 319\ K} = 2.98\ g/L$$

Objective 138. Calculate the partial pressure and molar fraction of a gas in a mixture.

1. A mixture of gases contains methane, argon, and nitrogen. If the partial pressure of argon is 23.40 mmHg, nitrogen is 67.45 mmHg, and the total pressure is 723.57 mmHg, what is the partial pressure of methane?

Solution

The total pressure of a mixture of gases is the sum of the individual partial pressures: $P_{total} = \sum P_{partial}$

$$P_{N_2} + P_{CH_4} + P_{Ar} = P_{total} \quad \Rightarrow \quad P_{CH_4} = P_{total} - P_{N_2} - P_{Ar}$$

$$P_{CH_4} = 723.57\ mmHg - 67.45\ mmHg - 23.40\ mmHg = 632.72\ mmHg$$

2. A gas sample has the following partial pressures: P(oxygen) = 234 mmHg, P(nitrogen) = 579 mmHg, and P(water) = 282 mmHg. What is the mole fraction of water in the gas mixture?

Solution

The mole fraction of each gas in a mixture: $X_{gas\ A} = \frac{moles\ A}{total\ moles} = \frac{P_{gas\ A}}{P_{total}}$ (the ratio between the partial pressure of the gas and the total pressure of the mixture)

$$P_{total} = P_{oxygen} + P_{nitrogen} + P_{water} = 234 + 579 + 282 = 1095 \; mmHg$$

$$X_{water} = \frac{P_{water}}{P_{total}} = \frac{282 \; mmHg}{1095 \; mmHg} = 0.258$$

The mole fraction is a dimensionless number.

---

3. A mixture of gases contains 0.31 mol CH_4, 0.25 mol C_2H_6, and 0.29 mol C_3H_8. The total pressure is 1.50 atm. Calculate the partial pressure of each gas.

Solution

Total number of moles: $0.31 + 0.25 + 0.29 = 0.85 \; mol$

$$P_{CH_4} = X_{CH_4} \times P_{total} = \frac{0.31 \; mol \; CH_4}{0.85 \; mol \; total} \times 1.50 \; atm = 0.55 \; atm$$

$$P_{C_2H_6} = X_{C_2H_6} \times P_{total} = \frac{0.25 \; mol \; C_2H_6}{0.85 \; mol \; total} \times 1.50 \; atm = 0.44 \; atm$$

$$P_{C_3H_8} = X_{C_3H_8} \times P_{total} = \frac{0.29 \; mol \; C_3H_8}{0.85 \; mol \; total} \times 1.50 \; atm = 0.51 \; atm$$

Check: is the sum of partial pressures equal to the total pressure?

$$0.55 + 0.44 + 0.51 = 1.50 \; atm$$

Objective 139.   Calculate the root mean square speed of the molecules of an ideal gas.

1. Calculate the average speed of an oxygen molecule at room temperature (25 °C).

Solution

We use the kinetic-molecular theory formula:

$$u_{rms} = \sqrt{\frac{3RT}{M}} = \sqrt{\frac{3 \times 8.314 \; \frac{J}{mol \; K} \times 298 \; K}{3.200 \times 10^{-2} \; kg/mol}} = 482 \; m/s$$

Note that the molar mass of the gas must be expressed in kg/mol in order for all units to cancel out. This is the only case when molar mass is in kg/mol. Also, note that the value of R that we must here is not the same as the value we used in all gas law studied.

Objective 140.　Calculate quantities of reactants or products using gas stoichiometry.

1.　What volume of $NO_{(g)}$ at 750 mmHg and 20°C can be made by the reaction of 0.512 g of copper with an excess of nitric acid according to the reaction:
$$3Cu_{(s)} + 8HNO_{3\,(aq)} \rightarrow 3Cu(NO_3)_{2\,(aq)} + 2NO_{(g)} + 4H_2O_{(l)}$$

Solution

Gas stoichiometry is no different than normal stoichiometry, but may use gas parameters instead of mass. We apply normal stoichiometry first:

$$0.512\ g\ Cu \times \frac{1\ mol\ Cu}{63.546\ g} \times \frac{2\ mol\ NO}{3\ mol\ Cu} = 0.005371\ mol\ NO\ obtained$$

Then we use the ideal gas law to find the volume in the conditions given:

$$PV = nRT \quad \Rightarrow \quad V = \frac{nRT}{P} = \frac{0.005371\ mol\ NO\ \times 0.0821\ \frac{L\ atm}{mol\ K} \times 293\ K}{750\ mmHg\ \times \frac{1\ atm}{760\ mmHg}} = 0.131\ L\ NO$$

2.　Calculate the volume of nitrogen will be produced by the decomposition of 5.63 g of sodium azide at a pressure of 1060 mmHg and a temperature of 39.3°C.
$$2NaN_{3\,(s)} \rightarrow 2Na_{(s)} + 3N_{2\,(g)}$$

Solution

$$5.63\ g\ NaN_3 \times \frac{1\ mol\ NaN_3}{65.01\ g} \times \frac{3\ mol\ N_2}{2\ mol\ NaN_3} = 0.130\ mol\ N_2$$

The amount of nitrogen gas produced can now be converted into a volume using the ideal gas law:

$$V = \frac{nRT}{P} = \frac{0.130\ mol\ NO\ \times 0.0821\ \frac{L\ atm}{mol\ K} \times 312.4\ K}{1060\ mmHg\ \times \frac{1\ atm}{760\ mmHg}} = 2.40\ L\ N_2$$

3.　The combustion of butane produces both carbon dioxide and water vapor. If 4.215 g of butane (C_4H_{10}) is burned in excess oxygen in a 3.15 liter container, what is the partial pressure of carbon dioxide if the container is at a temperature of 88.6°C?

Solution

The combustion of butane represents burning it in air (oxygen) with the formation of carbon dioxide and water:

$$2C_4H_{10} + 13O_2 \rightarrow 8CO_2 + 10H_2O$$

From stoichiometry:

$$4.215\ g\ C_4H_{10} \times \frac{1\ mol\ C_4H_{10}}{58.122\ g} \times \frac{8\ mol\ CO_2}{2\ mol\ C_4H_{10}} = 0.290\ mol\ CO_2$$

The amount of carbon dioxide produced can now be converted into a pressure using the ideal gas law:

$$P = \frac{nRT}{V} = \frac{0.290 \ mol \ \times 0.0821 \ \frac{L \ atm}{mol \ K} \times 361.7 \ K}{3.15 \ L} = 2.73 \ atm$$

If needed, the pressure of water vapor can be calculated in a similar manner.

Worksheet 17.   Gas Laws

The exercises and problems in this section will allow you to practice the topic until you understand it well.

1.   A gas occupying a volume of 50.4 L at a pressure of 2.56 atm is allowed to expand at constant temperature until its pressure reaches 0.996 atm. What is its final volume?

2.   A sample of air occupies 6.8 L when the pressure is 5.6 atm. What pressure is required in order to compress it to 250 mL at constant temperature?

3.   A sample of gas has a volume of 345 mL at 25.0°C. What will be its volume at 100.0°C at constant pressure?

4.   A 2.33 L volume of methane gas is heated from 298K at constant pressure. At what temperature will the gas occupy 12.0 L?

5.   If a gas has a pressure of 12.56 atm at 216°C, what is its pressure at -15.6°C at constant volume?

6.   A certain amount of gas at 25°C and at a pressure of 1.00 atm is contained in a closed steel vessel. At what temperature will the gas reach a pressure of 10.00 atm?

7.   A flexible container has 0.555 mol of gas in it and has a pressure of 1.215 atm. If 0.145 mol of gas is added to the container at constant temperature, what is the new pressure of the gas?

8. A gas-filled balloon having a volume of 50.0 L at 743 mmHg and 25°C is allowed to rise to the stratosphere, where the temperature and pressure are -22°C and 6.25×10^{-3} atm, respectively. Calculate the final volume of the balloon.

9. A small container of gas was allowed to expand into a much larger one. If the small container had a volume of 50.0 ml at 1.65 atmospheres pressure and 22.0°C and the large container had a volume of 2.50 L and a final temperature of 212°F, what is the final pressure of the gas?

10. A sample of gas with a volume of 22.4 L at 6.25 atmospheres pressure and a temperature of 25.5°C is allowed to expand to a pressure of 2.05 atm at a temperature of -15.5°C. What is the final volume of the gas?

11. A sample of carbon dioxide kept in a container of volume 525 mL and at a temperature of 0.0°C exerts a pressure of 3.55 atm. Calculate the number of moles of gas present.

12. Given that 0.456 moles of carbon monoxide gas are present in a container of volume 2.65 L. Calculate the pressure of the gas (in mmHg) at a temperature is -12°C.

13. At STP, 0.280 L of a gas has a mass of 0.400 g. Calculate the molar mass of the gas.

14. Calculate the density of carbon dioxide gas in grams per liter at 2.50 bar and 95°F.

15. Air contains 21% oxygen by volume. What is the partial pressure of oxygen in air when the atmospheric pressure is 0.85 atm?

16. A mixture of gases contains 0.156 mol oxygen, 0.336 mol nitrogen, and 0.0112 mol carbon dioxide. The total pressure is 2.55 atm. Calculate the mole fraction and the partial pressure of each gas.

17. Calculate the average speed of a carbon dioxide molecule at -25 °C.

18. Calculate the volumes of hydrogen gas and oxygen gas at 1.00 atm and 25°C necessary to make 10.0 g water.

Self-assessment

Using the scale indicated, rate your understanding of each learning objective at the completion of this lesson. Identify the areas where your understanding is weak or medium and discuss with your class mates and/or instructor. Write down specific questions you still have at the completion of this topic.

Learning objective	Self-assessment 3 = strong, 2 = medium, 1 = weak, 0 = not done
	3 2 1 0
	3 2 1 0
	3 2 1 0
	3 2 1 0
	3 2 1 0
	3 2 1 0
	3 2 1 0
	3 2 1 0
	3 2 1 0
	3 2 1 0
	3 2 1 0

Lesson 18 –   Liquids, Solids, and Intermolecular Forces

Learning Objectives

In this lesson you will learn:

- To calculate the **density** of a crystalline solid given its **unit cell** parameters
- To calculate the **atomic radius** or other characteristic of a **crystalline solid**
- To calculate the amount of **heat** involved in **phase changes** for a pure substance
- To determine the main type of **intermolecular forces** in a given compound

Pre-requisites: Units and measurement; Moles; Molecular structure; Thermochemistry.

Self-study questions

Before you start studying the worked examples, you should be able to formulate answers to the questions below. Use a textbook of your choice, or an online source of information, to find the answers.

1. What is the difference between polar and nonpolar bonds?
2. What is a dipole?
3. What is a net dipole moment?
4. List the main types of intermolecular forces.
5. When do hydrogen bonds occur?
6. What is a phase change?
7. List all the phase changes by name.
8. What happens to the temperature during a phase change?
9. List the types of solids (by internal structure).
10. What is a unit cell?
11. List the main types of cubic unit cells.
12. Give the average number of particles per each type of cubic unit cell.
13. Make a drawing for each type of cubic unit cells and show which atoms are adjacent (touch).

Worked examples

This section contains several solved examples that cover the learning objectives listed above. Study each example carefully and make notes in the workbook to check every example that you understood. Repeat several times what you don't understand at first. It should become clearer as you keep working on the examples.

Objective 141. Calculate the density of a crystalline solid given its unit cell parameters.

1. Lithium crystallizes in a body-centered cubic unit cell with edge length 350.9 pm. Calculate the density of Li.

Discussion

The density of a metal (or a crystalline solid in general) is a property that originates from the crystal structure. The unit cell is the smallest entity that maintains the properties of the entire solid, so if we find the density of the unit cell itself, we have the density of the solid.

$$density\ of\ unit\ cell = \frac{mass\ of\ unit\ cell}{volume\ of\ unit\ cell} = \frac{mass\ of\ all\ particles\ in\ the\ unit\ cell}{volume\ of\ unit\ cell}$$

$$= \frac{number\ of\ atoms\ per\ cell\ \times mass\ of\ one\ atom}{cube\ of\ edge\ length\ of\ unit\ cell} = \frac{n \times \frac{MM}{N_A}}{a^3}$$

where n is the average number of particles (atoms or ions) per unit cell, MM is the molar mass of the element or ion as appropriate, N_A is Avogadro's number, and a is the edge length of the unit cell. Remember the average number of particles per type of cubic unit cell:

Type of unit cell	Average # of particles per cell
Simple cubic	1
Body centered cubic	2
Face centered cubic	4

Solution

The first thing to do is convert the edge length in cm, since the density will be in g/cm^3 :

$$350.9\ pm\ \times \frac{1\ m}{10^{12}\ pm} \times \frac{100\ cm}{1\ m} = 3.509 \times 10^{-8}\ cm$$

$$d = \frac{2\ atoms \times 6.941\ \frac{g}{mol}}{6.022 \times 10^{23}\ \frac{atoms}{mol} \times (3.509 \times 10^{-8}\ cm)^3} = 0.5335\ g/cm^3$$

Objective 142. Calculate the atomic radius or other characteristic of a crystalline solid

1. Rubidium crystallizes in a body-centered cubic unit cell. Its density is 1.63 g/cm^3. Calculate the atomic radius of rubidium.

Solution

The formula for density derived above can be used to calculate other things, such as the edge length, the number of particles per cell, the molar mass of the solid, or even Avogadro's number, when the rest of the parameters are known. Here, we need to remember the relationship between atomic radius and edge length, which depends on the type of cubic cell. Review Appendix C.

$$d = \frac{n \times \frac{MM}{N_A}}{a^3} = \frac{n \times MM}{N_A \times a^3} \quad \Rightarrow \quad a = \sqrt[3]{\frac{n \times MM}{N_A \times d}} = \sqrt[3]{\frac{2 \; atoms \times 85.4678 \frac{g}{mol}}{6.022 \times \frac{10^{23} atoms}{mol} \times 1.63 \frac{g}{cm^3}}} = 5.58 \times 10^{-8} cm$$

For a body centered unit cell:

$$r = \frac{a\sqrt{3}}{4} = \frac{5.58 \times 10^{-8} cm \times \sqrt{3}}{4} = 2.42 \times 10^{-8} \; cm$$

Now let's convert this value to pm, a more convenient unit for atomic distances:

$$2.42 \times 10^{-8} \; cm \times \frac{10^{10} \; pm}{1 \; cm} = 242 \; pm$$

Similar problems under this section can ask:

- Identify the metal
- Identify the type of unit cell
- Determine Avogadro's number calculated by this method

Derive an equation for each of these further types of problems involving cubic unit cells.

Objective 143. Calculate the amount of heat involved in phase changes for a pure substance.

1.   How much energy is required to convert 44.9 g of ice at −28.0°C to steam at 143°C ?

Discussion

We need to supply heat to transform ice into water and further into steam. The following diagram represents how temperature varies with heat supplied, and will allow you to better understand the changes of phase.

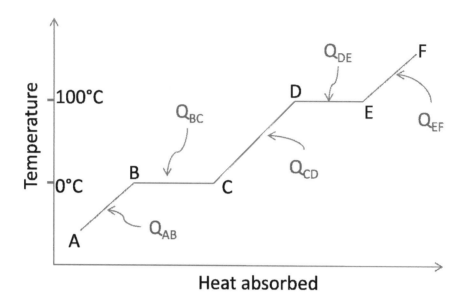

The different stages in the process of converting ice to steam are represented by the letters A through F.
*   A—B represents the heating of ice from the initial temperature up to 0°C
*   B—C represents the melting of ice, when temperature stays constant, and all the heat absorbed is used to change phase from solid to liquid (liquid state has more energy than solid)
*   C—D represents the heating of water from 0°C to 100°C
*   D—E represents the boiling of water, when the temperature stays constant while the liquid water absorbs heat to convert to gas phase (steam)
*   E—F represents the further heating of steam above 100°C.

Each of the 5 processes represented in the diagram require their own quantities of heat, which will be calculated differently:

A—B is warming up a substance, and the heat is calculated according to the calorimetry equation:

$$Q_{AB} = m_{ice} \times s_{ice} \times \Delta T_{AB}$$

B—C is a change of phase and requires the enthalpy of fusion (melting) of water:

$$Q_{BC} = \Delta H_{fusion}(H_2O) \times moles\ H_2O$$

C—D is again calorimetry:

$$Q_{CD} = m_{water} \times s_{water} \times \Delta T_{CD}$$

D—E is another change of phase:

$$Q_{DE} = \Delta H_{vaporization}(H_2O) \times moles\ H_2O$$

E—F is again calorimetry:

$$Q_{EF} = m_{steam} \times s_{steam} \times \Delta T_{EF}$$

In all of the above, the mass of the substance will be the same no matter the state, so:

$$m_{ice} = m_{water} = m_{steam}$$

The three specific heats of H_2O are different for the three states of matter of water. You can look them up:

$$specific\ heat\ of\ ice\ = s_{ice} =\ 2.09\ J/g\,°C$$
$$specific\ heat\ of\ water\ = s_{water} =\ 4.18\ J/g\,°C$$
$$specific\ heat\ of\ steam\ = s_{steam} =\ 1.84\ J/g\,°C$$

Also, the enthalpies of fusion and vaporization of water are published:

$$enthalpy\ of\ fusion\ of\ ice = \Delta H_{fus}\ =\ 6.02\ kJ/mol$$
$$enthalpy\ of\ vaporization\ of\ water =\ \Delta H_{vap}\ =\ 40.7\ kJ/mol$$

Because these last two quantities are given in kJ/mol, we need to convert the mass of ice given in moles:

$$44.9\ g\ ice\ \times\ \frac{1\ mol\ H_2O}{18.015\ g} = 2.49\ mol\ H_2O$$

Solution

Now we can calculate all the heats required:

$$Q_{AB} = 44.9\ g\ \times 2.09\frac{J}{g°C} \times 28.0°C = 2627\ J$$

$$Q_{BC} = 6.02\frac{kJ}{mol} \times 2.49\ mol = 14.99\ kJ = 14990\ J$$

$$Q_{CD} = 44.9\ g\ \times 4.18\frac{J}{g°C} \times 100°C = 18768\ J$$

$$Q_{DE} = 40.7\frac{kJ}{mol} \times 2.49\ mol = 101.343\ kJ = 101343\ J$$

$$Q_{EF} = 44.9\ g\ \times 1.84\frac{J}{g°C} \times 43°C = 3552\ J$$

Obviously all the heats must be in the same unit, because the total heat is the sum of all 5 heats:

$$Q_{total} = Q_{AB} + Q_{BC} + Q_{CD} + Q_{DE} + Q_{EF} = 141281\,J = 141\,kJ$$

This is the final answer to the proper number of significant figures.

---

2.   How much energy is required to take 150 g of ice at -10°C and convert it to water at 37°C?

Solution

Hint: in this case, you do not need the full diagram. Whatever the problem wants can be fit into the diagram above. Here, ice is at -10°C, it melts, and it is heated to 37°C, so segments D—E and E—F are not needed, and the changes in temperature are obviously different. You can finish this problem on your own now.

Objective 144.   Determine the main type of intermolecular forces in a given compound.

1.   Indicate the main type of intermolecular forces that exist in the following substances or mixtures:
   a.   Methane
   b.   Water
   c.   Hydrogen chloride
   d.   Sodium chloride (solid)
   e.   Sodium chloride (aq)
   f.   Sulfur tetrachloride

Discussion

In order to determine the type of intermolecular forces in a compound, we need to identify: whether the compound is ionic or covalent, whether it is pure or in solution, and whether its molecule (if covalent) is nonpolar or polar. The following flow-chart will help with this decision process.

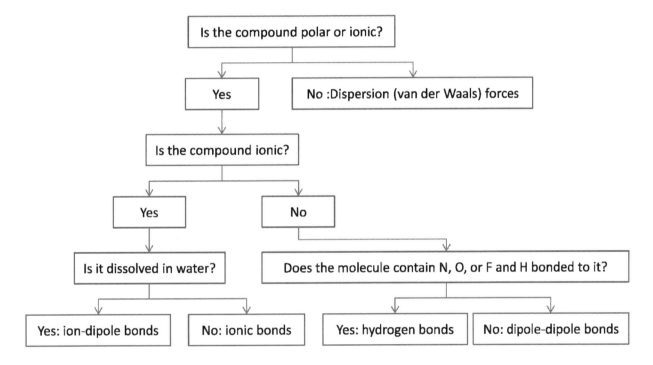

Solutions

a.   Methane

Methane has a tetrahedral geometry:

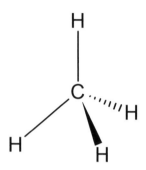

There is a small difference in electronegativity between C and H, but even though each bond in itself is slightly polar, the symmetrical geometry of the molecule means that all individual dipole moments cancel out, and overall the molecule is non-polar. For this reason, the intermolecular forces observed between methane molecules are **dispersion (or van der Waals) forces**.

b.   Water

Remember the geometry of the water molecule:

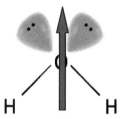

The molecule is polar because the individual bond dipoles do not cancel out. Thus, water molecules are polar and **dipole-dipole** forces exist. However, because water contains hydrogen atoms bonded to oxygen, there are also **hydrogen bonds**, which are stronger. To form hydrogen bonds, the molecule must contain F, O, or N, as well as H atoms bonded to one of these atoms.

c.   Hydrogen chloride

The molecule is linear and the H—Cl bond is polar, and so HCl has **dipole-dipole** forces between its molecules. There are no H bonds in this molecule.

d.   Sodium chloride (solid)

Ionic attraction forces exist between the Na^+ and Cl^- ions in solid state.

e.   Sodium chloride (aq)

In solution, the ions are surrounded by water molecules and form hydrated ions. We call these **ion-dipole** forces.

f.   Sulfur tetrachloride

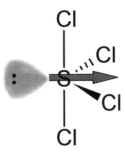

The geometry of this molecule (see-saw) is such that two dipoles are opposite each other and cancel out, but the other two (equatorial ones) do not, and so the molecule is polar and the intermolecular forces are **dipole-dipole**.

Worksheet 18.   Liquids, Solids, and Intermolecular Forces

The exercises and problems in this section will allow you to practice the topic until you understand it well.

1.   Tungsten crystallizes in a body-centered cubic unit cell with edge length 316.5 pm. Calculate its density.

2.   Gold crystallizes in a face-centered cubic unit cell with edge length 407.8 pm. Calculate its density.

3.   Polonium (Po) crystallizes in a simple cubic unit cell and has a density of 9.196 g/cm^3. Calculate the atomic radius of polonium.

4.   Palladium crystallizes in a face-centered cubic unit cell. Its density is 12.0 g/cm^3. Calculate the atomic radius of palladium.

5. Iron crystallizes in a body-centered cubic unit cell. Its 7.87 is density g/cm^3. Calculate the atomic radius of iron.

6. An unknown element crystallizes in a face-centered cubic unit cell with an edge length of 382.4 pm. The solid has a density of 22.59 g/cm^3. Identify the element.

7. Barium metal (density = 3.50 g/cm^3) crystallizes as BCC lattice with a cell edge length of 502 pm. Determine Avogadro's number calculated by this method.

8. Calculate the energy needed to take 325 ml of water at 20°C and convert it to steam at 100°C.

9. Calculate the energy needed to take 150 g of ice at -10°C and convert it to water at 37°C.

10. Calculate the energy needed to convert 23.3 g of ice at −13.0°C to steam at 183°C.

11. Indicate the main type of intermolecular forces that exist in each of the following substances or mixtures:
    a.   Carbon dioxide

    b.   Sulfur dioxide

    c.   Nitrogen gas

    d.   Ammonia

    e.   Ethanol (CH_3CH_2OH)

    f.   Calcium chloride dissolved in water

    g. SF_4

12. Use the diagram in the figure below for the questions that follow.

Phase Diagram for a Hypothetical Substance

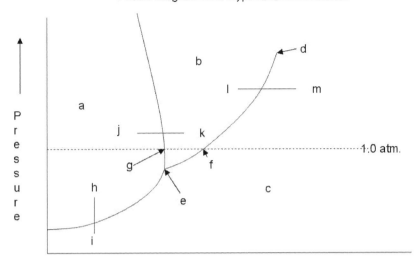

a. What is represented by point **e** on the diagram in the figure?

b. What is represented by point **f** on the diagram in the figure?

c. What is represented by point **d** on the diagram in the figure?

d. What is represented by point **c** on the diagram in the figure?

e. What is represented by point **a** on the diagram in the figure?

f. What phase change is represented in going from point **h** to point **i** along the line segment shown in the figure?

g. What phase change is represented in going from point **k** to point **j** along the line segment shown in the figure?

Self-assessment

Using the scale indicated, rate your understanding of each learning objective at the completion of this lesson. Identify the areas where your understanding is weak or medium and discuss with your class mates and/or instructor. Write down specific questions you still have at the completion of this topic.

Learning objective	Self-assessment 3 = strong, 2 = medium, 1 = weak, 0 = not done			
	3	2	1	0
	3	2	1	0
	3	2	1	0
	3	2	1	0

Lesson 19 –   Solutions and Colligative Properties

Learning Objectives

In this lesson you will learn:

- To convert between various ways of expressing the **concentration** of a solution
- To calculate the **molality** of a **saturated solution**
- To calculate the **effective concentration** of all particles in a solution
- To calculate numerical **colligative properties** of a solution: **freezing point depression**, **boiling point elevation**, **vapor pressure depression**, **osmotic pressure**

Pre-requisites: Solutions and concentration; Chemical reactions in solution.

Self-study questions

Before you start studying the worked examples, you should be able to formulate answers to the questions below. Use a textbook of your choice, or an online source of information, to find the answers.

1. What is molarity?
2. What is molality?
3. What is mole fraction?
4. What is mass percent composition?
5. What is a saturated solution?
6. What is the definition of solubility (as a quantitative property)?
7. What is a strong electrolyte?
8. What is a weak electrolyte?
9. What are colligative properties?
10. What is the van't Hoff factor?
11. What is meant by freezing point depression?
12. What is meant by boiling point elevation?
13. What is vapor pressure?
14. What is meant by vapor pressure depression?
15. What is osmotic pressure?

Worked examples

This section contains several solved examples that cover the learning objectives listed above. Study each example carefully and make notes in the workbook to check every example that you understood. Repeat several times what you don't understand at first. It should become clearer as you keep working on the examples.

Objective 145. Convert between various ways of expressing the concentration of a solution.

Complete the table below by converting between various types of concentrations from the quantities given. In all cases, the solvent is water, and assume that you have at your disposal exactly 100.00 mL of solution each time.

#	Solute	Density g/mL	Moles of solute	Molarity mol/L	Molality mol/kg solvent	Mass %	Mole fraction of solute
1	NaOH	1.1655		4.37			
2	H_2SO_4	1.0687				10.00	
3	CH_3COOH	1.0383			0.714		
4	HCl			6.016		20.00	

Discussion

Generally speaking:

$$concentration = \frac{quantity\ of\ solute}{quantity\ of\ solution\ or\ solvent}$$

Remember the various types of expressing the concentration of a solution:

$$M = \frac{n}{V} \quad \left(molarity = \frac{number\ of\ moles}{volume\ of\ solution\ in\ L}\right)$$

$$m = \frac{n}{m_{solvent}} \quad \left(molality = \frac{number\ of\ moles}{mass\ of\ solvent\ in\ kg}\right)$$

$$m\% = \frac{m_{solute}}{m_{solution}} \times 100 \quad \left(mass\ percent\ solute = \frac{mass\ of\ solute}{mass\ of\ solution} \times 100\right)$$

$$V\% = \frac{V_{solute}}{V_{solution}} \times 100 \quad \left(volume\ percent = \frac{volume\ of\ solute}{volume\ of\ solution} \times 100\right)$$

$$X_{solute} = \frac{n_{solute}}{n_{total}} \quad \left(mole\ fraction\ of\ solute = \frac{moles\ of\ solute}{moles\ solute + moles\ solvent}\right)$$

Solutions

In the table above, some of these quantities are given and we need to determine everything else. Let's proceed.

1. We have the density of the NaOH solution and its molarity. We need to find molality, mass percent of NaOH, and the mole fraction of NaOH. We also have the total volume of the solution (100.00 mL).

We can determine the moles first:

$$n = MV = 4.37 \frac{mol}{L} \times 100.00 \; mL = 437 \; mmol = 0.437 \; mol \; NaOH$$

In order to determine the molality, we need the mass of the solvent. From the volume of solution and its density we find its mass:

$$m = dV = 1.1655 \frac{g}{mL} \times 100.00 \; mL = 116.55 \; g \; solution$$

To find the mass of the solvent, we need to find and subtract the mass of the solute:

$$0.437 \; mol \; NaOH \; \times 40.00 \frac{g}{mol} = 17.48 \; g \; NaOH$$

$$116.55 \; g \; solution - 17.48 \; g \; NaOH = 99.07 \; g \; H_2O$$

Now we can calculate the molality:

$$m = \frac{0.437 \; mol \; NaOH}{0.09907 \; kg \; H_2O} = 4.41 \; m$$

The mass percent of NaOH:

$$\frac{17.48 \; g \; NaOH}{116.55 \; g \; solution} \times 100 = 15.00 \; \% \; NaOH$$

We need the moles of water to calculate the mole fraction:

$$\frac{99.07 \; g \; H_2O}{18.015 \; g/mol} = 5.499 \; mol \; H_2O$$

The mole fraction of NaOH:

$$\frac{0.437 \; mol \; NaOH}{0.437 + 5.499 \; mol \; total} = 0.0736$$

2. We have density and mass percent of sulfuric acid. We can find the mass of the solution and immediately the masses of solute and solvent:

$$m = dV = 1.0687 \frac{g}{mL} \times 100.00 \; mL = 106.87 \; g \; solution$$

$$106.87 \; g \; solution \times \frac{10.00}{100} = 10.687 \; g \; H_2SO_4$$

$$106.87 \; g \; solution \times \frac{90.00}{100} = 96.183 \; g \; H_2O$$

Moles of solute:

$$\frac{10.687 \; g \; H_2SO_4}{98.078 \; g/mol} = 0.1090 \; mol \; H_2SO_4$$

Molarity:

$$M = \frac{n}{V} = \frac{0.1090 \; mol}{0.10000 \; L} = 1.090 \; M$$

Molality:

$$m = \frac{0.1090 \; mol}{0.096183 \; kg \; H_2O} = 1.133 \; m$$

Mole fraction:

$$\frac{96.183 \; g \; H_2O}{18.015 \; g/mol} = 5.339 \; mol \; H_2O$$

$$\frac{0.1090 \; mol \; H_2SO_4}{0.1090 + 5.339} = 0.02000$$

3. We have density, molality, and volume of solution. These three quantities are unrelated so we cannot calculate molarity directly. We will need to set up an equation.

First we can determine the mass of the solution:

$$1.0383 \frac{g}{mL} \times 100.00 \; mL = 103.83 \; g \; solution$$

Let's denote the moles of solute (acetic acid) x. The mass of solute will thus be $60.052x$ (using the molar mass of acetic acid).

We express molality as a function of the unknown number of moles, x :

$$m = \frac{x \; mol \; CH_3COOH}{\dfrac{103.83 \; g \; solution - 60.052x \; g \; CH_3COOH}{1000 \; g/kg}} = \frac{1000x}{103.83 - 60.052x} = 0.714 \quad (given \; molality)$$

We solve for x:

$$1000x = 0.714(103.83 - 60.052x) = 74.135 - 42.877x$$

$$1042.877x = 74.135$$

$$x = 0.0711 \; mol \; CH_3COOH$$

Now we can calculate everything else. Molarity:

$$\frac{0.0711 \; mol}{0.10000 \; L} = 0.711 \; M$$

Mass of acetic acid:

$$0.0711 \; mol \; \times 60.052 \frac{g}{mol} = 4.27 \; g \; CH_3COOH$$

Mass of water:

$$103.83 \; g \; solution - 4.27 \; g \; CH_3COOH = 99.56 \; g \; H_2O$$

Moles of water:

$$\frac{99.56 \; g \; H_2O}{18.015 \; g/mol} = 5.527 \; mol \; H_2O$$

Mass percent acid:

$$\frac{4.27 \; g}{103.83 \; g} \times 100 = 4.11\% \; CH_3COOH$$

Mole fraction:

$$\frac{0.0711}{5.527 + 0.0711} = 0.0127$$

4. We have the molarity, volume, and mass percent of the solution. We can calculate other quantities directly:

Moles of solute:

$$6.016 \frac{mol}{L} \times 0.10000\ L = 0.6016\ mol\ HCl$$

Mass of solute:

$$0.6016\ mol\ \times 36.461 \frac{g}{mol} = 21.95\ g\ HCl$$

Mass of solution:

$$\frac{21.95\ g\ HCl}{mass\ solution} \times 100 = 20.00 \quad \Rightarrow \quad mass\ solution = \frac{21.95 \times 100}{20.00} = 109.75\ g$$

Mass of solvent:

$$109.75\ g\ solution - 21.95\ g\ HCl = 87.80\ g\ H_2O$$

Moles of solvent:

$$\frac{87.80\ g\ H_2O}{18.015\ g/mol} = 4.874\ mol\ H_2O$$

Molality:

$$\frac{0.6016\ mol\ HCl}{0.08780\ kg\ H_2O} = 6.852\ m$$

Density:

$$\frac{109.75\ g\ solution}{100.00\ mL} = 1.0975\ g/mL$$

Mole fraction:

$$\frac{0.6016}{0.6016 + 4.874} = 0.1099$$

Here is the final, completed table:

#	Solute	Density g/mL	Moles of solute	Molarity mol/L	Molality mol/kg solvent	Mass %	Mole fraction of solute
1	$NaOH$	1.1655	0.437	4.37	4.41	15.00	0.0736
2	H_2SO_4	1.0687	0.1090	1.090	1.133	10.00	0.02000
3	CH_3COOH	1.0383	0.0711	0.711	0.714	4.11	0.0127
4	HCl	1.0975	0.6016	6.016	6.852	20.00	0.1099

Objective 146. Calculate the molality of a saturated solution.

1. Using the solubility chart in Appendix D. determine the molality of a saturated solution of sodium nitrate at 20.0°C.

Solution

At 20.0°C we determine that the solubility of sodium nitrate is 88.0 g per 100.0 g water. This allows us to determine the molality:

Moles of solute:

$$\frac{88.0 \ g \ NaNO_3}{84.99 \ g/mol} = 1.04 \ mol \ NaNO_3$$

Molality:

$$\frac{1.04 \ mol}{0.1000 \ kg \ water} = 10.4 \ m$$

As we saw earlier, we can also calculate the mass percent composition of a saturated solution. We cannot calculate molarity and other mole-related concentration types unless we have the density of the solution.

Objective 147. Calculate the effective concentration of all particles in a solution.

Determine the concentration of all ions in each of the indicated solutions and complete the table below:

Compound	Concentration	Dissociation	Cation concentration	Anion concentration	Total species concentration
$NaNO_3$	0.500 M	$Na^+ + NO_3^-$	0.500 M	0.500 M	1.000 M
$CaCl_2$	0.250 M	$Ca^{2+} + 2Cl^-$	0.250 M	0.500 M	0.750 M
$Al_2(SO_4)_3$	0.500 m	$2Al^{3+} + 3SO_4^{2-}$	1.00 m	1.50 m	2.50 m

Solutions

Review the dissociation of salts in aqueous solution. The concentration of each ion in solution is dependent on how many of each ion are present in the formula unit of a salt. The total concentration of species in solution is the sum of all ion concentrations, as they add up. We need this concentration in the next objective.

Objective 148. Calculate the freezing point depression, boiling point elevation, and vapor pressure depression of a solution.

In each case below, assume that exactly 10.00 g of the substance indicated is dissolved in exactly 100.00 g water, and that the van't Hoff factor for each compound is equal to the number of particles resulting from 100% dissociation. Calculate the colligative properties: freezing point depression, boiling point elevation, and vapor pressure depression at 75°C by filling in the table below.

#	Solute	Van't Hoff	Moles solute	Molality Solute	Freezing point °C	Boiling point °C	Vapor pressure mmHg 75°C
1	Sucrose						
2	Na_2SO_4						

Solutions

Colligative properties depend on the number of particles in solution, and not on the nature of those particles. The total concentration of ions in a solution of a dissociated compound is what counts. We simplify the concentrations above by using what we call the van't Hoff factor, which is the number of particles that result from the 100% dissociation of a compound in solution.

Freezing point depression:

$$\Delta T_f = K_f \times m \times i$$

where K_f is the freezing point depression constant of the solvent (look it up), m is the molality of the solute, and i is the van't Hoff factor. Similarly, the boiling point elevation:

$$\Delta T_b = K_b \times m \times i$$

Data for a few solvents is given in the table below.

Solvent	Normal freezing point °C	K_f °C/m	Normal boiling point °C	K_b °C/m
Water	0.0	1.86	100.0	0.52
Benzene	5.5	5.12	80.1	2.53
Ethanol	-117.3	1.99	78.4	1.22
Acetic acid	16.6	3.90	117.9	2.93
Cyclohexane	6.6	20.0	80.7	2.79

Vapor pressure depression:

$$\Delta P = X_{solute} \times P^0_{solvent} \times i$$

where X_{solute} is the mole fraction of all the species that represent the solute (all ions, for example), and $P^0_{solvent}$ is

289

the vapor pressure of the pure solvent (this is Raoult's law). The vapor pressure of the solvent depends on temperature.

1. Sucrose

Sucrose ($C_{12}H_{22}O_{11}$), or sugar, is a covalent compound and it does not dissociate into ions. Thus, its van't Hoff factor is 1, and the effective concentration in solution is equal to the concentration of sucrose.

Moles of sucrose:

$$\frac{10.0 \ g \ sucrose}{342.297 \ g/mol} = 0.0292 \ mol \ sucrose$$

Molality:

$$\frac{0.0292 \ mol}{0.100 \ kg \ water} = 0.292 \ m$$

Freezing point depression:

$$\Delta T_f = 1.86 \times 0.292 \times 1 = 0.543 \ °C$$

Since the freezing point of a solution goes down from that of the solvent (depression), the new freezing point of this solution will be -0.541°C.

Boiling point elevation:

$$\Delta T_b = 0.515 \times 0.292 \times i = 0.150 \ °C$$

The boiling point of this solution will be 100.15 °C.

Vapor pressure:

$$\frac{100.0 \ g \ H_2O}{18.015 \ g/mol} = 5.551 \ mol \ H_2O$$

$$X_{sucrose} = \frac{0.0292}{0.0292 + 5.551} = 0.00524$$

$$\Delta P = 0.00524 \times 289.1 \ mmHg = 1.52 \ mmHg$$

The value 289.1 mmHg is the vapor pressure of water at 75°C (look up other values in Appendix E.) Vapor pressure goes down, so the new vapor pressure of this solution will be:

$$289.1 - 1.52 = 287.6 \ mmHg$$

2. Sodium sulfate

Sodium sulfate dissociates into three ions so the van't Hoff factor is 3.

Molality:

$$\frac{10.0 \ g \ Na_2SO_4}{142.042 \ g/mol} = 0.0704 \ mol \ Na_2SO_4$$

$$\frac{0.0704 \ mol}{0.100 \ kg} = 0.704 \ m$$

Freezing point depression:

$$\Delta T_f = 1.853 \times 0.704 \times 3 = 3.91\,°C$$

Boiling point elevation:

$$\Delta T_b = 0.515 \times 0.704 \times 3 = 1.09\,°C$$

Vapor pressure:

$$X_{solute} = \frac{0.0704 \times 3}{0.0704 + 5.551} = 0.0367$$

$$\Delta P = 0.0367 \times 289.1\,mmHg = 10.7\,mmHg$$

$$289.1 - 10.7 = 278.4\,mmHg$$

The completed table:

#	Solute	Van't Hoff	Moles solute	Molality Solute	Freezing point °C	Boiling point °C	Vapor pressure mmHg 75°C
1	Sucrose	1	0.0292	0.292	-0.541	100.15	287.6
2	Na_2SO_4	3	0.0704	0.704	-3.91	101.09	285.5

Objective 149. Calculate the osmotic pressure of a solution.

Calculate the osmotic pressure of a 0.0500 M solution of aluminum sulfate at 25.0°C.

Solution

The osmotic pressure of a solution can be calculated with the formula:

$$\pi = M \times R \times T \times i$$

where M is the molarity of the solution, R is the ideal gas constant (0.0821 L atm / mol K) and T is the absolute temperature. Osmotic pressure could not be calculated in the previous problem, because it depends on molarity rather than molality or mole fraction, and thus the densities of the solutions should have been known. We assume complete dissociation of aluminum sulfate and no ion pairing:

$$Al_2(SO_4)_3 \rightarrow 2Al^{3+} + 3SO_4^{2-}$$

$$\pi = 0.0500\frac{mol}{L} \times 0.0821\frac{L\,atm}{mol\,K} \times 298\,K \times 5 = 6.12\,atm$$

Worksheet 19. Colligative properties

The exercises and problems in this section will allow you to practice the topic until you understand it well.

1. Complete the table below by converting between various types of concentrations from the quantities given. In all cases, the solvent is water, and assume that you have at your disposal exactly 100.00 mL of solution each time.

#	Solute	Molar mass g/mol	Density g/mL	Moles of solute	Molarity mol/L	Molality mol/kg solvent	Mass %	Mole fraction of solute
1	H_2SO_4		1.3070		5.33			
2	CH_3COOH		1.0055				5.00	
3	NaOH		1.5290			25.00		
4	NH_3			0.2304		2.451		

2. Complete the table below. Refer to the solubility chart in the worked examples section. All solutions below are saturated solutions of the indicated salt at the indicated temperature.

#	Solute	Molar mass g/mol	Temperature (°C)	Solubility g/100 g solvent	Moles of solute	Molality (mol/kg solvent)	Mass %
1	KNO_3		50				
2	$CuSO_4$		25				
3	KI		5				
4	NH_4Cl		90				
5	$KClO_3$		60				

3. Show the dissociation of the following compounds in aqueous solution and calculate the effective concentration of the ions present.

Compound	Van't Hoff factor	Concentration	Dissociation	Cation concentration	Anion concentration	Total species concentration
HCl		1.50 M				
$AlCl_3$		0.360 M				
$K_2Cr_2O_7$		1.25 m				
$MgSO_4$		0.750 m				
Na_2SO_4		0.225 m				

4. Complete the table below. In each case, assume that exactly 10.00 g of the substance indicated is dissolved in exactly 100.00 g water, and that the van't Hoff factor for each compound is equal to the number of particles resulting from 100% dissociation.

#	Solute	Van't Hoff factor	Moles of solute	Molality of solute	Mole fraction of solute	Freezing point °C	Boiling point °C	Vapor pressure 50°C mmHg
1	$NaNO_3$							
2	$CaCl_2$							
3	$AlCl_3$							
4	$K_2Cr_2O_7$							
5	$Al_2(SO_4)_3$							

5. Calculate molarity of a sodium chloride solution that has an osmotic pressure of 16.0 atm at 20.0 °C.

Self-assessment

Using the scale indicated, rate your understanding of each learning objective at the completion of this lesson. Identify the areas where your understanding is weak or medium and discuss with your class mates and/or instructor. Write down specific questions you still have at the completion of this topic.

Learning objective	Self-assessment 3 = strong, 2 = medium, 1 = weak, 0 = not done
	3 2 1 0
	3 2 1 0
	3 2 1 0
	3 2 1 0
	3 2 1 0

Lesson 20 –   Kinetics

Learning Objectives

In this lesson you will learn:

- To express the **rate of a reaction** relative to each reactant and each product
- To calculate a simple rate of reaction
- To calculate the **half-life** or **rate constant** of a reaction
- To calculate the **time needed** for a reaction to proceed
- To calculate the **concentration of reactant** left after a specific amount of time
- To determine the **rate law** of a reaction using the **method of initial rates**
- To calculate the **activation energy** of a reaction
- To predict the rate law of a reaction from the **mechanistic steps**
- To identify the **catalyst** and the **intermediate** in a **reaction mechanism**

Pre-requisite: Units and measurement. Balancing chemical reactions.

Self-study questions

Before you start studying the worked examples, you should be able to formulate answers to the questions below. Use a textbook of your choice, or an online source of information, to find the answers.

1. What is meant by rate of reaction?
2. What is the difference between instantaneous rate and initial rate?
3. What is the rate law?
4. What is a reaction order?
5. What is the rate constant?
6. Is there a relationship between reaction orders and stoichiometric coefficients?
7. What common values reaction orders take?
8. What is the method of initial rates?
9. What is an integrated rate law?
10. What type of graph will result in a linear plot for reaction orders 0, 1, and 2?
11. What is half life?
12. Is half-life constant?
13. What is a reaction mechanism?
14. What is molecularity?
15. What is an intermediate?
16. How is the rate law related to the reaction mechanism?
17. Do rate constants change with temperature?
18. What is activation energy?
19. What is a transition state?
20. What is A in the Arrhenius equation?
21. What can be plotted using the Arrhenius equation in order to determine the activation energy?
22. What is a catalyst?

Worked examples

This section contains several solved examples that cover the learning objectives listed above. Study each example carefully and make notes in the workbook to check every example that you understood. Repeat several times what you don't understand at first. It should become clearer as you keep working on the examples.

The information compiled in the table below will be very useful for most numeric problems in this lesson.

Order	Rate law	Rate constant units	Concentration-time equation	Half-life	Linear plot
0	$Rate = k$	$mol\, L^{-1}\, s^{-1}$	$[A] = [A]_0 - kt$	$t_{1/2} = \dfrac{[A]_0}{2k}$	$[A]$ vs. t
1	$Rate = k[A]$	s^{-1}	$\ln[A] = \ln[A]_0 - kt$ Or $\ln \dfrac{[A]}{[A]_0} = -kt$	$t_{1/2} = \dfrac{\ln 2}{k}$	$\ln[A]$ vs. t
2	$Rate = k[A]^2$	$L\, mol^{-1}\, s^{-1}$	$\dfrac{1}{[A]} = \dfrac{1}{[A]_0} + kt$	$t_{1/2} = \dfrac{1}{k[A]_0}$	$\dfrac{1}{[A]}$ vs. t

Objective 150.   Express the rate of reaction relative to each reactant and each product.

1.   Express the rate of the reaction below in terms of the rate of disappearance of each reactant and the rate of formation of each product.
$$5Br^-_{(aq)} + BrO_3^-{}_{(aq)} + 6H^+{}_{(aq)} \rightarrow 3Br_2{}_{(aq)} + 3H_2O_{(l)}$$

Discussion

The rate of a reaction, as a mathematical expression, is:

$$Rate\ of\ reaction = \frac{change\ in\ concentration}{change\ in\ time} = -\frac{d[reactant]}{dt} = \frac{d[product]}{dt}$$

where **d** represents an infinitesimal (very small) change, and the square brackets represent concentration.

From stoichiometry, we see that for each bromate ion that reacts, it takes 5 bromide ions and 6 protons, in order to form 3 bromine molecules and 3 water molecules. Clearly, the 5 bromide ions and the 6 protons must react <u>at the same time</u> as one bromate ion. This means that the reaction rate of bromide must be 5 times higher than that of the bromate, and the reaction rate of protons must be 6 times higher than that of bromate. I chose bromate as a reference because its stoichiometric coefficient is 1. Since reactants are consumed (they "disappear"), we indicate their rates as negative, and since products are formed (they "appear"), we indicate their rates as positive This is just a convention.

Solution

The relative rates in this reaction will be:

$$-\frac{d[BrO_3^-{}_{(aq)}]}{dt} = -\frac{1}{5}\frac{d[Br^-{}_{(aq)}]}{dt} = -\frac{1}{6}\frac{d[H^+{}_{(aq)}]}{dt} = \frac{1}{3}\frac{d[Br_2{}_{(aq)}]}{dt} = \frac{1}{3}\frac{d[H_2O_{(l)}]}{dt}$$

What this relationship is saying is that we need to take one fifth of the rate of disappearance of bromide (faster) to equal the rate of disappearance of bromate (slower). Or, that the **rate of disappearance** of bromate ions is only a third of the **rate of formation** of water molecules. And so on. We express each rate, using the sign convention, relative to the other rates by using stoichiometry.

2.   The rate of disappearance of hydrogen in the reaction below is 0.102 M/s. Determine the rate of formation of ammonia.
$$N_2 + 3H_2 \rightarrow 2NH_3$$

Solution

First let's write the relative rates as seen above:

$$-\frac{d[N_2]}{dt} = -\frac{1}{3}\frac{d[H_2]}{dt} = \frac{1}{2}\frac{d[NH_3]}{dt}$$

This means that a third of the rate of hydrogen disappearance should equal half of the rate of formation of ammonia. This is because in the same time that 3 molecules (or moles) of hydrogen react, two molecules (or moles) of ammonia are made.

Now we can calculate the numerical rate, by dropping the negative sign (it is only for convention). We extract the term that interests us, as a function of what is given:

$$\frac{d[NH_3]}{dt} = \frac{2}{3}\frac{d[H_2]}{dt} = \frac{2}{3} \times 0.102\frac{M}{s} = 0.0680 \ M/s$$

Is the answer correct? Yes, half of this rate equals a third of the hydrogen consumption rate.

Objective 151. Calculate a simple rate of reaction

1. The reaction below follows the rate expression given. Calculate the reaction rate when $[NH_4^+] = 0.44 \ M$ and $[NO_2^-] = 0.020 \ M$. The rate constant is $4.8 \times 10^{-4} M^{-1}s^{-1}$.

$$NH_4^+ + NO_2^- \rightarrow N_2 + 2H_2O \quad ; \quad Rate = k[NH_4^+][NO_2^-]$$

Discussion

In general, for a generic reaction A + B → products, the rate will be expressed as follows:

$$Rate = k[A]^x[B]^y$$

where k is the rate constant, and the concentration of each reactant in the rate law expression is raised to a power called the reaction order with respect to that reactant. The reaction orders are determined experimentally and generally have nothing to do with the stoichiometric coefficients.

Solution

$$Rate = 4.8 \times 10^{-4} \ M^{-1}s^{-1} \times 0.44 \ M \times 0.020 \ M = 4.2 \times 10^{-6} \ M/s$$

The units for rate are always M/s.

2. The reaction below follows the rate law given. When $[H_2] = 0.080 \ M$ and $[NO] = 0.050 \ M$, the rate is $3.8 \times 10^{-6} \ M/s$. Calculate the rate constant.

$$2H_2 + 2NO \rightarrow 2H_2O + N_2 \quad ; \quad Rate = k[H_2][NO]^2$$

Solution

In this case, the rate depends on the second power of the NO concentration (we say that the reaction is second order in NO and first order in H_2).

$$Rate = k[H_2][NO]^2 \quad \Rightarrow \quad k = \frac{Rate}{[H_2][NO]^2} = \frac{3.8 \times 10^{-6} \ M/s}{(0.080 \ M)(0.050 \ M)^2} = 0.019 \ M^{-2} \ s^{-1}$$

Note that the units for the rate constant depend on the reaction orders. In this case, the reaction is third order overall and thus the rate constant units are $M^{-2}\, s^{-1}$, or $L^2\, mol^{-2}\, s^{-1}$.

Objective 152. Calculate the half-life or rate constant of a reaction

1. The half-life of a second-order reaction when $[A]_0 = 0.082$ M was 28 minutes. What is the half-life when $[A]_0 = 0.026$ M ?

Solution

Consult the table provided at the beginning of the lesson. Notice that the half-life of a first order reaction is always constant. For a reaction order other than 1, the half-life depends on the initial concentration of the reactant, $[A]_o$. From the first concentration we determine the rate constant:

$$t_{1/2} = \frac{1}{k[A]_o} \quad \Rightarrow \quad k = \frac{1}{t_{1/2}[A]_o} = \frac{1}{28 \text{ min} \times 0.082\ M} = 0.436\, min^{-1}\, M^{-1}$$

Now we calculate the new half-life:

$$t_{1/2} = \frac{1}{k[A]_o} = \frac{1}{0.436\, min^{-1}\, M^{-1} \times 0.026\ M} = 88.3\ min$$

Does the answer make sense? Yes: the half time is inversely proportional to the initial reactant concentration (for a second order reaction), and so a lower starting concentration will result in a larger half-life, meaning the reaction will be slower.

Objective 153. Calculate the time needed for a reaction to proceed.

1. The half-life of a first-order reaction is 46.0 s. What is the time required for 90.0% of the reactant to decompose?

Solution

The reaction is of the form: $A \rightarrow products$. The rate law is of the form:

$$Rate = k[A] \quad \text{(first order in A)}.$$

From the table provided above, we need the concentration-time equation (also called the integrated rate law) for a first order reaction, which will allow us to perform calculations related to concentration and time, as you might imagine. The equation is:

$$ln\frac{[A]}{[A]_o} = -kt$$

Where $[A]$ represents the concentration of reactant A left after time t has elapsed. The problem says that 90.0% of the reactant decomposes. That means that 10.0% (of the initial concentration) is left after the amount of time in question:

$$[A] = \frac{10.00}{100}[A]_o$$

We do not need to know the actual remaining concentration, because it is relative to the initial concentration, which will cancel out:

$$ln\frac{[A]}{[A]_o} = ln\frac{\frac{10.00}{100}[A]_o}{[A]_o} = ln\frac{0.100[A]_o}{[A]_o} = ln\,0.100 = -kt$$

This is why we used the second form of the equation from the table. We can find the time elapsed if we know the rate constant. The problem does not give a rate constant, but gives the half-life. Since this is a first order reaction, we can find the rate constant from the half-life:

$$t_{1/2} = \frac{ln\,2}{k} \quad \Rightarrow \quad k = \frac{ln\,2}{t_{1/2}} = \frac{0.693147}{46.0\ s} = 0.0151\ s^{-1}$$

Now we can solve for the time elapsed:

$$t = -\frac{ln\,0.1}{k} = -\frac{-2.30259}{0.0151\ s^{-1}} = 153\ s$$

---

2. It takes 52 min for the concentration of a reactant in a first-order reaction to drop from 0.46 M to 0.13 M at 25°C. How long will it take for the reaction to be 25% complete?

Solution

Again, we are dealing with a first order reaction. From the first set of data we can calculate the rate constant:

$$ln\frac{[A]}{[A]_o} = -kt \quad \Rightarrow \quad ln\frac{0.13\ M}{0.46\ M} = -k(52\ \text{min}) = -1.264$$

$$k = \frac{1.264}{52\ min} = 0.0243\ min^{-1}$$

Now that we have the rate constant, we can find the time needed for the reaction to be 25% complete, which means **75% of the reactant is left over**.

$$ln\frac{0.75\,[A]_0}{[A]_o} = -(0.0243\ min^{-1})\,t \quad \Rightarrow \quad t = \frac{ln\,0.75}{-0.0243\ min^{-1}} = 12\ min$$

Does the answer make sense? Yes, it takes 12 minutes for 25% to react, and it takes 52 minutes for 72% to react, which is what 0.13M represents compared to the initial 0.46 M. A shorter time is needed for a smaller percentage of the reactant to be consumed.

Objective 154.   Calculate the concentration of reactant left after a specific amount of time.

1.   The rate constant of the second-order reaction below is $0.90 \ M^{-1}s^{-1}$. Starting with a concentration of NOBr of 0.12 M, what is the concentration of NOBr after 60 seconds?

$$2NOBr \ \rightarrow 2NO + Br_2$$

Solution

The reaction is second order, so the equation we need is the following:

$$\frac{1}{[A]} = \frac{1}{[A]_o} + kt$$

Since we know the rate constant and the initial concentration, we can plug in the numbers and then solve for [A]:

$$\frac{1}{[A]} = \frac{1}{0.12 \ M} + 0.90 \ M^{-1}s^{-1} \times 60.0 \ s = 8.333 \ M^{-1} + 54 \ M^{-1} = 62.333 \ M^{-1}$$

$$[A] = \frac{1}{62.333 \ M^{-1}} = 0.0160 \ M$$

Does the answer make sense? Yes, the concentration is decreasing, and since the rate constant is large (compare to other rate constants we calculated earlier), the reaction is fast, and so after 60 seconds the leftover reactant is low (*0.016/0.12 = 13% leftover*).

Objective 155. Determine the rate law of a reaction using the method of initial rates.

1. The rate data for the reaction between F_2 and ClO_2 is given in the table below. Determine the rate law for this reaction.

[F_2] (M)	[ClO_2] (M)	Initial Rate (M/s)
0.10	0.010	1.2×10^{-3}
0.10	0.040	4.8×10^{-3}
0.20	0.010	2.4×10^{-3}

Discussion

The problem gives us a list of initial reaction rates at given starting concentrations of the reactants. We need to determine the rate law expression.

The rate law expression will be of the general form:

$$rate = k\,[F_2]^x\,[ClO_2]^y$$

where x and y are the partial reaction orders with respect to F_2 and ClO_2. In order to have a complete expression for the rate law, we need to determine these reaction orders, as well as the rate constant k. The method described here is called the method of initial rates.

Solution

Let's label the lines in the table of data 1,2, and 3. What we are looking for is two sets of data in which the concentrations of all reactants but one are kept constant. There are only two reactants, and we notice that the concentration of F_2 is constant in lines 1 and 2. We plug the data from these lines into the generic rate law expression from above and we obtain:

$$1.2 \times 10^{-3} = k\,(0.10)^x\,(0.010)^y \quad (1)$$

$$4.8 \times 10^{-3} = k\,(0.10)^x\,(0.040)^y \quad (2)$$

Next, we want to divide equations (1) and (2) one by the other, in order to cancel out the rate constant, as well as the term in x, which equals 1:

$$\frac{1.2 \times 10^{-3}}{4.8 \times 10^{-3}} = \frac{\cancel{k}\,\cancel{(0.10)^x}\,(0.010)^y}{\cancel{k}\,\cancel{(0.10)^x}\,(0.040)^y} = \frac{(0.010)^y}{(0.040)^y} = \left(\frac{0.010}{0.040}\right)^y$$

We notice that the numbers are in a ratio of 1:4 in each fraction:

$$\frac{1}{4} = \left(\frac{1}{4}\right)^y$$

Alternatively, we can divide (2) by (1) in order to have the larger numbers on top:

$$\frac{4.8 \times 10^{-3}}{1.2 \times 10^{-3}} = \left(\frac{0.040}{0.010}\right)^y \quad \Rightarrow \quad 4 = (4)^y$$

Either way, we can see, from simple visual inspection, that the value of y for which the equation above is true is 1. Thus, we found one of our partial reaction orders:

$$y = 1$$

Now that we know one variable, we can repeat the process by choosing two sets the data that will lead to finding the value of x, for example sets 3 and 1, which keep the concentration of ClO_2 constant.

$$2.4 \times 10^{-3} = k \, (0.20)^x \, (0.010)^1 \quad (3)$$

$$1.2 \times 10^{-3} = k \, (0.10)^x \, (0.010)^1 \quad (1)$$

If we divide (3) by (1) we obtain:

$$\frac{2.4 \times 10^{-3}}{1.2 \times 10^{-3}} = \frac{k \, (0.20)^x \, (0.010)^1}{k \, (0.10)^x \, (0.010)^1} \quad \Rightarrow \quad 2 = 2^x$$

Coincidently, $x = 1$ too. Of course, the two orders are don't have to be the same, although in many cases they can be.

Because now we know the two reaction orders, we can solve for the rate constant:

$$1.2 \times 10^{-3} = k \, (0.10)^1 \, (0.010)^1 \quad \Rightarrow \quad k = \frac{1.2 \times 10^{-3} \, M/s}{0.10 \, M \times 0.010 \, M} = 1.2 \, M^{-1}s^{-1}$$

Finally, we can write the complete rate law expression:

$$rate = 1.2 \, M^{-1}s^{-1} \, [F_2][ClO_2]$$

What if the exponential equations are not so simple in other problems? Many times, you can still use visual inspection to solve them. Examples:

$$4 = 2^x \; ; \; x \; must \; be \; 2$$

$$\frac{1}{3} = 3^x \; ; \; x = -1$$

If you run into more complicated expression, you can always apply logarithms to solve the equation. Reaction orders are usually small positive integers, but sometimes they can be fractional or even negative.

Objective 156.   Calculate the activation energy of a reaction.

1.   A reaction at 250°C is 2500 times faster than at 150°C. What is the activation energy of the reaction?

Discussion

The rate constant of a reaction stays constant as long as the temperature is the same. But rate constants do depend on temperature, through the Arrhenius equation:

$$k = A\,e^{-\frac{E_a}{RT}} \quad or \quad \ln(k) = \ln(A) - \frac{E_a}{RT}$$

Where A is called the pre-exponential factor, E_a is the activation energy of the reaction, R is the ideal gas constant, and T is the absolute temperature. The units of the pre-exponential factor are identical to those of the rate constant and will vary depending on the order of the reaction.

Solution

In this type of problem, we know the ratio between two rate constants and we need to find the activation energy. This simplifies the problem because we can simplify the equation. We write the equation for the two situations:

$$k_1 = A\,e^{-\frac{E_a}{RT_1}} \quad (1)$$

$$k_2 = A\,e^{-\frac{E_a}{RT_2}} \quad (2)$$

We know that the reaction at temperature $T_1 = 250\,°C$ is 2500 times faster than at $T_2 = 150\,°C$, which means that:

$$k_1 = 2500\,k_2$$

We can divide equations (1) and (2) and cancel out the pre-exponential factor:

$$\frac{k_1}{k_2} = \frac{e^{-\frac{E_a}{RT_1}}}{e^{-\frac{E_a}{RT_2}}} = e^{-\left(\frac{E_a}{RT_1} - \frac{E_a}{RT_2}\right)}$$

We apply *ln* to both sides of the equation:

$$ln\left(\frac{k_1}{k_2}\right) = ln\left(e^{-\left(\frac{E_a}{RT_1} - \frac{E_a}{RT_2}\right)}\right) = -\left(\frac{E_a}{RT_1} - \frac{E_a}{RT_2}\right) = -\frac{E_a}{R}\left(\frac{1}{T_1} - \frac{1}{T_2}\right) = -\frac{E_a}{R}\left(\frac{T_2 - T_1}{T_1 T_2}\right)$$

We extract the activation energy:

$$E_a = -\frac{ln\left(\frac{2500k_2}{k_2}\right) \times R \times T_1 \times T_2}{T_2 - T_1} = -\frac{ln(2500) \times 8.314\frac{J}{K\,mol} \times 523\,K \times 423\,K}{423\,K - 523\,K}$$

$$E_a = 143907\frac{J}{mol} = 144\frac{kJ}{mol}$$

Objective 157.   Predict the rate law of a reaction from the mechanistic steps.

1.   The reaction:
$$2N + Cl_2 \rightarrow 2NOCl$$
is known to follow the mechanism below:

$$NO + Cl_2 \rightarrow NOCl_2 \quad (slow)$$
$$NOCl_2 + NO \rightarrow 2NOCl \quad (fast)$$

What is the predicted rate of reaction?

Solution

A reaction mechanism is a series of steps that, when added together, yield the overall reaction. Some steps can be fast and some can be slow. The rate of the overall reaction depends on the rate of the slow step. The rate law for the slow step has partial reaction orders that are the same as the stoichiometric coefficients of the reactants showing in the slow step.

Thus, the rate law of the reaction above is predicted to be:

$$Rate = k[NO][Cl_2]$$

because both NO and Cl_2 have a coefficient of 1 in the balanced slow step. This is the <u>only case where reaction orders are the same as coefficients</u>.

Objective 158. Identify the catalyst and the intermediate in a reaction mechanism.

1. The reaction:

$$Tl^+ + 2Ce^{4+} \rightarrow Tl^{3+} + 2Ce^{3+}$$

Follows the mechanism:

$$Ce^{4+} + Mn^{2+} \rightarrow Ce^{3+} + Mn^{3+}$$

$$Ce^{4+} + Mn^{3+} \rightarrow Ce^{3+} + Mn^{4+}$$

$$Tl^+ + Mn^{4+} \rightarrow Tl^{3+} + Mn^{2+}$$

Identify the catalyst and the intermediate in this reaction.

Discussion

A catalyst must have the following features:
- Is not a reactant or a product of the overall reaction
- Must be retrieved unchanged at the end of the reaction

An intermediate must have the following features:
- Is not a reactant or a product of the overall reaction
- Is formed in one of the mechanistic steps
- Is consumed before the end of the last step

Solution

Given the definitions above, we can determine that Mn^{2+} has the characteristics of a catalyst (it enters the reaction in step 1 and is retrieved in step 3).

We also determine that more than one species have the characteristics on an intermediate: both Mn^{3+} and Mn^{4+} are formed in initial steps and consumed in subsequent steps. They are both intermediates (we can have more than one).

The following table summarizes the species involved in this reaction:

Reactants	Tl^+, Ce^{4+}
Products	Tl^{3+}, Ce^{3+}
Intermediates	Mn^{3+}, Mn^{4+}
Catalyst	Mn^{2+}

Worksheet 20. Kinetics

The exercises and problems in this section will allow you to practice the topic until you understand it well.

1. Express the rate of the reaction below in terms of the rate of disappearance of each reactant and the rate of formation of each product. Then, assuming that the rate of formation of the chromium(III) ion is 0.252 M/s, calculate:
    a. The rate of disappearance of the dichromate ion
    b. The rate of disappearance of hydrogen ions
    c. The rate of formation of ferric ions

$$Cr_2O_7^{2-} + 6Fe^{2+} + 14H^+ \rightarrow 2Cr^{3+} + 7H_2O + 6Fe^{3+}$$

2. Express the rate of the reaction below in terms of the rate of disappearance of each reactant and the rate of formation of each product. Then, assuming that the rate of consumption of oxygen gas is 0.756 M/s, calculate:
    a. The rate of consumption of ethane
    b. The rate of formation of carbon dioxide
    c. The rate of formation of water

$$2C_2H_6 + 7O_2 \rightarrow 4CO_2 + 6H_2O$$

3. The reaction between F_2 and ClO_2 follows the rate law:
$$rate = 1.2\ M^{-1}s^{-1}\ [F_2][ClO_2]$$
Calculate the rate of this reaction when the concentrations of F_2 and ClO_2 are 0.0225 M and 0.0331 M respectively.

4. The reaction $2H_2 + 2NO \rightarrow 2H_2O + N_2$ follows the rate law:
$$rate = k\ [H_2][NO]^2$$
If the rate of the reaction when [H₂] = 0.080 M and [NO] = 0.050 M is $3.8 \times 10^{-6}\ M/s$, calculate the rate constant.

5. A first order reaction has a rate constant of $2.40 \times 10^{-3}\ s^{-1}$. What is the time needed for the reaction to be 66% complete?

6. The half-life of a first-order reaction is 12 minutes. What percent of the initial reactant concentration is left over after one hour?

7. The half-life of a second-order reaction when [A]₀ = 0.0480 M was 16 minutes. What is the half-life of the same reaction when [A]₀ = 0.108 M?

8. It takes 66 hours for the concentration of a reactant in a second order reaction to drop from 1.25 M to 0.750 M. How long will it take for the reaction to be 80% complete?

9. The rate constant of the second-order reaction below is $0.090\ M^{-1}s^{-1}$. If a concentration of [NOBr]=0.025 M is found after 120 seconds, what is the initial concentration of NOBr?

$$2NOBr \rightarrow 2NO + Br_2$$

10. The rate data for the reaction between reactants A and B is given in the table below. Determine the rate law for this reaction and calculate the rate constant.

[A] (M)	[B] (M)	Initial Rate (M/s)
1.50	1.50	3.20×10^{-1}
1.50	2.50	3.20×10^{-1}
3.00	1.50	6.40×10^{-1}

11. The rate data for the reaction between reactants CH_3COCH_3, Br_2 and H^+ is given in the table below. Determine the rate law for this reaction and calculate the rate constant.

[CH$_3$COCH$_3$] (M)	[Br$_2$] (M)	[H$^+$] (M)	Initial Rate (M/s)
0.30 M	0.050 M	0.050 M	5.7×10^{-5}
0.30 M	0.10 M	0.050 M	5.7×10^{-5}
0.30 M	0.050 M	0.10 M	1.2×10^{-4}
0.40 M	0.050 M	0.20 M	3.1×10^{-4}

12. The rate constant for a reaction at 35°C is four times the rate constant at 5°. What is the activation energy of the reaction?

13. The reaction:
$$2H_2 + 2NO \rightarrow N_2 + H_2O$$
    is known to follow the mechanism below:

$$H_2 + 2NO \rightarrow N_2O + H_2O \quad (slow)$$
$$N_2O + H_2 \rightarrow N_2 + H_2O \quad (fast)$$

    What is the predicted rate of reaction? Identify the intermediate(s) in this reaction mechanism.

14. The reaction:
$$CO + NO_2 \rightarrow CO_2 + NO$$
    is known to follow the mechanism below:

$$2NO_2 \rightarrow NO_3 + NO \quad (slow)$$
$$NO_3 + CO \rightarrow CO_2 \quad (fast)$$

    What is the predicted rate of reaction? Identify the intermediate(s) in this reaction mechanism.

15. The reaction:
$$2N_2O_{(g)} \rightarrow 2N_{2\,(g)} + O_{2\,(g)}$$
    Follows the mechanism :
$$Cl_{2\,(g)} \rightarrow 2Cl_{(g)}$$
$$N_2O_{(g)} + Cl_{(g)} \rightarrow N_{2\,(g)} + ClO_{(g)}$$
$$ClO_{(g)} + ClO_{(g)} \rightarrow Cl_{2\,(g)} + O_{2\,(g)}$$

    Identify the catalyst and the intermediate(s) in this reaction.

16. The reaction:
$$S_2O_8^{2-} + 2I^- \rightarrow 2SO_4^{2-} + I_2$$
    Follows the mechanism :
$$Fe^{3+} + 2I^- \rightarrow Fe^{2+} + I_2$$
$$S_2O_8^{2-} + Fe^{2+} \rightarrow 2SO_4^{2-} + Fe^{3+}$$

    Identify the catalyst and the intermediate(s) in this reaction.

Self-assessment

Using the scale indicated, rate your understanding of each learning objective at the completion of this lesson. Identify the areas where your understanding is weak or medium and discuss with your class mates and/or instructor. Write down specific questions you still have at the completion of this topic.

Learning objective	Self-assessment 3 = strong, 2 = medium, 1 = weak, 0 = not done
	3 2 1 0
	3 2 1 0
	3 2 1 0
	3 2 1 0
	3 2 1 0
	3 2 1 0
	3 2 1 0
	3 2 1 0
	3 2 1 0

Lesson 21 – Equilibrium

Learning Objectives

In this lesson you will learn:

- To write the **expression of the equilibrium constant** for a given reaction
- To calculate the **equilibrium constant** for a given reaction
- To use the equilibrium constant to determine concentrations (or pressures) of species at **equilibrium**
- To calculate the **reaction quotient** and determine whether a system is at equilibrium
- To apply **Le Chatelier's principle** to predict **changes** in a system at equilibrium

Pre-requisite: Balancing chemical reaction; Stoichiometry.

Self-study questions

Before you start studying the worked examples, you should be able to formulate answers to the questions below. Use a textbook of your choice, or an online source of information, to find the answers.

1. What is meant by equilibrium?
2. Does a reaction stop completely at equilibrium?
3. What is the equilibrium constant?
4. How is the equilibrium constant of the direct (left to right) reaction related to the constant of the inverse (right to left) reaction?
5. What equilibrium constants can be written for a reaction in gas phase?
6. There are some rules that apply to heterogeneous equilibria when it comes to equilibrium constant expressions. What are they?
7. By looking at the numerical value for the equilibrium constant, how can you predict whether reactants are favored or products are favored?
8. What is the reaction quotient and why is it useful?
9. What does Le Chatelier's principle say? Why is it useful?
10. What is the effect of a catalyst on equilibrium?
11. How can the equilibrium constant be related to rate constants? When is this relationship valid?

Worked examples

This section contains several solved examples that cover the learning objectives listed above. Study each example carefully and make notes in the workbook to check every example that you understood. Repeat several times what you don't understand at first. It should become clearer as you keep working on the examples.

Objective 159. Write the expression of the equilibrium constant for a given reaction

1. Write the expression of the equilibrium constant for the chemical reaction below:
$$5Br^-_{(aq)} + BrO_3^-{}_{(aq)} + 6H^+_{(aq)} \rightleftharpoons 3Br_2{}_{(aq)} + 3H_2O_{(l)}$$

Solution

The equilibrium constant is a ration between the product of concentrations of all reaction products, each raised to a power equal to its stoichiometric coefficient, and the product of concentrations of all reactants, each raised to a power equal to its stoichiometric coefficient. Pure solids and pure liquids are excluded from the equilibrium constant. Thus, the expression of the equilibrium constant for the reaction given is:

$$K_C = \frac{\left[Br_{2\,(aq)}\right]^3}{\left[Br^-_{(aq)}\right]^5\left[BrO_3^-{}_{(aq)}\right]\left[H^+_{(aq)}\right]^6}$$

Note that the equilibrium constant is denoted K (upper case), while the rate constant is k (lower case)

2. Write the expressions of the equilibrium constants K_c and K_p for the reaction below:
$$N_{2\,(g)} + 3H_{2\,(g)} \rightleftharpoons 2NH_{3\,(g)}$$

Solution

For reactions in gas phase, we can write two equilibrium constants, one that includes concentrations, and one that includes pressures, since pressure is a quantity that is more easily measurable for gases than concentration is.

$$K_C = \frac{\left[NH_{3\,(g)}\right]^2}{\left[N_{2\,(g)}\right]\left[H_{2\,(g)}\right]^3}$$

$$K_P = \frac{P^2_{NH_{3\,(g)}}}{P_{N_{2\,(g)}} \times P^3_{H_{2\,(g)}}}$$

Objective 160. Calculate the equilibrium constant for a given reaction

1. Consider the reaction below.
$$CO_{(g)} + 2H_{2\,(g)} \rightleftharpoons CH_3OH_{(g)}$$
The numbers of moles present at equilibrium are: 0.960 mol CO, 1.91 mol H_2, and 1.50 mol CH_3OH. The volume of the reaction vessel is 10.0 L. Calculate the equilibrium constant for this reaction.

Solution

For any equilibrium problem, we should start by writing the expression of the equilibrium constant:

$$K = \frac{[CH_3OH_{(g)}]}{[CO_{(g)}][H_{2\,(g)}]^2}$$

Since we have the moles of all species at equilibrium, and the volume of the container, we can calculate the concentrations at equilibrium:

$$[CH_3OH_{(g)}] = \frac{1.50\ mol}{10.0\ L} = 0.150\ M$$

$$[CO_{(g)}] = \frac{0.960\ mol}{10.0\ L} = 0.0960\ M$$

$$[H_{2\,(g)}] = \frac{1.91\ mol}{10.0\ L} = 0.191\ M$$

And now the equilibrium constant:

$$K_C = \frac{0.150\ M}{0.0960\ M \times (0.191\ M)^2} = 42.8\ M^{-2}$$

The units of the equilibrium constant depend on the stoichiometric coefficients and will generally be molar units raised to some exponent (positive, negative, or zero). Many books leave out the units for the equilibrium constant, because they can vary.

---

2. The equilibrium constant for the reaction:

$$2HCl_{(g)} \rightleftharpoons H_{2\,(g)} + Cl_{2\,(g)}$$

is 4.17×10^{-31} at 25°C. Calculate K_c and K_p for the reaction:

$$H_{2\,(g)} + Cl_{2\,(g)} \rightleftharpoons 2HCl_{(g)}$$

Solution

As you notice, the second reaction is the reverse of the first reaction. The equilibrium constant for a reaction that goes in the opposite sense is the inverse of the constant for the direct reaction, thus:

$$K_C' = \frac{1}{K_C} = \frac{1}{4.17 \times 10^{-31}} = 2.40 \times 10^{30}$$

The relationship between K_C and K_P is:

$$K_P = K_C(RT)^{\Delta n}$$

where T is the temperature in Kelvin and Δn is the change in the number of moles (products – reactants), and R is the ideal gas constant in units of L and atm.

For this reaction:

$$\Delta n = moles\ products - moles\ reactants = 2 - 2 = 0$$

so $K_P = K_C$

3. For the reaction below:

$$2CO_{(g)} + O_{2(g)} \rightleftharpoons 2CO_{2(g)}$$

K_C is 2.24×10^{22} at 1273 °C. Calculate K_P for this reaction at the same temperature.

Solution

$$\Delta n = 2 - 3 = -1$$

$$K_P = K_C(RT)^{\Delta n} = 2.24 \times 10^{22} \, (0.0821 \times 1546 \, K)^{-1} = \frac{2.24 \times 10^{22}}{0.0821 \times 1546} = 1.76 \times 10^{16}$$

4. The equilibrium partial pressures of N_2, O_2 and NO in the reaction:

$$N_{2(g)} + O_{2(g)} \rightleftharpoons 2NO_{(g)}$$

are 0.15, 0.33 and 0.050 atm, respectively at 2200°C. What is the value of K_P and that of K_C for this reaction ?

Solution

Since we have the partial pressures of all gases at equilibrium, we can calculate the equilibrium constant directly:

$$K_P = \frac{P_{NO}^2}{P_{N_2}P_{O_2}} = \frac{(0.050 \, atm)^2}{0.15 \, atm \, \times 0.33 \, atm} = 0.051$$

Since there is no change in the overall number of moles, $K_P = K_C$ in this case too.

Objective 161. Use the equilibrium constant to determine concentrations (or pressures) of species at equilibrium

1. Consider the reaction below:

$$NH_4COONH_{2\,(s)} \rightleftharpoons 2NH_{3\,(g)} + CO_{2\,(g)}$$

The reaction starts with only the solid reactant. When it reaches equilibrium, the total pressure inside the container is 0.363 atm at 40°C. calculate the equilibrium constant K_P.

Solution

The fact that the reaction starts only with the solid reactant means that there are no products present at the beginning of the reaction. Thus, all the pressure in the vessel at equilibrium is due to the two gases formed:

$$P_{total} = P_{NH_3} + P_{CO_2} = 0.363 \, atm$$

What we need to determine is:

$$K_P = P_{NH_3}^2 P_{CO_2}$$

We don't know the partial pressures of the two gases, but we know the total pressure, and we also know that the two gases are produced in a ratio of 2:1 from stoichiometry. Since gas pressure is proportional to the amount of gas (review Avogadro's law), it means that the ratio of the two partial pressures is the same as the stoichiometric coefficients:

$$P_{NH_3} = 2P_{CO_2}$$

Thus:

$$2P_{CO_2} + P_{CO_2} = 3P_{CO_2} = 0.363 \, atm \quad \Rightarrow \quad P_{CO_2} = 0.121 \, atm$$

$$P_{NH_3} = 2P_{CO_2} = 0.242 \, atm$$

We can now calculate K_P:

$$K_P = (0.242)^2(0.121) = 7.09 \times 10^{-3}$$

---

2. Consider the reaction below:

    $$COCl_{2 \, (g)} \rightleftharpoons CO_{(g)} + Cl_{2 \, (g)}$$

    The reaction starts with 0.0300 mol $COCl_2$ in a 1.50 L container at 800 K. At equilibrium, the pressure of CO is 0.497 atm. Calculate K_P and K_C for this reaction.

Solution

Here, we know the starting concentration, and we know the partial pressure of one product. Since the two products are made in a ratio of 1:1, and the reaction was started with only the reactant present, we can deduct from stoichiometry that the partial pressure of Cl_2 is the same as that of CO:

$$P_{Cl_2} = P_{CO} = 0.497 \, atm$$

We know the amount of reactant in moles at the beginning of the reaction. Since we have the other parameters, we can apply the ideal gas law to convert that into a pressure:

$$P = \frac{nRT}{V} = \frac{0.0300 \, mol \times 0.0821 \, \frac{L \, atm}{mol \, K} \times 800. \, K}{1.50 \, L} = 1.314 \, atm \, COCl_2$$

We will construct a table to illustrate the situation more clearly. We will list the amounts of all species at the beginning of the reaction and at equilibrium, in the form of pressures in atm:

	$COCl_2$	CO	Cl_2
Initial	1.314	0	0
Change			
Equilibrium	x	0.497	0.497

We're going to call this an ICE table (from the initials on the left). On the *Initial* row, we list the starting partial pressure of the reactant, and zero for the two products because there is none of them at the beginning. On the **Equilibrium** row, we list the known partial pressures of the two products, and an unknown for the pressure of $COCl_2$. We'll leave the **Change** row empty because it does not help in this problem.

In order to calculate K_P, we need to know the pressure of the reactant as well. From the stoichiometry, we notice that the amount of $COCl_2$ that is consumed in the reaction must equal the amount of either product, because the stoichiometry is 1:1:1. Thus, in order to form 0.497 atm of, say, CO, the same amount, 0.497 atm, of $COCl_2$ must react. It is OK to use pressures instead of moles, as we saw previously. Thus, the pressure of $COCl_2$ left over is the initial pressure minus what was consumed in the reaction:

$$P_{COCl_2} = 1.314\ atm - 0.497\ atm = 0.817\ atm$$

This number is our unknown x in the table above. The equilibrium constant expression is:

$$K_P = \frac{P_{CO}P_{Cl_2}}{P_{COCl_2}} = \frac{0.497 \times 0.497}{0.817} = 0.302$$

3. Consider the reaction below:

$$H_{2\ (g)} + CO_{2\ (g)} \rightleftharpoons H_2O_{(g)} + CO_{(g)}$$

The reaction starts with 0.300 moles of CO and 0.300 moles of H_2O in a 1.00 L container. The equilibrium constant K_C is 0.534 at 700°. Calculate the concentrations of all species at equilibrium.

Solution

Since the volume of the container is 1.00 L, the starting concentrations of CO and H_2O are 0.300 M each. We will construct and ICE table to illustrate what is happening:

	H_2	CO_2	H_2O	CO
Initial	0	0	0.300	0.300
Change				
Equilibrium				

As you can see, the reaction starts with some quantities of products. This is fine, as all these reactions are equilibria, and so they will proceed in either direction until equilibrium is reached.

We don't know anything about the quantities of H_2 and CO_2 produced, so we will use an unknown. Let's say x is the concentration of H_2 produced in the reaction. According to the stoichiometry of the balanced reaction, in order to produce x moles of H_2, the same amount of CO_2 will also be produced, and also x moles of CO, as well as x moles of H_2O, will be consumed. The table now becomes:

	H_2	CO_2	H_2O	CO
Initial	0	0	0.3	0.3
Change	x	x	$-x$	$-x$
Equilibrium				

We indicate the species consumed as negative amounts, and the species produced as positive amounts. At equilibrium, the total concentrations will be the sum between the initial ones and the change:

	H_2	CO_2	H_2O	CO
Initial	0	0	0.3	0.3
Change	x	x	$-x$	$-x$
Equilibrium	x	x	$0.3. -x$	$0.3. -x$

Agreed? If we start with 0.3 mol of a reactant and x is consumed, we will have $0.3 - x$ at the end (we dropped the significant zeros to make calculations easier).

The equilibrium constant is calculated from the concentrations at equilibrium:

$$K_C = \frac{[H_2O][CO]}{[H_2][CO_2]}$$

We actually know the value of K, and we must solve for the unknown x:

$$K_C = \frac{(0.3 - x)(0.3 - x)}{x \times x} = \frac{(0.3 - x)^2}{x^2} = 0.534$$

Because this equation contains the unknown x to second power everywhere, it can be solved easily by taking square root of both sides:

$$\sqrt{\frac{(0.3 - x)^2}{x^2}} = \sqrt{0.534} \quad \Rightarrow \quad \frac{0.3 - x}{x} = 0.731$$

$$0.3 - x = 0.731x \quad \Rightarrow \quad 0.3 = 1.731x \quad \Rightarrow \quad x = 0.173$$

What is the significance of this result? Remember, x was the concentration of H_2 produced, and every other quantity is a function of this x. We can now complete the table with the actual concentrations at equilibrium:

	H_2	CO_2	H_2O	CO
Initial	0	0	0.300	0.300
Change	0.173	0.173	-0.173	-0.173
Equilibrium	**0.173**	**0.173**	**0.127**	**0.127**

The numbers in the Equilibrium row are the concentrations of all species at equilibrium. Are they correct? Let's check:

$$K_C = \frac{0.127^2}{0.173^2} = 0.539$$

The answer is very close, due to rounding off the intermediate concentrations.

Objective 162.   Calculate the reaction quotient and figure out whether a system is at equilibrium

1. Given the data in the table below, predict which direction the reaction will proceed or indicate "at equilibrium"

Equilibrium	Kc	Concentrations (mol/L)				Q	Predict direction
$H_{2\,(g)} + CO_{2\,(g)} \rightleftharpoons H_2O_{\,(g)} + CO_{\,(g)}$	4.20	[H_2]	[CO_2]	[H_2O]	[CO]		
		0.567	1.25	2.36	0.849		
$N_{2\,(g)} + 3H_{2\,(g)} \rightleftharpoons 2NH_{3\,(g)}$	0.0822	[N_2]	[H_2]	[NH_3]			
		1.568	2.158	8.520			

Solutions

The reaction quotient, Q, has the same expression as the equilibrium constant, but it refers to concentrations (or pressures) of species at some random point during the course of the reaction, not at equilibrium.

Let's calculate the quotients for the two situations above:

$$Q_1 = \frac{[H_2O][CO]}{[H_2][CO_2]} = \frac{2.36 \times 0.849}{0.567 \times 1.25} = \mathbf{2.83}$$

The reaction quotient is less than the equilibrium constant. This means that the quantity on top of the fraction line is less in the quotient than it is in the constant. This implies that the concentrations of the "products" as the reaction is written are less than what they would be at equilibrium. Thus, the reaction will proceed from **left to right** in order to reach equilibrium.

$$Q_2 = \frac{\left[NH_{3\,(g)}\right]^2}{\left[N_{2\,(g)}\right]\left[H_{2\,(g)}\right]^3} = \frac{8.520^2}{1.568 \times 2.158^3} = \mathbf{4.607}$$

In this case, the quotient is greater than the equilibrium constant, and so the reaction will proceed from **right to left** in order to decrease the concentration of ammonia and increase those of the reactants until equilibrium is reached.

Objective 163.   Apply Le Chatelier's principle to predict changes in a system at equilibrium.

1. Predict how the equilibrium position of the reaction below will change for each of the changes applied.

$$PCl_{5\,(g)} \rightleftharpoons PCl_{3\,(g)} + Cl_{2\,(g)} \qquad \Delta H = 92.5\ kJ$$

   a.   Increasing temperature

   b.   Increasing volume

   c.   Increasing pressure

   d.   Increasing the concentration of PCl_3

   e.   Removing Cl_2

   f.   Adding Ne

   g.   Adding a solution of NaOH

Solutions

According to Le Chatelier's principle, when a stress is applied to a system at equilibrium, the system reacts to counteract the effect of the stress.

a. The temperature is increased. Because the enthalpy of the reaction is positive, it means that the reaction is endothermic from left to right. Increasing temperature means supplying more heat to the reaction. The system reacts by trying to consume the extra heat, which favors the endothermic reaction. Thus, the equilibrium will shift to the **right** in order to consume the extra heat.

b. Increasing volume. The system will react in order to accommodate the larger volume. Since the reaction is in gas phase, a larger number of moles will occupy a larger volume, and so the equilibrium will shift towards the side with a larger number of moles, which is to the **right**.

c. Increasing pressure. From gas laws we know that increasing pressure is the opposite of increasing volume. Applying the previous reasoning in this case, we conclude that an increase in pressure causes the system to react by shifting towards the side with fewer moles of gas, which is the **left** side.

d. Increasing the concentration of PCl_3. The system reacts such that the extra PCl_3 added will be consumed, and thus it shifts to the **left**.

e. Removing Cl_2. The system reacts to compensate for the removal of a product, by producing more. Thus, the equilibrium shifts to the **right**.

f. Adding Ne. An inert gas is added to the system. Assuming no change in volume or pressure, the inert gas should not affect the equilibrium at all, so **no shift** in equilibrium is expected.

g. Adding a solution of NaOH. At first look it seems that no change is expected in this case either. However, remember (see Objective 49) that NaOH in solution reacts with halogens, in this case chlorine gas. Thus, this is the same as chlorine from the system (this time through chemical means), and thus the equilibrium will shift to the **right**.

Worksheet 21. Equilibrium

1. Write the expression of the equilibrium constant for the chemical reaction below:
$$Cr_2O_7^{2-}{}_{(aq)} + 6Fe^{2+}{}_{(aq)} + 14H^+{}_{(aq)} \rightleftharpoons 2Cr^{3+}{}_{(aq)} + 7H_2O_{(l)} + 6Fe^{3+}{}_{(aq)}$$

2. Write the expressions of the equilibrium constants K_c and K_p for the reaction below:
$$2C_2H_{6\,(g)} + 7O_{2\,(g)} \rightleftharpoons 4CO_{2\,(g)} + 6H_2O_{(g)}$$

3. Consider the reaction below.
$$N_{2\,(g)} + 3H_{2\,(g)} \rightleftharpoons 2NH_{3\,(g)}$$

The numbers of moles present at equilibrium are: 15.68 mol N_2, 21.58 mol H_2, and 85.20 mol NH_3. The volume of the reaction vessel is 10.0 L. Calculate the equilibrium constants K_c and K_p for this reaction at 325°C.

4. From the data obtained in the problem above, the equilibrium constants K_c and K_p for the reaction below:
$$2NH_{3\,(g)} \rightleftharpoons N_{2\,(g)} + 3H_{2\,(g)}$$

5. The equilibrium constant K_c for the reaction below is 3.8×10^{-5} at 750°C:
$$I_{2\,(g)} \rightleftharpoons 2I_{(g)}$$

What is the value of K_p at the same temperature?

6. The equilibrium constant K_C for the reaction below is 57.0 at 700°C:
$$I_{2\,(g)} + H_{2\,(g)} \rightleftharpoons 2HI_{(g)}$$

If at equilibrium $[I_{2\,(g)}] = 0.100\ M$ and If $[H_{2\,(g)}] = 0.400\ M$, what is the concentration of $HI_{(g)}$ at equilibrium?

7. The equilibrium constant K_P for the reaction below is 1500 at 400°C:
$$2NH_{3\,(g)} \rightleftharpoons N_{2\,(g)} + 3H_{2\,(g)}$$

If the partial pressures of nitrogen gas and hydrogen gas are 0.25 atm and 0.35 atm respectively, what is the partial pressure of ammonia at equilibrium (and at the same temperature)?

8. The equilibrium constant K_C for the reaction below is 3.8×10^{-5} at 750°C:
$$I_{2\,(g)} \rightleftharpoons 2I_{(g)}$$

Starting with 0.0456 moles of I_2 in a 2.30 L flask, calculate the equilibrium concentration of I_2 at that temperature.

9. Consider the reaction below:

$$H_{2\,(g)} + CO_{2\,(g)} \rightleftharpoons H_2O_{(g)} + CO_{(g)}$$

Initially 0.80 moles of H_2 and 0.80 mole CO_2 are placed in a 5.0 L flask. The equilibrium constant K_c is 4.20 at a certain temperature. Calculate the concentrations of all species at equilibrium.

10. Given the data in the table below, predict which direction the reaction will proceed or indicate "at equilibrium".

Equilibrium	K_c	Concentrations (mol/L)				Q	Predict direction
$I_{2\,(g)} \rightleftharpoons 2I_{(g)}$	3.8×10^{-5}	$[I_2]$	$[I]$				
		0.012	0.056				
$H_{2\,(g)} + Br_{2\,(g)} \rightleftharpoons 2HBr_{(g)}$	2.18×10^6	$[H_2]$	$[Br_2]$	$[HBr]$			
		0.0538	0.0260	55.26			
$H_{2\,(g)} + CO_{2\,(g)} \rightleftharpoons$ $H_2O_{(g)} + CO_{(g)}$	4.20	$[H_2]$	$[CO_2]$	$[H_2O]$	$[CO]$		
		1.25	0.358	0.488	1.45		

11. Predict how the equilibrium position of the reaction below will change for each of the changes applied.

$$SO_{2\,(g)} + Cl_{2\,(g)} \rightleftharpoons SO_2Cl_{2\,(g)}$$

a. Removing SO_2

b. Adding Cl_2

c. Removing $SOCl_2$

d. Increasing pressure

e. Increasing volume

f. Adding N_2

12. Predict how the equilibrium position of the reaction below will change for each of the changes applied.

$$2SO_{2\,(g)} + O_{2(g)} \rightleftharpoons 2SO_{3\,(g)}, \quad \Delta H = -198\ kJ$$

a. Decreasing temperature

b. Decreasing pressure

c. Decreasing volume

d. Decreasing the concentration of SO_2

e. Adding a catalyst

f. Removing SO_3

Self-assessment

Using the scale indicated, rate your understanding of each learning objective at the completion of this lesson. Identify the areas where your understanding is weak or medium and discuss with your class mates and/or instructor. Write down specific questions you still have at the completion of this topic.

Learning objective	Self-assessment 3 = strong, 2 = medium, 1 = weak, 0 = not done
	3 2 1 0
	3 2 1 0
	3 2 1 0
	3 2 1 0
	3 2 1 0

Lesson 22 –   Acids and Bases

Learning Objectives

In this lesson you will learn:

- To write a chemical equation that shows the **dissociation of an acid or a base** in solution.
- To calculate **pH** and **hydrogen ion concentration** of a solution of **strong acid**
- To calculate **pH, pOH** and **hydroxide ion concentration** of a solution of **strong base**
- To calculate the **acidity constant** for an acid and the **basicity constant** for a base
- To calculate pH and **percent ionization** in a solution of a **weak acid**
- To calculate pH, pOH and **percent ionization** in a solution of a **weak base**
- To calculate pH when two solutions of an acid (or a base) are **mixed**
- To calculate the **acidity or basicity constant** given the pH
- To predict the products of **hydrolysis of a salt** in aqueous solution
- To calculate the pH of a **salt solution**
- To calculate the pH at the **equivalence point** in a weak acid/strong base **titration**
- To calculate the pH at the equivalence point in a weak base/strong acid **titration**

Pre-requisites: Chemical reactions in solution; Equilibrium.

Self-study questions

Before you start studying the worked examples, you should be able to formulate answers to the questions below. Use a textbook of your choice, or an online source of information, to find the answers.

1. What is an acid?
2. What is a base?
3. What is a salt?
4. What is meant by dissociation in solution?
5. What is the difference between strong acids and weak acids?
6. What is the difference between strong bases and weak bases?
7. What is an acidity constant?
8. What is a basicity constant?
9. What is meant by hydrolysis?
10. What is a titration?
11. What is the equivalence point?

Worked examples

This section contains several solved examples that cover the learning objectives listed above. Study each example carefully and make notes in the workbook to check every example that you understood. Repeat several times what you don't understand at first. It should become clearer as you keep working on the examples.

Objective 164. Write a chemical equation that shows the dissociation of an acid or a base in solution.

1. Write chemical reactions that describe the dissociation of each acid or base below. Write an equilibrium constant expression when appropriate.
   a. HCl
   b. H_2SO_4
   c. CH_3COOH
   d. $Ca(OH)_2$
   e. CH_3NH_2

Solutions

a. HCl
   Hydrochloric acid is a strong acid and it dissociates completely in water:

$$HCl + H_2O \rightarrow H_3O^+ + Cl^-$$

b. H_2SO_4
   Sulfuric acid has two dissociation steps, being a diprotic acid. The first dissociation step is strong:

$$H_2SO_4 + H_2O \rightarrow HSO_4^- + H_3O^+$$

The second dissociation step consists in the ionization of the hydrogen sulfate ion. This is a weak acid:

$$HSO_4^- + H_2O \rightleftharpoons SO_4^{2-} + H_3O^+$$

For a weak acid we can write an equilibrium constant, which is called acidity constant when it refers to the dissociation of an acid:

$$Ka_2 = \frac{[SO_4^{2-}][H_3O^+]}{[HSO_4^-]}$$

c. CH_3COOH
   Acetic acid is a weak acid and its dissociation is an equilibrium:

$$CH_3COOH + H_2O \rightleftharpoons CH_3COO^- + H_3O^+$$

$$K_a = \frac{[CH_3COO^-][H_3O^+]}{[CH_3COOH]}$$

d. $Ca(OH)_2$
   Calcium hydroxide is a strong base:

$$Ca(OH)_2 \rightarrow Ca^{2+} + 2OH^-$$

e. CH_3NH_2
   Methylamine is a weak base and its dissociation resembles that of ammonia:

$$CH_3NH_2 + H_2O \rightleftharpoons CH_3NH_3^+ + OH^-$$

$$K_b = \frac{[CH_3NH_3^+][OH^-]}{[CH_3NH_2]}$$

Objective 165.   Calculate pH and hydrogen ion concentration for a solution of strong acid.

1.   Calculate the concentration of H^+ and OH^- ions and the pH of a 1.2×10^{-3} M HCl solution.

Solution

A strong acid is completely dissociated in aqueous solution, as we saw, and thus its hydrogen ion concentration will be equal to the acid concentration:

$$[H_3O^+] = 1.2 \times 10^{-3}\ M$$

In aqueous solutions, there are always hydrogen ions as well as hydroxide ions, due to the auto ionization of water:

$$H_2O\ (acid) + H_2O\ (base) \rightleftharpoons OH^-\ (conjugate\ base) + H_3O^+\ (conjugate\ acid)$$

The ionic product of water always holds, in pure water as well as in any solution:

$K_w = [H_3O^+][OH^-] = 1.0 \times 10^{-14}\ M^2$ (units are usually discarded)

Thus, we can calculate the concentration of the hydroxide ions even in a solution of a strong acid:

$$[OH^-] = \frac{K_w}{[H_3O^+]} = \frac{1.0 \times 10^{-14}\ M^2}{1.2 \times 10^{-3}\ M} = 8.1 \times 10^{-12}\ M$$

Does this answer make sense? Yes, in a solution of a strong acid, the hydroxide ion concentration is very small (but not zero).

Finally, we can calculate the pH:

$$pH = -log([H_3O^+]) = -\log(1.2 \times 10^{-3}) = 2.92$$

For pH, we retain <u>as many decimals as we have significant digits</u> in the concentration. pH is a **dimensionless** quantity.

2.   Calculate the hydrogen ion concentration of a solution having a pH of 1.82.

Solution

To go from pH to concentration we apply the inverse decimal logarithm, which is an exponential:

$$[H_3O^+] = 10^{-pH} = 10^{-1.82} = 0.015\ M$$

Objective 166.   Calculate pH, pOH and hydroxide ion concentration for a solution of strong base.

> 1.   Calculate the concentration of OH⁻ ions, the pH and the pOH of a 0.065 M Ca(OH)₂ solution.

Solution

The strong base is completely dissociated in aqueous solution:

$$Ca(OH)_2 \rightarrow Ca^{2+} + 2OH^-$$

From the stoichiometry of this reaction, it can be seen that the concentration of OH^- ions is double that of the calcium hydroxide (there are two hydroxide ions per calcium hydroxide formula unit):

$$[OH^-] = 2 \times 0.065 = 0.13 \ M$$

The quantity that can be calculated directly is pOH, which is the equivalent of pH for hydroxide ion:

$$pOH = -log([OH^-]) = -\log(0.13) = 0.89$$

From the ionic product of water we can derive the relationship: $pH + pOH = 14$

Thus,

$$pH = 14 - pOH = 14 - 0.89 = 13.11$$

> 2.   Calculate the hydroxide ion concentration of a solution having a pH of 10.66.

Solution

We can proceed two ways: either we calculate pOH first:

$$pOH = 14 - 10.66 = 3.34$$

$$[OH^-] = 10^{-pOH} = 10^{-3.34} = 4.57 \times 10^{-4} \ M$$

Or we can calculate the hydrogen ion concentration and then use the ionic product:

$$[H_3O^+] = 10^{-pH} = 10^{-10.66} = 2.19 \times 10^{-11} \ M$$

$$[OH^-] = \frac{K_w}{[H_3O^+]} = \frac{1.0 \times 10^{-14} \ M^2}{2.19 \times 10^{-11} \ M} = 4.57 \times 10^{-4} \ M$$

> 3.   What mass of NaOH is needed to prepare 500.0 mL solution with a pH of 12.50?

Solution

$$pOH = 14 - 12.50 = 1.50$$

The target hydroxide ion concentration is:

$$[OH^-] = 10^{-pOH} = 10^{-1.50} = 0.032 \, M$$

NaOH is a strong base so its concentration in the solution will be that of the hydroxide ion. We calculate the moles and then the mass of NaOH needed:

$$n = MV = 0.032 \frac{mol}{L} \times 0.5000 \, L = 0.016 \, mol \, NaOH \, needed$$

$$0.016 \, mol \times 40.00 \frac{g}{mol} = 0.64 \, g \, NaOH$$

Objective 167.   Calculate the acidity constant for an acid or the basicity constant for a base.

1. Benzoic acid has an acidity constant $K_a = 6.5 \times 10^{-5}$. Calculate pK_a of benzoic acid.

Solution

The "pX" notation stands for "$-log(X)$" in all quantities, as in pH and pOH. Thus:

$$pK_a = -\log(K_a) = -\log(6.5 \times 10^{-5}) = 4.19$$

2. Ammonia has a basicity constant $K_b = 1.8 \times 10^{-5}$. Calculate pK_b of ammonia.

Solution

$$pK_b = -\log(K_b) = -\log(1.8 \times 10^{-5}) = 4.74$$

3. The 3 dissociation constants of phosphoric acid, given in pK_a notation, are in Appendix E. Calculate the corresponding acidity constants K_a.

Solution

Dissociation constants are given in p notation because these numbers are simpler than the scientific format used for the actual constant values. We can easily transform them in numbers. The three pKa's of phosphoric acid are:

$$pKa_1 = 2.12 \quad \Rightarrow \quad Ka_1 = 10^{-2.12} = 7.59 \times 10^{-3}$$

$$pKa_2 = 7.21 \quad \Rightarrow \quad Ka_2 = 10^{-7.21} = 6.17 \times 10^{-8}$$

$$pKa_3 = 12.67 \quad \Rightarrow \quad Ka_3 = 10^{-12.67} = 2.14 \times 10^{-13}$$

Objective 168.   Calculate pH and percent ionization in a solution of a weak acid

1.   Calculate the pH of a 0.200 M benzoic acid solution ($K_a = 6.5 \times 10^{-5}$) and the percent ionization of benzoic acid in this solution.

Solution

All calculations involving weak acids or bases are equilibria and we can do them with the help of "ICE" tables.

The dissociation of benzoic acid:

$$C_6H_5COOH + H_2O \rightleftharpoons C_6H_5COO^- + H_3O^+$$

	$[C_6H_5COOH]$	$[C_6H_5COO^-]$	$[H_3O^+]$
Initial	0.200	0	0
Change	$-x$	x	x
Equilibrium	$0.2 - x$	x	x

The ICE table describes mathematically what happens in the equilibrium above. Upon dissolution in water, benzoic acid starts to dissociate from the initial concentration of 0.200 M. Since it is a weak acid (we know this because we are given an acidity constant, not because we are in the section on weak acids), it will not dissociate completely, so we use the unknown x for the amount (concentration really) of acid that dissociates. As we saw previously, since the stoichiometry is 1:1, we get the same amounts of hydrogen ions and benzoate ions. Solving for x will give us what we need in the end, the concentration of H_3O^+ ions, which will lead to pH.

$$K_a = \frac{[C_6H_5COO^-][H_3O^+]}{[C_6H_5COOH]} = \frac{x^2}{0.2 - x} = 6.5 \times 10^{-5}$$

In order to find the value of x, we need to solve a quadratic equation. Let's find the proper form for it.

$$x^2 = 6.5 \times 10^{-5}\,(0.2 - x)$$

$$x^2 = 1.3 \times 10^{-5} - 6.5 \times 10^{-5}x$$

$$x^2 + 6.5 \times 10^{-5}x - 1.3 \times 10^{-5} = 0$$

We now have the quadratic equation form, where:

$$a = 1 \quad b = 6.5 \times 10^{-5} \quad c = -1.3 \times 10^{-5}$$

You can use any quadratic equation solver to get the solutions, which are:

$$x_1 = 0.00357 \quad and \quad x_2 = -0.00364$$

What is the significance of x? In our table, x is the concentration of hydrogen (and benzoate) ions, so it must be a positive number. Thus:

$$x = [H_3O^+] = [C_6H_5COO^-] = 0.00357\ M$$

And:
$$pH = -\log(0.00357) = 2.45$$

Percent ionization means what percent of the acid is actually dissociated:

$$percent\ ionization = \frac{concentration\ of\ dissociated\ acid}{total\ acid\ concentration} \times 100$$

The concentration of the dissociated acid is the hydrogen (or benzoate) ion concentration. Thus:

$$percent\ ionization = \frac{0.00357\ M}{0.200\ M} \times 100 = 1.85\ \%$$

Does the answer make sense? Yes, we are dealing with a weak acid, and weak acids (or bases) dissociate very little. Values less than 5% are actually quite common. The percent ionization depends on concentration; dilute acids actually ionize more than concentrated acids.

Objective 169.   Calculate pH, pOH and percent ionization in a solution of a weak base

1. Calculate the pH and percent ionization of a 0.100 M aqueous NH_3 solution. $K_b = 1.8 \times 10^{-5}$.

Solution

$$NH_3 + H_2O \rightleftharpoons NH_4^+ + OH^-$$

We follow the same steps as in the previous problem, since the situation is similar.

	$[NH_3]$	$[NH_4^+]$	$[OH^-]$
Initial	0.100	0	0
Change	$-x$	x	x
Equilibrium	$0.1 - x$	x	x

$$K_b = \frac{[NH_4^+][OH^-]}{[NH_3]} = \frac{x^2}{0.1 - x} = 1.8 \times 10^{-5}$$

$$x^2 = 1.8 \times 10^{-5}\ (0.1 - x)$$

$$x^2 = 1.8 \times 10^{-6} - 1.8 \times 10^{-5}x$$

$$x^2 + 1.8 \times 10^{-5}x - 1.8 \times 10^{-6} = 0$$

Solving the quadratic equation leads to:
$$x = [NH_4^+] = [OH^-] = 0.00133\ M$$

Since we have the concentration of OH^- ions, we can calculate pOH and then pH:

$$pOH = -log([OH^-]) = -log(0.00133) = 2.88$$
$$pH = 14 - 2.88 = 11.12$$

$$percent\ ionization = \frac{0.00133\ M}{0.100\ M} \times 100 = 1.33\ \%$$

Objective 170.   Calculate pH or pOH when two solutions are mixed.

1.   What is the pH of a solution prepared by mixing 30.9 mL of HCl solution with pH=2.28 and 23.9 mL of HCl solution with pH = 5.19?

Solution

We are mixing two solutions of acid. The final solution will have a volume equal to the sum of the two volumes being mixed, and the total number of moles in the final solution will be the sum of the moles of acid in each solution. From the pH of each solution we can determine the concentration of the hydrogen ions:

$$[H^+]_1 = 10^{-pH_1} = 10^{-2.28} = 5.25 \times 10^{-3}\ M$$

$$[H^+]_2 = 10^{-pH_2} = 10^{-5.19} = 6.46 \times 10^{-6}\ M$$

Before performing the calculations, we anticipate that the concentration of the resulting solution will be between the concentrations of the two solutions above, and so will be the pH. Let's calculate:

$$[H^+]_{final} = \frac{n_1 + n_2}{V_1 + V_2} = \frac{M_1 V_1 + M_2 V_2}{V_1 + V_2} = \frac{5.25 \times 10^{-3}\ M \times 30.9\ mL + 6.46 \times 10^{-6}\ M \times 23.9\ mL}{30.9\ mL + 23.9\ mL}$$

$$[H^+]_{final} = 2.96 \times 10^{-3} M$$

$$pH = -\log(2.96 \times 10^{-3}) = 2.53$$

Objective 171.   Calculate the acidity or basicity constant given the pH.

1.   The pH of a 0.0100 M weak monoprotic acid is 6.20. Calculate the acidity constant of the acid.

Solution

We are given the concentration of a solution of a weak acid and its pH and we need to calculate the acidity constant. Let's call the acid HA and write a generic dissociation reaction:

$$HA + H_2O \rightleftharpoons H_3O^+ + A^-$$

Now let's set up the ICE table and see what we know and what we need:

	$[HA]$	$[H_3O^+]$	$[A^-]$
Initial	0.0100	0	0
Change	$-x$	x	x
Equilibrium	$0.01 - x$	x	x

Is x really an unknown? No, not really, we know the pH, and thus we can calculate the concentration of H_3O^+, which is x, and all other quantities that depend on it:

$$x = [H_3O^+] = 10^{-6.20} = 6.31 \times 10^{-7} \ M$$

We can put this value in our table:

	$[HA]$	$[H_3O^+]$	$[A^-]$
Initial	0.0100	0	0
Change	-6.31×10^{-7}	6.31×10^{-7}	6.31×10^{-7}
Equilibrium	$0.01 - 6.31 \times 10^{-7}$	6.31×10^{-7}	6.31×10^{-7}

Thus, we can calculate the constant:

$$K_a = \frac{[H_3O^+][A^-]}{[HA]} = \frac{(6.31 \times 10^{-7})^2}{0.01 - 6.31 \times 10^{-7}} = \frac{3.98 \times 10^{-13}}{0.01} = 3.98 \times 10^{-11}$$

What I did at the denominator is neglect the value 6.31×10^{-7}, which is much smaller (negligible) compared to 0.01 and it does not really affect the calculation when we round off numbers.

The resulting acidity constant is very small, which signifies we are dealing with a very weak acid. This is consistent with the fact that the pH of the solution is quite close to neutral, so our answer makes sense.

---

2. The pH of a 0.300 M solution of a weak base is 10.66. What is the K_b of the base?

Solution

We will do something very similar but applied to a generic base B:

$$B + H_2O \rightleftharpoons BH^+ + OH^-$$

$$pOH = 14 - 10.66 = 3.34$$

$$[OH^-] = 10^{-3.34} = 4.57 \times 10^{-4} \ M$$

	$[B]$	$[BH^+]$	$[OH^-]$
Initial	0.0100	0	0
Change	-4.57×10^{-4}	4.57×10^{-4}	4.57×10^{-4}
Equilibrium	$0.300 - 4.57 \times 10^{-4}$	4.57×10^{-4}	4.57×10^{-4}

$$K_b = \frac{[BH^+][OH^-]}{[B]} = \frac{(4.57 \times 10^{-4})^2}{0.300 - 4.57 \times 10^{-4}} = \frac{2.09 \times 10^{-7}}{0.300} = 6.96 \times 10^{-7}$$

Objective 172.   Predict the products of hydrolysis of a salt in aqueous solution.

1.   For each salt below, indicate whether hydrolysis occurs. If so, write a chemical equation describing the hydrolysis process and predict whether the solution will be acidic or basic.
   a.   sodium chloride
   b.   potassium nitrite
   c.   ammonium nitrate
   d.   ammonium acetate

Discussion

Hydrolysis is the reaction of an ion with water. In order to determine whether hydrolysis will occur when a salt is dissolved in water, we need to do the following:
- break the salt down into ions
- analyze the cation and anion and identify their conjugate acid and base
- determine whether one (or both) of the above are weak
- if the answer is no, then no hydrolysis occurs; if at least one is weak, then hydrolysis will take place

Let's understand this process by example.

Solutions

a.   sodium chloride

Dissociation in solution:

$$NaCl_{(s)} \xrightarrow{in\ water} Na^+_{(aq)} + Cl^-_{(aq)}$$

The conjugate acid of Cl^- is HCl, a **strong** acid. The conjugate base of Na^+ is $NaOH$, a **strong** base.

Since both conjugate acid and conjugate base of our ionic species are **strong**, there is **no hydrolysis** for this salt. Only ions derived from **weak** acids or bases will hydrolyze.

b.   potassium nitrite

Dissociation in solution:

$$KNO_{2\ (s)} \xrightarrow{\text{in water}} K^+_{(aq)} + NO_2^-{}_{(aq)}$$

The conjugate acid of NO_2^- is HNO_2, a **weak** acid. The conjugate base of K^+ is KOH, a **strong** base.

Because one of the two ions derives from a weak acid/base, that ion will undergo hydrolysis. In this case, the nitrite ion will hydrolyze, meaning it will react with water and regenerate its conjugate acid:

$$NO_2^- + H_2O \rightleftharpoons HNO_2 + OH^-$$

The hydrolysis process generates hydroxide ions in solution. Thus, a salt that is formed from a **weak acid and a strong base** will undergo **basic hydrolysis**. The pH of a solution of potassium nitrite will be **basic** (above 7).

c.   ammonium nitrate

Dissociation in solution:

$$NH_4NO_{3\ (s)} \xrightarrow{\text{in water}} NH_4^+{}_{(aq)} + NO_3^-{}_{(aq)}$$

The conjugate acid of NO_3^- is HNO_3, a **strong** acid. The conjugate base of NH_4^+ is NH_3, a **weak** base.

Because one of the two ions derives from a weak acid/base, that ion will undergo hydrolysis. In this case, the ammonium ion will hydrolyze, meaning it will react with water and regenerate its conjugate base:

$$NH_4^+ + H_2O \rightleftharpoons NH_3 + H_3O^+$$

The hydrolysis process generates hydrogen ions in solution. Thus, a salt that is formed from a **strong acid and a weak base** will undergo **acidic hydrolysis**. The pH of a solution of ammonium nitrate will be **acidic** (below 7).

d.   ammonium acetate

Dissociation in solution:

$$NH_4COOH_{(s)} \xrightarrow{\text{in water}} NH_4^+{}_{(aq)} + CH_3COO^-{}_{(aq)}$$

The conjugate acid of CH_3COO^- is CH_3COOH, a **weak** acid. The conjugate base of NH_4^+ is NH_3, a **weak** base. Because both ions derive from weak acids/bases, they will both undergo hydrolysis:

$$NH_4^+ + H_2O \rightleftharpoons NH_3 + H_3O^+$$

$$CH_3COO^- + H_2O \rightleftharpoons CH_3COOH + OH^-$$

Both hydronium and hydroxide ions are produced in solution. To predict whether the solution is acidic or basic we need to take into account the dissociation constants of the weak acid and weak base. In this case, they happen to be exactly the same in value, so a solution of ammonium acetate is predicted to be neutral. If the K_a of the acid was larger than the K_b of the base, the solution would have been acidic (and vice versa).

Objective 173. Calculate the pH of a solution of a salt.

1. Calculate the pH of a 0.25 M CH₃COONa solution.

Solution

As we saw in the previous objective, a salt can lead to a non-neutral pH when dissolved in water, due to hydrolysis. The complete dissociation of the sodium acetate in solution:

$$CH_3COONa \xrightarrow{\text{in water}} CH_3COO^- + Na^+$$

The acetate and sodium ion concentrations are both 0.25 M. As we saw previously, only acetate will undergo hydrolysis, not sodium:

$$CH_3COO^- + H_2O \rightleftharpoons CH_3COOH + OH^-$$

The solution will become basic. By using an ICE table, we can calculate the pH.

	$[CH_3COO^-]$	$[CH_3COOH]$	$[OH^-]$
Initial	0.25	0	0
Change	$-x$	x	x
Equilibrium	$0.25 - x$	x	x

Because this is a basic hydrolysis, we can write a K_b expression:

$$K_b = \frac{[CH_3COOH][OH^-]}{[CH_3COO^-]}$$

What particular K_b is this? Nothing that is published, it is the basicity constant of acetate ion, and it is not available. By using a trick, we can determine its value. Let's modify the expression above:

$$K_b = \frac{[CH_3COOH][OH^-][H_3O^+]}{[CH_3COO^-][H_3O^+]}$$

I multiplied both top and bottom by $[H_3O^+]$, which normally cancels out, so it does not change the equilibrium constant. But, I can isolate two separate terms:

$$K_b = \frac{[CH_3COOH]}{[CH_3COO^-][H_3O^+]} \times ([OH^-][H_3O^+])$$

This is the exact same expression. But, what is the first fraction? It is the inverse of the acidity constant of acetic acid, see Objective 164 part c. What is the second part, the product in parentheses? It is the ionic product of water, see Objective 165. Thus, our K_b becomes:

$$K_b = \frac{1}{K_a} \times K_w = \frac{K_w}{K_a}$$

where the acidity constant of acetic acid and the ionic product of water are known constants. This equation is actually true for the conjugate base of any weak acid, and vice versa. In our case:

$$K_b = \frac{1.0 \times 10^{-14}}{1.8 \times 10^{-5}} = 5.56 \times 10^{-10}$$

This is the basicity constant of acetate ion, and now we can solve our problem.

$$K_b = \frac{x^2}{0.25 - x} = 5.56 \times 10^{-10}$$

Before we delve into solving the quadratic equation, I will show you another trick. Because this basicity constant is very small, it means that the concentration of hydroxide ions (our x) that will result from it will be very small too. In fact it will be much smaller than the 0.25 M acetate ion concentration, so we can safely assume that x is negligible compared to 0.25. The expression is thus simplified:

$$\frac{x^2}{0.25} = 5.56 \times 10^{-10} \quad \Rightarrow \quad x^2 = 1.39 \times 10^{-10} \quad \Rightarrow \quad x = \sqrt{1.39 \times 10^{-10}} = 1.19 \times 10^{-5}\ M$$

x is indeed very small so our approximation is valid. Since x is the hydroxide ion concentration, we calculate:

$$pOH = -\log(1.19 \times 10^{-5}) = 4.93 \quad ; \quad pH = 14 - 4.93 = 9.07$$

As predicted, the solution of sodium acetate is basic.

---

2. Calculate the pH of a 0.34 M NH_4Cl solution.

Solution

Dissociation in water:

$$NH_4Cl \xrightarrow{in\ water} NH_4^+ + Cl^-$$

Which of these two ions will hydrolyze? The ammonium, of course, as we saw before:

$$NH_4^+ + H_2O \rightleftharpoons NH_3 + H_3O^+$$

We thus predict that the resulting solution will be acidic. Let's set up the ICE table:

	$[NH_4^+]$	$[H_3O^+]$	$[NH_3]$
Initial	0.34	0	0
Change	$-x$	x	x
Equilibrium	$0.34 - x$	x	x

$$K_a = \frac{[H_3O^+][NH_3]}{[NH_4^+]} = \frac{x^2}{0.34 - x}$$

This is the acidity constant of the ammonium ion. Applying the same deduction as in the previous problem, this constant can be calculated from the basicity constant of its conjugate base ammonia, which is known:

$$K_a = \frac{K_w}{K_b} = \frac{1.0 \times 10^{-14}}{1.8 \times 10^{-5}} = 5.56 \times 10^{-10}$$

It just happens that it has the same value as that of the acetate ion.

$$\frac{x^2}{0.34 - x} = 5.56 \times 10^{-10}$$

$$\frac{x^2}{0.34} = 5.56 \times 10^{-10} \quad \Rightarrow \quad x^2 = 1.89 \times 10^{-10} \quad \Rightarrow \quad x = \sqrt{1.89 \times 10^{-10}} = 1.37 \times 10^{-5} \, M$$

$$pH = -\log(1.37 \times 10^{-5}) = 4.86$$

As predicted, the solution is acidic. You can now calculate the pH of any salt that undergoes hydrolysis.

Objective 174. Calculate the pH at the equivalence point in a weak acid/strong base titration.

1. Calculate the pH at the equivalence point in the titration of 50.0 mL 0.100 *M* HCOOH with 0.100 *M* NaOH.

Solution

In this titration, formic acid is neutralized by sodium hydroxide:

$$HCOOH + NaOH \rightarrow HCOONa + H_2O$$

Formic acid is **monoprotic**. Notice that it is the H bound to O that is acidic, and not the H bound to C. This is an important detail that will be explained in organic chemistry.

At the equivalence point, all the acid has been neutralized and there is no excess of base. All that there is in solution is the salt, sodium formate: $HCOONa$, dissociated into ions:

$$HCOONa \rightarrow HCOO^- + Na^+$$

Since this salt is made from a weak acid and a strong base, the formate ion will hydrolyze and the sodium ion will not:

$$HCOO^- + H_2O \rightleftharpoons HCOOH + OH^-$$

This is extremely similar to the sodium acetate problem. From this point on, it is a hydrolysis problem. We only need to determine the concentration of the formate ion in solution. We need to apply stoichiometry for that.

Moles of formic acid to start with:

$$50.0 \ mL \ \times 0.100 \frac{mol}{L} = 5.00 \ mmol \ HCOOH$$

For complete titration, since the neutralization reaction is 1:1, 5.00 mmol NaOH is needed. The reactants are consumed, and 5.00 mmol $HCOONa$ is formed.

Let's determine what volume of NaOH solution is needed in the complete titration:

$$V = \frac{n}{M} = \frac{5.00 \ mmol \ NaOH \ needed}{0.100 \ mol/L} = 50.0 \ mL \ solution$$

This result was predictable because the acid and the base solutions have the same concentration.

Thus, the total volume of solution is: $50.0 \ mL \ acid + 50.0 \ mL \ base = 100.0 \ mL \ total \ solution$

The concentration of formate ion at the equivalence point:

$$M = \frac{n}{V} = \frac{5.00 \ mmol \ HCOONa}{100.0 \ mL \ solution} = 0.0500 \ M$$

Now we can construct the ICE table.

	$[HCOO^-]$	$[HCOOH]$	$[OH^-]$
Initial	0.05	0	0
Change	$-x$	x	x
Equilibrium	$0.05 - x$	x	x

$$K_b = \frac{[HCOOH][OH^-]}{[HCOO^-]} = \frac{x^2}{0.05 - x} = \frac{K_w}{K_a} = \frac{1.0 \times 10^{-14}}{1.77 \times 10^{-4}} = 5.62 \times 10^{-11}$$

I used the acidity constant of formic acid to calculate the basicity constant of the formate ion. You can find the K_a of formic acid in Appendix E. as pKa.

$$\frac{x^2}{0.05 - x} = \frac{x^2}{0.05} = 5.62 \times 10^{-11} \quad \Rightarrow \quad x = 1.68 \times 10^{-6}$$

$$pOH = 5.78 \quad \Rightarrow \quad pH = 8.22$$

The solution is basic, so the answer is reasonable.

Objective 175. Calculate the pH at the equivalence point in a weak base/strong acid titration.

1. Calculate the pH at the equivalence point in the titration of 20.0 mL 0.400 M NH_3 with 0.400 M HCl.

Solution

This is the same problem, except we are titrating a weak base with a strong acid. I will summarize the steps briefly:

$$20.0 \; mL \; \times 0.400 \frac{mol}{L} = 8.00 \; mmol \; NH_3$$

$$NH_3 + HCl \rightarrow NH_4Cl$$

8.00 mmol HCl will be consumed as well, and 8.00 mmol NH_4Cl will be produced.

Concentrations are the same for both base and acid solutions, so the volume of HCl consumed will be 20.0 mL.

$$[NH_4^+] = \frac{8.00 \; mmol}{40.0 \; mL} = 0.200 \; M$$

Hydrolysis:

$$NH_4^+ + H_2O \rightleftharpoons NH_3 + H_3O^+$$

ICE table:

	$[NH_4^+]$	$[H_3O^+]$	$[NH_3]$
Initial	0.2	0	0
Change	$-x$	x	x
Equilibrium	$0.2 - x$	x	x

$$K_a = \frac{[H_3O^+][NH_3]}{[NH_4^+]} = \frac{x^2}{0.2 - x} = \frac{x^2}{0.2} = 5.56 \times 10^{-10}$$

$$x = 1.05 \times 10^{-5} = [H_3O^+] \; ; \; pH = 4.98$$

Worksheet 22.   Acids and Bases

The exercises and problems in this section will allow you to practice the topic until you understand it well.

1. Write chemical reactions that describe the dissociation of each acid or base below. Write an equilibrium constant expression when appropriate.

   a.   HBr

   b.   HCOOH

   c. $H_2C_2O_4$

   d.   LiOH

   e. NH_3

   f. $C_2H_5NH_2$

2. Calculate the concentration of H^+ and OH^- ions and the pH of a 2.5×10^{-2} M HNO_3 solution.

3. Calculate the hydrogen ion concentration of a solution having a pH of 3.44.

4. Calculate the hydroxide ion concentration of a solution having a pH of 7.50.

5. Calculate the concentration of OH^- ions, the pH and the pOH of a 0.223 M NaOH solution.

6. Calculate the mass of $Ca(OH)_2$ needed to prepare 250.0 mL solution with a pH of 13.00.

7. The 3 dissociation constants of citric acid, given in pK_a notation, are in Appendix E. Calculate the corresponding acidity constants K_a.

8. Calculate the pH of a 0.0500 M formic acid solution and the percent ionization.

$K_a = 1.8 \times 10^{-4}$

$pH = 2.02$

$\dfrac{0.009496}{0.0500} \times 100 = 19.0\%$

9. Calculate the pH and percent ionization of a 0.100 M aqueous dimethylamine solution.

$pK_a : 10.73$

$K_a = 1.8 \times 10^{-11}$

$pH = 5.86$

$\dfrac{1.3 \times 10^{-6}}{0.1} \times 100 = 0.0086\%$

10. Calculate the pH of 250.0 mL of an aqueous solution containing 1.115 g of the strong acid trifluoromethane sulfonic (CF_3SO_3H) acid.

$$\frac{1.115 g\ CF_3SO_3H}{1} \cdot \frac{1 mol}{138.008 g} = \frac{0.00805\ mol}{250 ml} \cdot \frac{10^3 ml}{1 L} = 0.03221 M$$

$$pH = 1.49$$

11. Calculate the pH of a solution prepared by mixing 50.5 mL of HCl solution with pH=1.15 and 125.5 mL of HCl solution with pH=3.33.

$$\frac{0.07079 \times 50.5 mL + 7.67 \times 10^{-4} \times 125.5 mL}{50.5 ml + 125.5 mL} = 0.0206 M$$

$$pH = 1.69$$

12. Calculate the pH of a solution prepared by mixing 24.5 mL of $Ca(OH)_2$ solution with pH=12.28 and 33.5 mL of $Ca(OH)_2$ with pH=11.19.

13. A solution of formic acid has a pH of 3.26. Calculate the original molarity of the solution and the percent ionization of the acid.

14. For each salt below, indicate whether hydrolysis occurs. If so, write a chemical equation describing the hydrolysis process and predict whether the solution will be acidic or basic.
    a. Silver nitrate

    b. Potassium perchlorate

    c. Sodium hypochlorite

15. Calculate the pH of a 0.112 M NaCN solution.

16. Calculate the pH of a 0.225 M solution of NH_4Cl.

17. Calculate the pH at the equivalence point in the titration of 30.0 mL 0.150 M CH_3COOH with 0.120 M NaOH.

18. Calculate the pH at the equivalence point in the titration of 25.00 mL of 0.200 *M* HCl with 0.200 *M* methylamine.

Self-assessment

Using the scale indicated, rate your understanding of each learning objective at the completion of this lesson. Identify the areas where your understanding is weak or medium and discuss with your class mates and/or instructor. Write down specific questions you still have at the completion of this topic.

Learning objective	Self-assessment 3 = strong, 2 = medium, 1 = weak, 0 = not done
	3 2 1 0
	3 2 1 0
	3 2 1 0
	3 2 1 0
	3 2 1 0
	3 2 1 0
	3 2 1 0
	3 2 1 0
	3 2 1 0
	3 2 1 0
	3 2 1 0
	3 2 1 0

Lesson 23 –   Buffers

Learning Objectives

In this lesson you will learn:

- To determine what compounds make up a **buffer** and write chemical reactions that explain **how a buffer works**
- To calculate the **pH of a buffer** solution
- To calculate the **molar ratio** of the compounds needed to make a buffer of given pH
- To calculate the **pH of a buffer** after a certain amount of **acid or base is added**

Pre-requisites: Acids and bases.

Self-study questions

Before you start studying the worked examples, you should be able to formulate answers to the questions below. Use a textbook of your choice, or an online source of information, to find the answers.

1. What is a buffer and what is its purpose?
2. What types of buffers exist?
3. What is buffer capacity?

Worked examples

This section contains several solved examples that cover the learning objectives listed above. Study each example carefully and make notes in the workbook to check every example that you understood. Repeat several times what you don't understand at first. It should become clearer as you keep working on the examples.

Objective 176.   Determine what compounds make up a buffer and write chemical reactions that explain how a buffer works.

1. In each of the following cases, the formula of a substance is given. Suggest a second substance that, when added to a solution of the first, will make a buffer. If no buffer is possible explain why. If a buffer is possible, write chemical reactions that show how the buffer will resist drastic changes in pH upon addition of a strong acid or a strong base.
    a. CH_3COOH
    b. HCl
    c. NH_3
    d. $NaNO_2$
    e. NaH_2PO_4

Solutions

In order to have a buffer, we must have one of the two types of mixtures below:

- A **weak acid** plus a salt <u>of the same acid</u> with a **strong base**
- A **weak base** plus a salt <u>of the same base</u> with a **strong acid**

In other words, you need a weak acid and its conjugate base, or a weak base and its conjugate acid to form a buffer. The other requirement is that the counter cation (or anion) does not hydrolyze. Let's see how.

a. CH_3COOH

Acetic acid is a weak acid, so it **can** make a buffer. We need to add a salt of itself (an acetate in this case) with a strong base, such as NaOH. Thus, sodium acetate, CH_3COONa, is the other component we can add. Of course, we can use an acetate of another metal that forms a strong base, such as lithium, potassium, etc.

How does a buffer work? A buffer resists drastic changes in pH upon addition of strong acid OR strong base. The buffer must be prepared to neutralize either acid or base, so that is why it has two components. An acetate buffer, then, has two active components: CH_3COOH and CH_3COONa. The buffer "resists" to changes in pH by neutralizing the offending acid or base added to it. Here is how.

If a strong base is added, the acetic acid reacts with it:

$$CH_3COOH + OH^- \rightleftharpoons CH_3COO^- + H_2O$$

The buffer works if this equilibrium is shifted to the right, meaning that the strong base (OH^-) was consumed. Should this equilibrium be shifted to the right? Intuition says yes, because it is a neutralization reaction. But since we are dealing with equilibria here, let's analyze the reverse reaction:

$$CH_3COO^- + H_2O \rightleftharpoons CH_3COOH + OH^-$$

Where have we seen this reaction before? In Objective 172. What was the equilibrium constant K_b of this second reaction?

$$K_b = 5.56 \times 10^{-10}$$

What does it mean when the equilibrium constant is very small? That the equilibrium lies to the left (very little products, and lots of reactants unreacted). Well, if this equilibrium lies to the left, then the one above, its reverse, lies to the right.

What about when strong acid is added to the buffer? The other active component is the acetate ion, from the sodium acetate:

$$CH_3COO^- + H_3O^+ \rightleftharpoons CH_3COOH + H_2O$$

In order for this half of the buffer to work (and neutralize excess acid added to it), the equilibrium above must lie to the right as written. What is the reverse of this equilibrium? The dissociation of acetic acid. What kind of acid is acetic acid? A weak one. What does it mean? That it dissociates very little, of the order of <5% (Objective 168). Thus, since the acetic acid really does not like to stay dissociated, the equilibrium above is indeed shifted heavily to the right.

You should realize the importance of using a weak acid to make a buffer. What if we used a strong acid? It would be dissociated, so the equilibrium above will be shifted to the left for a strong acid, and you don't have a buffer.

It is also important that the counter ion, in this case sodium ion, does not hydrolyze, because if it did this would complicate the situation and the chemical reactions would be more complex than they already are.

b.   HCl

What kind of acid is HCl? Can it make a buffer? NO.

c. NH_3

Ammonia is a weak base, and so it needs its conjugate acid, the ammonium ion. This can be supplied as NH_4Cl, because the chloride ion does not hydrolyze (it derives from the strong acid HCl). Upon addition of acid:

$$NH_3 + + H_3O^+ \rightleftharpoons NH_4Cl + H_2O \ (shifted \ right \ as \ we \ saw \ in \ hydrolysis \ of \ NH_4^+)$$

Upon addition of base:

$$NH_4^+ + OH^- \rightleftharpoons NH_3 + H_2O$$

This regenerates the weak base, which dissociates very little.

d. $NaNO_2$

What is $NaNO_2$? A salt. Can it make a buffer? Sure, if it is the salt of a weak acid. What is the acid from which it is derived? Nitrous acid, HNO_2 , a weak acid. So the missing component in this case is HNO_2.

Upon addition of base:

$$HNO_2 + OH^- \rightleftharpoons NO_2^- + H_2O \ (shifted \ right \ as \ we \ saw \ in \ the \ hydrolysis \ of \ NO_2^-)$$

Upon addition of acid:

$$NO_2^- + H_3O^+ \rightleftharpoons HNO_2 + H_2O$$

The exact same reasoning applies here as the acetic buffer example.

e. NaH_2PO_4

What is NaH_2PO_4 ? A salt, but an acidic salt. Thus, it is dissociated as follows:

$$NaH_2PO_4 \rightarrow Na^+ + H_2PO_4^-$$

Can it make a buffer? It can. In more than one way, in fact. The dihydrogen phosphate ion can be either a conjugate base (to phosphoric acid), or it can be an acid in itself. Thus, the following two combinations are buffers:
- A mixture of NaH_2PO_4 and H_3PO_4
- A mixture of NaH_2PO_4 and Na_2HPO_4

Both buffers can actually be prepared, and they would differ by the pH value that they keep relatively constant, as you will see in the next objective. Let's see how the two phosphate buffers work.

- A mixture of NaH_2PO_4 and H_3PO_4

Addition of acid:
$$H_2PO_4^- + H_3O^+ \rightleftharpoons H_3PO_4 + H_2O$$

Phosphoric acid is relatively weak so the equilibrium lies to the right.

Addition of base:
$$H_3PO_4 + OH^- \rightleftharpoons H_2PO_4^- + H_2O$$

$H_2PO_4^-$ is a weaker acid than H_3PO_4, so it prefers to stay undissociated, meaning that the equilibrium above lies to the right as well.

- A mixture of NaH_2PO_4 and Na_2HPO_4

Addition of acid:
$$HPO_4^{2-} + H_3O^+ \rightleftharpoons H_2PO_4^- + H_2O$$
Addition of base:
$$H_2PO_4^- + OH^- \rightleftharpoons HPO_4^{2-} + H_2O$$

Both of these equilibria are clearly shifted to the right, so any offending acid or base is immediately neutralized.

To amuse you even further, I will just mention that the salts NaH_2PO_4 and NaH_2PO_4 can actually act as buffers <u>by themselves</u> (they are **self-buffered**), due to the fact that the products of neutralization of either acid or base are weak acids or bases themselves and thus stay undissociated for the most part. In fact, any **acidic** salt of a **polyprotic weak acid** is self-buffered. The same is true for a base counterpart.

Objective 177.　Calculate the pH of a buffer solution.

1. Calculate the pH of a buffer solution that contains 0.82 M benzoic acid (C_6H_5COOH) and 0.75 M sodium benzoate (C_6H_5COONa). $K_a = 6.5 \times 10^{-5}$ for benzoic acid.

Solution

The "best invention since sliced bread" may actually be the Henderson-Hasselbalch (in short H.H.) equation, which allows us to calculate the pH of a buffer in one shot by plugging in some numbers. Here is the equation for acidic buffers:

$$pH = pK_a + log \frac{[conjugate\ base]}{[acid]}$$

All we need is the pK_a of the weak acid used (published) and the concentrations of the two components. The equation then yields the pH. Applied to this problem:

$$pK_a = -log(6.5 \times 10^{-5}) = 4.19\ (we\ saw\ this\ before)$$

$$pH = 4.19 + log \frac{[C_6H_5COO^-]}{[C_6H_5COOH]} = 4.19 + log \frac{0.75\ M}{0.82\ M} = 4.15$$

The benzoate ion concentration comes from the complete dissociation of sodium benzoate, which is 0.75 M.

2. Calculate the pH of a buffer solution containing 0.25 $M\ NH_3$ and 0.30 $M\ NH_4Cl$. $K_b = 1.8 \times 10^{-5}$ for ammonia.

Solution

This is a basic buffer, and we employ the basic form of the H.H. equation:

$$pOH = pK_b + log \frac{[conjugate\ acid]}{[base]}$$

Here, the base is ammonia and the conjugate acid is the ammonium ion from the ammonium chloride.

$$pOH = pK_b + log \frac{[NH_4^+]}{[NH_3]} = 4.76 + log \frac{0.30}{0.25} = 4.84\ ;\quad pH = 9.18$$

3. Calculate the pH of a buffer solution containing 0.10 $M\ Na_2HPO_4$ and 0.15 $M\ KH_2PO_4$. pK_a's for phosphoric acid are 2.12, 7.21 and 12.67.

Solution

These are two acidic salts, but we saw in the previous objective how such salts actively form buffers (sodium and potassium ions are spectators, of course). The only question here is which of the three pK_a's to use. It helps to write out the three dissociation steps of phosphoric acid, individually:

$$H_3PO_4 + H_2O \rightleftharpoons H_2PO_4^- + H_3O^+\ (pKa_1)$$
$$H_2PO_4^- + H_2O \rightleftharpoons HPO_4^{2-} + H_3O^+\ (pKa_2)$$

$$HPO_4^{2-} + H_2O \rightleftharpoons PO_4^{3-} + H_3O^+ \quad (pKa_3)$$

Which pK_a has the two phosphate ions in the same equation (as acid/conjugate base pair)? It is pKa_2. Thus:

$$pH = pKa_2 + log\frac{[HPO_4^{2-}]}{[H_2PO_4^-]} = 7.21 + log\frac{0.10\ M}{0.15\ M} = 7.03$$

Of course, you must be able to recognize the conjugate base and the acid in the two salts given. This should not be a problem by now.

Objective 178. Calculate the molar ratio of compounds needed to make a buffer of given pH.

1. You are asked to go into the lab and prepare an acetic acid-sodium acetate buffer solution with a pH of 3.81. What molar ratio of CH_3COONa to CH_3COOH should be used?

Solution

$$pH = pK_a + log\frac{[conjugate\ base]}{[acid]} = 4.74 + log\frac{[CH_3COO^-]}{[CH_3COOH]}$$

We now have the target pH of this buffer. The unknown is the ratio under the log, so let's call it X:

$$\frac{[CH_3COO^-]}{[CH_3COOH]} = X \quad so \quad pH = 4.74 + log(X) = 3.81$$

$$log(X) = 3.81 - 4.74 = -0.93 \quad \Rightarrow \quad X = 10^{-0.93} = 0.12$$

As long as we mix acetate and acetic acid in a molar ratio of 0.12:1, the pH of the resulting buffer will be 3.81.

2. The pH of a bicarbonate/carbonic acid buffer is 6.60. What is the ratio of the concentration of H_2CO_3 to HCO_3^- in the buffer?

Solution

$$pH = pK_a + log\frac{[conjugate\ base]}{[acid]} = 6.37 + log\frac{[HCO_3^-]}{[H_2CO_3]} = 6.60$$

$$6.37 + log(X) = 6.60 \quad \Rightarrow \quad X = 1.70$$

Be careful here, before you move to the next problem. X was defined as:

$$\frac{[HCO_3^-]}{[H_2CO_3]} = X$$

The problem is asking for the inverse ratio:

$$\frac{[H_2CO_3]}{[HCO_3^-]} = \frac{1}{X} = \frac{1}{1.70} = 0.59$$

Objective 179.   Calculate the pH of a buffer after a certain amount of acid or base is added.

1.   10.0 mL of 0.200 M FCH_2COOH is titrated against 0.100 M $NaOH$. What will be the solution pH after the
     addition of 10.0 mL of NaOH solution? After 20.0 mL total? After 25.0 mL total? pK_a = 2.59 for FCH_2COOH.

Solution

The reaction during titration is:

$$FCH_2COOH + NaOH \rightarrow FCH_2COONa + H_2O$$

In order to calculate the pH at different points during the titration, we need to know exactly what is in the solution.
The starting amount of acid is:

$$10.0\ mL \times 0.200\frac{mol}{L} = 2.00\ mmol\ FCH_2COOH$$

We will determine how much base (in mmol) is added in each of the three cases given.

First case:

$$10.0\ mL \times 0.100\frac{mol}{L} = 1.00\ mmol\ NaOH$$

If 1.00 mmol base is added to 2.00 mmol acid, and since the stoichiometry is 1:1, then the base is limiting and the
acid is in excess. The 1.00 mmol base is consumed and thus 1.00 mmol salt is made. The solution will contain:

$$1.00\ mmol\ FCH_2COONa\ \ and\ 2.00 - 1.00 = 1.00\ mmol\ FCH_2COOH$$

The solution contains the weak acid and its sodium salt. What is this combination? A buffer. Thus, we can use the
H.H. equation to calculate the pH of the buffer:

$$pH = pK_a + log\frac{[FCH_2COO^-]}{[FCH_2COOH]} = 2.59 + log\frac{1.00\ mmol}{1.00\ mmol} = 2.59$$

Because the volume is the same for both compounds, we can just use the mmol instead of the concentration.

Second case:

$$20.0\ mL \times 0.100\frac{mol}{L} = 2.00\ mmol\ NaOH$$

Now the number of moles of base is the same as that of acid, so we are at the equivalence point. How do we
calculate the pH at the equivalence point in the titration of a weak acid with a strong base? From the hydrolysis of
the conjugate base, see Objective 172.

$$[FCH_2COO^-] = \frac{2.00\ mmol}{10.0 + 20.0\ mL} = 00667\ M$$

	$[FCH_2COO^-]$	$[FCH_2COOH]$	$[OH^-]$
Initial	0.0667	0	0
Change	$-x$	x	x
Equilibrium	$0.0667 - x$	x	x

$$K_b = \frac{[FCH_2COOH][OH^-]}{[FCH_2COO^-]} = \frac{x^2}{0.0667 - x} = \frac{K_w}{K_a} = \frac{1.0 \times 10^{-14}}{10^{-2.59}} = 3.89 \times 10^{-12}$$

$$\frac{x^2}{0.0667} = 3.89 \times 10^{-12} \quad \Rightarrow \quad x = 5.09 \times 10^{-7} M = [OH^-]$$

$$pOH = 6.29 \quad \Rightarrow \quad pH = 7.71$$

The solution is very slightly basic, because of the hydrolysis of the very weak conjugate base.

Third case:

$$25.0 \ mL \times 0.100 \frac{mol}{L} = 2.50 \ mmol \ NaOH$$

Now the base is in excess. What we have in solution is 2.00 mmol FCH_2COONa and 0.50 mol $NaOH$ excess. This mixture is not a buffer. We have a <u>strong base</u> and a <u>salt</u>. The presence of the strong base dominates over everything else, so the concentration of the hydroxide ions in solution will be given primarily by the concentration of excess base, we can neglect everything else. Thus:

$$[OH^-] = \frac{0.50 \ mmol \ NaOH}{10.0 + 25.0 \ mL} = 0.0143 \ M$$

$$pOH = 1.85 \quad and \ pH = 12.15$$

The solution is very basic due to the excess of strong base. As you can see, the contribution of the excess of base to pH is much larger than the hydrolysis of the salt (second case), so it is safe to assume that all other effects are negligible.

Worksheet 23. Buffers

The exercises and problems in this section will allow you to practice the topic until you understand it well.

1. In each of the following cases, the formula of a substance is given. Please suggest a second substance that, when added to a solution of the first, will make a buffer. If no buffer is possible indicate NB or similar. If a buffer is possible, then write chemical reactions that show how the buffer will resist drastic changes in pH upon addition of a strong acid or a strong base. \ plural

   a. $HCOOH$

   $HCOONa$

   $HCOONa_{(aq)} + H^+_{(aq)} \rightleftharpoons HCOOH_{(aq)} + Na^+_{(aq)}$

   $HCOOH_{(aq)} + OH^-_{(aq)} \rightleftharpoons HCOO^-_{(aq)} + H_2O_{(\ell)}$

   b. $KClO_2$ Buffer salt $HClO_2$
)

   KOH ↓ $HClO_2$ $HClO_2_{(aq)} + OH^-_{(aq)} \rightleftharpoons ClO_2^-_{(aq)} + H_2O_{(\ell)}$
   strong   weak
                                                      $KClO_2 + H^+ \rightleftharpoons HClO_2_{(aq)} + K^+_{(aq)}$

   Amine

   c. CH_3NH_2 Basic $CH_3NH_3^+ + OH^- \rightleftharpoons CH_3NH_2 + H_2O_{(\ell)}$
   I'm confused.
                                                    $CH_3NH_2 + H^+ \rightleftharpoons CH_3NH_3^+$

   $CH_3NH_3^+$

   CH_3NH_3Cl

   d. $HClO_4$
   ↓
   Strong Acid , cannot make a buffer

                                                    $HS^- + OH^-_{(aq)} \rightleftharpoons S^{2-}_{(aq)} + H_2O_{(\ell)}$

   e. Na_2S Basic Salt
                                                    $S^{2-}_{(aq)} + H^+_{(aq)} \rightleftharpoons HS^-_{(aq)}$
   $NaOH$ ↓ HS^-
   strong   weak

   f. $NaNO_3$
   $NaOH$ HNO_3 Cannot make a Buffer because its
   strong   strong   conj acids & conj Bases are both
              Neutral Salt   strong

365

2. Calculate the pH of a buffer containing 0.45 M CH_3COOH and 0.35 M CH_3COONa.

$$K_a = 1.8 \times 10^{-5}$$

$$pH = 4.74 + \log\left[\frac{(0.35)}{(0.45)}\right]$$

$$\boxed{pH = 4.6}$$

3. Calculate the pH of a buffer containing 0.200 M Na_2HPO_4 and 0.250 M Na_3PO_4.

4. The pH of a CH_3COONa / CH_3COOH buffer is 4.22. Calculate the ratio of $[CH_3COO^-]$ / $[CH_3COOH]$.

5. Calculate the pH of a buffer solution prepared by dissolving 6.54 g of cyanic acid (HCNO) and 55.26 g of sodium cyanate (NaCNO) in enough water to make 0.750 L of solution.

6. You have 500.0 mL of a buffer solution containing 0.225 M acetic acid and 0.302 M sodium acetate. Calculate the pH of this solution before and after adding three separate increments of 25.0 mL of 0.500 M NaOH solution (four calculations total).

Before:

$$pH = 4.74 + \log\left[\frac{0.302}{0.225}\right]$$

$$\boxed{pH = 4.87}$$

$$500\,mL \cdot \frac{1L}{10^3 mL} \quad \bigcirc \quad \frac{0.225\ \text{acetizated}}{} = 0.1125\ mol\ Acetate$$

$$CH_3COOH + OH^- \rightarrow CH_3COO^- + H_2O(l)$$

0.1125 mol + 0.0125 mol		
0.0125 mol	0.0125 mol	+ 0.0125 mol
0.1	$\emptyset$	0.0125

$$25 \cdot \frac{1L}{10^3 mL} \cdot \frac{0.5\,mol\ NaOH}{1L} =$$

$$50 \cdot \frac{1L}{10^3 mL} \cdot \frac{0.5}{1L} = 0.025\ mol$$

$[CH_3COOH] = 0.19 M$

$$\boxed{pH = 4.95 \text{ (after the first 25mL)}}$$

$$CH_3COOH + OH^- \rightarrow CH_3COO^- + H_2O(l)$$

0.1125	0.025 mol	$\emptyset$
-0.025	-0.025 mol	+ 0.025 mol
0.0875	$\emptyset$	0.025 mol
.55		

$[CH_3COOH] = 0.159 M$

$$\boxed{pH = 5.02 \text{ (after the second 25mL)}}$$

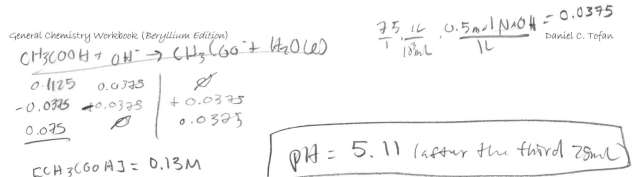

$$\frac{75}{1} \frac{1L}{10^3 mL} \cdot \frac{0.5 mol \, NaOH}{1L} = 0.0375$$

$$CH_3COOH + OH^- \rightarrow CH_3CO_2^- + H_2O (l)$$

$$
\begin{array}{ccc}
0.1125 & 0.0375 & \varnothing \\
-0.0375 & +0.0375 & +0.0375 \\
\hline
0.075 & \varnothing & 0.0375
\end{array}
$$

$[CH_3CO_2A] = 0.13M$

$\boxed{pH = 5.11 \text{ (after the third 75 mL)}}$

7. Calculate the pH of a 0.150 M NH_3 / 0.150 M NH_4Cl buffer after the addition of 10.0 mL of 0.0500 M HCl to 90.0 mL of the buffer.   Brønsted   conj Acid   strong acid

$$\frac{90 mL}{1} \cdot \frac{1L}{10^3 mL} \cdot \frac{0.150 mol}{1L} NH_3 = 0.0135 mol \qquad \frac{10 mL}{1} \cdot \frac{1L}{10^3 mL} \cdot \frac{0.0300 \, mol \, HCl}{1L} = 3 \times 10^{-4}$$

$$NH_3 + H^+ \rightarrow NH_4^+$$

$$
\begin{array}{c}
B \\
D \\
A
\end{array}
\begin{array}{ccc}
0.0135 + & 3\times10^{-4} & \varnothing \\
-3\times10^{-4} & -3\times10^{-4} & +3\times10^{-4} \\
0.0132 \, mol & & \\
\hline
0.1 L &
\end{array}
$$

$K_b \approx 1.8 \times 10^{-5}$

$pK_a = 4.74$

$pH = 4.74 + log\left[\dfrac{(0.132)}{(0.150)}\right]$

$[NH_3] = 0.132$

$\boxed{pH = 4.69}$

8. A buffer is made by mixing 100.0 mL of 0.250 M acetic acid and 100.0 mL of 0.350 M sodium acetate. Calculate the pH of the buffer. Then calculate the mass of solid NaOH needed to raise the pH of this buffer by exactly 1.00 pH units (assume no change in volume upon reaction with the solid NaOH).

Self-assessment

Using the scale indicated, rate your understanding of each learning objective at the completion of this lesson. Identify the areas where your understanding is weak or medium and discuss with your class mates and/or instructor. Write down specific questions you still have at the completion of this topic.

Learning objective	Self-assessment 3 = strong, 2 = medium, 1 = weak, 0 = not done
	3　2　1　0
	3　2　1　0
	3　2　1　0
	3　2　1　0

Lesson 24 – Solubility Equilibria

Learning Objectives

In this lesson you will learn:

- To calculate the concentration of ions in a **saturated solution** of an "**insoluble**" compound
- To calculate the **solubility product** of a compound from solubility data
- To calculate the **molar solubility** of a compound from the solubility product
- To calculate the **pH** of a solution of an insoluble acid or base
- To calculate the pH or concentration of reagent needed for **selective precipitation** of an ion in a solution
- To calculate the solubility of a salt using the **common ion effect**

Pre-requisites: Chemical reactions in solution; Equilibrium.

Self-study questions

Before you start studying the worked examples, you should be able to formulate answers to the questions below. Use a textbook of your choice, or an online source of information, to find the answers.

1. What is meant by equilibrium?
2. How do we know when a salt is insoluble?
3. What is a saturated solution?
4. What is the definition of solubility?
5. What is a solubility product?
6. What is selective precipitation?
7. What is the common ion effect?

[handwritten notes:]
a small % of the salt can dissolve
when all that can be dissolved is dissolved
How much of a substance can be dissolved
Ksp =
what precipitates first)
the decrease in solubility of an ionic precipitate
by the addition of a soluble compound with an
ion in common w/ the precipitate.
Le Chatelier's principle .

Worked examples

This section contains several solved examples that cover the learning objectives listed above. Study each example carefully and make notes in the workbook to check every example that you understood. Repeat several times what you don't understand at first. It should become clearer as you keep working on the examples.

Objective 180.   Calculate the concentration of ions in a saturated solution of an "insoluble" compound.

---

1.   Calculate the concentration of I^- in a saturated AgI solution.

Solution

According to the solubility rules, silver iodide is "insoluble". But nothing is completely insoluble, all such salts actually dissolve to some extent. When solid silver iodide is added to water, there is an equilibrium:

$$AgI_{(s)} \rightleftharpoons Ag^+_{(aq)} + I^-_{(aq)}$$

How much of the solid salt dissociates into ions? Very little, but again, not zero. Each insoluble salt has a dissociation constant, denoted K_{sp} and called **solubility product**. Consult 0for a list of solubility products. The value for silver iodide is 8.3×10^{-17}. This particular salt is less soluble than some, but more soluble than others. The smaller the value of K_{sp}, the less soluble the salt. The expression of K_{sp} is that of a normal equilibrium constant:

$$K_{sp} = [Ag^+][I^-]$$

The solubility product is the product of the concentrations of the ions in solution (raised to powers equal to coefficients if different than 1). The solid substance, as usual, is not part of the equilibrium constant.

The problem asks for the concentration of one of the ions in a saturated solution. A saturated solution will have dissolved as much of the salt as possible. We can construct an ICE table to help understand the process and find this concentration.

	$[Ag^+]$	$[I^-]$
Initial	0	0
Change	x	x
Equilibrium	x	x

We do not put $AgI_{(s)}$ in the table because only species that affect equilibrium show up in there. Thus:

$$K_{sp} = [Ag^+][I^-] = x^2 = 8.3 \times 10^{-17}$$

We can solve for x directly:

$$x = \sqrt{8.3 \times 10^{-17}} = 9.1 \times 10^{-9} \, M = [I^-]$$

Objective 181.   Calculate the solubility product of a compound from solubility data.

1.   The solubility of SrF_2 is 0.107 g/L. Calculate the solubility product of this salt.

Solution

In this problem we calculate K_{sp} from the solubility of the salt. First we need to convert this solubility in g/L into a molarity:

$$0.107g\frac{SrF_2}{L} \times \frac{1\ mol\ SrF_2}{125.617\ g} = 8.55 \times 10^{-4}\ mol\ SrF_2\ /L$$

This number represents the concentration of strontium fluoride that dissolves in the solution. The dissociation of the salt is:

$$SrF_{2\ (s)} \rightleftharpoons Sr^{2+}{}_{(aq)} + 2F^-{}_{(aq)}$$

$$K_{sp} = [Sr^{2+}][F^-]^2$$

From the stoichiometry we can see that the concentration of strontium ions is that of the salt itself, and the concentration of fluoride ions is double that:

$$K_{sp} = (8.55 \times 10^{-4})(2 \times 8.55 \times 10^{-4})^2 = 2.50 \times 10^{-9}$$

Objective 182.   Calculate the molar solubility of a compound from the solubility product.

1.   The solubility product of calcium fluoride is 4.0×10^{-11}. Calculate its molar solubility.

Solution

In this problem we go from solubility product to solubility. We saw the difference in the previous problem. The solubility of the salt is the molar concentration of the dissociated salt. If the salt contains one ion in a 1:1 ratio to the salt itself, such as Ca^{2+} in this case, by determining the concentration of this ion in solution we determine the solubility of the entire salt, as they are the same.

$$CaF_{2\ (s)} \rightleftharpoons Ca^{2+}{}_{(aq)} + 2F^-{}_{(aq)}$$

$$K_{sp} = [Ca^{2+}][F^-]^2$$

Of course, we could determine the fluoride ion concentration, and the solubility of the salt would be half of that, since there are two fluorides per formula unit. Let's stick with the simpler one.

	$[Ca^{2+}]$	$[F^-]$
Initial	0	0
Change	x	$2x$
Equilibrium	x	$2x$

Since there are twice as many fluoride ions produced by dissociation than calcium ions, what goes in the table is $2x$ for fluoride. Thus:

$$K_{sp} = x(2x)^2 = 4x^3 = 4.0 \times 10^{-11}$$

$$x = \sqrt[3]{\frac{4.0 \times 10^{-11}}{4}} = 2.2 \times 10^{-4} \, M = [Ca^{2+}]$$

Because we defined x as the concentration of the calcium ion, the number obtained represents the molar solubility of calcium fluoride as well.

Objective 183. Calculate the pH of a solution of an insoluble acid or base.

1.   Calculate the pH of a saturated solution of $Zn(OH)_2$.

Solution

Why is pH mentioned in this lesson? Because many hydroxides are insoluble, and hydroxides imply hydroxide ions, and so the pH and solubility equilibria can be related.

$$Zn(OH)_{2 \, (s)} \rightleftharpoons Zn^{2+}{}_{(aq)} + 2OH^-{}_{(aq)}$$

$$K_{sp} = [Zn^{2+}][OH^-]^2 = 1.2 \times 10^{-17}$$

From the solubility product, we employ ICE to solve for the hydroxide ion concentration, which will lead to pH.

	$[Zn^{2+}]$	$[OH^-]$
Initial	0	0
Change	x	$2x$
Equilibrium	x	$2x$

$$K_{sp} = x(2x)^2 = 4x^3 = 1.2 \times 10^{-17} \quad \Rightarrow \quad x = 1.4 \times 10^{-6} = [Zn^{2+}]$$

$$[OH^-] = 2x = 2.8 \times 10^{-6}$$

$$pOH = -\log(2.8 \times 10^{-6}) = 5.54 \quad ; \quad pH = 8.46$$

The slightly basic pH is consistent with a slightly soluble base.

2.   Calculate the concentration of aluminum ions in a solution of aluminum hydroxide with a pH equal to 7.4

Solution

$$Al(OH)_{3 \, (s)} \rightleftharpoons Al^{3+}{}_{(aq)} + 3OH^-{}_{(aq)}$$

Now the pH is given, which means that the pH is maintained at a certain value (perhaps with the aid of a buffer). The concentration of the aluminum ions will adjust so that K_{sp} holds.

$$pOH = 14 - 7.4 = 6.6 \quad ; \quad [OH^-] = 10^{-6.6} = 2.5 \times 10^{-7} \, M$$

We now plug this value into the expression of K_{sp} and solve for the aluminum ion concentration:

$$K_{sp} = [Al^{3+}][OH^-]^3 = x(2.5 \times 10^{-7})^3 = 4.6 \times 10^{-33}$$

$$x = \frac{4.6 \times 10^{-33}}{(2.5 \times 10^{-7})^3} = 2.9 \times 10^{-13} \; M = [Al^{3+}]$$

---

3. The pH of a saturated solution of a generic base MOH is 9.68. Calculate the solubility product of MOH.

Solution

MOH is a generic insoluble salt of a monovalent cation:

$$MOH_{(s)} \rightleftharpoons M^+_{(aq)} + OH^-_{(aq)}$$

The concentrations of the cation and hydroxide ion are the same, so after determining the latter from pH we can calculate the solubility product:

$$pOH = 14 - 9.68 = 4.32 \quad ; \quad [OH^-] = 10^{-4.32} = 4.79 \times 10^{-5} \; M = [M^+]$$

$$K_{sp} = [M^+][OH^-] = (4.79 \times 10^{-5})^2 = 2.29 \times 10^9$$

Objective 184.   Calculate the pH or concentration of reagent needed for the selective precipitation of an ion in a solution.

1. What ion will precipitate first, as a hydroxide, from a solution that is initially 0.0400 M in both Cu^{2+} and Ni^{2+}? At what pH will that precipitation occur?

Solution

Both copper and nickel form insoluble hydroxides:

$$Cu(OH)_{2\,(s)} \rightleftharpoons Cu^{2+}_{(aq)} + 2OH^-_{(aq)}$$
$$K_{sp} = [Cu^{2+}][OH^-]^2 = 2.2 \times 10^{-20}$$

$$Ni(OH)_{2\,(s)} \rightleftharpoons Ni^{2+}_{(aq)} + 2OH^-_{(aq)}$$
$$K_{sp} = [Ni^{2+}][OH^-]^2 = 2.0 \times 10^{-15}$$

Upon addition of hydroxide ions (in the form of a strong base such as NaOH, for example), the hydroxide that will precipitate first is the less soluble one, because its solubility product, being lower, will be reached first. Thus, Cu^{2+} will selectively precipitate from this solution once the pH reaches a certain value. Let's find out for what concentration of hydroxide ions that can happen.

$$K_{sp} = [0.400][OH^-]^2 = 2.2 \times 10^{-20}$$

$$[OH^-] = \sqrt{\frac{2.2 \times 10^{-20}}{0.400}} = 2.4 \times 10^{-10} \ M$$

$$pOH = -log(2.4 \times 10^{-10}) = 9.63 \ ; \ pH = 4.37$$

What does this result mean? That cupric hydroxide is very insoluble, and will precipitate even in an acidic solution.

Objective 185. Calculate the solubility of a salt using the common ion effect.

1. What is the molar solubility of $AgCl$ in a solution made by dissolving 10.0g of $CaCl_2$ in 1.00 L of solution?

Solution

In this problem, we are dissolving silver chloride, an "insoluble" salt, not into water, but into a solution that contains calcium chloride. Let's see how that affects the calculation.

Calcium chloride is soluble and thus completely dissociated:

$$CaCl_2 \rightarrow Ca^{2+} + 2Cl^-$$

When silver chloride is added to this solution, it also dissociates a little:

$$AgCl_{(s)} \rightleftharpoons Ag^+_{(aq)} + Cl^-_{(aq)}$$

What is different is that there is a common ion, chloride, already present in solution when the silver chloride dissociates. This will affect the initial concentration of the chloride ion in the calculation. Let's determine that initial concentration:

$$\frac{10.0 \ g \ CaCl_2}{110.984 \ g/mol} = 0.0901 \ mol \ CaCl_2 \ in \ 1.00 \ L \ solution$$

There are two chloride ions per formula unit and so the concentration of chloride is double that of the salt:

$$[Cl^-] = 2 \times 0.0901 \ M = 0.180 \ M$$

The solubility of the silver chloride as a whole will be the concentration of the silver ions in solution. We cannot use chloride ions because there is another source of chloride. Now we can construct the ICE table and calculate the silver ion concentration:

	$[Ag^+]$	$[Cl^-]$
Initial	0	0.180
Change	x	$0.180 + x$
Equilibrium	x	$0.180 + x$

As discussed, there is an initial concentration of chloride already in solution, and that enters our calculation.

$$K_{sp} = [Ag^+][Cl^-] = x(0.18 + x) = 1.8 \times 10^{-10}$$

$$0.18x + x^2 = 1.8 \times 10^{-10}$$

$$x^2 + 0.18x - 1.8 \times 10^{-10} = 0$$

By solving the quadratic equation we get:

$$x = 1.00 \times 10^{-9} M = [Ag^+]$$

We can avoid using the quadratic if we make the approximation that x will be much smaller than 0.18 (which is what we expect for the solubility of such salts). Then the equation is simplified:

$$x(0.18 + x) = 1.8 \times 10^{-10} \quad \Rightarrow \quad 0.18x = 1.8 \times 10^{-10} \quad \Rightarrow \quad x = 1.00 \times 10^{-9} M$$

We get the same result either way. The quadratic equation usually provides an exact solution, but approximations are valid when we work with such small quantities.

Since this is the effective concentration of silver ions in solution, this value will be the molar solubility of solver chloride under the given condition. This type of problem uses what we call the **common ion effect**.

Worksheet 24.   Solubility Equilibria

The exercises and problems in this section will allow you to practice the topic until you understand it well.

1.   Calculate the concentration of barium ions in a saturated barium sulfate solution.

2.   The molar solubility of $MnCO_3$ is 4.2×10^{-6} M. What is the solubility product of this salt?

3.   Calculate the concentration of Pb^{2+} in a solution that is 0.0125 M in Cl^-.

4.   The solubility of silver phosphate is 6.7×10^{-3} g/L. Calculate its solubility product.

5.   The solubility of an ionic compound M_2X_3 (molar mass = 288 g/mol) is 3.6×10^{-17} g/L. Calculate its solubility product.

6. Calculate the pH of a saturated solution of $Al(OH)_3$.

7. The solubility product of silver carbonate, Ag_2CO_3, is 8.1×10^{-12}. Calculate its solubility in g/L.

8. What ion will precipitate first, as a hydroxide, from a solution that is initially 0.0250 M in both Zn^{2+} and Fe^{2+} ?
    At what pH will that precipitation occur?

9. Calculate the molar solubility of $Fe(OH)_2$ at pH=7.00.

10. Calculate the molar solubility of $BaSO_4$ in a solution containing $0.250\ M\ SO_4^{2-}$ ions.

11. Calculate the mass of $CaCO_3$ that will dissolve in 250 mL of 0.050 M $Ca(NO_3)_2$.

Self-assessment

Using the scale indicated, rate your understanding of each learning objective at the completion of this lesson. Identify the areas where your understanding is weak or medium and discuss with your class mates and/or instructor. Write down specific questions you still have at the completion of this topic.

Learning objective	Self-assessment 3 = strong, 2 = medium, 1 = weak, 0 = not done
	3 2 1 0
	3 2 1 0
	3 2 1 0
	3 2 1 0
	3 2 1 0
	3 2 1 0

Lesson 25 – Thermodynamics

Learning Objectives

In this lesson you will learn:

- To determine how the **entropy** of a reaction or physical process changes
- To calculate the **entropy change** in a chemical reaction
- To calculate the **free energy change** in a chemical reaction
- To calculate the **freezing or boiling point** of a substance from thermodynamic data
- To calculate a thermodynamic quantity for a reaction and identify when a reaction is **spontaneous**

Pre-requisites: Balancing chemical reactions; Solutions and concentration.

Self-study questions

Before you start studying the worked examples, you should be able to formulate answers to the questions below. Use a textbook of your choice, or an online source of information, to find the answers.

1. What is enthalpy?
2. What is entropy?
3. What is free energy?
4. What does it mean for a reaction to be spontaneous?

Worked examples

This section contains several solved examples that cover the learning objectives listed above. Study each example carefully and make notes in the workbook to check every example that you understood. Repeat several times what you don't understand at first. It should become clearer as you keep working on the examples.

Objective 186.   Determine how the entropy of a reaction or physical process changes.

1.   For each of the following processes, indicate whether the entropy increases, decreases or stays the same.
   a. $2SO_{2\,(g)} + O_{2\,(g)} \rightarrow 2SO_{3\,(g)}$

   b. $I_{2\,(s)} \rightarrow I_{2\,(g)}$

   c. $Mg^{2+}_{(aq)} + 2OH^{-}_{(aq)} \rightarrow Mg(OH)_{2\,(s)}$

   d. $AgCl_{(s)} \rightarrow Ag^{+}_{(aq)} + Cl^{-}_{(aq)}$

Solutions

Entropy is a measure of disorder and thus it generally increases with the degree of freedom of the substance. This means that the same substance will have higher entropy in liquid state than it does in solid state and even higher entropy in gas state.

a. $2SO_{2\,(g)} + O_{2\,(g)} \rightarrow 2SO_{3\,(g)}$

In this reaction, all species are in gas state so there is no change in phase to help us. Still, on the left we have three moles of gases, and on the right we have two moles. Two smaller molecules combine into a larger molecule, so it is apparent that the entropy **decreases** because the atoms have less freedom in a larger molecule than they do in a simpler one.

b. $I_{2\,(s)} \rightarrow I_{2\,(g)}$

This is the sublimation of iodine. The entropy **increases** because the substance goes from solid to gas state.

c. $Mg^{2+}_{(aq)} + 2OH^{-}_{(aq)} \rightarrow Mg(OH)_{2\,(s)}$

Two ions in aqueous solution (liquid state) combine to form a precipitate (solid), and thus entropy **decreases**.

d. $AgCl_{(s)} \rightarrow Ag^{+}_{(aq)} + Cl^{-}_{(aq)}$

This is the opposite of the above, and so the entropy **increases**.

Objective 187. Calculate the entropy change in a chemical reaction.

1. Determine ΔS^0 for the reaction below when the following quantities are given:

$$SO_{3\,(g)} + H_2O_{\,(l)} \rightarrow H_2SO_{4\,(l)}$$

Compound	$S^o \left(\dfrac{J}{mol\ K}\right)$
$SO_{3\,(g)}$	256.2
$H_2O_{\,(l)}$	69.9
$H_2SO_{4\,(l)}$	156.9

Solution

We are given the standard entropies of the species involved in the chemical reaction above. Like enthalpy, the entropy change in a reaction can be calculated from the standard entropies of reactants and products:

$$\Delta S^\circ = \sum \Delta S^o \ (products) - \sum \Delta S^o \ (reactants)$$

$$\Delta S^\circ = S^o(H_2SO_4) - \left(S^0(SO_3) + S^o(H_2O)\right)$$

$$\Delta S^\circ = 1\ mol\ H_2SO_4 \times 156.9\frac{J}{mol\ K} - \left(1\ mol\ SO_3 \times 256.2\ \frac{J}{mol\ K} + 1\ mol\ H_2O \times 69.9\ \frac{J}{mol\ K}\right) = -169.2\frac{J}{K}$$

Does the answer make sense? We combine a gas and a liquid to make another liquid, so the entropy should decrease, and indeed the change in entropy is negative.

2. Calculate the entropy change when 49.0 kg of sulfuric acid are made according to the previous reaction.

Solution

Thermodynamic quantities such as enthalpy, entropy, and free energy depend on the quantity of reactants and products. In the previous problem, we calculated an entropy change of $= -169.2\ J/K$. That number applies to the quantities in the balanced chemical reaction, which means for 1 mol of H_2SO_4 in this case. When we have a different quantity given, we must use a proportion.

$$49.0\ kg\ H_2SO_4 \times \frac{1\ mol}{98.08\ g/mol} \times \frac{1000\ g}{kg} = 500.\ mol\ H_2SO_4$$

$$\frac{-169.2\ J/K}{1\ mol\ H_2SO_4} = \frac{x}{500.\ mol\ H_2SO_4} \quad \Rightarrow \quad x = 84.6\frac{kJ}{K}$$

Objective 188.   Calculate the free energy change in a chemical reaction.

1.   Calculate the standard free energy for the reaction given.

$$2\,CH_3OH_{(l)} + 3\,O_{2\,(g)} \rightarrow 2\,CO_{2\,(g)} + 4\,H_2O_{(l)}$$

Compound	$\Delta G_f^o \left(\dfrac{kJ}{mol}\right)$
$CH_3OH_{(l)}$	-166.3
$O_{2\,(g)}$	0.00
$CO_{2\,(g)}$	-394.4
$H_2O_{(l)}$	-237.1

Solution

The free energies of formation for all species in the reaction are given. Like enthalpy, the change in free energy of a reaction can be determined from the free energies of formation of reactants and products:

$$\Delta G^\circ = \sum \Delta G_f^o(products) - \sum \Delta G_f^o\ (reactants)$$

$$\Delta G^\circ = \left(2\ \text{mol}\ CO_{2\,(g)}\right) \times \Delta G_f^o\left(CO_{2\,(g)}\right) + \left(4\ \text{mol}\ H_2O_{(l)}\right)$$

$$\times\ \Delta G_f^o\left(H_2O_{(l)}\right) - \left(\left(2\ \text{mol}\ CH_3OH_{(l)}\right) \times \Delta G_f^o\left(CH_3OH_{(l)}\right) + \left(3\ \text{mol}\ O_{2\,(g)}\right) \times \Delta G_f^o\left(O_{2\,(g)}\right)\right)$$

$$\Delta H^\circ = \left(2\ \text{mol}\ CO_{2\,(g)}\right) \times \left(-394.4\frac{kJ}{mol}\right) + \left(4\ \text{mol}\ H_2O_{(l)}\right) \times \left(-237.1\frac{kJ}{mol}\right) - \left(2\ \text{mol}\ CH_3OH_{(l)}\right)$$

$$\times\left(-166.3\frac{kJ}{mol}\right) - \left(3\ \text{mol}\ O_{2\,(g)}\right) \times \left(0\frac{kJ}{mol}\right)$$

$$\Delta G^\circ = -1405\ kJ$$

2. Calculate the standard free energy change at 25°C for the reaction below from the given thermodynamic data.

$$2\ NO_{(g)} + O_{2\ (g)} \rightarrow 2\ NO_{2\ (g)}$$

Compound	$\Delta H_f^o\ \left(\dfrac{kJ}{mol}\right)$	$S^o\ \left(\dfrac{J}{mol\ K}\right)$
$NO_{(g)}$	90.25	210.8
$O_{2\ (g)}$	0.00	205.1
$NO_{2\ (g)}$	33.18	240.1

Solution

We are given enthalpies of formation and entropies for reactants and products. We can use them to calculate the changes in enthalpy and entropy in the reaction given:

$$\Delta H^o = \left(2\ \text{mol}\ NO_{2\ (g)}\right) \times \left(33.18\,\frac{kJ}{mol}\right) - \left(1\ \text{mol}\ O_{2\ (g)}\right) \times \left(0\,\frac{kJ}{mol}\right) - \left(2\ \text{mol}\ NO_{(g)}\right) \times \left(90.25\,\frac{kJ}{mol}\right)$$

$$\Delta H^o = -114.1\ kJ$$

$$\Delta S^o = \left(2\ \text{mol}\ NO_{2\ (g)}\right) \times \left(240.1\,\frac{J}{mol\ K}\right) - \left(1\ \text{mol}\ O_{2\ (g)}\right) \times \left(205.1\,\frac{J}{mol\ K}\right) - \left(2\ \text{mol}\ NO_{(g)}\right) \times \left(210.8\,\frac{J}{mol\ K}\right)$$

$$\Delta S^o = -146.5\,\frac{J}{K}$$

From this data, we can use the relationship between all three thermodynamic quantities to find the free energy:

$$\Delta G = \Delta H - T\Delta S$$

We just need to pay attention to units:

$$\Delta G = -114.1\ kJ - 298\ K\ \times \left(-146.5\,\frac{J}{K}\right) \times \frac{1\ kJ}{1000\ J} = -70.5\ kJ$$

The negative value for the free energy means that the reaction will proceed spontaneously at 25 °C.

Objective 189. Calculate a thermodynamic quantity for a reaction from given data and identify when a reaction is spontaneous.

1. We are given the thermodynamic data for the reaction:

$$CuS_{(s)} + H_{2\,(g)} \rightleftharpoons H_2S_{(g)} + Cu_{(s)}$$

Compound	$\Delta G_f^o \left(\dfrac{kJ}{mol}\right)$	$\Delta H_f^o \left(\dfrac{kJ}{mol}\right)$
$CuS_{(s)}$	-53.6	-53.1
$H_2S_{(g)}$	-33.6	-20.6

a. Calculate ΔG^0 and ΔH^0 at 298 K and 1 atm pressure.
b. Will this reaction proceed spontaneously at 298 K and 1 atm pressure?
c. Calculate ΔS^0 at 298 K and 1 atm pressure.
d. Calculate the equilibrium constant
e. Determine the lowest temperature at which the reaction is spontaneous

Solutions

a. Calculate ΔG^0 and ΔH^0 at 298 K and 1 atm pressure.

Why are we not given the data for $H_{2\,(g)}$ and $Cu_{(s)}$? Because enthalpies of formation, as well as free energies of formation, are zero for <u>elements in their natural state</u>.

$$\Delta G^o = -33.6 - (-53.6) = 20.0\ kJ$$

$$\Delta H^o = -20.6 - (-53.1) = 32.5\ kJ$$

b. Will this reaction proceed spontaneously at 298 K and 1 atm pressure?

ΔG^o is positive, and thus the reaction will NOT be spontaneous under these conditions.

c. Calculate ΔS^0 at 298 K and 1 atm pressure.

$$\Delta G^o = \Delta H^0 - T\Delta S^o = 0 \quad \Rightarrow \quad \Delta S^o = \frac{\Delta H^0 - \Delta G^o}{T} = \frac{32.5\ kJ - 20.0\ kJ}{298\ K} \times \frac{1000\ J}{kJ} = 41.9\frac{J}{K}$$

d. Calculate the equilibrium constant at 268 K

The relationship between free energy and equilibrium constant is:

$$\Delta G^o = -RT\ln K$$

$$\ln K = -\frac{\Delta G^o}{RT} = -\frac{20000\ J}{8.314\frac{J}{mol\ K} \times 298\ K} = -8.07$$

$$K = e^{-8.07} = 3.13 \times 10^{-4}$$

e. Determine the lowest temperature at which the reaction is spontaneous

The reaction becomes spontaneous above the temperature where ΔG^o becomes zero. Then:

$$T = \frac{\Delta H^0}{\Delta S^o} = \frac{32500\ I}{41.9\frac{J}{K}} = 775\ K$$

At temperatures above 775 K, this reaction will become spontaneous. You can check by calculating ΔG^o at a temperature of your choice greater than 775 K.

Objective 190. Calculate the freezing or boiling point from thermodynamic data.

1. Given the following data, calculate the boiling point of HCOOH (formic acid).

Compound	$\Delta H_f^o \left(\frac{kJ}{mol}\right)$	$S^o \left(\frac{J}{mol\ K}\right)$
$HCOOH_{(l)}$	-410	130
$HCOOH_{(g)}$	-363	251

Solution

When a substance changes phase (boiling, freezing, etc.), it is at equilibrium. A system at equilibrium has $\Delta G = 0$.

$$\Delta G^o = \Delta H^0 - T\Delta S^o = 0 \quad \Rightarrow \quad \Delta H^0 = T\Delta S^o \quad \Rightarrow \quad T = \frac{\Delta H^0}{\Delta S^o}$$

We will calculate the change in enthalpy and entropy for the process:

$$HCOOH_{(l)} \rightleftharpoons HCOOH_{(g)}$$

which represents the boiling of formic acid.

$$\Delta H^o = \left(1\ mol\ HCOOH_{(g)}\right) \times \left(-363\frac{kJ}{mol}\right) - \left(1\ mol\ HCOOH_{(l)}\right) \times \left(-410\frac{kJ}{mol}\right) = 47\ kJ$$

$$\Delta S^o = \left(1\ mol\ HCOOH_{(g)}\right) \times \left(251\frac{J}{mol\ K}\right) - \left(1\ mol\ HCOOH_{(l)}\right) \times \left(130\frac{J}{mol\ K}\right) = 121\ \frac{J}{K}$$

$$T = \frac{47000\ J}{121\ J/K} = 388\ K = 115\ °C$$

Worksheet 25. Thermodynamics

The exercises and problems in this section will allow you to practice the topic until you understand it well.

1. For each of the following processes, indicate whether the entropy increases, decreases or stays the same.

   a. $2NH_{3\,(g)} \rightarrow N_{2\,(g)} + 3H_{2\,(g)}$

   b. $Br_{2\,(g)} \rightarrow Br_{2\,(l)}$

   c. $4Al_{(s)} + 3O_{2\,(g)} \rightarrow 2Al_2O_{3\,(s)}$

   d. $2KClO_{3\,(s)} \rightarrow 2KCl_{(s)} + 3O_{2\,(g)}$

2. Determine ΔS^0 for the reaction below when the following quantities are given:

$$SO_{2\,(g)} + NO_{2\,(g)} \rightarrow SO_{3\,(g)} + NO_{(g)}$$

Compound	$S^o \left(\dfrac{J}{mol\,K} \right)$
$SO_{2\,(g)}$	248.5
$NO_{2\,(g)}$	240.5
$SO_{3\,(g)}$	256.2
$NO_{(g)}$	210.6

3. Calculate the entropy change when 65.8 g NO_2 react according to the previous reaction.

4. Calculate the standard free energy for the reaction given.

$$CaC_{2\,(s)} + 2H_2O_{(l)} \rightarrow C_2H_{2\,(g)} + Ca(OH)_{2\,(aq)}$$

Compound	$\Delta G_f^o \left(\dfrac{kJ}{mol}\right)$
$CaC_{2\,(s)}$	-64.9
$H_2O_{(l)}$	-237.1
$C_2H_{2\,(g)}$	209.2
$Ca(OH)_{2\,(aq)}$	-867.6

5. Calculate the free energy change when 250.0 g C_2H_2 are produced according to the previous reaction.

6. Given the following data, calculate the boiling point of mercury.

Compound	$\Delta H_f^o \left(\dfrac{kJ}{mol}\right)$	$S^o \left(\dfrac{J}{mol\,K}\right)$
$Hg_{(l)}$	0	77.4
$Hg_{(g)}$	60.8	174.7

7.   We are given the thermodynamic data for the reaction:

$$SbCl_{5\,(g)} \rightleftharpoons SbCl_{3\,(g)} + Cl_{2\,(g)}$$

Compound	$\Delta G_f^o \left(\dfrac{kJ}{mol}\right)$	$\Delta H_f^o \left(\dfrac{kJ}{mol}\right)$
$SbCl_{5\,(g)}$	-334	-394
$SbCl_{3\,(g)}$	-301	-314

a.   Calculate ΔG^0 and ΔH^0 at 298 K and 1 atm pressure.

b.   Will this reaction proceed spontaneously at 298 K and 1 atm pressure?

c.   Calculate ΔS^0 at 298 K and 1 atm pressure.

d.   Calculate the equilibrium constant

e.   Determine the lowest temperature at which the reaction is spontaneous

Self-assessment

Using the scale indicated, rate your understanding of each learning objective at the completion of this lesson. Identify the areas where your understanding is weak or medium and discuss with your class mates and/or instructor. Write down specific questions you still have at the completion of this topic.

Learning objective	Self-assessment 3 = strong, 2 = medium, 1 = weak, 0 = not done
	3 2 1 0
	3 2 1 0
	3 2 1 0
	3 2 1 0
	3 2 1 0

Lesson 26 – Electrochemistry

Learning Objectives

In this lesson you will learn:

- To "build" **galvanic cells** given any two **half reactions** and their **standard reduction potentials**.
- To write an **electrochemical cell notation** and calculate its **electromotive force**
- To calculate the **electromotive force** or other parameter of a **concentration cell**
- To calculate the amount and/or mass of substance produced in **electrolysis** or another parameter of an **electrolytic cell**

Pre-requisites: Balancing redox reactions in solution; Acids and bases.

Self-study questions

Before you start studying the worked examples, you should be able to formulate answers to the questions below. Use a textbook of your choice, or an online source of information, to find the answers.

1. What is a galvanic cell?
2. What do we call galvanic cells in day to day life?
3. What is a half reaction?
4. What are standard reduction potentials?
5. What is electromotive force?
6. What is a concentration cell?
7. What is electrolysis?
8. What is the difference between charge, current, and voltage?
9. What is Faraday's number?
10. What is a common application of electrolysis?

Worked examples

This section contains several solved examples that cover the learning objectives listed above. Study each example carefully and make notes in the workbook to check every example that you understood. Repeat several times what you don't understand at first. It should become clearer as you keep working on the examples.

Objective 191.   "Build" galvanic cells given any two half reactions and their standard reduction potentials. Write the electrochemical cell notation and calculate its electromotive force.

1.   In each of the tables below, two half reactions are given (identified by their numbers in the table of standard reduction potentials in Appendix H. Use the two half reactions to "construct" a galvanic cell that will produce a positive voltage (electromotive force). Complete the table template below for each set.

   a.   37 and 29

   b.   9 and 19

   c.   12 and 24

Half reaction	Potential
Rearranged:	
Balanced redox reaction:	
Cell notation:	E°=

Discussion

Galvanic cells utilize the power of redox reactions to produce electricity. In order to have a working galvanic cell (which is what we know as a battery), we must combine two half reactions, an oxidation and a reduction, in such a way that we have a positive voltage. That is the condition for a galvanic cell to function spontaneously and produce electricity.

In Appendix H. we have standard reduction potentials. The half reactions that show a positive reduction potential represent reactions that tend to happen spontaneously. Those that have negative reduction potentials will tend to do the opposite, meaning to occur in the reverse direction, as oxidations. The higher the reduction potential the more likely a species will get reduced (and the more powerful reducing agent it will be), and vice versa.

Solutions

a.   The two half reactions give are:

$$(37)\ Mg^{2+} + 2e \rightarrow Mg \quad E^0 = -2.37\ V$$
$$(29)\ Cd^{2+} + 2e \rightarrow Cd \quad E^0 = -0.40\ V$$

Let's put them in our table.

Half reaction	Potential
$Mg^{2+} + 2e^- \rightarrow Mg$	$-2.37\ V$
$Cd^{2+} + 2e^- \rightarrow Cd$	$-0.40\ V$

These are both reductions. In a galvanic cell we must have a redox reaction, so one of the two will have to become an oxidation. When a reduction is reversed to become an oxidation, its potential changes sign. The overall potential of the galvanic cell will be the sum of the two potentials, the reduction and the oxidation. Which of the two can we transform into an oxidation, such that the sum of the resulting potentials is positive? The first half reaction:

Half reaction	Potential
$Mg^{2+} + 2e^- \rightarrow Mg$	$-2.37\,V$
$Cd^{2+} + 2e^- \rightarrow Cd$	$-0.40\,V$
Rearranged: $Mg \rightarrow Mg^{2+} + 2e^-$	$2.37\,V$

The sum of the two potentials will be +1.97 V, so the resulting galvanic cell will work spontaneously and will produce close to 2 V of electricity.

The balanced redox reaction will be the sum of the two half reactions, as we saw in balancing redox reactions in solution. The electrochemical cell notation is a special way of writing electrochemical (galvanic) cells in a short notation. Here it is:

$$Mg \mid Mg^{2+} \parallel Cd^{2+} \mid Cd$$

We list the species getting oxidized on the left, a vertical bar, the product of oxidation, then a double bar (which represents the salt bridge), the species getting reduced, bar, and finally the product of reduction. This is a convention – oxidation always comes first. If there are coefficients other than 1 in the balanced redox reaction, they are **not shown**. Only the identity of the species involved is shown.

Now we can complete the table:

Half reaction	Potential
$Mg^{2+} + 2e^- \rightarrow Mg$	$-2.37\,V$
$Cd^{2+} + 2e^- \rightarrow Cd$	$-0.40\,V$
Rearranged: $Mg \rightarrow Mg^{2+} + 2e^-$	$2.37\,V$
Balanced redox reaction: $Mg + Cd^{2+} \rightarrow Mg^{2+} + Cd$	$1.97\,V$
Cell notation: $Mg \mid Mg^{2+} \parallel Cd^{2+} \mid Cd$	$E° = +1.97\,V$

b.   9 and 19

Half reaction	Potential
$Br_2 + 2e^- \rightarrow 2Br^-$	$1.07\,V$
$Sn^{4+} + 2e^- \rightarrow Sn^{2+}$	$0.15\,V$
Rearranged: $Sn^{2+} \rightarrow Sn^{4+} + 2e^-$	$-0.15\,V$
Balanced redox reaction: $Br_2 + Sn^{2+} \rightarrow 2Br^- + Sn^{4+}$	$0.92\,V$
Cell notation: $Sn^{2+} \mid Sn^{4+} \parallel Br_2 \mid Br^-$	$E° = +0.92\,V$

This time both reduction potentials were positive, but one is larger. We rearranged the second half reaction and converted it into an oxidation so that the overall potential is positive. Notice how the coefficient of the bromide ion in the balanced redox reaction is not shown in the cell notation.

c.   12 and 24

Half reaction	Potential
$Ag^+ + e^- \rightarrow Ag$	$0.80\ V$
~~$Ni^{2+} + 2e^- \rightarrow Ni$~~	~~$-0.25\ V$~~
Rearranged: $Ni \rightarrow Ni^{2+} + 2e^-$	$0.25\ V$
Balanced redox reaction: $Ni + 2\ Ag^+ \rightarrow Ni^{2+} + 2\ Ag$	$1.05\ V$
Cell notation: $Ni \mid Ni^{2+} \parallel Ag^+ \mid Ag$	$E° = +1.05\ V$

This case was easier because one potential was positive and one was negative, so clearly by reversing the half reaction with a negative potential we are guaranteed an overall positive outcome. Notice that balancing the redox reaction was necessary to have the same number of electrons transferred. Multiplying a half reaction by any coefficient <u>does not change the numerical value of its reduction potential</u>!

Objective 192.   Calculate the electromotive force or other parameter of a concentration cell.

1.   Calculate the electromotive force of a cell consisting of a $Pb \mid Pb^{2+}$(0.020 M) half-cell and a Pt/H^+(0.010 M)$\mid H_2$(g, 1 atm) half-cell.

Discussion

The voltage, or electromotive force $E°$, that we calculated for galvanic cells in the previous objective, is valid when the concentrations of all aqueous species are 1.0 M, and the pressures of any gas phase species are 1.00 atm. In real galvanic cells, concentrations are almost never 1.0 M. the Nernst equation allows us to calculate the electromotive force of any galvanic cell for any concentration of the species involved:

$$E = E° - \frac{0.0592}{n} log\ Q$$

where $E°$ is the standard electromotive force as calculated in the previous objective for 1.0 M concentrations, n is the number of electrons transferred between the oxidation and the reduction half reactions, and Q is the reaction quotient of the balanced redox reaction taking place in the electrochemical cell (see Objective 162).

Solution

Our galvanic cell is given in cell notation:

$$Pb \mid Pb^{2+}\ (0.020\ M) \parallel Pt/H^+\ (0.010\ M) \mid H_2\ (1 atm)$$

This cell notation is more complete than what we saw before, because it lists the concentrations or pressures of the species in the cell. It also shows that an inert platinum electrode is used for the hydrogen ion / hydrogen gas half reaction. Such an electrode is needed to conduct the electricity, but it is not part of the redox reaction. The reaction quotient will have to include the concentrations and pressures of products and those of the reactants.

What is the chemical reaction taking place in this cell? From the oxidation (on left) and reduction (on right) in the cell notation we can piece together and balance the overall redox reaction:

$$Pb + 2H^+ \rightarrow Pb^{2+} + H_2$$

Since Pb is oxidized to Pb^{2+}, the number of electrons transferred is 2. The Nernst equation for this cell becomes:

$$E = E° - \frac{0.0592}{2} log \frac{[Pb^{2+}] \times P_{H_2}}{[H^+]^2}$$

We only need to calculate E° for this cell. From the table of potentials we get:

$$(22)\ Pb^{2+} + 2e \rightarrow Pb \quad E^0 = -0.13\ V$$
$$(20)\ 2H^+ + 2e \rightarrow H_2 \quad E^0 = 0.00\ V$$

As we know by now, half reaction (22) will be reversed and become the oxidation, and so the overall potential will be:

$$E^o = +0.13\ V$$

Now we can solve the big equation:

$$E = 0.13 - \frac{0.0592}{2} log \frac{0.020\ M \times 1.00\ atm}{(0.010\ M)^2} = 0.06\ V$$

As you can see, the potential is different in these given conditions compared to standard 1.0 M concentrations.

---

2. The measured voltage of the cell Pt(s) | H$_2$(1.0 atm) | H$^+$(aq) || Ag$^+$(0.200 M) | Ag(s) is 1.07 V at 25 $°C$. Calculate the pH of the solution.

Solution

In this problem we are given the electromotive force and need to calculate the pH, because hydrogen ions are involved again. The redox reaction is:

$$H_2 + 2Ag^+ \rightarrow 2H^+ + 2Ag$$

The Nernst equation:

$$E = E° - \frac{0.0592}{2} log \frac{[H^+]^2}{[Ag^+]^2 \times P_{H_2}}$$

Calculate E° for this cell. From the table of potentials we get:

$$(12)\ Ag^+ + e \rightarrow Ag \quad^+ \quad E^0 = 0.80\ V$$
$$(20)\ 2H^+ + 2e \rightarrow H_2 \quad E^0 = 0.00\ V$$

To make this cell work, we will reverse half reaction (20), so hydrogen gas will be oxidized and silver ions will be reduced. The cell potential is thus +0.80 V. we will solve for the hydrogen ion concentration below.

$$1.07 = 0.80 - \frac{0.0592}{2} log \frac{[H^+]^2}{(0.200 \text{ M})^2 \times 1.00 \text{ atm}}$$

$$0.27 = -\frac{0.0592}{2} log \frac{x^2}{0.04}$$

$$log \frac{x^2}{0.04} = -9.12 \quad \Rightarrow \quad \frac{x^2}{0.04} = 10^{-9.12} = 7.59 \times 10^{-10}$$

$$x^2 = 3.03 \times 10^{-11} \quad \Rightarrow \quad x = 5.51 \times 10^{-6} = [H^+]$$

$$pH = -\log(5.51 \times 10^{-6}) = 5.26$$

Objective 193. Calculate the amount and/or mass of substance produced in electrolysis or another parameter of an electrolytic cell.

1. How many faradays are transferred in an electrolytic cell when a current of 5.0 amperes flows for 7.0 hours?

Solution

$$charge(C) = current\ (A) \times time\ (s) = 5.0\ A \times 7.0\ h \times 3600 \frac{s}{h} = 126000\ C$$

2. What mass of nickel would be electroplated by passing a constant current of 13.3 A through a solution of $NiSO_4$ for 280.0 min?

Solution

Electric current can be used to reduce metal ions to the free metal, by supplying electrons. The charge passed through the solution is:

$$13.3\ A \times 280 \min \times 60\ s/min = 223440\ C$$

To relate charge to mass of nickel, we convert the charge into moles of electrons, using Faraday's number:

$$223440\ C \times \frac{1\ mol\ e^-}{96500\ C} = 2.32\ mol\ e^-$$

How is nickel reduced to the free metal?

$$Ni^{2+} + 2e^- \rightarrow Ni$$

The Ni^{2+} ions from the solution of nickel sulfate are reduced to the metal form by accepting 2 electrons per nickel. Thus:

$$2.32\ mol\ e^- \times \frac{1\ mol\ Ni^{2+}}{2\ mol\ e^-} \times \frac{1\ mol\ Ni}{1\ mol\ Ni^{2+}} = 1.16\ mol\ Ni\ can\ be\ obtained$$

$$1.16 \; mol \; Ni \times 58.693 \frac{g}{mol} = 68.0 \; g \; Ni$$

---

3. How long will it take to produce 87.5 g of aluminum metal by the reduction of aluminum ion in an electrolytic cell with a current of 3.0 A?

Solution

Let's determine how many moles of electrons are needed to make this much aluminum metal according to the reduction:

$$Al^{3+} + 3e^- \rightarrow Al$$

$$\frac{87.5 \; g \; Al}{26.98 \; g/mol} = 3.24 \; mol \; Al$$

$$3.24 \; mol \; Al \; \times \; \frac{3 \; mol \; e^-}{1 \; mol \; Al} = 9.72 \; mol \; e^- \; needed$$

$$9.72 \; mol \; e^- \times 96500 \frac{C}{mol} = 938836 \; C$$

$$\frac{938836 \; C}{3.0 \; A} = 312945 \; s = 86.9 \; hours$$

Other quantities such as the intensity of the current or the molar mass of an unknown metal can be determined in the same way from electrolysis.

Worksheet 26.   Electrochemistry

The exercises and problems in this section will allow you to practice the topic until you understand it well.

1.   In each of the tables below, two half reactions are given (identified by their numbers in the table of standard reduction potentials in Appendix H. Use the two half reactions to "construct" a galvanic cell that will produce a positive voltage (electromotive force). Complete the table template below for each set.

   a.   17 and 21

Half reaction	Potential
Rearranged:	
Balanced redox reaction:	
Cell notation:	E°=

   b.   6 and 9

Half reaction	Potential
Rearranged:	
Balanced redox reaction:	
Cell notation:	E°=

   c.   3 and 26

Half reaction	Potential
Rearranged:	
Balanced redox reaction:	
Cell notation:	E°=

   d.   4 and 28

Half reaction	Potential
Rearranged:	
Balanced redox reaction:	
Cell notation:	E°=

e.   7 and 13

Half reaction	Potential
Rearranged:	
Balanced redox reaction:	
Cell notation:	E°=

f.   17 and 32

Half reaction	Potential
Rearranged:	
Balanced redox reaction:	
Cell notation:	E°=

g.   20 and 30

Half reaction	Potential
Rearranged:	
Balanced redox reaction:	
Cell notation:	E°=

2.   Calculate the electromotive force of a cell consisting of a $Ag|Ag^+(0.091\ M)$ half-cell and a $Pt/H^+(pH = 8.00)\ |\ H_2(g, 1\ atm)$ half-cell.

3. Calculate the electromotive force of a cell consisting of a $Zn|Zn^{2+}(0.055\ M)$ half-cell and a $Pt/H^+(0.98\ M)\ |\ H_2(g, 2\ atm)$ half-cell.

4. The measured voltage of the cell $Pt_{(s)}\ |\ H_2(1.0\ atm)|H^+(aq)\ ||\ Ag^+(0.180\ M)\ |\ Ag_{(s)}$ is 1.15 V at 25 $°C$. Calculate the pH of the solution.

5. How many faradays are transferred in an electrolytic cell when a current of 8.0 amperes flows for 8.0 hours?

6. What mass of nickel would be electroplated by passing a constant current of 5.4 A through a solution of $NiSO_4$ for 360 min?

7. How long will it take to produce 32.5 g of aluminum metal by the reduction of aluminum ion in an electrolytic cell with a current of 7.80 A?

8. Calculate the charge needed to deposit 25.0 g silver from a silver nitrate solution.

9. The passage of 0.750 A for 25.0 min deposited 0.369 g of a divalent metal. Identify the metal.

Self-assessment

Using the scale indicated, rate your understanding of each learning objective at the completion of this lesson. Identify the areas where your understanding is weak or medium and discuss with your class mates and/or instructor. Write down specific questions you still have at the completion of this topic.

Learning objective	Self-assessment 3 = strong, 2 = medium, 1 = weak, 0 = not done
	3 2 1 0
	3 2 1 0
	3 2 1 0

Lesson 27 – Coordination Chemistry

Learning Objectives

In this lesson you will learn:
- To name **coordination compounds**
- To determine the **geometry around the metal ion**, **crystal field orbital splitting**, and **magnetic properties** of a coordination compound
- To calculate **absorbance**, concentration, or other parameters using **Beer's law**

Pre-requisites: Atomic structure; Classes of compounds and nomenclature; Molecular structure.

Self-study questions

Before you start studying the worked examples, you should be able to formulate answers to the questions below. Use a textbook of your choice, or an online source of information, to find the answers.

1. What is a coordination compound?
2. What is a ligand?
3. What are the common geometries of metal ions in coordination compounds?
4. What is meant by crystal field splitting?
5. What is the spectrochemical series?
6. What is meant by high spin?
7. What is meant by low spin?
8. What is meant by diamagnetic?
9. What is meant by paramagnetic?
10. What is the meaning of Beer's law? Is there a Wine's law?

Worked examples

This section contains several solved examples that cover the learning objectives listed above. Study each example carefully and make notes in the workbook to check every example that you understood. Repeat several times what you don't understand at first. It should become clearer as you keep working on the examples.

Objective 194. **Given the formula of a coordination compound, determine its name, geometry around the metal ion, crystal field orbital splitting, and magnetic properties.**

1. Complete the table for each coordination compound given.
   a. $[Mn(en)_2(F)(I)]NO_3$

   b. $Na_2[CuCl_4]$ (tetrahedral)

Show dissociation in aqueous solution	List all ligands	Oxidation # for transition metal	Electron configuration of	
			Free metal	Metal ion
Name of compound	Draw geometry of complex ion		Draw orbital diagram and fill in electrons	
Magnetic properties			High spin (HS) or low spin (LS)?	

Solutions

Coordination compounds differ from normal salts of transition metals by the fact that there are neutral molecules or charged ions that bind directly to the metal ion and form what we call a complex ion. These entities are called ligands. Ligands can be monodentate (they bind through only one atom) or polydentate (they bind through multiple atoms). What makes them behave in this manner is the fact that they have extra pairs of electrons, which transition metals like because they have some empty orbitals ready to accept such extra electron pairs.

In order to name coordination compounds and understand their electronic structure, we need to understand their dissociation in aqueous solution. We will fill out the table template above with all the information in one exercise, because all the sub-questions are related to each other.

a. $[Mn(en)_2(F)(I)]NO_3$

The complex ion is indicated in square brackets, and any counter ions, positive or negative, are outside. In solution, complex ions are entities of their own, and do not break apart. This compound dissociates in water as follows:

$$[Mn(en)_2(F)(I)]NO_3 \rightarrow [Mn(en)_2(F)(I)]^+ + NO_3^-$$

How do we know that this complex ion carries a +1 charge? We don't. We figure it out from the counter ions. Since we have one nitrate ion, which we know is a -1 anion, we imply the charge on the complex ion.

Now we are going to list the ligands in the complex ion:
- *en* is ethylenediamine, a neutral molecule
- F^-, the fluoride ion, is called *fluoro* when it acts as a ligand

- I^-, the iodide ion, is called *iodo* when it acts as a ligand

Most ligands are either neutral molecules, or ions. The names of many ligands are different than the normal names of the entities they represent. As a further example, water is called aqua when it is a ligand. Consult the list of ligands in Appendix I. for the names of some common ligands.

The next step is to determine the oxidation number of the metal ion inside the complex ion. This is important for nomenclature, as well as for electronic structure. The sum of all charges of the ligands plus the charge of the metal ion equals the charge of the complex ion. Thus:

$$x + 2 \times 0 + (-1) + (-1) = +1 \quad \Rightarrow \quad x = +3$$

The metal ion is Mn^{3+}. This is not obvious without analyzing the composition of the complex ion, as manganese is more common in the +2 oxidation state.

Now we can name our compound. The following rules apply for naming coordination compounds:

1) The positive ion is named first, whether it is the complex ion or not

2) Within the complex ion, ligands are named first, in alphabetical order, and then the metal ion is named

3) The number of each ligand appearing in the complex ion is indicated by a prefix from the table below (middle column). BUT: if the name of the ligand itself already contains **any of the prefixes** from the middle column, then the **last column** is used to indicate how many of that ligand (you will see in examples)

4) If the complex ion is positive (or if we have a neutral coordination compound), the name of the metal ion does not change; if the complex ion is negative, then the name of the metal ion will be changed to include the suffix -ate

5) The name of the metal is listed followed by the oxidation number in parentheses, as a **roman numeral**

6) The name of the negative ion comes last, without any prefix to indicate how many

Here is the table of prefixes mentioned in the rules:

2	di	bis
3	tri	tris
4	tetra	tetrakis
5	penta	pentakis
6	hexa	hexakis
7	hepta	
8	octa	
9	nona	
10	deca	

Let's name our coordination compound. The complex ion is positively charged, so we name it first. The ligands, in alphabetical order, are: ethylenediamine, fluoro, and iodo. There are two ethylenediamine ligands, so we should use the prefix di- in front of it. But wait: ethylene**di**amine already contains the prefix "di" as part of its name, so we are not allowed to use any of these prefixes again. Instead, we will use **bis**. Because the complex ion is positive, the name of the metal ion remains manganese, and we add (III) to indicate its oxidation number. Lastly, we add "nitrate" to name the counter ion. The name of this coordination compound is thus:

Bis- ethylenediamine-fluoro-iodo-manganese(III) nitrate. Looks complicated, right? It is. The dashes are not required in the name, and you will see coordination compounds named without dashes. That leads to some very long and ugly words, and for that reason I prefer to use dashes to separate the various parts. This compound is a nitrate, and a complex one.

What about the geometry? Coordination compounds adopt a certain geometry around the metal ion, which is one of the known geometries from the molecular structure section. Ethylenediamine is a bidentate ligand, meaning it binds to metals using two atoms, which are nitrogen atoms. That is a total of four bonds. Counting the other two (fluoro and iodo), we determine that there are 6 bonds formed by ligands to the metal ion. This number is called the **coordination number**. When 6 bonds are around a central atom/ion, the geometry is octahedral. We can sketch the geometry of this complex as follows:

$$\text{F}$$

(structure of the Mn complex with ethylenediamine ligands, F above and I below)

I represented the two ethylenediamine molecules in square the plane, with the fluoro and iodo above and below. We are not looking at isomerism for now, so it really doesn't matter how you draw these compounds. You just need to have the right number of bonds on the central metal, and the correct geometry.

What is the electron configuration of ground state manganese? $[Ar]4s^2\, 3d^5$. What is the electron configuration of the Mn^{3+} ion? Remember, we remove electrons starting from the s orbitals, and so the ion configuration will be $[Ar]4s^0\, 3d^4$. We will place these electrons on the d orbitals of the metal in an orbital diagram that we will draw.

When ligands bind to the metal ion, they distort the shape and energy levels of the d orbitals. This effect is what we call crystal field splitting. The positioning of the d orbitals depends on the geometry of the complex ion. We will only consider three geometries: octahedral (coordination number, C.N., = 6), tetrahedral (C.N. = 4), and square planar (C.N. = 4 as well).

The following three diagrams show how the d orbitals of a transition metal split up depending on the geometry:

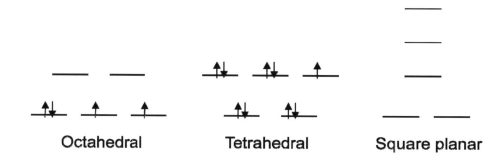

Electrons follow the same rules when occupying these orbitals as they do in regular atomic or molecular orbitals. However, the difference in energy between the groups of orbitals can differ based on the type of ligands attached to the metal ion. The following order is called the spectrochemical series:

$$I^- < Br^- < Cl^- < F^- < OH^- < H_2O < (COO)_2^{2-} < NH_3 < en < NO_2^- < CN^-$$

Ligands on the left cause a small splitting and they are called weak field ligands. Ligands on the right cause a large splitting and are called strong field ligands. The cut-off, for our purposes, will be water (aqua). Ligands up to and including water will be weak, and the ones to the right of water will be strong.

If the ligand field is weak, then electrons can occupy all orbitals, one per orbital, before a second electron is added to any orbital. If the ligand field is strong, then orbitals of lower energy MUST be filled completely before electrons are allowed on higher energy orbitals. If there is a mix of strong and weak field ligands, the strong field ones will win.

Let's place the 4 d orbitals of our manganese ion on the d orbitals. Because the geometry is octahedral, the first split pattern applies.

Since the ligand field is strong (due to the presence of ethylenediamine), the fourth electron will pair up with another electron in one of the lower energy orbitals. If all ligands were weak, then we would have seen the fourth electron on one of the two higher energy d orbitals, with its spin pointing up.

These two types of configurations are called high spin and low spin. A strong crystal field leads to a low spin configuration, because electrons are paired up as much as possible, and the number of unpaired electrons (spins) is minimized. If the crystal field is weak, then we have a high spin situation, because the number of unpaired spins is maximized. Our manganese complex is a low spin one.

Finally, the magnetic properties. If there are ANY unpaired electrons in the metal ion orbitals, then the coordination compound is paramagnetic. If ALL electrons are paired up, the compound is diamagnetic. We can now fill the table completely, as follows:

Show dissociation in aqueous solution	List all ligands	Oxidation # for transition metal	Electron configuration of	
			Free metal	Metal ion
$[Mn(en)_2(F)(I)]NO_3$ $\rightarrow [Mn(en)_2(F)(I)]^+ + NO_3^-$	en F^- I^-	+3	$[Ar]4s^2\,3d^5$	$[Ar]4s^0\,3d^4$

Name of compound	Draw geometry of complex ion	Draw orbital diagram and fill in electrons
$Bis-ethylenediamine$ $-fluoro-iodo$ $-manganese(III)\ nitrate$	F, N, Mn, N, N, N, I	
Magnetic properties $paramagnetic$		**High spin (HS) or low spin (LS)?** $Low\ spin$

b. $Na_2[CuCl_4]$ (tetrahedral)

The geometry is specified because the coordination number is 4, and there are two possible geometries for that, as we saw. You cannot tell which geometry is adopted by each compound with C.N. = 4, so you will be given this info.

The charge of the complex ion is -2, implied from the two sodium counter ions. The ligands are all chloro, Cl^-, four of them. The oxidation number on Cu must be +2: $+2 + 4(-1) = -2$.

Because the complex ion is negatively charged, the name of the metal will become cup**rate**. The name is then: Sodium tetra-chloro-cuprate(II). Since all ligands are weak fields, the complex will be high spin. The rest of the information should be straightforward. Let's see the table:

Show dissociation in aqueous solution	List all ligands	Oxidation # for transition metal	Electron configuration of	
			Free metal	Metal ion
$Na_2[CuCl_4] \rightarrow 2Na^+$ $+ [CuCl_4]^{2-}$	Cl^-	+2	$[Ar]4s^1\,3d^{10}$	$[Ar]4s^0\,3d^9$

Name of compound	Draw geometry of complex ion	Draw orbital diagram and fill in electrons
$Sodium\ tetra-chloro$ $-cuprate(II)$	Cl, Cu^{2+}, Cl, Cl, Cl	
Magnetic properties $paramagnetic$		**High spin (HS) or low spin (LS)?** $High\ spin$

Objective 195.   Calculate absorbance, concentration, or other parameters using Beer's law.

1. A solution with a concentration of 0.14 M is measured to have an absorbance of 0.43. Another solution of the same chemical is measured under the same conditions and has an absorbance of 0.37. What is the concentration of the second solution?

Solution

Beer's law: $A = \varepsilon c l$

where A is the absorbance of a solution, ε is the extinction coefficient of the compound dissolved (a constant for each compound at a given wavelength), c is the molarity of the solution, and l is the path length (the thickness of the layer of solution through which the light passes on its way to the detector).

The two measurements described in this problem refer to the same compound, so the extinction coefficient is the same. We can apply Beer's law for each situation:

$$A_1 = \varepsilon c_1 l$$
$$A_2 = \varepsilon c_2 l$$

"Under the same conditions" means that the path length is the same too. We can divide the two equations in order to find the unknown concentration:

$$\frac{A_1}{A_2} = \frac{c_1}{c_2} \quad \Rightarrow \quad c_2 = \frac{A_2 \times c_1}{A_1} = \frac{0.37 \times 0.14 \, M}{0.43} = 0.12 \, M$$

2. A solution is prepared to be 0.400 M. A 10.00 mL sample of this solution is placed in a 250.00 mL volumetric flask and diluted to the mark. A sample of the diluted solution is placed in a 1.00 cm cuvette and its absorbance is measured at 550 nm, yielding a value of 0.785. Determine the extinction coefficient of the substance based on this one measurement.

Solution

The first dilution:

$$M_1 V_1 = M_2 V_2 \quad \Rightarrow \quad M_2 = \frac{M_1 V_1}{V_2} = \frac{0.400 \, M \times 10.00 \, mL}{250.00 \, mL} = 0.0160 \, M$$

$$\varepsilon = \frac{A}{c \, l} = \frac{0.785}{0.0160 \, M \times 1.00 \, cm} = 49.1 \, M^{-1} cm^{-1}$$

The wavelength does not enter the calculation, but we need to specify at what wavelength the extinction coefficient was measured, as it is wavelength dependent.

Worksheet 27. Coordination Chemistry

The exercises and problems in this section will allow you to practice the topic until you understand it well.

1. Complete the table for each coordination compound given.
    a. $K_3[Fe(CN)_6]$

Show dissociation in aqueous solution	List all ligands	Oxidation # for transition metal	Electron configuration of	
			Free metal	Metal ion
Name of compound	Draw geometry of complex ion		Draw orbital diagram and fill in electrons	
Magnetic properties			High spin (HS) or low spin (LS)?	

    b. $[Cr(en)_3]_2(SO_4)_3$

Show dissociation in aqueous solution	List all ligands	Oxidation # for transition metal	Electron configuration of	
			Free metal	Metal ion
Name of compound	Draw geometry of complex ion		Draw orbital diagram and fill in electrons	
Magnetic properties			High spin (HS) or low spin (LS)?	

c.   [Cr(OH$_2$)$_3$Br$_3$]

Show dissociation in aqueous solution	List all ligands	Oxidation # for transition metal	Electron configuration of	
			Free metal	Metal ion
Name of compound	Draw geometry of complex ion		Draw orbital diagram and fill in electrons	
Magnetic properties			High spin (HS) or low spin (LS)?	

d.   K$_4$[Fe(CN)$_6$]

Show dissociation in aqueous solution	List all ligands	Oxidation # for transition metal	Electron configuration of	
			Free metal	Metal ion
Name of compound	Draw geometry of complex ion		Draw orbital diagram and fill in electrons	
Magnetic properties			High spin (HS) or low spin (LS)?	

e.   [Co(en)$_3$]Cl$_3$

Show dissociation in aqueous solution	List all ligands	Oxidation # for transition metal	Electron configuration of	
			Free metal	Metal ion
Name of compound	Draw geometry of complex ion		Draw orbital diagram and fill in electrons	
Magnetic properties			High spin (HS) or low spin (LS)?	

f.   K$_2$[Cu(OH)$_4$(NH$_3$)$_2$]

Show dissociation in aqueous solution	List all ligands	Oxidation # for transition metal	Electron configuration of	
			Free metal	Metal ion
Name of compound	Draw geometry of complex ion		Draw orbital diagram and fill in electrons	
Magnetic properties			High spin (HS) or low spin (LS)?	

g. [Pt(NH$_3$)$_2$(OH$_2$)Cl]$_3$PO$_4$ (square planar)

Show dissociation in aqueous solution	List all ligands	Oxidation # for transition metal	Electron configuration of	
			Free metal	Metal ion
Name of compound	Draw geometry of complex ion		Draw orbital diagram and fill in electrons	
Magnetic properties			High spin (HS) or low spin (LS)?	

h. [Zn(NH$_3$)$_4$]SO$_4$ (tetrahedral)

Show dissociation in aqueous solution	List all ligands	Oxidation # for transition metal	Electron configuration of	
			Free metal	Metal ion
Name of compound	Draw geometry of complex ion		Draw orbital diagram and fill in electrons	
Magnetic properties			High spin (HS) or low spin (LS)?	

i.   [Pt(en)$_3$](NO$_3$)$_4$

Show dissociation in aqueous solution	List all ligands	Oxidation # for transition metal	Electron configuration of	
			Free metal	Metal ion
Name of compound	Draw geometry of complex ion		Draw orbital diagram and fill in electrons	
Magnetic properties			High spin (HS) or low spin (LS)?	

j.   [Co(NH$_3$)$_2$(en)(Cl)$_2$]$_2$SO$_4$

Show dissociation in aqueous solution	List all ligands	Oxidation # for transition metal	Electron configuration of	
			Free metal	Metal ion
Name of compound	Draw geometry of complex ion		Draw orbital diagram and fill in electrons	
Magnetic properties			High spin (HS) or low spin (LS)?	

k. $[Cr(NH_3)_6]_2[NiCl_4]_3$

Show dissociation in aqueous solution	List all ligands	Oxidation # for transition metal	Electron configuration of	
			Free metal	Metal ion
Name of compound	Draw geometry of complex ion		Draw orbital diagram and fill in electrons	
Magnetic properties			High spin (HS) or low spin (LS)?	

l. $K_3[Co(NO_2)_6]$

Show dissociation in aqueous solution	List all ligands	Oxidation # for transition metal	Electron configuration of	
			Free metal	Metal ion
Name of compound	Draw geometry of complex ion		Draw orbital diagram and fill in electrons	
Magnetic properties			High spin (HS) or low spin (LS)?	

2.   A solution with a concentration of 0.225 M is measured to have an absorbance of 0.970. Another solution of the same chemical is measured under the same conditions and has an absorbance of 1.343. What is the concentration of the second solution?

413

3. The extinction coefficient of a particular chemical is 225 $M^{-1}cm^{-1}$. What is the concentration of a solution made from this chemical if a 1.00 cm sample has an absorbance of 1.33?

4. A stock solution is prepared to be 0.250 M. Various dilutions are made from this solution and their absorbencies are measured. Use the data below to fill in the blanks with the appropriate results.

Preparation of sample for measurement			Wavelength = 470 nm		Wavelength = 540 nm		Measured sample	
Volume of stock solution (mL)	Volume of water added (mL)	Volume after dilution (mL)	Absorbance	Extinction coefficient ($M^{-1}cm^{-1}$)	Absorbance	Extinction coefficient ($M^{-1}cm^{-1}$)	Path length (cm)	Concentration of solution (M)
4.00	0		1.225		0.783		1.00	
10.00	15.00						1.00	
5.00		100.00					2.00	
10.00							2.00	0.0250
		250.00					10.00	6.50×10^{-3}

5. Consider an electrochemical cell made of: a nickel electrode immersed in a 1M $NiSO_4$ solution (beaker A), a chromium electrode immersed in a 1M $Cr_2(SO_4)_3$ solution (beaker B), and a salt bridge containing 1 M potassium sulfate. Answer the following questions:

A. Complete the table below.

Half reaction	Potential
Rearranged:	
Balanced redox reaction:	
Cell notation:	E°=

B. Check all true statements below
   a. electrons flow from beaker A to beaker B
   b. electrons flow from beaker B to beaker A
   c. the concentration of nickel ions increases
   d. the concentration of nickel ions decreases
   e. the concentration of chromium ions increases
   f. the concentration of chromium ions decreases
   g. the nickel is the anode
   h. the chromium is the anode
   i. sulfate ions will move to beaker A when the cell works
   j. sulfate ions will move to beaker B when the cell works
   k. potassium ions will move to beaker A when the cell works
   l. potassium ions will move to beaker B when the cell works
   m. the nickel electrode will be **heavier** at the end of the experiment
   n. the chromium electrode will be **heavier** at the end of the experiment
   o. the absorbance of the solution in beaker A should increase
   p. the absorbance of the solution in beaker B should increase
   q. if the poles of the voltmeter are switched, the voltage indicated will change sign

C. How will be the conductivity of the solution in beaker A **at the end** of the experiment compared to the beginning?
   i. higher
   ii. the same
   iii. lower

D. How will be the conductivity of the solution in beaker B **at the end** of the experiment compared to the beginning?
   i. higher
   ii. the same
   iii. lower

E. How will be the conductivity of the solution in beaker A compared to that of the solution in beaker B **at the beginning** of the experiment?
   i. higher
   ii. the same
   iii. lower

F. How will be the conductivity of the solution in beaker A compared to that of the solution in beaker B **at the end** of the experiment?
   i. higher
   ii. the same
   iii. lower

Self-assessment

Using the scale indicated, rate your understanding of each learning objective at the completion of this lesson. Identify the areas where your understanding is weak or medium and discuss with your class mates and/or instructor. Write down specific questions you still have at the completion of this topic.

Learning objective	Self-assessment 3 = strong, 2 = medium, 1 = weak, 0 = not done
	3 2 1 0
	3 2 1 0

Lesson 28 – Nuclear Chemistry

Learning Objectives

In this lesson you will learn:

- To write balanced chemical equations for **nuclear reactions**
- To perform calculations related to the **kinetics** of nuclear reactions

Pre-requisites: Atomic structure; Balancing simple chemical reactions; Kinetics.

Self-study questions

Before you start studying the worked examples, you should be able to formulate answers to the questions below. Use a textbook of your choice, or an online source of information, to find the answers.

1. What particles are inside the nucleus of an atom?
2. What do we call atoms with the same number of protons but different numbers of neutrons?
3. What are nuclear reactions?
4. What are some of the common particles encountered in nuclear reactions?
5. What principles are followed in balancing nuclear reactions?
6. What type of kinetics is followed by all radioactive decompositions?

Worked examples

This section contains several solved examples that cover the learning objectives listed above. Study each example carefully and make notes in the workbook to check every example that you understood. Repeat several times what you don't understand at first. It should become clearer as you keep working on the examples.

Objective 196. Write balanced chemical equations for nuclear reactions.

1. Complete and balance the following nuclear reactions. Replace the X's with the correct particle.

 a. $^{126}_{50}Sn \rightarrow {}^{0}_{-1}e + X$

 b. $^{210}_{88}Ra \rightarrow {}^{4}_{2}He + X$

 c. $^{235}_{92}U \rightarrow {}^{87}_{35}Br + X + 2{}^{1}_{0}n$

Discussion

Nuclear reactions deal with the decomposition of the nucleus of an atom into other particles. The most common particles encountered in nuclear chemistry are:

- Alpha particles (helium nuclei): ${}^{4}_{2}He$

- Beta particles (electrons): ${}^{0}_{-1}e$

- Positrons: ${}^{0}_{+1}e$

- Neutrons: ${}^{1}_{0}n$

- Protons: ${}^{1}_{+1}p$

- Deuterium nuclei: ${}^{2}_{1}H$

- Gamma radiation: ${}^{0}_{0}\gamma$ (no mass or charge, just energy)

In nuclear chemistry we use isotopic notation, because we are dealing with particles inside the nucleus. The general principle is that mass and charge are conserved, so when identifying the missing particles in a nuclear reaction, we apply this basic principle.

Solutions

a. $^{126}_{50}Sn \rightarrow {}^{0}_{-1}e + X$

Let's rewrite the missing particle ${}^{m}_{c}X$, where m and c refer to mass and charge. Because both are conserved, the sum of the masses of all reactant particles must equal the sum of masses of all product particles, and the same applies to charge. Thus:

$$126 = 0 + m \quad and \quad 50 = (-1) + c$$

This results in:

$$m = 126 \quad and \quad c = 51$$

Our mystery particle is $^{126}_{51}Sb$, an isotope of antimony.

b. $^{210}_{88}Ra \rightarrow {}^{4}_{2}He + X$

$$210 = 4 + m \quad and \quad 88 = 2 + c$$

So:

$$X \; is \; {}^{206}_{86}Rn$$

c. $^{235}_{92}U \rightarrow {}^{87}_{35}Br + X + 2{}^{1}_{0}n$

$$235 = 87 + m + 2 \quad and \quad 92 = 35 + c + 0$$

So:

$$X = {}^{146}_{57}La$$

---

2.   Write balanced nuclear equations for the following processes:
   a.   Alpha emission of ^{162}Re
   b.   Beta emission of ^{188}W
   c.   Electron capture of ^{138}Sm
   d.   Positron emission of ^{125}Ba

Solutions

a.   Alpha emission of ^{162}Re

Emission means an alpha particle is eliminated (becomes a product). The equation should be:

$$^{162}_{75}Re \rightarrow {}^{4}_{2}He + {}^{158}_{73}Ta$$

b.   Beta emission of ^{188}W

$$^{188}_{74}W \rightarrow {}^{0}_{-1}e + {}^{188}_{75}Re$$

c.   Electron capture of ^{138}Sm

$$^{138}_{62}Sm + {}^{0}_{-1}e \rightarrow {}^{138}_{61}Pm$$

d.   Positron emission of ^{125}Ba

$$^{125}_{56}Ba \rightarrow {}^{0}_{+1}e \rightarrow {}^{125}_{55}Cs$$

---

3. ^{232}Th decays to ^{228}Th. What is the numbers of α and β-particles produced?

Solution

$$^{232}_{90}Th \rightarrow {}^{228}_{90}Th + x\ {}^{4}_{2}He + y\ {}^{0}_{-1}e$$

The element is the same, but a lighter isotope is produced. We know that the β-particles have no mass, so no matter how many are emitted, the mass would stay the same. Since the mass decreases by 4, it means that one α-particle is emitted. If this is the case, then the equation becomes:

$$^{232}_{90}Th \rightarrow {}^{228}_{90}Th + {}^{4}_{2}He + y\ {}^{0}_{-1}e$$

Since charge needs to be balanced, we determine that $y = 2$. The complete equation:

$$^{232}_{90}Th \rightarrow {}^{228}_{90}Th + {}^{4}_{2}He + 2\ {}^{0}_{-1}e$$

4. The mechanism of the following reaction (I* = ^{128}I) is given:

$$^{*}IO_{4(aq)}^{-} + 2I_{(aq)}^{-} + H_2O_{(l)} \rightarrow {}^{*}I_{2(s)} + IO_{3(aq)}^{-} + OH_{(aq)}^{-}$$

Indicate whether each of the following statements is true or false.

a. I^{-} is oxidized to IO_3^{-}
b. IO_4^{-} is reduced to IO_3^{-}
c. I_2 is formed from I^{-}
d. I_2 is formed from I^{-} and IO_4^{-}

Solution

This is a mechanistic problem. The iodine marked with an asterisk is a marked isotope. That means that a particular isotope of iodine is used to track what happens to that iodine in the reaction mechanism. Let's analyze each statement:

a. I^{-} is oxidized to IO_3^{-}

True, because the iodine in both of these species is not marked

b. IO_4^{-} is reduced to IO_3^{-}

False, as the periodate ion contains a marked iodine, whereas the iodate does not

c. I_2 is formed from I^{-}

False, the marked isotope in I_2^{*} cannot originate from the non-marked iodide

d. I_2 is formed from I^{-} and IO_4^{-}

Possible, it depends on whether both iodine atoms in I_2^{*} are marked isotopes, or only one is. If the latter is true, then the statement is true. If not, the statement is false.

Objective 197.   Perform calculations related to the kinetics of nuclear reactions.

1. The half-life of indium-111, a radioisotope used in studying the distribution of white blood cells, is $t_{1/2} = 2.805$ days. Calculate the decay constant of ^{111}In.

Solution

Nuclear reactions follow first order kinetics, which makes them easy to understand and calculate. The decay constant is simply the rate constant of the radioactive decay, which is calculated from the half-life:

$$k = \frac{\ln 2}{t_{1/2}} = \frac{\ln 2}{2.805 \ days} = 0.247 \ day^{-1}$$

2. Fluorine-18 has a half-life of 109.8 minutes. What percentage of a fluorine-18 sample remains after 24 min? After 24 hours? After 24 days?

Solutions

We use the first order time-concentration equation:

$$ln\frac{[A]}{[A]_o} = \ln X = -kt$$

We used the unknown X for the ratio [A] to [A]$_o$ as this will make the calculations easy.

First we need the rate constant:

$$k = \frac{\ln 2}{t_{1/2}} = 6.31 \times 10^{-3} \ min^{-1}$$

$$\ln X = -6.31 \times 10^{-3} \ min^{-1} \times 24 \min \quad \Rightarrow \quad X = e^{(-6.31\times10^{-3} \times 24)} = 0.859$$

Thus, 85.9% is left over after 24 minutes elapse.

$$\ln X = -6.31 \times 10^{-3} \ min^{-1} \times 24 \ h \ \times \frac{60 \ min}{1 \ h} \quad \Rightarrow \quad X = 0.000113$$

Only 0.113% reactant is left over after 24 hours.

$$\ln X = -6.31 \times 10^{-3} \ min^{-1} \times 24 \ days \times \frac{24 \ h}{day} \times \frac{60 \ min}{1 \ h} \quad \Rightarrow \quad X = 1.78 \times 10^{-95}$$

After 24 days, the leftover is essentially zero. The reaction is relatively fast.

3. Carbon-14 has a half-life of 5730 years, and currently living organisms decay at the rate of 15.3 disintegrations/min per gram of carbon. Carbon-14 dating of an old object indicated a decay rate of 11.5 disintegrations/min per gram of carbon. What is the age if the object?

Solution

First we need the rate constant:

$$k = \frac{\ln 2}{t_{1/2}} = 1.21 \times 10^{-4} \; year^{-1}$$

The number of disintegrations per minute can be used as a measure of how much carbon-14 is left in the sample, and thus it can be used instead of concentration. The concentration-time equation will allows us to find the time elapsed and thus date the ancient object:

$$ln\frac{[A]}{[A]_o} = -kt$$

$$ln\frac{11.5}{15.3} = -0.286 = -(1.21 \times 10^{-4} \; year^{-1})t$$

$$t = \frac{0.286}{1.21 \times 10^{-4} \; year^{-1}} = 2360 \; years$$

Worksheet 28. Nuclear Chemistry

The exercises and problems in this section will allow you to practice the topic until you understand it well.

1. Complete and balance the following nuclear reactions. Replace the X's with the correct particle.

a. $^{77}_{37}Rb \rightarrow {}^{0}_{1}e + X$

b. $^{76}_{36}Kr + {}^{0}_{-1}e \rightarrow X$

c. $^{90}_{38}Sr \rightarrow {}^{0}_{-1}e + X$

d. $^{49}_{25}Mn \rightarrow {}^{0}_{1}e + X$

e. $^{247}_{100}Fm \rightarrow {}^{4}_{2}He + X$

f. $^{37}_{18}Ar + {}^{0}_{-1}e \rightarrow X$

g. $^{188}_{80}Hg \rightarrow {}^{188}_{79}Au + X$

h. $^{218}_{85}At \rightarrow {}^{214}_{83}Bi + X$

i. $^{234}_{90}Th \rightarrow {}^{234}_{91}Pa + X$

j. $^{24}_{11}Na \rightarrow {}^{24}_{12}Mg + X$

k. $^{135}_{60}Nd \rightarrow {}^{135}_{59}Pr + X$

l. $^{170}_{78}Pt \rightarrow {}^{166}_{76}Os + X$

m. $^{109}_{47}Ag + {}^{4}_{2}He \rightarrow X$

n. $^{10}_{5}B + {}^{4}_{2}He \rightarrow X + {}^{1}_{0}n$

o. $^{235}_{92}U \rightarrow {}^{160}_{62}Sm + {}^{72}_{30}Zn + X{}^{1}_{0}n$

p. $^{246}_{96}Cm + {}^{12}_{6}C \rightarrow X + 4{}^{1}_{0}n$

2. Write balanced nuclear equations for the following processes:

a. Positron emission of ^{165}Ta

b. Beta emission of ^{157}Eu

c. Electron capture of ^{126}Ba

d. Alpha emission of ^{146}Sm

e. Positron emission of ^{125}Ba

3. The decay constant of thallium-201 is 0.228 day^{-1}. Calculate the half-life of thallium-201.

4. The half-life for the decay of ^{67}Ga is 78.25 h. Calculate the percentage of this isotope remaining after 199 hours.

5. Plutonium-239 has a decay constant of 2.88 x 10^{-5} year^{-1}. What percentage of a Plutonium-239 sample remains after 1000 years? After 25,000 years? After 100,000 years?

6. If 23% of a certain radioisotope decays in 5.3 years, what is the half-life of this isotope?

7. The half-life of Tl-206 decay to Pb-206 is 4.20 minutes. If 1.00 g sample of Tl-206 reacts, how much is left after 600 seconds?

Self-assessment

Using the scale indicated, rate your understanding of each learning objective at the completion of this lesson. Identify the areas where your understanding is weak or medium and discuss with your class mates and/or instructor. Write down specific questions you still have at the completion of this topic.

Learning objective	Self-assessment 3 = strong, 2 = medium, 1 = weak, 0 = not done
	3 2 1 0
	3 2 1 0

Practice final exam

This is a practice exam that you can use to prepare for a full year final exam in this course. I suggest that you work on this exam on your own, in order to assess your understanding of the material in a format that will be very close to what you might expect in a final exam. Then, a full solution to the practice exam is presented, so that you can check your work. Good luck!

1. How long will it take to produce 49 g of aluminum metal by the reduction of aluminum ion in an electrolytic cell with a current of 8.5 A?
   A)   5.7 h
   B) 4.5×10^6 s
   C) 2.1×10^4 s
   D)   17 h
   E) 1.7×10^6 s

2. What mass of oxygen gas is needed for the complete combustion of 76.6 g of ethylene (C_2H_4) to form carbon dioxide and water?
   A)   29.1 g
   B)   87.4 g
   C)   131.1 g
   D)   262 g
   E)   43.7 g

3. How many grams of sulfur are there in 28.8 g of iron(III) sulfate?
   A)   2.31 g
   B)   6.08 g
   C)   119.8 g
   D)   359 g
   E)   6.93 g

4. How many unpaired electrons are there in the complex ion hexacyanomanganate(II)?
   A)   3
   B)   4
   C)   0
   D)   2
   E)   1

5. The molecular geometry of carbon dioxide is best described as
   A)   linear.
   B)   bent.
   C)   trigonal planar.
   D)   tetrahedral.
   E)   none of these.

6. A 175. mL sample of 0.642 M NH_4NO_3 is diluted with water to a total volume of 450. mL. What is the ammonium nitrate concentration in the resulting solution?
   A)   1.65 M
   B)   0.250 M
   C)   4.01 M
   D)   0.123 M
   E)   0.606 M

7. The heat of neutralization of hydrochloric acid by sodium hydroxide is given below:
$$HCl_{(aq)} + NaOH_{(aq)} \rightarrow NaCl_{(aq)} + H_2O_{(l)} \;; \Delta H^o = -56.2 kJ/mol$$

   How much heat is released when 270. mL of 1.485 M HCl is mixed with 185. mL of 1.177 M NaOH?
   A)   22.5 kJ
   B)   10.3 kJ
   C)   140 kJ
   D)   258 kJ
   E)   12.2 kJ

8. Neutralization of an 85.00 mL sample of a sulfuric acid solution required 47.80 mL of 0.2490 M sodium hydroxide. What is the concentration of the original sulfuric acid solution?
   A)   0.14 M
   B)   0.8856 M
   C)   0.2801 M
   D)   0.07001 M
   E)   0.2214 M

9. The best name for $[Ru(NH_3)_2(en)](NO_3)_2$ is
   A)   (ethylenediamine)diammineruthenium(II) nitrate.
   B)   diamminebis(ethylenediamine)ruthenium(III) nitrate.
   C)   diammine(ethylenediamine)ruthenium(II) nitrate.
   D)   diammine(ethylenediamine)nitratoruthenium(III).
   E)   bis(ethylene)diamminenitratoruthenate(II).

10. Complete and balance the following redox equation using the set of smallest whole-number coefficients.

$$BrO_3^-{}_{(aq)} + Sb^{3+}{}_{(aq)} \rightarrow Br^-{}_{(aq)} + Sb^{5+}{}_{(aq)} \quad (acidic\ solution)$$

Now sum the coefficients of all species in the balanced equation. (Remember the coefficients that are equal to one.) The sum of the coefficients is

   A)   4
   B)   12
   C)   13
   D)   17
   E)   None of these.

11. How much energy is required to convert 84.2 g of ice at −49.4°C to steam at 113°C?

specific heat of ice = 2.09 J/g °C
specific heat of water = 4.18 J/g °C
specific heat of steam = 1.84 J/g °C
$\Delta H_{fus} = 6.02 \; kJ/mol$
$\Delta H_{vap} = 40.7 \; kJ/mol$

A)　3980 kJ
B)　46,100 kJ
C)　264 kJ
D)　280 kJ
E)　247 kJ

12. When 0.7981 g of benzoic acid was burned in a calorimeter containing 1.000 kg of water, a temperature rise of 2.99°C was observed. What is the heat capacity of the bomb calorimeter, excluding the water? (The heat of combustion of benzoic acid is -26.42 kJ/g)
    A) 94.8 kJ/°C
    B) 7.05 kJ/°C
    C) 99 kJ/°C
    D) 16.9 kJ/°C
    E) 2.87 kJ/°C

13. What is the pH of a 0.024 M $Ca(OH)_2$ solution?
    A) 15.32
    B) 10.27
    C) 12.38
    D) 12.68
    E) 10.96

14. A certain binary compound (XY) has a molar solubility of 2.1×10^{-6} mol/L. What is K_{sp} for this compound?
    A) 1.8×10^{-11}
    B) 4.2×10^{-6}
    C) 8.4×10^{-6}
    D) 4.4×10^{-12}
    E) 1.4×10^{-3}

15. Complete and balance the following redox equation:

$$MnO_4^- + Br^- \rightarrow Mn^{2+} + Br_2 \quad (acidic\ solution)$$

The sum of the smallest whole-number coefficients is
    A) 6
    B) 17
    C) 21
    D) 29
    E) 43

16. Calculate the pH of a buffer solution that contains 0.55 M benzoic acid (C_6H_5COOH) and 0.18 M sodium benzoate (C_6H_5COONa).
    A)   9.33
    B)   8.52
    C)   4.67
    D)   3.71
    E)   18.67

17. The best name for $K[Cr(NH_3)_2Cl_2SO_4]$ is
    A)   potassium diamminedichlorosulfatochromium(III).
    B)   potassium diamminedichlorosulfatochromate(II).
    C)   potassium diamminedichlorochromatium(III) sulfate.
    D)   potassium diamminedichlorochromate(II) sulfate.
    E)   potassium diamminedichlorosulfatochromate(III).

18. What is the concentration of nitrate ion in a solution formed by mixing 44.70 mL of 0.2114 M calcium nitrate with 31.05 mL of 0.1416 M sodium nitrate?
    A)   0.2408 M
    B)   0.3075 M
    C)   0.1828 M
    D)   0.2313 M
    E)   0.2083 M

19. How much heat is required to raise the temperature of 258 g of water from 27.4°C to 56.4°C? (The specific heat of water is 4.184 J/g °C.)
    A) 3.56×10^2 kJ
    B) 3.13×10^4 kJ
    C) 3.13×10^1 kJ
    D) 6.09×10^1 kJ
    E) 3.24×10^2 kJ

20. Hydrogen iodide decomposes according to the equation $2HI_{(g)} \rightleftharpoons H_{2\,(g)} + I_{2\,(g)}$. For this reaction, $K_c = 0.0156$ at $400\,^{\circ}C$. If 0.410 mol HI is injected into a 2.50 L reaction vessel at $400\,^{\circ}C$, what will the concentration of HI be at equilibrium?
    A)   0.205 M
    B)   0.131 M
    C)   0.0821 M
    D)   0.0328 M
    E)   0.148 M

21. Calculate the standard cell *emf* for the following cell:

$$Mg \mid Mg^{2+} \parallel NO_3^- \text{ (acid soln)} \mid NO_{(g)} \mid Pt$$

   A)   3.33 V
   B)   1.41 V
   C)   -1.41 V
   D)   8.46 V
   E)   -8.46 V

22. How many unpaired electrons are present in a ground-state titanium atom?

   A)   1
   B)   2
   C)   0
   D)   3
   E)   4

23. How much heat is released to the surroundings when 7.19 g of aluminum reacts with excess iron(III) oxide to give aluminum oxide and metallic iron? (The heats of formation of iron(III) oxide and aluminum oxide are -822 kJ/mol and -1670. kJ/mol, respectively.)

   A)   113 kJ
   B)   3050 kJ
   C)   452 kJ
   D)   226 kJ
   E)   332 kJ

24. The data below were determined for the reaction $S_2O_8^{2-} + 3I^- \rightarrow 2SO_4^{2-} + I_3^-$

Expt. #	$[S_2O_8^{2-}]$	$[I^-]$	Initial Rate
1	0.038	0.060	1.4×10^{-5} M/s
2	0.076	0.060	2.8×10^{-5} M/s
3	0.076	0.030	1.4×10^{-5} M/s

The rate law for this reaction must be:
A)   rate = $k[S_2O_8^{2-}][I^-]^3$
B)   rate = $k[S_2O_8^{2-}]$
C)   rate = $k[S_2O_8^{2-}]^2[I^-]^2$
D)   rate = $k[I^-]$
E)   rate = $k[S_2O_8^{2-}][I^-]$

25. Calculate the sodium ion concentration in a solution formed by diluting 15.00 mL of a 0.792 M sodium phosphate solution to a final volume of 50.00 mL.
A)   7.92 M
B)   0.0792 M
C)   0.238 M
D)   0.713 M
E)   2.64 M

26. 15.2 g of magnesium chloride is dissolved in 650. mL of 0.548 hydrochloric acid. The chloride concentration in the resulting solution is
    A) 0.939 M
    B) 0.794 M
    C) 0.756 M
    D) 1.33 M
    E) 1.04 M

27. A single manganese ion with a +2 charge has
    A) 27 electrons.
    B) 23 electrons.
    C) 53 electrons.
    D) 25 electrons.
    E) 57 electrons.

28. What is the pH of a 0.0349 M solution of nitrous acid?
    A) 1.46
    B) 2.38
    C) 5.59
    D) 2.33
    E) 5.47

29. The solubility of barium carbonate is 0.0014 g per 100. g of water at 20°C. How many moles of barium ions will dissolve in 6.50 kg of water at this temperature?
    A) 4.6×10^{-4}
    B) 4.6×10^{-5}
    C) 5.0×10^{-4}
    D) 4.6×10^{-6}
    E) 4.3×10^{-3}

30. Calculate the pH of 14.2 mL of 1.4×10^{-3} M HCl.
    A) 11.15
    B) 16.85
    C) 2.85
    D) 6.57
    E) 20.57

31. Consider the following standard reduction potentials in acid solution:

$$Cr^{3+} + 3e^- \rightarrow Cr \qquad\qquad\qquad E° = -0.74 \text{ V}$$
$$Co^{2+} + 2e^- \rightarrow Co \qquad\qquad\qquad E° = -0.28 \text{ V}$$
$$MnO_4^- + 8H^+ + 5e^- \rightarrow Mn^{2+} + 4H_2O \qquad E° = +1.51 \text{ V}$$

The *weakest reducing agent* listed above is
A) Cr^{3+}
B) Cr
C) Mn^{2+}
D) Co
E) MnO_4^-

32. How many faradays are transferred in an electrolytic cell when a current of 7.0 amperes flows for 11.0 hours?
A) 2.4×10^{-2} F
B) 2.1×10^3 F
C) 4.8×10^{-2} F
D) 8.0×10^{-4} F
E)   2.9 F

33. In the complex ion $[Fe(CN)_6]^{4-}$, the oxidation number of Fe is
A)   +1.
B)   +2.
C)   +3.
D)   -4.
E)   +6.

34. In the coordination compound $K_2[Co(en)Cl_4]$, the coordination number (C.N.) and oxidation number (O.N.) of cobalt are
    A)   C.N. = 6; O.N. = +2.
    B)   C.N. = 6; O.N. = +3.
    C)   C.N. = 5; O.N. = +2.
    D)   C.N. = 5; O.N. = +4.
    E)   C.N. = 4; O.N. = +3.

35. What mass of K_2CO_3 is needed to prepare 500. mL of a solution having a potassium ion concentration of 0.274 M?
    A)   18.9 g
    B)   37.9 g
    C)   5.36 g
    D)   9470 g
    E)   9.47 g

36. What is the pH of a 0.26 M solution of NH_4Cl?
    A) 2.67
    B) 4.92
    C) 2.66
    D) 11.33
    E) 9.08

37. The electron configuration of a Cr^{3+} ion is
    A) $[Ar]3d^5$.
    B) $[Ar]4s^13d^2$.
    C) $[Ar]3d^3$.
    D) $[Ar]4s^13d^5$.
    E) $[Ar]4s^23d^4$.

38. Potassium crystallizes in a body-centered cubic unit cell with edge length 532.1 pm. Calculate the density of K.
    A) 0.02204 g/cm^3
    B) $8.619 \times 10^5 \text{ g/cm}^3$
    C) $4.31 \times 10^5 \text{ g/cm}^3$
    D) 0.431 g/cm^3
    E) 0.8619 g/cm^3

39. What is the hydrogen ion concentration in a solution formed by mixing 34.87 mL of 0.2233 M hydrochloric acid with 16.27 mL of 0.1468 M potassium hydroxide?
    A)   0.1056 M
    B)   0.1548 M
    C)   0.1523 M
    D)   0.1990 M
    E)   0.4786 M

40. Consider an electrochemical cell constructed from the following half cells, linked by a KCl salt bridge.
    - a Fe electrode in 1.0 M $FeCl_2$ solution
    - a Sn electrode in 1.0 M $Sn(NO_3)_2$ solution
    When the cell is running spontaneously, which choice includes *only* true statements and no false ones?
    A)   The tin electrode loses mass and the tin electrode is the cathode.
    B)   The tin electrode gains mass and the tin electrode is the cathode.
    C)   The iron electrode gains mass and the iron electrode is the anode.
    D)   The iron electrode loses mass and the iron electrode is the cathode.
    E)   The iron electrode gains mass and the iron electrode is the cathode.

41. How many valence electrons does an atom of fluorine have?
    A)   9
    B)   6
    C)   5
    D)   7
    E)   1

42. Consider the following gas phase equilibrium system:
    $$PCl_{5\,(g)} \rightleftharpoons PCl_{3\,(g)} + Cl_{2\,(g)} \quad \Delta H^o = +87.8\ kJ/mol$$
    Which of the following statements is *false*?
    A)   Increasing the system volume shifts the equilibrium to the right.
    B)   Increasing the temperature shifts the equilibrium to the right.
    C)   A catalyst speeds up the approach to equilibrium and shifts the position of equilibrium to the right.
    D)   Decreasing the total pressure of the system shifts the equilibrium to the right.
    E)   Increasing the temperature causes the equilibrium constant to increase.

43. The density of mercury is 13.6 g/cm^3. How may liters does 494 g of Hg occupy?
    A) 6.72×10^3 L
    B) 3.63×10^4 L
    C)   6.718 L
    D) 3.63×10^{-2} L
    E) 6.72×10^6 L

44. Calculate ΔS^o for the reaction of 250. g of PbO with excess carbon according to the equation

$$2PbO_{(s)} + C_{(s)} \rightarrow 2Pb_{(s)} + CO_{2\,(g)}$$

$$S^o \; (J/K \cdot mol)$$

PbO(s)	69.45
C(s)	5.7
Pb(s)	64.89
CO$_2$(g)	213.6

   A)   199 J/K
   B)   228 J/K
   C)   223 J/K
   D)   111 J/K
   E)   445 J/K

45. How many 3d electrons does a V^{3+} ion have?
   A)   6
   B)   5
   C)   4
   D)   3
   E)   2

46. A piece of metal with a mass of 136 g is placed into a graduated cylinder that contains 50.00 mL of water, raising the water level to 99.00 mL. What is the density of the metal?
    A)   0.360 g/cm^3
    B)   2.78 g/cm^3
    C)   0.728 g/cm^3
    D)   2.72 g/cm^3
    E)   1.37 g/cm^3

47. In the complex ion $[ML_6]^{n+}$, M^{n+} has five d electrons and L is a strong field ligand. According to crystal field theory, the magnetic properties of the complex ion correspond to how many unpaired electrons?
    A)   0
    B)   1
    C)   2
    D)   3
    E)   5

48. A balloon contains 0.76 mol N_2, 0.18 mol O_2, 0.031 mol He and 0.026 mol H_2 at 725 mm Hg. What is the partial pressure of oxygen?
    A)   140 mmHg
    B)   134 mmHg
    C)   530 mmHg
    D)   725 mmHg
    E)   18 mmHg

49. A first-order reaction has a rate constant of $3.66 \times 10^{-3}\ s^{-1}$. The time required for the reaction to be 80.0% complete is
    A)   819 s
    B)   440 s
    C)   191 s
    D)   26.5 s
    E)   61 s

50. In liquid propanol (C_3H_8OH), which intermolecular forces are predominant?
    A)   Dispersion forces
    B)   Dipole-dipole
    C)   Hydrogen bonds
    D)   Ion-dipole
    E)   Dispersion and dipole-dipole

Answer sheet for practice final exam

1.
2.
3.
4.
5.
6.
7.
8.
9.
10.
11.
12.
13.
14.
15.
16.
17.
18.
19.
20.
21.
22.
23.
24.
25.
26.
27.
28.
29.
30.
31.
32.
33.
34.
35.
36.
37.
38.
39.
40.
41.
42.
43.
44.
45.
46.
47.
48.
49.
50.

Solutions to practice final exam

1. **How long will it take to produce 49 g of aluminum metal by the reduction of aluminum ion in an electrolytic cell with a current of 8.5 A?**

Review: Objective 193

$$Al^{3+} + 3e^- \rightarrow Al$$

$$\frac{49\ g\ Al}{26.98\ g/mol} = 1.8\ mol\ Al$$

$$1.8\ mol\ Al\ \times \frac{3\ mol\ e^-}{1\ mol\ Al} = 5.4\ mol\ e^-\ needed$$

$$5.4\ mol\ e^- \times 96500\frac{C}{mol} = 521100\ C$$

$$\frac{521100\ C}{8.5\ A} = 61306\ s = 17\ hours$$

2. **What mass of oxygen gas is needed for the complete combustion of 76.6 g of ethylene (C_2H_4) to form carbon dioxide and water?**

Review: Objective 84

$$C_2H_4 + 3O_2 \rightarrow 2CO_2 + 2H_2O$$

$$76.6\ g\ C_2H_4 \times \frac{1\ mol\ C_2H_4}{28.06\ g} \times \frac{3\ mol\ O_2}{1\ mol\ C_2H_4} \times \frac{32.00\ g\ O_2}{1\ mol\ O_2} = 262\ g\ O_2$$

3. **How many grams of sulfur are there in 28.8 g of iron(III) sulfate?**

Review: Objective 57, Objective 58

$$28.8\ g\ Fe_2(SO_4)_3 \times \frac{1\ mol\ Fe_2(SO_4)_3}{399.88\ g} \times \frac{3\ mol\ S}{1\ mol\ Fe_2(SO_4)_3} \times \frac{32.07\ g}{1\ mol\ S} = 6.93\ g\ S$$

4. **How many unpaired electrons are there in the complex ion hexacyanomanganate(II)?**

Review: Objective 194

Mn^{2+} has the electron configuration $4s^0 3d^5$ and thus has 5 electrons available. The ligand field is strong (cyano ligands are strong field ligands), and thus the complex will be low spin. There are 6 ligands so the complex is octahedral. The splitting and orbital diagram will be as follows:

Thus, there is one unpaired electron.

Octahedral

5. **The molecular geometry of carbon dioxide is best described as**

Review: Objective 116

$$\overset{\displaystyle ..}{\underset{\displaystyle ..}{O}} = C = \overset{\displaystyle ..}{\underset{\displaystyle ..}{O}}$$

The carbon dioxide molecule is linear.

6. **A 175 mL sample of 0.642 M NH_4NO_3 is diluted with water to a total volume of 450. mL. What is the ammonium nitrate concentration in the resulting solution?**

Review: Objective 75

$$M_1V_1 = M_2V_2 \quad ; \quad M_2 = \frac{M_1V_1}{V_2} = \frac{0.642 \frac{mol}{L} \times 175\ mL}{450.\ mL} = 0.250 \frac{mol}{L}$$

7. **The heat of neutralization of hydrochloric acid by sodium hydroxide is given below:**
$$HCl_{(aq)} + NaOH_{(aq)} \rightarrow NaCl_{(aq)} + H_2O_{(l)} \quad ; \quad \Delta H^o = -56.2 kJ/mol$$

How much heat is released when 270. mL of 1.485 M HCl is mixed with 185. mL of 1.177 M NaOH?

Review: Objective 127

The amounts of reactants are:
$$270.\ mL \times 1.485\ M = 400.95\ mmol\ HCl$$
$$185\ mL \times 1.177\ M = 217.75\ mmol\ NaOH$$

From this information we can see that NaOH is the limiting reactant. Thus, the amount of heat produced will be:

$$56.2\ \frac{kJ}{mol} \times 217.75\ mmol \times \frac{1\ mol}{1000\ mmol} \times \frac{1000\ J}{1\ kJ} = 12238\ J = 12.2\ kJ$$

8. **Neutralization of an 85.00 mL sample of a sulfuric acid solution required 47.80 mL of 0.2490 M sodium hydroxide. What is the concentration of the original sulfuric acid solution?**

Review: Objective 90

$$2NaOH + H_2SO_4 \rightarrow Na_2SO_4 + 2H_2O$$

$$n = MV = 47.80\ mL \times 0.2490\ \frac{mol}{L} = 11.9022\ mmol\ NaOH$$

$$11.9022\ mmol\ NaOH \times \frac{1\ mmol\ H_2SO_4}{2\ mmol\ NaOH} = 5.9511\ mmol\ H_2SO_4$$

$$M = \frac{n}{V} = \frac{5.9511\ mmol}{85.00\ mL} = 0.07001\ mol/L$$

9. **The best name for [Ru(NH₃)₂(en)](NO₃)₂ is**

Review: Objective 194

Since the ligands are all neutral and there are two nitrate ions outside of the complex ion, the charge on the Ru ion must be +2. According to the nomenclature rules, the name of this compound is diammine-ethylenediamine-ruthenium(II) nitrate.

10. **Complete and balance the following redox equation using the set of smallest whole-number coefficients.**

$$BrO_3^-{}_{(aq)} + Sb^{3+}_{(aq)} \rightarrow Br^-_{(aq)} + Sb^{5+}_{(aq)} \quad (acidic\ solution)$$

Now sum the coefficients of all species in the balanced equation. (Remember the coefficients that are equal to one.) The sum of the coefficients is

Review: Objective 47

Let's use a table like we did when we learned about redox reactions.

	$BrO_3^-{}_{(aq)} + Sb^{3+}_{(aq)} \rightarrow Br^-_{(aq)} + Sb^{5+}_{(aq)}$	Acidic
Multipliers	Half reactions	
× 1	$BrO_3^-{}_{(aq)} + 6H^+ + 6e^- \rightarrow Br^-_{(aq)} + 3H_2O$	
× 3	$Sb^{3+}_{(aq)} \rightarrow Sb^{5+}_{(aq)} + 2e^-$	
Sum of two half reactions	$BrO_3^-{}_{(aq)} + 6H^+ + \cancel{6e^-} + 3Sb^{3+}_{(aq)} \rightarrow Br^-_{(aq)} + 3H_2O + 3Sb^{5+}_{(aq)} + \cancel{6e^-}$	
Balanced reaction	$BrO_3^-{}_{(aq)} + 6H^+ + 3Sb^{3+}_{(aq)} \rightarrow Br^-_{(aq)} + 3H_2O + 3Sb^{5+}_{(aq)}$	

The sum of the coefficients is: 1 + 6 + 3 + 1 + 3 + 3 = 17

11. **How much energy is required to convert 84.2 g of ice at –49.4°C to steam at 113°C?**

specific heat of ice = 2.09 J/g °C
specific heat of water = 4.18 J/g °C
specific heat of steam = 1.84 J/g °C
$\Delta H_{fus} = 6.02\ kJ/mol$
$\Delta H_{vap} = 40.7\ kJ/mol$

Review: Objective 143

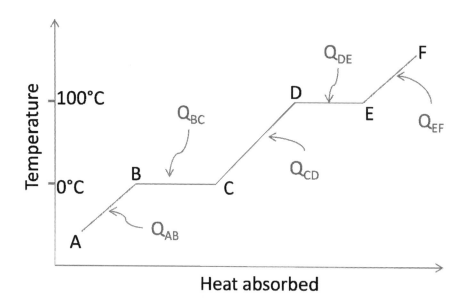

We are using the full phase change diagram, where point A is at -49.4°C and point F is at 113°C.

$$Q_{AB} = 84.2 \ g \ \times 2.09 \frac{J}{g°C} \times 49.4°C = 8693 \ J$$

$$Q_{BC} = 6.02 \frac{kJ}{mol} \times \frac{84.2 \ g \ H_2O}{18.02 \ g/mol} = 28.129 \ kJ = 28129 \ J$$

$$Q_{CD} = 84.2 \ g \ \times 4.18 \frac{J}{g°C} \times 100°C = 35196 \ J$$

$$Q_{DE} = 40.7 \frac{kJ}{mol} \times \frac{84.2 \ g \ H_2O}{18.02 \ g/mol} = 190.174 \ kJ = 190174 \ J$$

$$Q_{EF} = 84.2 \ g \ \times 1.84 \frac{J}{g°C} \times 13°C = 2014 \ J$$

$$Q_{total} = Q_{AB} + Q_{BC} + Q_{CD} + Q_{DE} + Q_{EF} = 264206 \ J = 264 \ kJ$$

12. **When 0.7981 g of benzoic acid was burned in a calorimeter containing 1.000 kg of water, a temperature rise of 2.99°C was observed. What is the heat capacity of the bomb calorimeter, excluding the water? (The heat of combustion of benzoic acid is -26.42 kJ/g)**

Review: Objective 121, Objective 126

From the heat of combustion of benzoic acid we calculate the total amount of heat released:

$$Q = \ 0.7981 \ g \ \times \frac{26420 \ J}{g} = 21086 \ J \ released$$

This heat is absorbed by the water and by the calorimeter:

$$Q = m_{H_2O} \times s_{H_2O} \times \Delta T + C_{cal} \times \Delta T$$

$$C_{cal} = \frac{Q - m_{H_2O} \times s_{H_2O} \times \Delta T}{\Delta T}$$

$$C_{cal} = \frac{21086\,J - 1000\,g \times 4.18\frac{J}{g\,°C} \times 2.99\,°C}{2.99\,°C} = 2872\frac{J}{°C} = 2.87 kJ/°C$$

13. **What is the pH of a 0.024 M Ca(OH)$_2$ solution?**

Review: Objective 166

$$Ca(OH)_2 \rightarrow Ca^{2+} + 2OH^-$$

$$[OH^-] = 2 \times 0.024 = 0.048\,M$$

$$pOH = -log([OH^-]) = -log(0.048) = 1.32$$

$$pH = 14 - pOH = 14 - 1.32 = 12.68$$

14. **A certain binary compound (XY) has a molar solubility of $2.1 \times 10^{-6}\,mol/L$. What is K_{sp} for this compound?**

Review: Objective 181

Because this is a binary salt, there will be one of each ion dissociated in solution, and the solubility of the salt is the actual concentration of either ion:

$$XY_{(s)} \rightleftharpoons X^{n+}_{(aq)} + Y^{n-}_{(aq)}$$

$$[X^{n+}] = [Y^{n-}] = [XY_{(aq)}] = 2.1 \times 10^{-6}\,mol/L$$

$$K_{sp} = [X^{n+}][Y^{n-}] = 4.41 \times 10^{-12}$$

15. **Complete and balance the following redox equation:**

$$MnO_4^- + Br^- \rightarrow Mn^{2+} + Br_2 \quad (acidic\ solution)$$

The sum of the smallest whole-number coefficients is

Review: Objective 47

We work this exactly like problem 10 and obtain the balanced redox reaction:

$$2MnO_4^- + 16H^+ + 10Br^- \rightarrow 2Mn^{2+} + 8H_2O + 5Br_2$$

Sum of coefficients is 43.

16. **Calculate the pH of a buffer solution that contains 0.55 M benzoic acid (C₆H₅COOH) and 0.18 M sodium benzoate (C₆H₅COONa).**

Review: Objective 177

The mixture of benzoic acid and sodium benzoate is a buffer. Thus, we calculate the pH of the buffer using the H.H. equation:

$$pH = pK_a + log\frac{[C_6H_5COONa]}{[C_6H_5COOH]} = 4.20 + log\frac{0.18\ M}{0.55\ M} = 3.71$$

17. **The best name for K[Cr(NH₃)₂Cl₂SO₄] is**

Review: Objective 194

Total charge of ligands: $2 \times 0 + 2 \times (-1) + (-2) = -4$. Charge of potassium ion is +1, therefore Cr must be +3.

The name is potassium diammine-dichloro-sulfato-chromate(III).

18. **What is the concentration of nitrate ion in a solution formed by mixing 44.70 mL of 0.2114 M calcium nitrate with 31.05 mL of 0.1416 M sodium nitrate?**

Review: Objective 73, Objective 78

We are mixing two solutions containing the nitrate ion.

The calcium nitrate solution is $2 \times 0.2114 = 0.4228\ M\ in\ NO_3^-$

The sodium nitrate solution is $0.1416\ M\ in\ NO_3^-$

The total molarity of nitrate in the final solution:

$$M_{NO_3^-} = \frac{M_1V_1 + M_2V_2}{V_1 + V_2} = \frac{0.4228\ M \times 44.70\ mL + 0.1416\ M \times 31.05\ mL}{44.70\ mL + 31.05\ mL} = 0.3075\ M\ NO_3^-$$

19. **How much heat is required to raise the temperature of 258 g of water from 27.4°C to 56.4°C? (The specific heat of water is 4.184 J/g °C.)**

Review: Objective 124

$$Q = m \times s \times \Delta T = 258\ g \times 4.184\frac{J}{g°C} \times (56.4°C - 27.4°C) = 31305\ J = 3.13 \times 10^1\ kJ$$

20. Hydrogen iodide decomposes according to the equation $2HI_{(g)} \rightleftharpoons H_{2\,(g)} + I_{2\,(g)}$. For this reaction, $K_c = 0.0156$ at $400\,^{\circ}C$. If 0.410 mol HI is injected into a 2.50 L reaction vessel at $400\,^{\circ}C$, what will the concentration of HI be at equilibrium?

Review: Objective 161

We use an ICE table to solve this problem. Initial concentration of HI is:

$$[HI] = \frac{0.410\ mol}{2.50\ L} = 0.164\ mol/L$$

	HI	H_2	I_2
Initial	0.164	0	0
Change	$-2x$	x	x
Equilibrium	$0.164 - 2x$	x	x

$$K_c = \frac{[H_2][I_2]}{[HI]^2} = \frac{x^2}{(0.164 - 2x)^2} = 0.0156$$

$$\frac{x}{0.164 - 2x} = \sqrt{0.0156} = 0.1249$$

$$x = 0.1249\,(0.164 - 2x) = 0.02048 - 0.2498x$$

$$1.2498x = 0.02048 \quad \Rightarrow \quad x = 0.0164\ M$$

$$[HI] = 0.164 - 2 \times 0.0164 = 0.131\ M$$

21. Calculate the standard cell emf for the following cell:
$$\mathbf{Mg \mid Mg^{2+} \parallel NO_3^- \ (acid\ soln) \mid NO_{(g)} \mid Pt}$$

Review: Objective 191

From the table of standard reduction potentials:

$$Mg \rightarrow Mg^{2+} + 2e^- \ : \ E^o_{ox} = +2.37\ V$$

$$NO_3^- + 4H^+ + 3e^- \rightarrow NO + 2H_2O \ : \ E^o_{red} = +0.96\ V$$

$$E^o_{cell} = E^o_{ox} + E^o_{red} = +3.33\ V$$

22. How many unpaired electrons are present in a ground-state titanium atom?

Review: Objective 96

Titanium is $4s^2 3d^2$, and the two 3d electrons are unpaired.

23. **How much heat is released to the surroundings when 7.19 g of aluminum reacts with excess iron(III) oxide to give aluminum oxide and metallic iron? (The heats of formation of iron(III) oxide and aluminum oxide are -822 kJ/mol and -1670. kJ/mol, respectively.)**

Review: Objective 120, Objective 121

$$2Al + Fe_2O_3 \rightarrow 2Fe + Al_2O_3$$

We know that the heats of formation of elements are zero.

$$\Delta H^o = \left(1 \text{ mol } Al_2O_{3\,(s)}\right) \times \Delta H_f^o\left(Al_2O_{3\,(s)}\right) - \left(1 \text{ mol } Fe_2O_{3\,(s)}\right) \times \Delta H_f^o\left(Fe_2O_{3\,(s)}\right)$$

$$\Delta H^o = -1670 \text{ kJ} - (-822 \text{ kJ}) = -848 \text{ kJ}$$

This amount of heat corresponds to the stoichiometry above, when 2 moles of aluminum react. For our given quantity:

$$7.19 \text{ g } Al \times \frac{1 \text{ mol } Al}{26.98 \text{ g}} \times \frac{848 \text{ kJ heat}}{2 \text{ mol } Al} = 113 \text{ kJ heat released}$$

24. **The data below were determined for the reaction** $S_2O_8^{2-} + 3I^- \rightarrow 2SO_4^{2-} + I_3^-$

Expt. #	$[S_2O_8^{2-}]$	$[I^-]$	Initial Rate
1	0.038	0.060	1.4×10^{-5} M/s
2	0.076	0.060	2.8×10^{-5} M/s
3	0.076	0.030	1.4×10^{-5} M/s

The rate law for this reaction must be:

Review: Objective 155

Using the method of initial rates:

$$rate = k\,[S_2O_8^{2-}]^x\,[I^-]^y$$

$$1.4 \times 10^{-5} = k\,(0.038)^x\,(0.060)^y \quad (1)$$

$$2.8 \times 10^{-5} = k\,(0.076)^x\,(0.060)^y \quad (2)$$

$$\frac{1.4 \times 10^{-5}}{2.8 \times 10^{-5}} = \frac{k\,(0.038)^x\,(0.060)^y}{k\,(0.076)^x\,(0.060)^y} = \left(\frac{0.038}{0.076}\right)^x$$

$$\frac{1}{2} = \left(\frac{1}{2}\right)^x \quad thus \ x = 1$$

$$2.8 \times 10^{-5} = k\,(0.076)^x\,(0.060)^y \quad (2)$$

$$1.4 \times 10^{-5} = k\,(0.076)^x\,(0.030)^y \quad (3)$$

$$\frac{2.8 \times 10^{-5}}{1.4 \times 10^{-5}} = \frac{k\,(0.076)^x\,(0.060)^y}{k\,(0.076)^x\,(0.030)^y} = \left(\frac{0.060}{0.030}\right)^y$$

$$2 = 2^y \quad thus\ y = 1$$

$$rate = k[S_2O_8^{2-}]\,[I^-]$$

25. **Calculate the sodium ion concentration in a solution formed by diluting 15.00 mL of a 0.792 M sodium phosphate solution to a final volume of 50.00 mL.**

Review: Objective 72, Objective 75

$$M_1V_1 = M_2V_2 \quad ; \quad M_2 = \frac{M_1V_1}{V_2} = \frac{0.792\,\frac{mol}{L} \times 15.00\ mL}{50.00\ mL} = 0.2376\,\frac{mol}{L}\ Na_3PO_4$$

$$[Na^+] = 0.2376 \times 3 = 0.713\,\frac{mol}{L}$$

26. **15.2 g of magnesium chloride is dissolved in 650. mL of 0.548 hydrochloric acid. The chloride concentration in the resulting solution is**

Review: Objective 71, Objective 78

From the solid salt:
$$15.2\ g\ MgCl_2 \times \frac{1\ mol\ MgCl_2}{95.211\ g} \times \frac{2\ mol\ Cl^-}{1\ mol\ MgCl_2} = 0.3193\ mol\ Cl^-$$

From the solution:

$$n = MV = 0.548\,\frac{mol}{L} \times 0.650L = 0.3562\ mol\ Cl^-$$

Total concentration of chloride:
$$M = \frac{0.3193\ mol + 0.3562\ mol}{0.650\ L} = 1.04\,\frac{mol}{L}$$

27. **A single manganese ion with a +2 charge has**

Review: Objective 98

Mn has Z=25, therefore the +2 ion has 23 electrons.

28. **What is the pH of a 0.0349 M solution of nitrous acid?**

Review: Objective 168

$$HNO_2 + H_2O \rightleftharpoons NO_2^- + H_3O^+$$

	$[HNO_2]$	$[NO_2^-]$	$[H_3O^+]$
Initial	0.0349	0	0
Change	$-x$	x	x
Equilibrium	$0.0349 - x$	x	x

$$K_a = \frac{[NO_2^-][H_3O^+]}{[HNO_2]} = \frac{x^2}{0.0349 - x} = 10^{-3.14} = 7.24 \times 10^{-4}$$

where 3.14 is the pK_a of nitrous acid.

$$x^2 = 7.24 \times 10^{-4} \, (0.0349 - x)$$

$$x^2 = 2.53 \times 10^{-5} - 7.24 \times 10^{-4}x$$

$$x^2 + 7.24 \times 10^{-4}x - 2.53 \times 10^{-5} = 0$$

$$x = 0.00468 \, M = [H_3O^+]$$

$$pH = -\log(0.00468) = 2.33$$

29. **The solubility of barium carbonate is 0.0014 g per 100. g of water at 20°C. How many moles of barium ions will dissolve in 6.50 kg of water at this temperature?**

Review: Objective 69

$$\frac{0.0014 \, g \, BaCO_3}{100. \, g \, water} = \frac{x}{6500 \, g \, water}$$

$$x = \frac{0.0014 \times 6500}{100} = 0.091 \, g \, BaCO_3$$

$$\frac{0.091 \, g \, BaCO_3}{197.36 \, g/mol} = 4.6 \times 10^{-4} \, mol \, BaCO_3$$

30. **Calculate the pH of 14.2 mL of 1.4 x 10^{-3} M HCl.**

Review: Objective 165

$$[H^+] = 1.4 \times 10^{-3} \, M$$

$$pH = -\log(1.4 \times 10^{-3}) = 2.85$$

31. Consider the following standard reduction potentials in acid solution:

$$Cr^{3+} + 3e^- \rightarrow Cr \qquad\qquad E° = \text{-0.74 V}$$
$$Co^{2+} + 2e^- \rightarrow Co \qquad\qquad E° = \text{-0.28 V}$$
$$MnO_4^- + 8H^+ + 5e^- \rightarrow Mn^{2+} + 4H_2O \qquad E° = \text{+1.51 V}$$

The *weakest reducing agent* listed above is

Review: Objective 191

The weakest reducing agent is the species least likely to get oxidized. Therefore, we are looking for the most negative oxidation potential, which would correspond to the Mn^{2+} ion (-1.51 V).

32. How many faradays are transferred in an electrolytic cell when a current of 7.0 amperes flows for 11.0 hours?

Review: Objective 193

$$charge(C) = current\ (A) \times time\ (s) = 7.0\ A\ \times 11.0\ h\ \times 3600\frac{s}{h} = 277200\ C$$

$$126000\ C \times \frac{1\ F}{96500\ C} = 2.9\ F$$

33. In the complex ion $[Fe(CN)_6]^{4-}$, the oxidation number of Fe is

Review: Objective 194

Cyanide ions are -1 each, thus Fe is +2.

34. In the coordination compound K₂[Co(en)Cl₄], the coordination number (C.N.) and oxidation number (O.N.) of cobalt are

Review: Objective 194

There is one bidentate ligand (en) and four chlorides, therefore the coordination number is 6. The charge on Co must be +2.

35. What mass of K₂CO₃ is needed to prepare 500. mL of a solution having a potassium ion concentration of 0.274 M?

Review: Objective 74

$$0.274\frac{mol}{L} \times 0.500\ L = 0.137\ mol\ K^+$$

$$0.137\ mol\ K^+ \times \frac{1\ mol\ K_2CO_3}{2\ mol\ K^+} \times \frac{138.21\ g}{1\ mol\ K_2CO_3} = 9.47\ g\ K_2CO_3$$

36. What is the pH of a 0.26 M solution of NH_4Cl?

Review: Objective 173

$$NH_4Cl \xrightarrow{in\ water} NH_4^+ + Cl^-$$

$$NH_4^+ + H_2O \rightleftharpoons NH_3 + H_3O^+$$

	$[NH_4^+]$	$[H_3O^+]$	$[NH_3]$
Initial	0.26	0	0
Change	$-x$	x	x
Equilibrium	$0.26 - x$	x	x

$$K_a = \frac{[H_3O^+][NH_3]}{[NH_4^+]} = \frac{x^2}{0.26 - x}$$

$$K_a = \frac{K_w}{K_b} = \frac{1.0 \times 10^{-14}}{1.8 \times 10^{-5}} = 5.56 \times 10^{-10}$$

$$\frac{x^2}{0.26 - x} = 5.56 \times 10^{-10}$$

$$\frac{x^2}{0.26} = 5.56 \times 10^{-10} \Rightarrow x^2 = 1.45 \times 10^{-10} \Rightarrow x = \sqrt{1.45 \times 10^{-10}} = 1.20 \times 10^{-5}\ M$$

$$pH = -\log(1.20 \times 10^{-5}) = 4.92$$

37. The electron configuration of a Cr^{3+} ion is

Review: Objective 98

Cr is $4s^1 3d^5$, therefore the +3 ion is $3d^3$.

38. Potassium crystallizes in a body-centered cubic unit cell with edge length 532.1 pm. Calculate the density of K.

Review: Objective 141

$$532.1\ pm \times \frac{1\ m}{10^{-12}\ pm} \times \frac{100\ cm}{1\ m} = 5.321 \times 10^{-10}\ cm$$

$$d = \frac{n \times MM}{N_A \times a^3} = \frac{2\ atoms \times 39.10\ \frac{g}{mol}}{6.022 \times 10^{23}\ \frac{atoms}{mol} \times (5.321 \times 10^{-8}\ cm)^3} = 0.8619\ g/cm^3$$

39. **What is the hydrogen ion concentration in a solution formed by mixing 34.87 mL of 0.2233 M hydrochloric acid with 16.27 mL of 0.1468 M potassium hydroxide?**

Review: Objective 93

This is a neutralization stoichiometry problem (titration) where we also have a limiting reagent situation.

$$34.87 \; mL \; \times 0.2233 \; M = 7.786 \; mmol \; HCl$$

$$16.27 \; mL \; \times 0.1468 \; M = 2.388 \; mmol \; KOH$$

$$HCl + KOH \; \rightarrow KCl + H_2O$$

We have only 2.388 mmol KOH, so KOH is the limiting reactant, thus HCl is in excess. Let's see by how much:

$$7.786 \; mmol \; HCl \; available - 2.388 \; mmol \; consumed = 5.398 \; mmol \; HCl \; excess$$

The hydrogen ion concentration will be given by the excess HCl, which is completely dissociated in solution.

$$[H^+] = [HCl]_{excess} = \frac{5.398 \; mmol}{34.87 \; mL + 16.27 \; mL} = 0.1056 \; M$$

40. **Consider an electrochemical cell constructed from the following half cells, linked by a KCl salt bridge.**
   - a Fe electrode in 1.0 M $FeCl_2$ solution
   - a Sn electrode in 1.0 M $Sn(NO_3)_2$ solution
   When the cell is running spontaneously, which choice includes *only* true statements and no false ones?

Review: Objective 191

Standard reduction potentials:

$$Fe^{2+} + 2e^- \rightarrow Fe \qquad E^o = -0.41 \; V$$

$$Sn^{2+} + 2e^- \rightarrow Sn \qquad E^o = -0.14 \; V$$

The galvanic cell will be:
$$Fe \mid Fe^{2+} \mid\mid Sn^{2+} \mid Sn$$

Thus, the iron electrode will oxidize and lose mass (anode), and the tin electrode will gain mass from the reduction of tin ions to tin metal, and thus be the cathode.

41. **How many valence electrons does an atom of fluorine have?**

Review: Objective 20

Fluorine has the electron configuration $1s^2 2s^2 2p^5$ and therefore has 7 valence electrons.

42. Consider the following gas phase equilibrium system:

$$PCl_{5\,(g)} \rightleftharpoons PCl_{3\,(g)} + Cl_{2\,(g)} \qquad \Delta H^o = +87.8\ kJ/mol$$

Which of the following statements is *false*?

Review: Objective 163

The false statement is "A catalyst speeds up the approach to equilibrium and shifts the position of equilibrium to the right", because a catalyst does not shift the position of the equilibrium.

43. The density of mercury is 13.6 g/cm^3. How may liters does 494 g of Hg occupy?

Review: Objective 6

This is a simple density problem:

$$V = \frac{m}{d} = \frac{494\ g}{13.6\ g/cm^3} = 36.3\ cm^3$$

$$36.3\ cm^3 \times \frac{1\ L}{1000\ cm^3} = 3.63 \times 10^{-2}\ L$$

44. Calculate ΔS^o for the reaction of 250. g of PbO with excess carbon according to the equation

$$2PbO_{(s)} + C_{(s)} \rightarrow 2Pb_{(s)} + CO_{2\,(g)}$$

	$S^o\ (J/K \cdot mol)$
PbO(s)	69.45
C(s)	5.7
Pb(s)	64.89
CO$_2$(g)	213.6

Review: Objective 187

$$\Delta S^\circ = \sum \Delta S^o\ (products) - \sum \Delta S^o\ (reactants)$$

$$\Delta S^\circ = S^o(Pb) + S^o(CO_2) - \left(S^o(PbO) + S^o(C)\right)$$

$$\Delta S^\circ = 2\ mol\ Pb \times 64.89\,\frac{J}{mol\ K} + 1\ mol\ CO_2 \times 213.6\,\frac{J}{mol\ K}$$
$$- \left(2\ mol\ PbO \times 69.45\,\frac{J}{mol\ K} + 1\ mol\ C \times 5.7\,\frac{J}{mol\ K}\right) = -198.8\,\frac{J}{K}$$

$$250.\,g\ PbO \times \frac{1\ mol}{223.20\ g/mol} = 1.12\ mol\ PbO$$

$$\frac{-198.8\ J/K}{2\ mol\ PbO} = \frac{x}{1.12\ mol\ PbO} \quad \Rightarrow \quad x = 111\,\frac{kJ}{K}$$

45. How many 3d electrons does a V^{3+} ion have?

Review: Objective 98

V^{3+} has 2 d electrons.

46. A piece of metal with a mass of 136 g is placed into a graduated cylinder that contains 50.00 mL of water, raising the water level to 99.00 mL. What is the density of the metal?

Review: Lessons 1 and 2.

This is called the determination of density by water displacement.

$$d = \frac{136\ g}{99.00\ mL - 50.00\ mL} = 2.78\frac{g}{mL}\ or\ 2.78\ g/cm^3$$

47. In the complex ion $[ML_6]^{n+}$, M^{n+} has five d electrons and L is a strong field ligand. According to crystal field theory, the magnetic properties of the complex ion correspond to how many unpaired electrons?

Review: Objective 194

The metal in question has the electron configuration $4s^0 3d^5$ and ligand field is strong, thus the complex will be low spin. There are 6 ligands so the complex is octahedral. The splitting and orbital diagram will be as follows:

Thus, there is one unpaired electron.

Octahedral

48. A balloon contains 0.76 mol N_2, 0.18 mol O_2, 0.031 mol He and 0.026 mol H_2 at 725 mm Hg. What is the partial pressure of oxygen?

Review: Objective 138

Total number of moles of gas:

$$0.76 + 0.18 + 0.031 = 0.971\ mol$$

Mole fraction of oxygen:

$$\frac{0.18\ mol\ O_2}{0.971\ mol\ total} = 0.185$$

Partial pressure of oxygen:

$$0.185 \times 725\ mmHg = 134\ mmHg$$

49. A first-order reaction has a rate constant of $3.66 \times 10^{-3} \ s^{-1}$. The time required for the reaction to be 80.0% complete is

Review: Objective 153

$$Rate = k[A]$$

$$[A] = \frac{20.0}{100}[A]_o \quad (80\% \ complete)$$

$$\ln\frac{[A]}{[A]_o} = \ln\frac{\frac{20.0}{100}[A]_o}{[A]_o} = \ln\frac{0.200[A]_o}{[A]_o} = \ln 0.200 = -kt$$

$$t = -\frac{\ln 0.2}{k} = -\frac{-1.609}{3.66 \times 10^{-3} \ s^{-1}} = 440 \ s$$

50. In liquid propanol (C_3H_8OH), which intermolecular forces are predominant?

Review: Objective 144

Propanol is a polar molecule, and it contains OH groups, so the predominant type of intermolecular forces are hydrogen bonds.

Answer key for practice final exam

1. D
2. D
3. E
4. E
5. A
6. B
7. E
8. D
9. C
10. D
11. C
12. E
13. D
14. D
15. E
16. D
17. E
18. B
19. C
20. B
21. A
22. B
23. A
24. E
25. D
26. E
27. B
28. D
29. A
30. C
31. C
32. E
33. B
34. A
35. E
36. B
37. C
38. E
39. A
40. B
41. D
42. C
43. D
44. C
45. E
46. B
47. B
48. B
49. B
50. C

Appendix A.   Classes of Inorganic Substances. Nomenclature and Oxidation numbers.

Elements

Elements are simple substances that cannot be decomposed into simpler ones through chemical means. Oxidation number = 0. Some nonmetals have polyatomic molecules.

Examples: H_2, Na, O_2, P_4, S_8, Ca

Oxides

Metal oxides

Compounds between oxygen and metals; these are generally ionic compounds, containing the oxide ion (O^{2-})

Li_2O	lithium ox**ide**
MgO	magnesium ox**ide**
Al_2O_3	aluminum ox**ide**
FeO	iron (II) ox**ide** (ferr**ous** oxide)
Fe_2O_3	iron (III) ox**ide** (ferr**ic** oxide)

Oxidation numbers: O = -2, metal = cation charge (except Hg_2^{2+}, where Hg = +1)

Nonmetal oxides

Compounds between oxygen and nonmetals; these are always covalent compounds; there can be more than one oxide of the same nonmetal.

CO	carbon monoxide
CO_2	carbon dioxide
SO_3	sulfur trioxide
P_2O_3	diphosphorus trioxide
P_2O_5	diphosphorus pentoxide

Oxidation numbers: O = -2 (except in F_2O, where O = +2), other nonmetal varies

Peroxides and superoxides

Oxides in which O has oxidation numbers higher than -2

Na_2O_2	sodium peroxide	(Na=+1, O=-1)
BaO_2	barium peroxide	(Ba=+2, O=-1)
KO_2	potassium superoxide	(K=+1, O=-1/2)
H_2O_2	hydrogen peroxide	(H=+1, O=-1)

Metal Hydrides

Compounds between metals and hydrogen. Generally only the more active metals (groups 1 – 3) form hydrides. These are generally ionic compounds containing the hydride ion (H^-). Some are covalent.

NaH	sodium hyd**ride**
CsH	cesium hyd**ride**
CaH_2	calcium hyd**ride**

Oxidation numbers: H = -1, metal = cation charge

Hydroxides

Compounds between cations and the hydroxide ion (OH^-). All hydroxides are also known as bases. However, there are other bases that are not necessarily metal hydroxides, such as NH_3 (ammonia), N_2H_4 (hydrazine) etc.

LiOH	lithium hydrox**ide**
$Ba(OH)_2$	barium hydrox**ide**
$Al(OH)_3$	aluminum hydrox**ide**
$Fe(OH)_3$	iron (III) (or fer**ric**) hydrox**ide**
$Fe(OH)_2$	iron (II) (or fer**rous**) hydrox**ide**

Oxidation numbers: O = -2, H = +1, metal = cation charge

Strength

Bases can be strong or weak, which is related to their ability to dissociate when dissolved in water (and produce *hydroxide ions*, OH^-). Group 1 and 2 metal hydroxides are all strong bases (although not all of them are very soluble). Beyond group 2 and including all transition metals are weak bases. Ammonia and hydrazine are also examples of weak bases.

Acids

Compounds between hydrogen and other nonmetals. Acids donate H^+ ions in solution as H_3O^+.

Binary acids

Acids that do not contain oxygen in their molecule – their name will end in –**ide.**

GROUP 17 (halogen family)

HF	Hydrofluoric acid or hydrogen fluoride	weak
HCl	Hydrochloric acid or hydrogen chloride	strong
HBr	Hydrobromic acid or hydrogen bromide	strong
HI	Hydroiodic acid or hydrogen iodide	strong

GROUP 16 (oxygen family)

H_2S	Hydrosulfuric acid or hydrogen sulfide	weak
H_2Se	Hydroselenic acid or hydrogen selenide	weak

| H_2Te | Hydrotelluric acid or hydrogen telluride | weak |

Other acids not containing oxygen:

| HCN | Hydrocyanic acid | very weak |
| HSCN | Thiocyanic acid | very weak |

Oxoacids

Acids containing oxygen in their molecule – their name will end in **–ic** (if high in oxygen) or **–ous** (if low in oxygen); if a nonmetal can have more than 2 oxoacids, then the prefixes **hypo-** (for low oxygen) or **per-** (for high oxygen) are used in addition to the endings

GROUP 17 (halogen family)

$HClO_4$	**Per**chlor**ic** acid	strong
$HClO_3$	Chlor**ic** acid	strong
$HClO_2$	Chlor**ous** acid	weak
HClO	**Hypo**chlor**ous** acid	weak
$HBrO_4$	**Per**brom**ic** acid	strong
$HBrO_3$	Brom**ic** acid	strong
$HBrO_2$	Brom**ous** acid	weak
HBrO	**Hypo**brom**ous** acid	weak
HIO_4	**Per**iod**ic** acid	strong
HIO_3	Iod**ic** acid	strong
HIO_2	Iod**ous** acid	weak
HIO	**Hypo**iod**ous** acid	weak

GROUP 16 (oxygen family)

H_2SO_4	Sulfur**ic** acid	strong
H_2SO_3	Sulfur**ous** acid	weak
H_2SeO_4	Selen**ic** acid	strong
H_2SeO_3	Selen**ous** acid	weak
H_6TeO_6	Tellur**ic** acid	weak
H_2TeO_3	Tellur**ous** acid	weak

GROUP 15 (nitrogen family)

HNO_3	Nitr**ic** acid	strong
HNO_2	Nitr**ous** acid	weak
H_3PO_4	Phosphor**ic** acid	weak
H_3PO_3	Phosphor**ous** acid	weak
H_3AsO_4	Arsen**ic** acid	weak
H_3AsO_3	Arsen**ous** acid	weak

GROUP 14 (carbon family)

H_2CO_3	Carbonic acid	very weak
H_2SiO_3	Silicic acid	very weak

GROUP 13 (Boron family)

H_3BO_3	Boric acid	weak

Acids of transition metals in high oxidation states:

H_2CrO_4	Chromic acid	strong
$H_2Cr_2O_7$	Dichromic acid	strong
$HMnO_4$	Permanganic acid	strong
H_2MnO_4	Manganic acid	weak

Most of these acids are not known in free form, but their salts are important.

Other oxoacids:

$H_2C_2O_4$	Oxalic acid	weak
$H_2S_2O_3$	Thiosulfuric acid	weak
$H_2S_4O_6$	Tetrathionic acid	weak

Organic Acids

HCOOH	Formic acid	weak
CH_3COOH	Acetic acid	weak
CH_3CH_2COOH	Propionic acid	weak
$CH_3CH_2CH_2COOH$	Butiric acid	weak
C_6H_5COOH	Benzoic acid	weak

Oxidation numbers: H=+1, O=-2, others vary (organic acids have special rules)

Strength

Acids can be strong or weak, which is related to their ability to dissociate when dissolved in water (and produce *hydronium ions*, H_3O^+). The strength of acids is determined experimentally, but can be predicted fairly accurately from their molecular structure. Examples above show the approximate strength for each acid.

Salts

Compounds between metal cations (or ammonium) and anions derived from acids. An anion is what results from the removal of one or more hydrogen ions (H^+) from an acid.

Rules for deriving anion names from acid names:

Binary acids: the ending –ide is appended to the root of the name of the nonmetal. For polyprotic acids, anions containing hydrogen get the name "hydrogen" inserted before the name of the anion. Examples:

Oxoacids:

the ending –ate is appended to the root of the name of the acid if that name ends in –ic;
the ending –ite is appended to the root of the name of the acid if that name ends in –ous;
the prefix –per or –hypo is kept in the name of the anion if present in the name of the acid

Examples of acid dissociation in aqueous solution with formation of anions:

$HCl \rightarrow H^+ + Cl^-$ chloride
$HClO_4 \rightarrow H^+ + ClO_4^-$ **per**chlor**ate**
$HClO_3 \rightarrow H^+ + ClO_3^-$ chlor**ate**
$HClO_2 \rightarrow H^+ + ClO_2^-$ chlor**ite**
$HClO \rightarrow H^+ + ClO^-$ **hypo**chlor**ite**

$H_3PO_4 \leftrightarrow H^+ + H_2PO_4^-$ dihydrogen phosph**ate**
$H_2PO_4^- \leftrightarrow H^+ + HPO_4^{2-}$ hydrogen phosph**ate**
$HPO_4^{2-} \leftrightarrow H^+ + PO_4^{3-}$ phosph**ate**

Binary salts

Salts between metal cations and anions derived from binary acids. The names of these salts end in –ide. Examples:

Halides (generic name given to salts between metal cations and anions derived from binary acids of halogens)

LiF	lithium fluor**ide**
CaF_2	calcium fluor**ide**
NaCl	sodium chlor**ide**
$FeCl_3$	ferric chlor**ide**
KBr	potassium brom**ide**
AgI	silver iod**ide**
PbI_2	lead (II) iod**ide**

Sulfides, selenides and tellurides

Na_2S	sodium sulf**ide**
CdS	cadmium sulf**ide**
Al_2S_3	aluminum sulf**ide**
Li_2Se	lithium selen**ide**
MgTe	magnesium tellur**ide**

Cyanides and thiocyanides:

KCN	potassium cyan**ide**
$Mg(SCN)_2$	magnesium thiocyan**ide**

Nitrides
Na_3N	sodium nitr**ide**
Mg_3N_2	magnesium nitr**ide**
AlN	aluminum nitr**ide**

Phosphides

Li_3P	lithium phosph**ide**
Sr_3P_2	strontium phosph**ide**

Arsenides

Na_3As	sodium arsen**ide**
Mg_3As_2	magnesium arsen**ide**

Carbides

Na_4C	sodium carb**ide**
Ca_2C	calcium carb**ide**

Other nonmetal hydrides (these are not salts, however)

NH_3	ammonia
PH_3	phosphine
AsH_3	arsine
CH_4	methane
SiH_4	silane
H_3B	borane

Salts derived from oxoacids

Compounds between metal cations and oxoanions

KNO_3	potassium nitr**ate**
$CuSO_4$	cupric sulf**ate**
$Al_2(SO_4)_3$	aluminum sulf**ate**
$LiClO_4$	lithium perchlor**ate**
$Mg_3(PO_4)_2$	magnesium phosph**ate**
$CaCO_3$	calcium carbon**ate**
$Ca(HCO_3)_2$	calcium hydrogen carbon**ate** (or calcium bicarbonate)

Oxidation numbers for elements in a salt: determine oxidation numbers separately for cations and anions as explained above.

Example: determine the oxidation numbers for all elements in ammonium dichromate: $(NH_4)_2Cr_2O_7$

This is a salt composed of the ammonium ion (NH_4^+) and the dichromate ion ($Cr_2O_7^{2-}$) in a ratio of 2:1. The *cation : anion* ratio is irrelevant in determining oxidation numbers in this case because each is a complex ion and we will determine the oxidation number for each element.

Ammonium ion: NH_4^+ : H = +1 (in all cases except H_2 and hydrides), thus N = -3 (sum of all oxidation numbers must equal the charge of the anion: 4x(+1) + 1x(-3) = +1)

Dichromate: $Cr_2O_7^{2-}$: O = -2 in all cases except F_2O, peroxides and superoxides, thus Cr = +6 (sum of all oxidation numbers must equal the charge of the anion: 2x(+6) + 7x(-2) = -2)

Appendix B.   Activity series of metals

The following table shows the activity series of metals.

Metal	Ion	Reactivity
Li	Li^+	React with acids and water to free H_2.
Rb	Rb^+	
K	K^+	
Ba	Ba^{2+}	
Sr	Sr^{2+}	
Ca	Ca^{2+}	
Na	Na^+	
Mg	Mg^{2+}	React with acids and water vapor to free H_2.
Al	Al^{3+}	
Mn	Mn^{2+}	React with acids free H_2 but not with water.
Zn	Zn^{2+}	
Cr	Cr^{3+}	
Fe	Fe^{2+}	
Cd	Cd^{2+}	
Co	Co^{2+}	
Ni	Ni^{2+}	
Sn	Sn^{2+}	
Pb	Pb^{2+}	
H_2	H^+	
Cu	Cu^{2+}	Do not react with acids to produce free H_2.
Ag	Ag^+	
Hg	Hg^{2+}	
Au	Au^{3+}	
Pt	Pt^{2+}	

Appendix C.   Determination of atomic radius in cubic unit cells

Simple cubic (atoms touch each other)

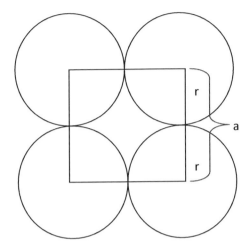

r = atomic radius
a = edge length

thus, a = 2r, so r = a/2

Face centered cubic (atoms across a face diagonal touch each other)

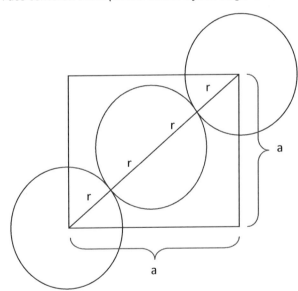

Since the diagonal measures r + 2r + r = 4r, where r = radius of
one atom, write an expression relating a to r using the Pythagorean Theorem.

$(4r)^2 = a^2 + a^2$

$16r^2 = 2a^2$

$r = \dfrac{a}{\sqrt{8}}$

Body centered cubic (atoms across the cube diagonal touch each other)

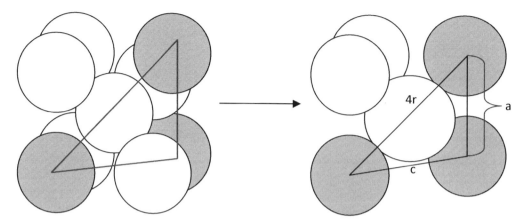

If we look at bcc closely, we can see the length of the body diagonal of the cell (d) where d = 4r (r is atomic radius)

The length of the remaining side of this triangle is the length of the diagonal line through the bottom of the unit cell, the length of which is determined by using Pythagorean Theorem on another triangle.

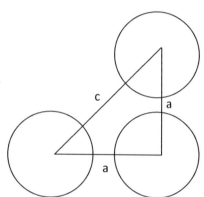

r = atomic radius
a = edge length
c = face diagonal

$c^2 = 2a^2$
$(4r)^2 = a^2 + 2a^2 = 3a^2$
$16r^2 = 3a^2$
$r^2 = 3a^2 / 16$

$$r = \frac{a\sqrt{3}}{4}$$

Appendix D.   Solubility curves for several inorganic salts

The chart below shows solubility curves for a number of inorganic salts. See legend on next page.

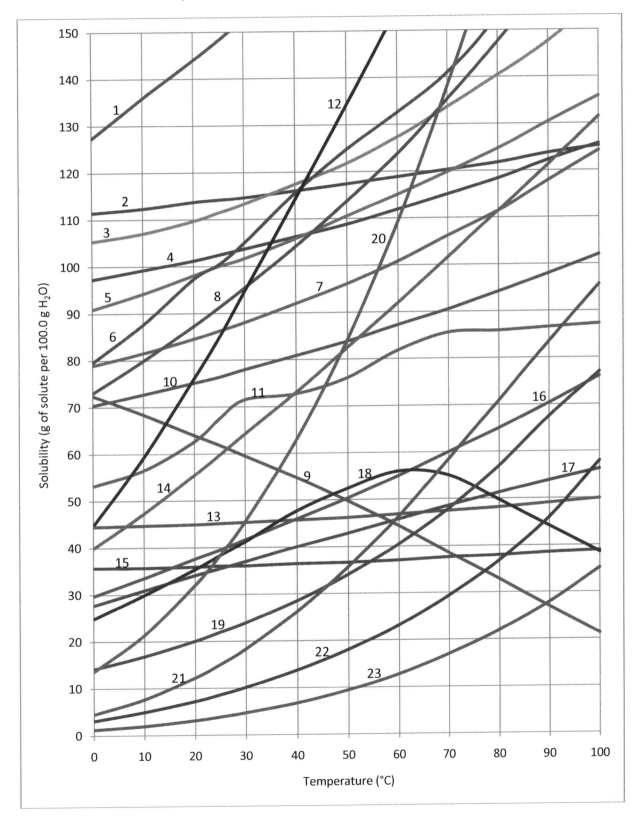

Legend

The number closest to each curve in the chart corresponds to the salt indicated in the table below.

$1 = KI$

$2 = K_2SO_3$

$3 = K_2CO_3$

$4 = MgBr_2$

$5 = BaBr_2$

$6 = NaClO_3$

$7 = CdI_2$

$8 = NaNO_3$

$9 = CdSeO_4$

$10 = (NH_4)_2SO_4$

$11 = NiCl_2$

$12 = CsI$

$13 = AlCl_3$

$14 = Pb(NO_3)_2$

$15 = NaCl$

$16 = NH_4Cl$

$17 = KCl$

$18 = CoSO_4$

$19 = CuSO_4$

$20 = KNO_3$

$21 = K_2Cr_2O_7$

$22 = KClO_3$

$23 = CsBrO_3$

Appendix E.   Vapor pressures of water

Temperature (°C)	Pressure (mmHg)	Temperature (°C)	Pressure (mmHg)	Temperature (°C)	Pressure (mmHg)	Temperature (°C)	Pressure (mmHg)
0	4.6	26	25.2	51	97.2	76	301.4
1	4.9	27	26.7	52	102.1	77	314.1
2	5.3	28	28.3	53	107.2	78	327.3
3	5.7	29	30	54	112.5	79	341
4	6.1	30	31.8	55	118	80	355.1
5	6.5	31	33.7	56	123.8	81	369.7
6	7	32	35.7	57	129.8	82	384.9
7	7.5	33	37.7	58	136.1	83	400.6
8	8	34	39.9	59	142.6	84	416.8
9	8.6	35	42.2	60	149.4	85	433.6
10	9.2	36	44.6	61	156.4	86	450.9
11	9.8	37	47.1	62	163.8	87	468.7
12	10.5	38	49.7	63	171.4	88	487.1
13	11.2	39	52.4	64	179.3	89	506.1
14	12	40	55.3	65	187.5	90	525.8
15	12.8	41	58.3	66	196.1	91	546
16	13.6	42	61.5	67	205	92	567
17	14.5	43	64.8	68	214.2	93	588.6
18	15.5	44	68.3	69	223.7	94	610.9
19	16.5	45	71.9	70	233.7	95	633.9
20	17.5	46	75.7	71	243.9	96	657.6
21	18.7	47	79.6	72	254.6	97	682.1
22	19.8	48	83.7	73	265.7	98	707.3
23	21.1	49	88	74	277.2	99	733.2
24	22.4	50	92.5	75	289.1	100	760
25	23.8						

Appendix F. Dissociation constants

Acidity constants

Acid	Formula	pK_{a1}	pK_{a2}	pK_{a3}
Acetic	CH_3COOH	4.74		
Acetylsalicylic	$C_8H_7O_2COOH$	3.48		
Acrylic	$HC_3H_3O_2$	4.26		
Aluminum ion	Al^{3+}	5.01		
Arsenic	H_3AsO_4	2.30	7.03	11.53
Arsenous	$HAsO_2$	9.18		
Ascorbic	$H_2C_6H_6O_6$	4.10	11.80	
Benzoic	C_6H_5COOH	4.20		
Boric	H_3BO_3	9.23		
Bromoacetic	$BrCH_2COOH$	2.90		
Butyric	$HC_4H_7O_2$	4.83		
Carbonic	H_2CO_3	6.37	10.25	
Chloroacetic	$ClCH_2COOH$	2.85		
Chlorous	$HClO_2$	1.92		
Chromium ion	Cr^{3+}	4.0		
Cinnamic	$HC_9H_7O_2$	4.44		
Citric	$H_3C_6H_5O_7$	3.13	4.76	6.40
Cyanic	$HCNO$	3.46		
Cyanuric	$HC_3H_2N_3O_3$	6.78		
Dichloroacetic	$Cl_2CHCOOH$	1.26		
Fluoroacetic	FCH_2COOH	2.59		
Formic	$HCOOH$	3.75		
Germanic	H_2GeO_3	9.0	12.4	
Hydrazoic	HN_3	4.72		
Hydrocyanic	HCN	9.23		

Acid	Formula	pK_{a1}	pK_{a2}	pK_{a3}
Hydrofluoric	HF	3.16		
Hydrogen peroxide	H_2O_2	11.65		
Hydroselenic	H_2Se	3.89	11.0	
Hydrosulfuric	H_2S	6.88	14.15	
Hydrotelluric	H_2Te	2.64	10.80	
Hypobromous	$HBrO$	9.24		
Hypochlorous	$HClO$	7.55		
Hypoiodous	HIO	10.64		
Hyponitrous	$H_2N_2O_2$	7.05	11.4	
Hypophosphorous	H_3PO_2	1.23		
Iodic	HIO_3	0.80		
Iodoacetic	ICH_2COOH	3.18		
Iron(II) ion	Fe^{2+}	6.74		
Iron(III) ion	Fe^{3+}	2.83		
Lactic	$HC_3H_5O_3$	3.08		
Maleic	$HOOCCH = CHCOOH$	1.84	6.07	
Malonic	$H_2C_3H_2O_4$	2.82	5.70	
Nitrous	HNO_2	3.14		
Oxalic	$H_2C_2O_4$	1.23	4.19	
Phenol	HOC_6H_5	10.00		
Phosphoric	H_3PO_4	2.12	7.21	12.67
Phosphorous	H_3PO_3	1.80	6.15	
Phthalic	$H_2C_8H_4O_4$	2.92	5.41	
Propionic	$HC_3H_5O_2$	4.87		
Salicylic	$HC_7H_5O_3$	1.96		
Selenic	H_2SeO_4	1.66		
Selenous	H_2SeO_3	2.64	8.27	

Acid	Formula	pK_{a1}	pK_{a2}	pK_{a3}
Succinic	$H_2C_4H_4O_4$	4.21	5.64	
Sulfuric	H_2SO_4	none	1.92	
Sulfurous	H_2SO_3	1.89	7.21	
Thiophenol	HSC_6H_5	6.49		
Trichloroacetic	Cl_3CCOOH	0.52		
Zinc ion	Zn^{2+}	8.96		

Basicity constants

Base	Formula	pK_{b1}	pK_{b2}
Ammonia	NH_3	4.76	
Aniline	$C_6H_5NH_2$	9.37	
Codeine	$C_{18}H_{21}O_3N$	6.05	
Diethylamine	$(C_2H_5)_2NH$	4.51	
Dimethylamine	$(CH_3)_2NH$	3.23	
Ethylamine	$C_2H_5NH_2$	3.36	
Hydrazine	N_2H_4	5.77	15.05
Hydroxylamine	$HONH_2$	9.04	
Methylamine	CH_3NH_2	3.38	
Morphine	$C_{17}H_{19}O_3N$	6.13	
Piperidine	$C_5H_{11}N$	2.88	
Pyridine	C_5H_5N	8.70	
Quinoline	C_9H_7N	9.20	
Triethanolamine	$C_6H_{15}O_3N$	6.24	
Triethylamine	$(C_2H_5)_3N$	3.28	
Trimethylamine	$(CH_3)_3N$	4.20	

Appendix G. Solubility products

Compound	K_{sp}	Compound	K_{sp}	Compound	K_{sp}
$Ag_2C_2O_4$	3.6×10^{-11}	BaS_2O_3	$1.6 \ 10^{-5}$	$Cr(OH)_3$	6.3×10^{-31}
Ag_2CO_3	8.1×10^{-12}	$BaSO_3$	8×10^{-7}	$Cu(OH)_2$	2.2×10^{-20}
Ag_2CrO_4	1.1×10^{-12}	$BaSO_4$	1.1×10^{-10}	$Cu(SCN)_2$	4.0×10^{-14}
Ag_2S	6×10^{-51}	Bi_2S_3	1×10^{-97}	$Cu_2[Fe(CN)_6]$	1.3×10^{-16}
Ag_2SO_4	1.4×10^{-5}	$BiOCl$	1.8×10^{-31}	Cu_2S	2.5×10^{-48}
Ag_3AsO_4	1.0×10^{-22}	$BiO(OH)$	4×10^{-10}	$Cu_3(AsO_4)_2$	7.6×10^{-36}
$AgBr$	5.3×10^{-13}	$Ca(IO_3)_2$	7.1×10^{-7}	$CuCl$	1.2×10^{-6}
$AgBrO_3$	5.5×10^{-5}	$Ca(OH)_2$	5.5×10^{-6}	$CuCN$	3.2×10^{-20}
$AgC_2H_3O_2$	2.0×10^{-3}	$Ca_3(PO_4)_2$	1×10^{-26}	$CuCO_3$	1.4×10^{-10}
$AgC_7H_5O_2$	2.5×10^{-5}	$Ca_5(PO_4)_3F$	1.0×10^{-60}	$CuCrO_4$	3.6×10^{-6}
$AgCl$	1.8×10^{-10}	$Ca_5(PO_4)_3OH$	1.0×10^{-36}	CuI	1.1×10^{-12}
$AgCN$	1.2×10^{-16}	$CaC_2O_4 \cdot H_2O$	1.96×10^{-8}	CuS	6×10^{-37}
AgI	8.3×10^{-17}	$CaCO_3$	3.8×10^{-9}	$Fe(OH)_2$	8.0×10^{-16}
$AgIO_3$	3.0×10^{-8}	$CaCrO_4$	7.1×10^{-4}	$Fe(OH)_3$	4×10^{-38}
AgN_3	2.0×10^{-8}	CaF_2	5.3×10^{-9}	$Fe_4[Fe(CN)_6]_3$	3.3×10^{-41}
$AgNO_2$	6.0×10^{-4}	$CaHPO_4$	1×10^{-7}	$FeAsO_4$	5.7×10^{-21}
$AgSCN$	1.0×10^{-12}	$CaSO_3$	6.8×10^{-8}	$FeCO_3$	3.2×10^{-11}
$AgSO_3$	1.5×10^{-14}	$CaSO_4$	9.1×10^{-6}	$FePO_4$	1.3×10^{-22}
$Al(OH)_3$	4.6×10^{-33}	$Cd(IO_3)_2$	2.3×10^{-8}	FeS	6×10^{-19}
$AlPO_4$	6.3×10^{-19}	$Cd(OH)_2$	2.5×10^{-14}	$Hg(SCN)_2$	2.8×10^{-20}
$Ba(IO_3)_2$	1.5×10^{-9}	$CdCO_3$	5.2×10^{-12}	$Hg_2(CN)_2$	5×10^{-40}
$Ba(OH)_2$	5×10^{-3}	CdS	8.0×10^{-27}	$Hg_2(SCN)_2$	3.0×10^{-20}
BaC_2O_4	2.3×10^{-8}	$Co(OH)_3$	1.6×10^{-44}	Hg_2Br_2	5.6×10^{-23}
$BaCO_3$	5.1×10^{-9}	$CoCO_3$	1.4×10^{-13}	Hg_2Cl_2	5.0×10^{-13}
$BaCrO_4$	2.2×10^{-10}	CoS	4.0×10^{-21}	Hg_2CrO_4	2.0×10^{-9}
BaF_2	1.0×10^{-6}	$Cr(OH)_2$	2×10^{-16}	Hg_2S	1.0×10^{-47}

Compound	K_{sp}
Hg_2SO_4	7.4×10^{-7}
HgI_2	4.5×10^{-29}
HgS	1.6×10^{-52}
Li_2CO_3	2.5×10^{-2}
Li_3PO_4	3.2×10^{-9}
LiF	3.8×10^{-3}
$Mg(OH)_2$	1.8×10^{-11}
$Mg_3(AsO_4)_2$	2.1×10^{-20}
$Mg_3(PO_4)_2$	1×10^{-25}
MgC_2O_4	7×10^{-7}
$MgCO_3$	3.5×10^{-8}
MgF_2	3.7×10^{-8}
$MgNH_4PO_4$	2.5×10^{-13}
$Mn(OH)_2$	1.9×10^{-9}
$MnCO_3$	1.8×10^{-11}
MnS	2.5×10^{-13}
$Ni(OH)_2$	2.0×10^{-15}
$NiCO_3$	6.6×10^{-9}
NiS	3×10^{-19}
$Pb(BrO_3)_2$	7.9×10^{-6}

Compound	K_{sp}
$Pb(IO_3)_2$	2.6×10^{-13}
$Pb(N_3)_2$	2.5×10^{-9}
$Pb(OH)_2$	1.2×10^{-5}
$Pb_3(AsO_4)_2$	4.0×10^{-36}
$PbBr_2$	4.0×10^{-5}
$PbCl_2$	1.6×10^{-5}
$PbCO_3$	7.4×10^{-14}
$PbCrO_4$	2.8×10^{-13}
PbF_2	2.7×10^{-8}
PbI_2	7.1×10^{-9}
PbS	3×10^{-29}
$PbSO_4$	1.6×10^{-8}
$Sc(OH)_3$	4.2×10^{-18}
ScF_3	4.2×10^{-18}
$Sn(OH)_2$	1.4×10^{-28}
SnS	1×10^{-26}
SrC_2O_4	4×10^{-7}
$SrCO_3$	1.1×10^{-10}
$SrCrO_4$	2.2×10^{-5}
SrF_2	2.5×10^{-9}

Compound	K_{sp}
$SrSO_3$	4×10^{-8}
$SrSO_4$	3.2×10^{-7}
$Tl(OH)_3$	6.3×10^{-46}
Tl_2CrO_4	9.8×10^{-15}
Tl_2S	6×10^{-22}
$TlBr$	3.4×10^{-6}
$TlBrO_3$	1.7×10^{-4}
$TlCl$	1.7×10^{-4}
TlI	6.5×10^{-8}
$TlIO_3$	3.1×10^{-6}
$TlSCN$	1.6×10^{-4}
$Zn(CN)_2$	3×10^{-16}
$Zn(IO_3)_2$	3.9×10^{-6}
$Zn(OH)_2$	1.2×10^{-17}
$Zn_3(PO_4)_2$	9.0×10^{-33}
ZnC_2O_4	2.7×10^{-8}
$ZnCO_3$	1.4×10^{-11}
ZnS	2×10^{-25}

486

Appendix H. Standard reduction potentials

Half reaction	E^o
(1) $F_2 + 2e^- \rightarrow 2F^-$	+2.87
(2) $Co^{3+} + e^- \rightarrow Co^{2+}$	+1.80
(3) $PbO_2 + 4H^+ + SO_4^{2-} + 2e^- \rightarrow PbSO_{4\,(s)} + 2H_2O$	+1.69
(4) $MnO_4^- + 8H^+ + 5e^- \rightarrow Mn^{2+} + 4H_2O$	+1.49
(5) $PbO_2 + 4H^+ + 2e^- \rightarrow Pb^{2+} + 2H_2O$	+1.46
(6) $Cl_2 + 2e^- \rightarrow 2Cl^-$	+1.36
(7) $Cr_2O_7^{2-} + 14H^+ + 6e^- \rightarrow 2Cr^{3+} + 7H_2O$	+1.33
(8) $O_2 + 4H^+ + 4e^- \rightarrow 2H_2O$	+1.23
(9) $Br_2 + 2e^- \rightarrow 2Br^-$	+1.07
(10) $NO_3^- + 4H^+ + 3e^- \rightarrow NO + 2H_2O$	+0.96
(11) $Hg^{2+} + 2e^- \rightarrow Hg$	+0.85
(12) $Ag^+ + e^- \rightarrow Ag$	+0.80
(13) $Fe^{3+} + e^- \rightarrow Fe^{2+}$	+0.77
(14) $I_2 + 2e^- \rightarrow 2I^-$	+0.54
(15) $Cu^+ + e^- \rightarrow Cu$	+0.52
(16) $Fe(CN)_6^{3-} + e^- \rightarrow Fe(CN)_6^{4-}$	+0.36
(17) $Cu^{2+} + 2e^- \rightarrow Cu$	+0.34
(18) $Cu^{2+} + e^- \rightarrow Cu^+$	+0.15
(19) $Sn^{4+} + 2e^- \rightarrow Sn^{2+}$	+0.15
(20) $2H^+ + 2e^- \rightarrow H_2$	0.00
(21) $Fe^{3+} + 3e^- \rightarrow Fe$	-0.04
(22) $Pb^{2+} + 2e^- \rightarrow Pb$	-0.13
(23) $Sn^{2+} + 2e^- \rightarrow Sn$	-0.14
(24) $Ni^{2+} + 2e^- \rightarrow Ni$	-0.25
(25) $Co^{2+} + 2e^- \rightarrow Co$	-0.29
(26) $PbSO_4 + 2e^- \rightarrow Pb + SO_4^{2-}$	-0.36

Half reaction	E^o
(27) $PbI_2 + 2e^- \rightarrow Pb + 2I^-$	-0.37
(28) $Cr^{3+} + e^- \rightarrow Cr^{2+}$	-0.40
(29) $Cd^{2+} + 2e^- \rightarrow Cd$	-0.40
(30) $Fe^{2+} + 2e^- \rightarrow Fe$	-0.41
(31) $Cr^{3+} + 3e^- \rightarrow Cr$	-0.74
(32) $Zn^{2+} + 2e^- \rightarrow Zn$	-0.76
(33) $2H_2O + 2e^- \rightarrow H_{2\,(g)} + 2OH^-$	-0.83
(34) $V^{2+} + 2e^- \rightarrow V$	-1.18
(35) $Mn^{2+} + 2e^- \rightarrow Mn$	-1.18
(36) $Al^{3+} + 3e^- \rightarrow Al$	-1.66
(37) $Mg^{2+} + 2e^- \rightarrow Mg$	-2.37

Appendix I. Common ligands

Formula	Name	Coordination sites
H_2O	aqua	1
NH_3	ammine (two m's	1
CO	carbonyl	1
NO	nitrosyl	1
C_5H_5N	pyridine	1
$NH_2CH_2CH_2NH_2$	ethylenediamine	2
$C_5H_4N - C_5H_4N$	dipyridyl	2
$P(C_6H_5)_3$	triphenylphosphine	1
$NH_2CH_2CH_2NHCH_2CH_2NH_2$	diethylenetriamine	3
Cl^-	chloro	1
OH^-	hydroxo	1
O^{2-}	oxo	1
O_2^-	peroxo	1
CN^-	cyano	1
N_3^-	azido	1
N^{3-}	nitrido	1
NH_2^-	amido	1
CO_3^{2-}	carbonato	1
$C_2O_4^{2-}$	oxalato	2
NO_3^-	nitrato	1
NO_2^-	nitrito	1
S^{2-}	sulfido	1
SCN^-	thiocyanato-S	1
NCS^-	thiocyanato-N	1
$-(CH_2 - N(CH_2COO^-)_2)_2$	ethylenediaminetetraacetato (EDTA)	4

Appendix J. Worksheet 0 solutions

1. Compute each of the following:

$$\frac{4}{15} \times \frac{3}{4} = \frac{3}{15} = 0.2$$

$$(1.25)^{-3} = 0.512$$

$$65\% \ of \ 525 = 341$$

$$55.845 + 2(14.007 + 4 \times 1.008) + 2(32.065 + 4 \times 16.00) = 284.05$$

$$\frac{12.01}{6.022 \times 10^{23}} = 1.99 \times 10^{-23}$$

$$2.18 \times 10^3 - 1.1 \times 10^2 = 2.18 \times 10^3 - 0.11 \times 10^3 = 2.07 \times 10^3$$

$$\ln 2^2 = 2 \ ln2 = 1.386$$

$$\log_3(27) = 3$$

$$2.18 \times 10^{-18} \times \left(\frac{1}{3^2} - \frac{1}{2^2}\right) = -3.03 \times 10^{-19}$$

$$\frac{80.912 \times \frac{555}{760}}{0.0821 \times 319} = 2.256$$

$$\frac{3 \times 8.315 \ \times 298}{3.200 \times 10^{-3}} = 2.32 \times 10^6$$

$$25.4 \times \frac{2.5}{100} \times \frac{1}{295.557} \times \frac{3}{5} \times 79.904 = 0.103$$

$$\sqrt[3]{\frac{4 \ \times 85.4678}{6.022 \times 10^{23} \ \times \ 1.63}} = 8.28 \times 10^{-8}$$

2. Expand the following:

$$(x - 2)(x + 2) = x^2 - 4$$

$$\frac{a}{b} + \frac{c}{d} = \frac{ad + bc}{bd}$$

$$\frac{2}{a + 1} - \frac{1}{a - 1} = \frac{2(a - 1) - (a + 1)}{a^2 - 1} = \frac{2a - 2 - a - 1}{a^2 - 1} = \frac{a - 3}{a^2 - 1}$$

$$\sqrt{64x^4} = 8x^2$$

$$\sqrt{3} + \sqrt{27} = \sqrt{3} + 3\sqrt{3} = 4\sqrt{3}$$

$$\frac{a-b}{\frac{1}{b}-\frac{1}{a}} = \frac{a-b}{\frac{a-b}{ba}} = ab$$

$$x^a \times x^b = x^{a+b}$$

$$\frac{x^a}{x^b} = x^{a-b}$$

$$(x^a)^b = x^{ab}$$

$$\ln(a \times b) = \ln a + \ln b$$

$$\ln\left(\frac{a}{b}\right) = \ln a - \ln b$$

$$\frac{x^{3a+2}}{x^{2a-1}} = x^{3a+2-(2a-1)} = x^{a+3}$$

$$\text{Solve for } E_a: \quad \frac{k_1}{k_2} = \frac{e^{-\frac{E_a}{RT_1}}}{e^{-\frac{E_a}{RT_2}}} = e^{-\left(\frac{E_a}{RT_1} - \frac{E_a}{RT_2}\right)}$$

$$\ln\left(\frac{k_1}{k_2}\right) = \ln\left(e^{-\left(\frac{E_a}{RT_1} - \frac{E_a}{RT_2}\right)}\right) = -\left(\frac{E_a}{RT_1} - \frac{E_a}{RT_2}\right) = -\frac{E_a}{R}\left(\frac{1}{T_1} - \frac{1}{T_2}\right) = -\frac{E_a}{R}\left(\frac{T_2 - T_1}{T_1 T_2}\right)$$

$$E_a = -\frac{\ln\left(\frac{k_1}{k_2}\right) R\, T_1 T_2}{T_2 - T_1}$$

3. Solve for x in each equation below:

$2.56\,x - 3.14 = 9.45$ $\qquad 2.56\,x = 12.59 \;\rightarrow\; x = 4.92$

$\dfrac{3x}{4} = 2$ $\qquad 3x = 8 \;\rightarrow\; x = 2.67$

$2(+3) + 3x + 12(-2) = 0$ $\qquad 6 + 3x - 24 = 0 \;\rightarrow\; 3x = 24 - 6 = 18 \;\rightarrow x = 6$

$4x - 9 = 2x + 5$ $\qquad 4x - 2x = 5 + 9 \;\rightarrow\; 2x = 14 \;\rightarrow\; x = 7$

$\dfrac{x}{2.5} = \dfrac{14.5}{50}$ $\qquad x = \dfrac{2.5 \times 14.5}{50} = 0.725$

$42 \text{ is } x\% \text{ of } 256$ $\qquad \dfrac{x}{100} \times 256 = 42 \;\rightarrow\; x = \dfrac{42 \times 100}{256} = 16.4$

$15.2 \text{ is } 3.5\% \text{ of } x$ $\qquad \dfrac{3.5\,x}{100} = 15.2 \;\rightarrow\; x = \dfrac{100 \times 15.2}{3.5} = 434$

$\dfrac{1}{x} = \dfrac{1}{10} - 3 \times 0.25$ $\qquad \dfrac{1}{x} = \dfrac{1}{10} - 0.75 = 0.1 - 0.75 = -0.65 \;\rightarrow\; x = -1.54$

$\dfrac{0.3611x}{x+200} = \dfrac{25}{100}$ $\qquad 100\,(0.3611x) = 25(x+200) \;\rightarrow\; 36.11\,x = 25x + 5000 \;\rightarrow$

$$11.11x \quad = 5000 \quad \rightarrow \quad x = 450$$

$$\frac{1000x}{256 - 110.98\,x} = 0.500 \qquad 1000x = 0.5\,(256 - 110.98x) = 128 - 55.49\,x$$

$$1055.49\,x = 128 \quad \rightarrow \quad x = 0.1213$$

$$\frac{(x-3)^2}{(x+3)^2} = 0.16 \qquad \sqrt{\frac{(x-3)^2}{(x+3)^2}} = \sqrt{0.16} \quad \rightarrow \quad \frac{x-3}{x+3} = 0.4 \quad \rightarrow \quad x - 3 = 0.4x + 1.2 \quad \rightarrow$$

$$0.6x = 4.2 \quad \rightarrow \quad x = 7$$

$$(x-2)(3x-4) = 0 \qquad 3x^2 - 4x - 6x + 8 = 0 \quad \rightarrow \quad 3x^2 - 10x + 8 = 0 \quad \rightarrow \quad x_1 = 2 \; ; \; x_2 = 1.33$$

$$x^2 = 6.5 \times 10^{-5}\,(0.2 - x) \qquad x^2 = 1.3 \times 10^{-5} - 6.5 \times 10^{-5}x \quad \rightarrow \quad x^2 + 6.5 \times 10^{-5}x \; - 1.3 \times 10^{-5} = 0$$

$$x_1 = 0.00357 \; ; \; x_2 = -0.00364$$

$$\begin{cases} 3x + 2y = 8 \\ y = x - 1 \end{cases} \qquad 3x + 2(x-1) = 8 \quad \rightarrow \quad 3x + 2x - 2 = 8 \quad \rightarrow \quad 5x = 10 \quad \rightarrow \quad x = 2 \text{ and } y = 1$$

$$2^x = 4 \qquad\qquad x = 2$$

$$3^x = 1 \qquad\qquad x = 0$$

$$\left(\frac{1}{x}\right)^3 = \frac{1}{8} \qquad\qquad \frac{1}{x^3} = \frac{1}{8} \quad \rightarrow \quad x = 2$$

$$\log_{10} x = 1.5 \qquad\qquad x = 10^{1.5} = 31.6$$

$$\ln(2x) = 2.4 \qquad\qquad \ln 2 + \ln x = 2.4 \quad \rightarrow \ln x = 2.4 - \ln 2 = 1.707 \quad \rightarrow \quad x = e^{1.707} = 5.51$$

$$\log(x^2) - \log(10) - 3 = 0 \qquad 2 \log x = \log 10 + 3 = 1 + 3 = 4 \quad \rightarrow \quad \log x = 2 \quad \rightarrow \quad x = 100$$

$$7 = \ln(5x) + \ln(7x - 2x)$$

$$7 = \ln(5x) + \ln(5x) = 2 \ln(5x) \quad \rightarrow \quad \ln 5 + \ln x = 3.5 \quad \rightarrow \quad \ln x = 1.89 \quad \rightarrow \quad x = 6.62$$

$$2^{-x} = \frac{1}{16} \qquad\qquad \frac{1}{2^x} = \frac{1}{16} = \frac{1}{2^4} \quad \rightarrow \quad x = 4$$

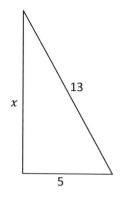

$$13^2 = x^2 + 5^2 \quad \rightarrow \quad 169 = x^2 + 25 \quad \rightarrow \quad x^2 = 144 \quad \rightarrow \quad x = 12$$

Index

Notes

Periodic Table of the Elements

Key:

Atomic number
Symbol
Name
Atomic mass

1	2	3	4	5	6	7	8	9	10	11	12	13	14	15	16	17	18
1 **H** Hydrogen 1.01																	2 **He** Helium 4.00
3 **Li** Lithium 6.94	4 **Be** Beryllium 9.01											5 **B** Boron 10.81	6 **C** Carbon 12.01	7 **N** Nitrogen 14.01	8 **O** Oxygen 16.00	9 **F** Fluorine 19.00	10 **Ne** Neon 20.18
11 **Na** Sodium 22.99	12 **Mg** Magnesium 24.31											13 **Al** Aluminium 26.98	14 **Si** Silicon 28.09	15 **P** Phosphorus 30.97	16 **S** Sulfur 32.07	17 **Cl** Chlorine 35.45	18 **Ar** Argon 39.95
19 **K** Potassium 39.10	20 **Ca** Calcium 40.08	21 **Sc** Scandium 44.96	22 **Ti** Titanium 47.87	23 **V** Vanadium 50.94	24 **Cr** Chromium 52.00	25 **Mn** Manganese 54.94	26 **Fe** Iron 55.85	27 **Co** Cobalt 58.93	28 **Ni** Nickel 58.69	29 **Cu** Copper 63.55	30 **Zn** Zinc 65.41	31 **Ga** Gallium 69.72	32 **Ge** Germanium 72.64	33 **As** Arsenic 74.92	34 **Se** Selenium 78.96	35 **Br** Bromine 79.90	36 **Kr** Krypton 83.80
37 **Rb** Rubidium 85.47	38 **Sr** Strontium 87.62	39 **Y** Yttrium 88.91	40 **Zr** Zirconium 91.22	41 **Nb** Niobium 92.91	42 **Mo** Molybdenum 95.94	43 **Tc** Technetium [98]	44 **Ru** Ruthenium 101.07	45 **Rh** Rhodium 102.91	46 **Pd** Palladium 106.42	47 **Ag** Silver 107.87	48 **Cd** Cadmium 112.41	49 **In** Indium 114.83	50 **Sn** Tin 118.71	51 **Sb** Antimony 121.76	52 **Te** Tellurium 127.60	53 **I** Iodine 126.90	54 **Xe** Xenon 131.29
55 **Cs** Caesium 132.91	56 **Ba** Barium 137.33	57 **La** Lanthanum 138.91	72 **Hf** Hafnium 178.49	73 **Ta** Tantalum 180.95	74 **W** Tungsten 183.84	75 **Re** Rhenium 186.21	76 **Os** Osmium 190.23	77 **Ir** Iridium 192.22	78 **Pt** Platinum 195.08	79 **Au** Gold 196.97	80 **Hg** Mercury 200.59	81 **Tl** Thallium 204.38	82 **Pb** Lead 207.2	83 **Bi** Bismuth 208.98	84 **Po** Polonium [209]	85 **At** Astatine [210]	86 **Rn** Radon [222]
87 **Fr** Francium [223]	88 **Ra** Radium [226]	89 **Ac** Actinium [227]	104 **Rf** Rutherfordium [261]	105 **Db** Dubnium [262]	106 **Sg** Seaborgium [266]	107 **Bh** Bohrium [264]	108 **Hs** Hassium [277]	109 **Mt** Meitnerium [268]	110 **Ds** Darmstadtium [271]	111 **Rg** Roentgenium [272]							

58 **Ce** Cerium 140.12	59 **Pr** Praseodymium 140.91	60 **Nd** Neodymium 144.24	61 **Pm** Promethium [145]	62 **Sm** Samarium 150.36	63 **Eu** Europium 151.96	64 **Gd** Gadolinium 157.25	65 **Tb** Terbium 158.93	66 **Dy** Dysprosium 162.50	67 **Ho** Holmium 164.93	68 **Er** Erbium 167.26	69 **Tm** Thulium 168.93	70 **Yb** Ytterbium 173.04	71 **Lu** Lutetium 174.97
90 **Th** Thorium 232.04	91 **Pa** Protactinium 231.04	92 **U** Uranium 238.03	93 **Np** Neptunium [237]	94 **Pu** Plutonium [244]	95 **Am** Americium [243]	96 **Cm** Curium [247]	97 **Bk** Berkelium [247]	98 **Cf** Californium [251]	99 **Es** Einsteinium [252]	100 **Fm** Fermium [257]	101 **Md** Mendelevium [258]	102 **No** Nobelium [259]	103 **Lr** Lawrencium [262]

Made in the USA
San Bernardino, CA
11 August 2020